PARALLEL CULTURES

Parallel Cultures

Majority/minority relations in the countries of
the former Eastern Bloc

Edited by
CHRISTOPHER LORD and OLGA STRIETSKA-ILINA

Routledge
Taylor & Francis Group

LONDON AND NEW YORK

First published 2001 by Ashgate Publishing

Reissued 2018 by Routledge
2 Park Square, Milton Park, Abingdon, Oxon OX14 4RN
711 Third Avenue, New York, NY 10017, USA

Routledge is an imprint of the Taylor & Francis Group, an informa business

Publisher's Note
The publisher has gone to great lengths to ensure the quality of this reprint but points out that some imperfections in the original copies may be apparent.

Disclaimer
The publisher has made every effort to trace copyright holders and welcomes correspondence from those they have been unable to contact.

A Library of Congress record exists under LC control number: 2001086757

ISBN 13: 978-1-138-72621-5 (hbk)
ISBN 13: 978-1-138-72620-8 (pbk)
ISBN 13: 978-1-315-19151-5 (ebk)

Foreword

SIR PETER USTINOV

As the world continues to exist, and even slightly improve its health, like a permanently convalescent patient it is afflicted by an endless variety of obscure but threatening illnesses; and so, like a single invalid, it is subject to relapses. At the very moment when we were entitled to think that we had outlived, at last, the virus of bigotry and conventional imperialism with the creation of an interdependent Europe, a rash of conflicts broke out, culminating in bloodless independence in some places, in wasteful and inhuman warfare in others. Lunatic theories like that of ethnic cleansing captured the vulnerable imagination of some, while others, seized with an obsolete idea of self-determination, ended up with an independence entailing no more than a national flag, an undistinguished anthem, and a valueless currency. In many cases, people had been more independent before independence.

Well, every sickness demands that we find an antidote. In Prague, I chanced across a group of younger scholars from many parts of Eastern Europe and especially from the new states of the former Soviet Union, eager to explore what they call 'Parallel Cultures'. The very title given to their work is a mark of respect for the unfamiliar and even for the seemingly uncouth. Among these people is a remarkable fellow called Christopher Lord, who, far from coming from the landlocked cultures of the Slavs, is a highly untypical, and indeed uninsular product of Britain. I have had the privilege of hearing his highly individual music, and can say that his interests are extremely wide, ranging from a passion for the musical modes of the Orthodox Church to the fate of the Eastern European Gypsies, not only in the Camps of Death, but also in the face of the state-of-the-art indifference of today. This diversity of interests is nothing to be derided. I suffer from it myself. On my seventieth birthday, I told my children that, at my age, I would soon have to decide what to do with my life. My son, with a wisdom not usually associated with middle age, agreed, but added, 'Don't hurry!'

I can only highly recommend a book which is not only thought-provoking and valuable, but is also a reaction on behalf of the human imagination, common sense, and generosity of spirit to the many manifestations of retrogressive thinking still prevalent today.

Vaud, Switzerland

List of Contributors

Madeleine Danova is a Senior Assistant Professor at Kliment Ohridsky University, Sofia, Bulgaria.

Gavril Flora is a lecturer in Sociology at the Christian University of Partium, Romania.

Christopher Lord is a lecturer at the Philosophy Faculty of Charles University, Prague, Czech Republic.

Kirill Shevchenko is a lecturer in Russian History at Moscow University of the Humanities.

Kateryna Stadnik is Head of the Sociological Service at the Centre for Political Studies, Donetsk, Ukraine.

Olga Strietska-Ilina is Head of the Analytical Section, National Training Fund, Prague.

Note from the Editors

The idea for this book first arose during a series of lectures and seminars on minority issues that were held in Prague – at Charles University, and at the now-vanished Prague Centre of the Central European University – between 1992 and 1995. After much discussion, the authors decided to undertake a study which would present a picture of minority cultures in the former Eastern Bloc, not by an exhaustive study of all such minorities (something that would have required a huge project) but by a series of carefully-chosen representative studies, so that the main types of minority population – religious, linguistic, political and so on – should be dealt with. There are still some important gaps. Our focus has been mainly European, and so large areas of the former USSR are not really addressed; but we hope that the reader will find not just useful studies of particular societies, but an organized whole. However, this does not mean that a uniform methodology or conceptual framework has been applied. Approaches to the study of nationalities and national minorities are as varied as the objects of study themselves, and each author has therefore made a separate (but again, complementary, we hope) approach to his or her subject.

The studies in this volume were supported by a collective research grant from the Research Support Scheme, for which we express our gratitude both to the RSS committee and staff and to Mr George Soros. We are also very grateful to Sir Peter Ustinov for his magnanimity in taking an interest in our project.

Olga Strietska-Ilina
Christopher Lord

1   Parallel Cultures

CHRISTOPHER LORD[1]

I. The Problem

The history of Europe can be interpreted from two points of view: as the history of Christianity, and as the history of the European states. These two points of view are not mutually exclusive: the European states have until recently also represented themselves as Christian bodies, and so the two histories can form an organic whole. At moments of great crisis – the Reformation is the obvious example – the link between the political and the 'spiritual' appears at the surface of events, but in the normal run of things these two histories of Europe would seem to go at different speeds. If we take the long view, the religious history, with its deep changes in morality and cosmology, would seem to have the profounder effect on the life of people (and not just 'religious' people; we are all religious, in the sense that we accept moral and cosmological traditions that have no other basis or claim to legitimacy than their historical acceptance by various organised religions; and we can also argue, following Weber, that modern social structures such as capitalism have themselves been produced through a transformation of religion); but at the beginning of the twenty-first century, we are biased in the other direction, and will tend to give the greater importance in our histories of the past to the kind of questions which present themselves to us in everyday life today: questions of politics, and of national politics in particular.

Since it is a theme which we will pick up again later in this study, let us make it clear at the outset that national politics (and nationalism in politics too) is inextricably linked with religion. In the European states this is explicit, since monarchs have often (up until the French Revolution, anyway) claimed divine authority for their wars, treaties and indeed all their other actions too; and since all the other nation states of the world have more or less been created in the image of a few European countries, this kind of image of state authority has become established as the global norm. Even if

---

[1] A draft of this chapter was presented at the third annual convention of the Association for the Study of Nationalities, held at Columbia University in April 1998.

the modern state is not necessarily Christian in its imagery and orientation, it still characteristically represents itself as standing for a definite moral order, in a local or national variant. Let us look briefly at the reasons for this peculiar development in the West.

The Romans took the political category of 'citizen' from the Greek city-states and adapted it, as the Greeks never did, to the purpose of imperial organisation; and this is the direct and explicit source of the equivalent concept in later European political culture. 'Citizen' still meant 'of the city', but now the city in question was Rome, whether the citizen actually lived in Italy, Africa or Britain. Most lived in northern and central Italy; but the citizens of Rome, whether culturally Latin or not, also provided a unified military and administrative ruling caste throughout the Empire.[2]

Although Athens, Sparta and other cities of the Greek-speaking Eastern Mediterranean world had at different times enjoyed a certain degree of political, military or cultural pre-eminence, the Greek system of city-states was inherently competitive, and leagues and alliances came and went as the monarchs and tyrants who led them rose and fell. Alexander's conquests – the amazing zenith of this struggle for pre-eminence among the Hellenic or Hellenised states – did unite a huge territory under his own personal rule, and under a more or less Greek cultural and political idea, but there was still no secure state concept – no legal or moral order – behind this domination, and the political unification achieved by his conquests did not survive Alexander himself. The Greek language and cultural idea also had a profound effect on the societies where Alexander's troops had taken over; but this can be seen as a demonstration that cultural imperialism is not enough to guarantee actual empire.

After Alexander's death, the Greek habit of rivalry and hunger for *kudos* re-asserted itself, and the different regions of his new empire at once began an internal struggle for power that reflected the competitive Greek political tradition on a new and larger scale. It was not until the rise and consolidation of Roman power that a single administrative centre was seen to be able to dominate a large and culturally diverse area, under a state concept which provided for stable, long-lasting and unified legal and political mechanisms.

---

[2] '[T]he same salutary maxims of government, which had secured the peace of Italy, were extended to the most distant conquests. A nation of Romans was gradually formed in the provinces, by the double expedient of introducing colonies, and of admitting the most faithful and deserving of the provincials to the freedom of Rome.' Gibbon, *Decline and Fall*, Chapter 2.

Rome did not rely on ephemeral personality cults or mystical religions (though it was big enough to accommodate these): the short sword was enough. For centuries, the legions guaranteed a peace and stability which rested on the rock of superior military organisation and technique, and which remains the pattern for state organisation today. The Empire, though, as military states will, eventually outgrew itself: over-stretching its resources at its frontiers as it softened internally; and, in an attempt to make the state administration more manageable, was permanently divided into a Western and an Eastern part during the reign of Diocletian (284-305). This corresponded to a cultural division between Greek-speakers and Latin-speakers (although this was not directly the reason for the division), and therefore introduced the idea – and demonstrated the fact – that the eternal-seeming and monolithic Empire could in principle be sub-divided in this way. The innovation was an immediate success: the two halves of the Empire rapidly ceased to be mere administrative units, and took on political and cultural lives of their own – became separate actors in history, indeed, reading their parts from different scripts.

It seems sometimes to be assumed that the further sub-division of the territories of the Empire into national units was the next logical step in this process, and just a matter of time. But it is important to realise that this further division into nation states (or rather into proto-nation states) only took place in the Western part of the Empire. The Western Roman provinces of Spain, Italy, Britain and Gaul formed the administrative basis for the modern countries of Spain, Italy, Britain and France. The other Western nation states, along with some Central European states not originally falling into either camp (Poland, Bohemia and Hungary), were formed later on in imitation of these basic units; although we should remember that there were also other important defining differences between the East and the West – the most important perhaps being the effect on the West of assimilating successive waves of non-Romanised Germanic populations. Another important difference, with a directly political impact, is that after the fall of Rome itself, the relationship of Church and State developed quite differently in the West and the East. The Catholic Church in the West took on an active and 'international' political function quite different from that of the Orthodox Church, which continued to see itself as sharing the legitimacy of the Empire and its institutions, and which therefore had no direct interest in challenging that legitimacy. Specifically, the rise of the Popes in the West had no immediate analogue in the East, where 'the patriarch of Constantinople never acquired either that independence of secular authority or that superiority to

other ecclesiastics that was achieved by the Pope.' (Russell, 1975, p. 387) [3]
The Eastern Empire, in any event, was subject to different forces, and did not
follow the same line of development. Rather, the Eastern or Byzantine
Empire continued to function for about a thousand years, still basically on the
Roman pattern of managing a polycultural Empire with a monocultural,
Greek-speaking, state administration, backed up by an official state religion;
and when it did eventually break up, the smaller units as a rule continued to
claim for themselves the dignity of Empire, still seeking to continue the
imperial Roman system on a smaller physical scale.

The cultural divergence of East and West did not neatly follow the
old Roman geographical and administrative divisions, though, since these
soon broke down under the stresses of the new situation (and especially after
the sack of Rome in 455 and the fall of the West); and in particular we can
see that the old provinces of Illyria (nominally Western) and Dacia
(nominally Eastern) fell in between the two large-scale cultural blocks. Illyria
and Dacia ceased to function as effective administrative or cultural units, and
their territory is still disputed by different religious, national and political
forces today. The identity and boundaries of Gaul were similarly disputed,
with the Latinised Gauls having to assimilate an important influx of Germans
from the East, but in this case the basic state idea did eventually re-surface –
as the Empire of the Franks. This in turn provided for a long intermediary
phase, before the component peoples and territories separated out into
'national' French and German parts.

The different state-political histories of the Eastern and the Western
Christian states are somewhat obscured by the fact that their modern
successors share a similar 'nation state' profile in international politics and
law. But in fact it is the Western nation state idea – meaning that which
developed in the successor states of the Western Empire – that has won. The
Byzantine Empire itself fizzled out in the end, losing its territory and its
power under the influence of the new forces of Islam and the House of
Osman. The Orthodox empires (attempts to continue the Eastern Roman
dignity on a smaller scale) of Russia and Bulgaria – the latter much reduced
in size and importance – are now officially national states on the Western
pattern, and the same is true of Turkey, which is the successor state to a
polycultural empire, the Ottoman, which was organised according to quite a

---

[3] Bertrand Russell also explains here the political circumstances under which the mediæval
Church in the West finally broke with the East. (It was over Pepin the Short's gift of
formerly Byzantine lands to the Papacy in 755 in return for official recognition of his
legitimacy; which passed to Charlemagne.)

different (Islamic/dynastic) plan. Other successor states temporarily established on the territory of the old Eastern Empire at one time or another, such as the Empires of Trebizond or Nicaea, or the Latin Empire set up after the Crusaders sacked Constantinople in 1204, have vanished without trace, defeated in the end by the national state system of the West.[4] Leaving Europe for a moment, we see that even the explicitly Islamic states of the Middle East, though looking back to the theocratic state idea of the Caliphate, have no alternative today but to conform to the Western nation-state pattern, even though this is a Western Christian pattern at root which in fact keeps them in a position of subordination to their fellow monotheists at an international level.

Now, in Europe we see that the Western nation state model rests on one fundamental principle: that the inhabitants share a common nationality, typically demonstrated by their use of a national language. This is the basis of their citizenship. It is only in a few marginal states (Iceland, for instance, or Armenia) where this is completely true; and in some other states (Belgium, Switzerland) this principle is completely compromised. But still, language and nationality are inextricably linked, with state bureaucracy in particular characteristically using a single standard language. In the countries where this is not true, such as Belgium, Switzerland, or now Britain, Spain and to some extent France (where local languages have recently achieved a degree of recognition, even or especially where state bureaucracy is concerned), we see this as a further evolution of the nation-state idea, and not as a non-national alternative system. In Belgium, for instance, it is the Catholic religious identity (opposed to the Calvinism of the Netherlands) which provides the historical basis of 'national' solidarity. The Swiss, despite their linguistic and in this case also religious divisions, do still have a strong sense of national identity. There are also some pluralistic European states that have dropped out of the picture. Finland before independence was an organic part of Sweden; Poland-Lithuania also functioned quite well without a unified national culture. This demonstrates immediately that the nationalist's self-image is a false one: his ideology, which seems so pure and a-political to him, in fact represents a powerful political programme: for the nationalisation of politics leads to the nationalisation of culture. The Swiss

---

[4] The adoption of Western norms is illustrated for example by Kemal Ataturk's creation of a 'national' political culture for Turkey; but the earliest establishment of Western states on Eastern territory was by military means, in the twelfth century, when the Crusaders established temporary states by conquest in Syria, Jerusalem and Antioch. But these were cultural and religious outposts: explicitly representing the values of the West, that is, and not just the ambitions of this or that dynasty or clique. (Lilie, 1993) is a thorough study.

version of national feeling, which is a relic from an earlier phase of the process of nation-building in Europe, shows us that loyalty to a state does not always mean loyalty to a monocultural national idea. Unusually, but for quite ordinary and simply-explicable reasons, the success of Switzerland as a political and military unit did not produce the characteristic West European Christian cultural homogenisation of its population; and the various denominations of Swiss seem to be able to coexist without putting too much strain on their *Volksgeister*.

Switzerland, though, is an exception, for Western European countries are usually differentiated by language; and if we look for the origin of this principle, we at once realise that the Western and Eastern Empires were differentiated by language, with the Western Empire (and Rome) using Latin, and the Eastern Empire (and Constantinople and Alexandria) using Greek. The Greek-speaking states failed in one way or another; were divided and invaded and re-made according to different plans. Only Greece itself, an Orthodox imperial remnant where a very mixed population (actually an Ottoman remnant population more than anything) speaks a reconstructed and modernised version of the old imperial tongue, still reminds us directly of the Eastern state and its system of government. Western countries imitate the Western Empire. Russia, a state which was set up to imitate the Eastern system, but with Old Church Slavonic used instead of written Greek as the language of religion and government, offers another historical mirror. As in Greece, the 'native' population (the 'Russians') comprises an artificially homogenised imperial population: a mix of Slavs, Finno-Ugrians, Turks, Armenians and others, united by the imposition of the Russian language and the domination of the imperial culture – though this imitation of the Roman imperial system, too, is perceived today as a national culture and tradition.

The characteristic cultural pattern of the Western nation states was formed by a movement in the reverse direction: the consolidation of local cultural patterns, to the point that they became continuous with the administration of state power. What this meant in practice was that the Latin of church and state administration failed to establish itself as the normal language of the people. Instead, local languages arose. In some cases, these were simply the local variants of Latin, isolated and regularised according to a local norm (Italian, French and Spanish, approximately, but with islands of other Gallo-Roman dialects also surviving, especially in rural areas); and in others, a different literary standard in the end prevailed (German and the languages of Britain). Some mediævalists argue that it was Britain which provided the model for this rebellion against the use of Latin. One reason for this was that, as in what was to become Germany, the language of the people had a distinctive and non-Latinate structure, and another (often overlooked) reason was that in the court cultures of Ireland and Wales, the British Isles already had a native high culture, with poetry, law and so on, which could provide a real alternative to the Roman model and tradition (with Welsh poets, for instance, performing in the castles of the Norman overlords after the invasion of 1066). Anyway, we can see that there were basically two cultural trajectories, defined by the use and spread of literacy. In the Roman Empire, both West and East, there had been a sharp diglossia, with the Empire and its functionaries using Latin or Greek, both very highly-developed literary languages, and the illiterate rabble using various peasant dialects (i.e. non-standard, un-standardised, and un-standardisable variants and hybrids of these and other languages). In the East, the successor states continued to use Greek for their state administration, but these states failed – although they did leave their imitators, Bulgaria and Russia, behind them as a reminder of what might have been. (What would become the First Bulgarian Empire was Christianised by the conversion of Khan Boris in 864, and what would become Russia by the conversion of Prince Saint Vladimir of Kiev in 988.) In the West, though, Latin became the language of the Church more than that of state power. This is basically because a unified religious identity survived in the ecclesiastical structures of Western Europe, even when state power was at its lowest ebb. In Italy, Latin was closer to the language of the people, it is true, but a careful look at the modern national language of Italy reveals that modern Italian, like modern French, represents on the one hand a middle course between two diverging dialect areas (Northern French versus Occitain, and the Gallo-Roman Northern Italian dialects versus the language of Rome itself), and on the other hand the acceptance of an arbitrary local standard (Ile-de-France French; Florentine Italian) more or less conforming in its general phonology to the arising consensus in the linguistic community as a whole: and so we see that the same processes of social renewal, and the corresponding generation of new social structures, took place in Italy too.

But the sad truth is that the middle ages were a period of decline and collapse in Western Europe. While the Church preserved the language of Rome in its monasteries, its liturgy, and its documents, power passed into the hands of the illiterate, and the imperial political system collapsed. However, the idea of such a system survived in people's minds, and this in the end proved decisive. When the Frankish warrior king Charlemagne accepted the dignity of Roman Emperor on Christmas Day 800, re-starting (Western)

European history by founding a large, centralised state authority, securely founded on military power on the one hand and an organised religious base on the other, the submission to the authority of the written word implicit in this gesture was only partial. While Latin had continued in use as an ecclesiastical language, and now once again became the official bureaucratic language of an 'imperial' state organisation, Western Europe had become a place of creoles and contact languages; and the babble of the rabble was gradually re-organising itself according to a different kind of system: a system of regional spoken norms that would in time result in stable national languages. These verbal and mental badges of nationality more than anything else succeed in dividing Europe: since the Frenchman and the Spaniard actually cannot understand one another, even though their languages are both transformations of imperial Latin.[5]

It is worth noting in passing that the isolation and establishment of single standard forms of national languages – both Latinate and non-Latinate – is something which in a sense runs counter to the natural flow of things. Given a minimally stable political background, so that the linguistic situation is not disrupted by large flows of people, the normal thing is for the divisions between dialect areas to become deeper. This, indeed, is the reason for the break-up of Latin in the first place. In places where the same language has been left to itself for a very long time (and a low level of literacy will help the process along too), we see that the division into local dialects (idiolects, more technically) can continue to the level of individual streets in villages. Welsh, for instance, is very highly fragmented in this way, as is Chinese (on a much larger scale). But the national language idea represents a change of course. Looking at French again, we see that it was the economic success of Paris which established Ile-de-France French as the high prestige variant, and this spoken variant became established as the written norm too. This, though, does not mean that it displaced an earlier written norm. Before the establishment of this national standard, even the most cultivated writers (the Troubadours) just wrote in the way they spoke, thus preserving the spoken dialects in a written form. English shows a similar variability, and this means that writing had a different (and more natural?) function, and a more direct relationship with speech. Without dictionaries, national schools, and other

---

[5] This is as good a place as any to express my gratitude to the Linguistic Circle of Prague for the privilege of being able to attend its meetings of 1996-97, which were organised around the theme of contacts between languages. Much of the material on language development in this study comes from the excellent lectures and discussions of the Circle.

basic tools, the homogenisation of spoken language was actually impossible anyway.

But once a standard written form (Parisian French; Florentine Italian; Oxford English) had been established, this had a powerful influence on the spoken language, since it was now possible to transmit a record of a single spoken standard throughout a more or less unified cultural and economic space. The eventual success of the kings of France, and the absorption of Burgundy and Provence, completed the process of standardisation there (though even today, various surviving dialects still attest to earlier stages in this development). We see, therefore, that the national language is the language of a new kind of social structure: it is the language of urbanism and mercantilism. A rural society has no real use for a national language, and can get by with a foreign language for its limited bureaucratic and intellectual needs if necessary. But the rise of urban mercantilism meant the rise of mercantile cities: Paris, London, and Amsterdam. These became centres of cultural standardisation generally, and of linguistic standardisation in particular. We will argue that they also played a vital role in establishing parallel culture locations, but as far as the associated national cultures were concerned, we see that the capital city soon fixed an official version of the national language. It is interesting to note that great cities sometimes as it were delegate the task of linguistic formation to smaller satellites. Standard English is not the language of London, but the language of Oxford and Cambridge Universities. Standard Italian is not the language of Rome, but that of the Florentine poets. So there may be a separation of functions; but even so, it is only with the political and commercial consolidation of nations around capital cities that the corresponding linguistic consolidation becomes possible. This is a Western European pattern, let us note. The national language, with standard spoken and written forms, is as much a West European development as the national state.

In parallel to this process of the formation of national languages – a process which still continues, incidentally, at least in the Balkans – the original religious continuity of Europe (which we can conveniently date from 324, when Constantine the Great, at the Council of Nicaea, established an official policy of legal and theological continuity between the Greek and Latin parts of the Empire) also saw a break-up into smaller organisational units. This process of variegation, intersecting with the linguistic diversification discussed above, eventually led to the establishment of national religions, expressed, naturally enough, in the corresponding national languages. The state, indeed, is from one perspective itself a religious structure, both in the sociological sense that it fixes formal standards of morality for those who live under its authority, and in the historical sense that the legal authority of the sovereign is originally derived from theological considerations. Since the French and American Revolutions, there have been other options, but during the period of formation of the Western national system, this state authority was explicitly derived from and linked to the moral and indeed divine authority of the priests who worked hand in glove with the temporal rulers. The modern state is certainly more atheistical, but the 'national feeling' promoted at international sporting events, during wars, and so on is in effect a transformed religious sentiment. Max Weber's seamless arguments demonstrate beyond conjecture that the 'spirit of capitalism' is a transformed religious feeling; and given the commercial nature of the modern nation state in general, we can argue that the unthinking loyalty to the state has the same basic source as the unthinking drive to acquire wealth described in Weber's classic study of capitalism: that the rise of nationalism and the rise of capitalism are at root the same phenomenon.[6] Weber also argues that the quality of modern national feelings – their emotional content, that is – relies not on national character (as one might naively suppose), but on this same transformation of religion, in local or national variants.

> The appeal to national character is generally a mere confession of ignorance, and in this case it is entirely untenable. To ascribe a unified national character to the Englishmen of the seventeenth century would be simply to falsify history. Cavaliers and Roundheads did not appeal to each other simply as two parties, but as radically distinct species of men, and whoever looks into the matter carefully must agree with them.... It was the power of religious influence, not alone, but more than anything else, which created the differences of which we are conscious today.
>
> (Weber, 1958, pp. 88-89)

It may seem strange at first sight that religion is able to perform this peculiar conjuring trick of claiming absolute, universal authority for its dogmas, and at the same time promoting some set of exclusive national or sectarian values on the basis of these supposedly universal truths; but it is a trick repeated

---

[6] 'A nation is not merely a historical category but a historical category belonging to a definite epoch, the epoch of rising capitalism. The process of elimination of feudalism and development of capitalism was at the same time a process of amalgamation of people into nations.' (Stalin, 1971, p. 56)

with such depressing regularity that it would be foolish to deny its central importance as a mechanism of moral formation and isolation. If we cast a comparative eye around, we will see that there are other alternatives. The modern Arab states, which have resisted national doctrinal variation, and also the use of local dialects and languages for liturgical purposes, have not fragmented in precisely this way. While such a rivalry as that between the Abbasid and Fatimid Caliphates (10th-11th centuries), or the creation of a separate Qarmathian state in Bahrein in 899, did rely on differing interpretations of religious dogma, Iraq does not nowadays claim a moral ascendancy over Saudi Arabia or Syria on the grounds of possessing a more perfect version of Islam. After all, these modern states have been created on the Western pattern, and not according to an Islamic plan at all. Monotheism does seem to produce a characteristic tendency to schism and heresy, but in the Middle East this tendency was arrested by the forces of orthodoxy a long time ago – apart, that is, from the Sunni vs. Shi'ite schism, which has recently isolated Iran in a parody of the Christian national differentiation just described. The Iranian Revolution was not just supposed to create a more perfect version of Islam in Iran; it was supposed to be the first stage of a revolution of Islam generally. But the cultural and political boundaries of the neighbouring Arab states proved resilient enough to resist the ideological revolution of Khomeini and his colleagues, and so the supposedly non-national, universal spiritual revolution became a national revolution in its objective results. In general, contemporary Islam seeks to resist the main stream of political and economic development in the world. If we accept that this main stream is Christian-national-capitalist in its origin, it is not such an illogical resistance to attempt. As a contemporary observer acutely notes, 'What uniquely characterises the current era is the organisation of religious forces... to frustrate the development process.' (Horowitz, 1991, p. 4) [7]

It is a complex issue, but from a historical point of view, the use of a standard liturgical Arabic would seem to be an important factor – at least, if we want to fit this development into a comparative scheme. On the one hand, we see that the Islamic world, despite its internal disagreements, still perceives itself as a single religious community (an idea which is now obsolete in the West); but on the other, the forced assimilation of this pattern

---

[7] In this stimulating essay, Horowitz argues that the opposition of religion to modernisation can also be seen in the Polish workers' resistance to the Marxist ideology of progress during the Solidarnosc period in Poland. The picture of the national priest or witch-doctor helping his people to stand up against the inhuman power of the machine is certainly a suggestive one, and rings true as far as Islam is concerned. Another example is the anti-evolution ideology of the American religious right.

to the nation state system of modern international politics has arguably prevented either side of this unbalanced duality from functioning to anybody's best advantage. At a state-political level, Islam remains unable completely to unite, and nationalism unable completely to divide, the followers of Mohammed. Either process could in principle lead to a next phase of development. Both together produce political and cultural stagnation, with if anything a retrograde tendency to take refuge in the lunatic fringe attitudes of fundamentalist schismatics. (Who are at the same time schismatics from nation-state solutions. As with the Christian ideology of mediæval Europe, there is a general claim to the universal truth of Islam.)

Turning to the Orthodox Church, we find a position closer to that of the West – but not identical. The Orthodox Church is, indeed, orthodox. It resembles Islam in that way. Like modern Islam, it has no use for rationalistic theology, in the sense in which we have come to understand this term in the West. No Aquinas and his followers. Stuck – deliberately – at the cultural level of the Greek Fathers, the Orthodox Church makes no systematic attempt to demonstrate the unity of scientific and religious truth, through the application of logic. Instead, as with Islamic theology,[8] there is the detailed elaboration of a system which explains everything – the Creation, the Flood, God and his angels; important things like that – but as revealed, fixed and permanent truth, and not (as with Aquinas and his revision of Aristotelianism) as something at the same time logically and rationalistically guaranteed. This is the heart of the matter. In the West, in line with Aristotelianism and rationalism generally, the Catholic Church eventually adopted a policy of welcoming science and the knowledge it offered. This was the official line, anyway, and it is easy to see the logic behind this

---

[8] This term needs some explanation. 'Given the absence of a system of theology of any kind generally recognised in the regions of the Moslem world, it is not legitimate to speak of an orthodox theology of Islam.' (Ibrahim and Sagadeev, 1990, p. 38) However, the drift in various fragmented schools of Islamic philosophy up to the twelfth century was generally in the direction of a reconstructed Greek rationalism, as first Syriac and then Arabic translations and commentaries on Aristotle, and some neo-Platonic writings, circulated. This trend was reversed by the Sufi al-Ghazali (1058-1111), whose polemical *Incoherence of the Philosophers* put mysticism, obedience and tradition (*naql*) back at the centre of Muslim thought, with a corresponding retreat for the *kamal* strand of philosophical disputation, for the 'Divine Science' synthesis of religion and logic proposed by Ibn Sina (Avicenna), and for speculative thought generally. Incidentally, the attempt of Ibn Rushd (Averroës) to refute al-Ghazali led by chance to a philosophical movement in the West – Averroism – which in turn provoked St. Thomas Aquinas to his epoch-making new synthesis of Christianity and Aristotelianism in the thirteenth century. So the new rationalism of the West – a key element in the Italian Renaissance – in a way had its root in the anti-rationalist turn taken by Islam a hundred years earlier.

choice. Since all truth is one, and since the official interpretation of the Scriptures is the perfect distillation of this truth, it follows from basic principles of dogma that any other disciplined reasoning – which meant philosophy, logic and even experimental science, when that came along – must also necessarily conform with this truth. This, to the devout, looked logically guaranteed, and it is a plan which demonstrates a certain nobility of purpose, too. The Jesuit scheme of learning took this approach, anyway: but things turned out badly. Science could at first be turned to the service of religion, confirming (apparently) various Church doctrines: by providing hard evidence of the Creation, the Flood, and so on... But the uneasy realisation that it was all a hallucination and an illusion gradually sabotaged this happy situation from the inside. A concrete example is provided by the science of astronomy. This was seen as the most perfectly theological of sciences, revealing the regularities in the divine will on the most grandiose scale imaginable. Sixteenth-century astronomy was extravagant in its interpretive function: it did not limit itself to mere observation of the heavens, but, like the Arab astronomy of the middle ages, took on board an elaborate cargo of astrology too. Among the learned, this was seen as the ideal link between science and dogma, and it was assumed that what was being uncovered by all this learning was not just the underlying mechanism of the universe, but at the same time the working of the divine will. Advanced intellectuals saw this as the path to a unified science and theology. But the weakness of this was precisely that it all formed a unified doctrinal system, and when science (dreary old mathematics, that is) revealed that it was the sun which was in the middle and the earth which went round and round, the whole thing came crashing down. This was why the Church had to oppose the new astronomy, and not simply for reasons of conservatism.

This gives us a metaphor for the whole conflict between religion and scientific rationality. The latter has its origins in the former, and as far as the modern West is concerned, it is in the fantastic speculations of metaphysical theology that the discipline of logical reasoning has its historical source. But promoting this scientific kind of reasoning has done no good to religion. It has undermined its own authority, and the only way out of this direct opposition of interests is to deny the reality of science. In a society dominated by a technology which has been produced as a direct result of experimental science, this is a difficult line to promote at anything higher than a 'grass roots' level; but still, there is a clear logic behind resistance of this kind, and we do indeed now find just this brand of reactionary fundamentalism arising throughout the monotheistic world – in California as much as in Tehran.

Orthodox Christianity, anyway, never made the mistake of the Jesuits: never suggested that there was any particular merit in rationalism or 'progress'. The eternal nature and principles of the cosmos were fixed forever in the fourth century, and the whole idea of doctrinal change is horrifying to the Orthodox. This, after all, is what led the Western Church to its schismatic position in the first place, and the result (in Orthodox eyes) has been a general decline of religion in the West, with a corresponding spread of atheism and evil.[9] The religious truth of the Orthodox Church is not demonstrated by reason: it is a religion of revelation and mystical experience, of the ecstatic adulation of the icons (representing 'the world glorified') and of trance states arrived at through the repetition of a cult formula (the Jesus Prayer).[10] Like Islam after al-Ghazali, the Orthodox Church makes no bones about resisting truth and reason if they get in the way of its dogmas.

The reason to discuss this here is that these patterns of doctrinal diversification (or not) are basic to the formation of differing state patterns of morality. St. Augustine, an author of great subtlety sometimes and monumental stupidity the rest of the time, was acute enough (on a good day, presumably) to realise that what really tied people together in social groups was a shared system of values – what we can call a shared morality.[11] The underlying pattern and historical source of the moralities established in the modern nation states of Europe is imperial Roman Christianity, and its differentiation into national systems is pre-dated by its differentiation into larger doctrinal groupings. To close the analysis of the Orthodox Church specifically, we see that despite the supposed doctrinal unity (and this does have some reality, since the authority of the official doctrines of the Church Fathers is never questioned), *de facto* 'national' variants have arisen here too, with linguistic separation playing an important role in this. In this way, Orthodoxy is intermediate between Western Christianity and Islam. The

---

[9] 'What was the instrument of the devil's slandering of God?... He used 'theology'. He first instituted a slight alteration in theology which, once it was accepted, he managed to increase more and more to the degree that Christianity became completely unrecognisable. This is what we call "Western theology".' (Kalomiros, 1996) Augustine, Latin in general, and Anselm and Aquinas in particular, are blamed for this development.

[10] 'In the mystic of the East... we see an example of man's complete regeneration... the super-consciousness of the ascetic of the East is concentrated in his flaming heart. There – within himself – he perceives the fire of the Godhead.' (Lodyzhensky, 1915, pp. 156-7)

[11] 'A people is a large gathering of rational beings united in fellowship by their agreement about the objects of their love.' (*City of God*, Book XIX, XXIV)

Romanian Orthodox Church uses Romanian, the Greek Orthodox Church uses Greek, and the Slav Orthodox Churches (Russian, Ukrainian, Bulgarian and Serbian) use the 'Old Church Slavonic' which is ancestral to all their contemporary standard written languages.

If the Western and Eastern derivatives of Roman Christianity have differed on their approaches to some basic religious and moral questions, they are united on one important question: their cooperative attitude to temporal power. This, after all, is their meal ticket. The equation of state morality and the eternal truths offered by the official religion of the day is a winning formula for both sides. Executions, wars and other morally delicate operations of the state can be carried out in a comforting glow of sanctity; and conversely, theological questions can be settled with the sword or the rack, should any disputes arise to threaten the position of the official religious authorities (which is by its nature somewhat precarious).

It is easy to see that the larger theological differences lead directly to differences of political culture. The absolutism of Habsburg Spain, for instance, was of a dual religious and secular nature. Because the Church and the state between them constructed a cooperative morality which guaranteed the unquestioned domination of both organisations, the Church was free to torture and kill its opponents in the name of Christian charity on the one hand, and the royal family was free to enrich itself with the gold of the New World on the other, with the decline into poverty and backwardness of the rest of the country seen as a natural consequence of following this divinely-ordained moral path. Another obvious example is the 'Protestant ethic' discussed by Weber. This, though, leads us to a later phase in the process of differentiation of national systems; and first we should consider the Reformation itself.

Martin Luther's rebellion against the values of the Roman Church was already a political act. By the 16th century, important cultural differences between the emerging national states and moral systems of Europe were already established, and the re-division of territory along Catholic and Protestant lines can be understood partly as a result of the stresses produced by these cultural differences. It might be that Western Europe without Luther could have preserved a united religion: but actually it did not. And once the logical possibility of theological reform in this revolutionary manner had been established, the way was open for Calvinism, Pietism, and the Puritan stream of Christianity, which, however marginal in its intellectual content, had a decisive influence on the formation of the Anglo-American school of nationalist/capitalist Christianity, and was therefore of decisive importance in setting the conditions for the rise of the modern state. After some wild swings, the Catholic vs. Protestant division settled into its now inevitable-seeming pattern. This did not in every case follow state boundaries, though, even in a general way. Switzerland, it is said, preserves its unique character and identity because and not in spite of its divided population. On the whole, though, this process encouraged the idea of a particular brand of Christianity for each country (especially in the Protestant countries; but also in Catholic Central Europe), and more generally drew attention to the fact that such variation was possible, and could be put to the service of the state. It sanctioned the idea that the state had the moral right to impose its own standards of behaviour on its citizens, and this was such a useful notion as far as those in power were concerned that it was installed even in those countries without an official national religion – though we see that the creation of national moralities has been slower and less complete in the Catholic countries, which still officially subscribe to the universal religion run by the Vatican and its officials.

The state still basically meant royal and aristocratic circles at the time of the Reformation, and religious differences had real practical consequences at these more elevated levels. In England, Henry VIII made the break from Rome that had the unforeseen consequence of founding the mighty Church of England (whose Christian Soldiers would soon march out to export its morality over a huge geographical area); while in Central Europe, the Jesuits concentrated their (rather successful) efforts to reverse the Reformation on the nobility, with the result that Protestantism acquired rather middle-class connotations: a grubby, commercial sort of belief, compared to the aristocratic grandeur of the Roman original, with its ancient traditions and impressive rituals. Real social change followed at all levels. In England, the decline of the Catholic element (which inconveniently included the better-educated levels of the aristocracy) led to a corresponding artistic and cultural decline at the top of society, with an anti-intellectual, anti-artistic, anti-foreign-nonsense attitude prevailing among the upper classes for centuries after; while in German Europe, as we have noted, the rise of the Protestant ethic and the middle classes is reasonably connected with the success of Luther and Calvin. This competed with the conservative Catholic ideology of the Austro-Hungarian Empire, which, though complicated in its own right, had important links with the absolutism of the Spanish branch of the Habsburg dynasty.

(The Czech historian Miroslav Hroch writes persuasively of the unresolved battle for control of Central Europe between the Catholic and Protestant factions; the result of which, he says, is a compromise which still persists today: the result of a general recognition that no decisive division of territory could be achieved by force. A similar compromise took place in political culture: 'The curious parallel existence of monarchic absolutism and the Estates system was typical for the Habsburg monarchy, where absolutist centralism didn't achieve complete success until the second half of the eighteenth century.' (Hroch, 2000, p. 26) This is an interesting case of the coexistence of two parallel *political* cultures: a phenomenon, however, which we will merely note and leave aside, since these two styles of government authority were not directly linked to the establishment of national identity, as we seek to identify it here.)

The examples of linked religious and political developments could be extended almost indefinitely. The Netherlands was divided into a Catholic part (Belgium) and a Protestant part (which we call the Netherlands today, or, less accurately, Holland). Catholic Scotland maintained an independent intellectual culture among the ruling elites. Throughout Western Europe, individual bishops and cardinals set up local administrations and political power-bases which left permanent political traces. And the general net effect of all this complicated development was to create divisions of territory which exhibited a dual character: the isolation of language communities, and the creation of corresponding officially-sponsored moralities, attached to their population blocks by such means as the promotion of heroic national mythologies or histories.

If we are looking at these developments in the long term, we should consider 'moralities' rather than just 'religions', because with the French Revolution a new age began. Officially-sponsored state morality lost the necessary link with Christianity. This was truly an epoch-making change, since the spread of the European style of state power – for instance in the pagan lands of the Slavs – had been eponymous with the spread of Christianity since time immemorial. The displacement of Christianity is still not absolute, but the modern state has been revolutionised: its morality is supposed to be free-standing, based on truths, like the American Constitutional truths, which are 'self-evident'. But scratch the surface of the Western national cultures and moral differences immediately reveal themselves. In taboo areas such as the beating or not of wives and children, or sexual matters such as attitudes and practices of homosexuality and prostitution, we see that the national boundaries clearly mark moral boundaries too. The fine grain of moral attitudes is suddenly altered, and the foreigner who crosses a national boundary suddenly does not automatically know what is expected as 'proper' behaviour in a given situation. These are illustrations of a general phenomenon: crossing a national frontier is experienced as a change of moral background conditions. In their prehistory, as we have said, these boundaries have close links with theological developments in official Christianity; but this is not the whole story. The modern nation-state idea also derives its authority from what is ultimately an assumption about anthropology: that populations are naturally divided into 'nations', more or less homogeneous groups speaking the same language, and sharing common features such as a common origin, a common purpose, and a common national culture. This idea is so attractive as a means of organising politics in particular that it has enjoyed increasing international currency for about the last one hundred and fifty years. Indeed, we can say that this is the idea which has replaced the sanction of Christian cosmological dogma as the real moral justification for having state formations in the first place. Both the state formations and the moralities which underlie them are historically derived from Western Christianity, as has been shown above; but the anthropological assumption – what we can call the *naive anthropological hypothesis* – can be called into question on other grounds too.

To give a concrete example of how this naive anthropological hypothesis has been translated into political action, the Czech philosopher Jan Patočka gives a concise and convincing account of the mechanism by which one nationalist movement – the Czech 'national programme' which inspired the thinkers and politicians of the nineteenth century, and which still forms the basis for the Czech national consciousness today – was formed. (Patočka, 1969)[12] This was important for the development of the whole pan-Slavist movement, and so its 'Slavonic messianism' had repercussions far outside the borders of Bohemia.[13] The philosophical basis and ultimate

---

[12] The phrase 'Slavonic messianism' comes from this article (p.53).

[13] Although it is argued (Bradley, 1984) that the idea of pan-Slavism was never well-defined among Czech nationalists themselves. According to Bradley, it was only with Masaryk that a coherent nationalist programme arose. The 'grotesque illusions' (p. 102) of the earlier nationalists were marked by a variety of competing and indeed incompatible ideologies, mostly 'intellectual' in their general character – which was a problem when it came to motivating the masses, who found nothing they could understand in these historical or philological fantasies. Bradley points out that there were important objective changes – population growth among the Czechs, and migration to cities in connection with industrialisation – which were just as important determinants of the rise of nationalism as the rather limited ideological programmes of the first nationalist theoreticians and activists.

intellectual authority for the thought of a sequence of Czech (and Slovak) activists leading from Jungmann, through Kollár and Palacký, and eventually to Masaryk and the formation of the Czechoslovak state, was provided by Herder's writings on the nation. These views were not studied or treated critically; they were embraced as a heroic political dogma on the one hand, and as philosophy of the most profound type on the other, and gradually amplified and consolidated by successive generations of nationalists. Herder's position was that the nation was something natural, to be compared to a family, and that a national language was therefore also something natural. 'Every distinct community is a nation, having its own national culture as it has its own language.' (Herder, 1969, p. 284) This led to a simple political position, namely that a national state, based on a national language, is the most natural form of state, compared with which a multi-national state was 'mechanical' and artificial. 'The most natural state is, therefore, *one* nation, an extended family with one national character. This it retains for ages and develops most naturally if the leaders come from the people and are wholly dedicated to it.' (*Ideas*, Book IX, IV; Herder, 1969, p. 324) Herder's position, as just cited, is simply expounded: stated in a couple of sentences as something self-evident. This is perhaps in part because he had already developed his ideas much more fully in a separate work, the 'Essay On The Origin Of Language' of 1772. In retrospect, the 'Ideas For A Philosophy Of The History Of Mankind', which was supposed to be the culminating grand synthesis of Herder's thought, is much less successful than his work on language. The 'Ideas' is an imaginative, forward-looking work in its way, but its argumentation is based on a great many scientific ideas which we cannot endorse today. These are not just ideas about philosophy or anthropology, but specific 'hard science' assertions about such subjects as electricity and phonetics, physiology and embryology: ideas which are just wrong. There are some pleasing echoes of classical writers such as Strabo, Eratosthenes and Vitruvius in Herder's imaginative explanations of the effects of climate on the human organism (this is the basic reason why different cultures exist in different places, he says), but if this talk of the winds and the effects of heat on the imagination can give the argumentation a certain specialised antiquarian appeal for some restricted circles of readers, it also reminds us why these Greek and Latin authors are so little read today.

The scientific theses are worked together with theological arguments and assertions in a manner which is also repugnant to the contemporary reader. ('By the divine gift of speech dormant reason was aroused.' Herder, 1969, p. 263) It is interesting to see how the argument progresses – Herder is certainly an intelligent author – but the book is a mere museum piece in scientific terms. The essay on language is more interesting; paradoxically, this is immediately because it contains less science. Its analysis is more rigorously philosophical in style, based on deductions from first principles, and does not rely much on observation – no more than that of David Hume, say, or other eighteenth-century philosophical authors. Again, the analysis of language is obsolete and inadequate in scientific terms, but in the treatment of language communities we find a more developed theory of the *Volk* and its nature; and the theory has an internal logic to it which is attractive up to a point. Herder claims that the nature of man is always to progress in his thinking, and that this progression can be seen both in the life of the individual, and in that of the communities he forms. This leads language, too, to change and develop, and the isolation of social groups therefore at the same time leads to the isolation of languages and cultures. These primæval language communities are then preserved by tradition. Since we cannot today accept the narrowly linguistic claims made in this work (that 'Oriental languages' – apparently he means Hebrew – contain more of the original animal sounds of speech than European languages, for instance, which is why they cannot be written down using alphabets), we should understand this as a theory about cultural formation; and in those terms it seems reasonable as far as it goes. Coherent, anyway. But it will not do as a universal theory about national languages. It is clear in retrospect that Herder's conception was fatally flawed by its Euro-centric assumptions. His theory assumes that society is naturally made up of independent, linguistically-differentiated and geographically-separated communities; but in the first place, this pattern, which seems so familiar in Europe, is not repeated in other developed societies, such as the Chinese and the Indian, and in the second place, Herder, already under the spell of the romantic ideas which would so much affect the next generation of German thinkers, saw a steady progression from the noble primitive to the modern national citizen, without imagining that the intervening developments of society (such minor factors as the rise and fall of Egypt, Greece and Rome, that is) might have played any decisive part in forming the basic structures of the modern European nation states. Although Herder does not discuss this much, his analysis is partly motivated by the search for the long-lost German national culture, political identity, and *Volksgeist*; but sadly, recent scholarship rejects precisely the idea that there ever was a primæval German national consciousness or character. Like the French one, this identity arose after the division of the Imperial Roman remnant population whose descendants were given a unified political structure and identity by the establishment of the Carolingian Empire, and involved the identification of the state principle with a cultural identity – something which had not occurred to anyone as a practical or theoretical possibility before then. (Brühl, 1994)[14] What we can call the Ossian view is triumphant: for Herder's whole intellectual plan is based on the notion that his theoretical nationalism would serve to preserve the ancient treasures of the *Volk*. He offers no empirical basis for his view of the nation, anyway. It is based on an account of language which was a general theory of culture as much as anything, and this theory, though interesting in its way, rests on the idea that the highly artificial linguistic and cultural situation in a few European countries at the end of the eighteenth century was the inevitable result and culmination of natural processes of human physiology. No-one today would support Herder's specific scientific claims as they stand; and it seems fair to point out that by expressing his theory of the *Volk* in terms of comparisons of the noble, free Europeans of the North and the degenerate savages of the rest of the world, and by establishing an ideological base for the destruction of multi-national states on 'scientific' grounds,[15] Herder unwittingly did much to set the stage for the Nazi Holocaust. His aim was benign, and his philosophy of history, of which this modern and progressive conclusion was supposed to be the triumphant result, had no specific political aim; but even so, when we learn that Goethe had advised him not under any circumstances to publish an earlier draft of the last chapter of the *Ideas*, in one paragraph of which the ideological position just discussed is stated, we can perhaps lament that Herder did not take this advice to heart and abandon his whole project. He was never happy with this last chapter, apparently. But there has been as much blood spilled over the ideas in that one exalted paragraph as over any other work of modern European scientific or philosophical literature.[16]

---

[14] Brühl follows Carl Erdmann (1935) in denying the existence of a German *Volk* in the middle ages. Analysis of documents shows that society was not organised according to such concepts; and the various populations who would later unite as Germans, far from being the guardians of an ancient sacred tradition and culture, saw themselves as independent, despite their cultural similarities. 'It is necessary to reject categorically any idea of a national consciousness, French or German, in the IXth and Xth centuries.' (p. 143; my translation)

[15] 'Since they are devoid of national character, it would be the curse of Fate which would condemn to immortality these forced unions, these lifeless monstrosities.' (Herder, 1969, p. 324)

[16] 'From the start of the Greek uprising against Ottoman rule in 1824 till the ethnic war on the territory of the unfortunate Yugoslavia in the 1990s, all the European wars were fought either for ethnic emancipation, ethnic unification, promotion of one nation state's power (whether real or alleged) or ethnic adjustment of the states' borders.' (Krejčí, 1996)

However, as Patočka points out, these anthropological theories were not central to Herder's own (equally idiosyncratic) political thought, even if a simplistic version of his theory of the nation subsequently formed a central part of Czech nationalist ideology, of East European nationalisms generally, of pan-Slavism, and ultimately of German National Socialism. (Indeed, we still see the shadow of Herder's thought lying across the international state system today.) A consistent theme of Herder's political writings is opposition to centralised political authority of any kind; and with its Ossian romanticism – its naive anthropological assumptions – removed, his theory of what constitutes a nation (a language community), in combination with this, would presumably have sanctioned a kind of atomistic and anarchistic fragmentation of the political organisation of society into hundreds or thousands of ethnically cleansed basic units. It is an original position, and must have seemed very interesting and modern at the time, but bears as little relation to practical political programmes as do the ideologies of Fourier or Blake. The Czech nationalist ideologues, though, seized on this treatment of nationality and especially of national languages by a famous German philosopher as just what they needed to combat Austro-Hungarian centralism; and so Herder's ungrounded speculations about the national basis of society were embedded as important facts into the Czech national mythology, and more generally into the European nationalist tradition. Like many a philosophical writer,[17] Herder is left to spin in his grave in despair at the way that his real arguments, over which he had laboured so long and hard, have been ignored and left behind: too difficult and too complicated. But to return to the main stream of our own arguments, we see that Herder's supposedly neutral and philosophical argumentation concerning the naturalness of nations and of national languages makes exactly the set of assumptions we have characterised above as the 'naive anthropological hypothesis'. The nationalistic conclusions are built into the premises of the arguments, even if it would take nineteenth-century Romanticism to make this apparent; and Herder could not have been expected to think this through in the 1780s.

---

[17] Let us spare a thought for poor old Spinoza, for instance. The doctrine of national self-determination springs ultimately from his *Ethics*, in which we find the idea that while the universe as a whole is morally neutral, the self-determination of the individual is necessarily good as far as he is concerned; and via the political programmes of the United States and the United Nations, *inter alia*, a highly modified form of this doctrine has now been institutionalised internationally as the basis for exclusivist political projects which Spinoza, the gentle intellectual and champion of toleration, would certainly have deplored.

To put this same process in quite another perspective, let us consider the view of the contemporary Africanist Jean-Loup Amselle about 'tribes' in Africa. Amselle suggests that the division of the African population into tribes is something that has been done by the white man. There is an unconscious cultural imperialism at work. Starting from the same naive anthropological hypothesis about nationalism, the nineteenth-century colonists and invaders who annexed large parts of Africa in the name of nationalist projects of self-aggrandisement of one sort or another set out to explain and catalogue the indigenous African population they found. Because they knew that primitive society – the 'noble savage' – came in monocultural units, they constructed a sort of sociobiology of Africa, combining ideas of evolutionary progress from the Bushmen and Pygmies to more 'advanced' peoples with rather approximate fieldwork in native villages. One aspect of the project was to identify the more advanced peoples as potential future partners. The French were particularly active and thorough in this work, and they soon had West Africa analysed into tribes in this way. (Amselle's own fieldwork and research has focused on Côte d'Ivoire, Mali and Guinea.) Government studies gave way to government schools, and soon these same theories were being taught to the government-selected locals as the facts of their 'tribal heritage'. Since only these people could then advance in the colonial hierarchy, this style of analysis was quickly propagated through the new 'tribal' elites, who in time became the representatives of their 'peoples' in the nationalistic political arrangements also put in place by the colonial powers. This vandalism has served to unravel the population structure, destroying the delicate equilibrium of forces which relates population to land, and introducing a European principle of territoriality (with its roots in Western Christianity and the collapse of the Roman Empire): and certain 'tribes' are now close to Western 'nations' in their aspirations for power and land. The obvious contemporary example of this process is Rwanda, where two components of a parallel cultural configuration have been separated out into proto-national ethnic adversaries. From the beginnings of German missionary activity in the country, individuals were assigned the bureaucratic status of Hutu, Tutsi or Twa (a pygmy group making up about 1 percent of the present population of Rwanda). It is interesting to note that the government of Paul Kagame, seeking to find an ideological basis for reconstructing the country after the 1994 genocide, chose an official position close to Amselle's view – *i.e.* that the division of the Rwandan population into Tutsi and Hutu elements was based on a false understanding of the nature of African society. (Rieff, 1996)

This seems like a very complete and logical approach. Amselle suggests that a better approach would be to develop a topological method in anthropology, starting from areas rather than 'tribes'. (Amselle, 1985) But the damage has already been done. Educated Africans have now been trained to think of themselves not only as having a natural loyalty to a nation invented and drawn on a map by a colonial power, basically for commercial reasons, but also as having a natural tribal identity, representing the pre-colonial society. But the dynamics of the population structure have been altered irrevocably (by guns, medicine, irrigation, disease, new foods, and so on – not forgetting that most powerful import, information): and so the 'tribal' identities, though certainly based on some real differences, now refer in their values to a different kind of network of relationships.

The explanation of European history as a history of nations has roughly the same kind of stratigraphy, we could say. The picture is complicated, of course, since different countries, nations and cultures exhibit different local patterns in their self-awareness, but overall there is a progression from the introduction of a recognisable state idea in the form of Roman citizenship to the national histories available today. Is this the only kind of pattern available in the world, though? It is not. Does every 'national language' necessarily contain a similar kind of 'national morality'? It does not. A look at India will show that there is another kind of alternative, even at the level of a 'nation' of hundreds of millions of people. Indeed, all the countries marked by contact with Indian Buddhism – China, Japan, Vietnam, Cambodia, Burma, Tibet, and various now-extinct Central Asian societies – show a social pattern which is inherently pluralistic, as far as religious or ideological allegiance is concerned. In India, this pluralism exists at all the levels of social organisation which are unified in the European national cultures: language, religion (or morality), territory and culture. While Sikhs, Hindus or Muslims do predominate in this or that village, city or region, and while the overall social organisation does conform more strongly to a Hindu pattern than to any other, the pluralism of India is not marginal or accidental: it is a structural feature of the whole society. Of the whole approach to society. If we look for a concrete reason for this, we will find it in the history of Buddhism.

As in the case of Roman Christianity in Europe, it was the religion of India that first provided a moral basis for a unified society, by legitimising a system of military and political domination. Hinduism, and its offshoot, Buddhism, provided a philosophy of society on the one hand, and on the other an ideology of power. This latter feature was not originally present in either the Roman or the Indian religion: but it is nevertheless a historical reality that this is how they were transformed into state ideologies. As Constantine connected Christianity with the Roman power, Ashoka united India under the banner of Buddhism. It is a sad irony that this religion of peace and benign government should have been adopted as a kind of penance by a king who had earned a reputation for ruthless brutality during his rise to power and conquest of India; but this is no more paradoxical than the adoption of Christianity by the Roman legions, which were hardly known for turning the other cheek, after all. But there is a profound difference between Christianity and Buddhism. The difference is one of exclusion versus inclusion. Christianity, like Islam and Judaism, is an ideology of exclusion – a cult of exclusion, to use the terminology I have developed elsewhere. (Lord, 1994; and see Lord, 1999, pp. 110ff, 'The cult aspect of exlusion in society') It says that there is only one answer, the Christian answer, and that all other answers are therefore wrong. This, anyway, has been the working assumption of many Christian leaders – military and political as well as spiritual. It is a pattern which is then repeated within Christianity, and within Christian society, with this or that faction promoting its own special brand of Christianity as the only true one; with, once again, the implicit or explicit complementary idea emerging that all the other alternatives (the other Christian factions) must therefore be wrong. Islam shows a broadly similar pattern. It is a logical consequence of adopting an exclusivist ideology and morality in the first place.

Buddhism, like the other beliefs connected with Hindu thought, represents a different, inclusivist, pattern. This is partly for internal historical reasons, and partly because it had to fit itself to a society which was already very variegated. The historical reasons are to do with the origin of Buddhism. Unlike Christianity and Islam, it was not a revolutionary creed, demanding a break from the old ways. On the contrary, Buddha was an orthodox Hindu, who did not see himself as challenging the established pattern of philosophy. His position (as far as it can reliably be reconstructed) was rather that he had reached a more perfect understanding. His philosophy is one of refinement. Through a still more perfect refinement than that suggested by the philosophy of the orthodox Brahmin tradition, that is, a still more perfect spiritual condition could be attained. This, anyway, is how Indian Buddhists interpreted his message, and this allowed Buddhist thought to flower in a society still dominated by the Hindu social and moral system. Indeed, these two strands of Indian thought were able to coexist throughout the life-cycle of Buddhism in India; and in those countries where Buddhist philosophy was exported, we see a similar pluralist, inclusivist tendency. So Japan, for instance, despite a culture which is strongly nationalistic, and chauvinistic in the sense of being violently opposed to foreigners and their works, was civilised by the introduction of elements of a Chinese high culture which contained a large measure of Buddhism; and as a result we see that there are a number of coexisting Japanese belief-systems (schools of Shinto and of Zen Buddhism). These are not in conflict with each other in the way that Christian and Islamic factions have historically been in conflict – despite the fact that Buddhism was a foreign system imposed on nature-loving Shinto, with which it had no immediate cultural connection.[18] Rather, these belief systems complement each other at the social level, and without compromising the Japanese cultural identity. This is because the individual feels no personal contradiction in believing in more than one religious or philosophical system at the same time, and this is because the systems of thought in question are morally and intellectually compatible (whereas the Christian sects traditionally present themselves as mutually exclusive, each deliberately making dogmatic claims which are unacceptable for its rivals – the Calvinist dogma of predestination providing a convenient example of this). While following the same basic pattern of Buddhist thought, then, each Buddhist school claims to offer a more perfect version of these ideas. The existence of other schools of thought is thus a confirmation that the whole complex tradition is alive and valid, rather than a threat to any one particular school. We see that the basic Buddhist inclusivist model is propagated throughout the system (of states civilised by contact with Buddhism), in the same way that the basic Christian or Muslim exclusivist model is propagated throughout the system of states civilised by or otherwise affected by these monotheistic systems of thought and belief.

(We should note, for completeness, that modern India actually offers a hybrid between these two models. While the effects of Hinduism and Buddhism are still profoundly felt, the success of Sikh and Muslim moral, religious and social models has complicated the picture so that we should analyse India as a pluralistic, inclusivist society on the large scale, but including islands of exclusivism among individual component cultures at a smaller scale. It is interesting to note that even Islam, which has definitely

---

[18] 'The question arises how the Japanese people could accept Buddhism, an alien religion, when they already had an indigenous faith that apparently satisfied their needs? The answer is that from the beginning the two religions had a great deal in common.' (Matsunaya and Matsunaya, 1974, Vol. 1, p. 5)

tended towards an exclusivist pattern, in India as elsewhere, was to some extent assimilated by the syncretist, inclusivist, Hindu tradition, so that hybrid Muslim/Hindu schools of religion flourished at one time.[19] But it would require a separate treatment to go into this in any depth.)

Why does Indian culture preserve a greater variety of cultural standards than Europe? It is not an empty question. The general tendency towards standardisation and homogenisation that we see in Europe, while not entirely absent, seems to have had much less effect on society in India. One reason is the function of language in society, and specifically the function of standard languages. In Europe, as we have seen, the social and political homogenisation which led eventually to the production of nation states was brought about through the agency of the standard languages of the Roman Empire, and of the Slav written language created in imitation of these. The situation in India was quite different, since the standard language of India was not (primarily) written, but spoken. Sanskrt (which means 'regular language') is a standardised version of the background spread of dialects (Prakrt), improved and regularised for the use of the ruling Brahmin caste. It is described in great detail in the earliest known philological study, that of Panini (c. 300 B.C.), and we know that it was regularised not for the needs of scribes and bureaucrats using written texts, but for the needs of a society whose documents were orally transmitted and stored in memory. The pronunciation of Sanskrt was highly variable from place to place, but what was preserved was its prosody, since this was essential for the construction of regular, chanted texts. A regular metrical structure was the essential thing. This device enabled some individuals to memorise texts of tens of thousands of lines, and shorter texts, even when full of the most difficult philosophical language, could be memorised at a single hearing (as the testimony of Chinese travellers tells us). So, a 'national' language for India is not the language of a particular ethnic group – although there are plenty of those to choose from. It is the language of the educated stratum of society. Indeed, it was forbidden for low-caste people to use or even to study Sanskrt. We see that contemporary India has quite easily accepted English in a similar way: not as the exclusive language of this or that ethnic group or region, but as a uniting language, whose use includes members of all the components of society above a certain level of education. While the impact of British imperialism had complicated effects, in this one aspect – linguistic change – much of the previous social structure was preserved, as indeed is normal during the process of cultural transfer.

---

[19] (Sen, 1961), Ch. 18, 'Medieval Mysticism of North India', pp. 97-102.

To draw together some of these strands, then, let us say that the stately progress of society towards the ideal of the homogeneous, monocultural nation state is not observed in India or in those Eastern countries marked by contact with Indian high culture. The success of Christianity at a world level depends to some extent on its philosophical depth; for the Western European culture, with its impressive artistic and scientific achievements, is Christian in its inspiration: and the success of Buddhism as a social, moral and religious model similarly relied on the superiority of its art, and of its philosophical formulations and concepts.[20] This, after all, was how it had succeeded in India itself.

This brings us back to the question of the anthropological assumption mentioned above: the assumption that since modern European history is interpreted from the point of view of nations and national projects, all history is correctly interpreted as the history of nations in some older form. The Indian 'nation', we have seen, is structured differently: according to the horizontal divisions of caste, with cultural and in particular linguistic differentiation also affected by this pattern, and not just following the territorial divisions that seem so natural to those of us with a Eurocentric intellectual background. Can we therefore construct an anthropological scheme which will give us another, more general kind of explanation?

Let us schematise the question as follows. The technologically least developed societies, we easily observe, are subjectively monocultural and homogeneous. Jungle villages occupied by naked hunters have no problems of minority populations. Modern European societies, too, are (in their own imagining) monocultural and homogeneous. So one kind of history is a history which untangles all the paths which have taken the primitive cultural units to this contemporary position. These paths are typically shown on maps, which neatly summarise the migrations and other movements by which this or that 'people' has advanced towards the present happy situation.

An alternative scheme for European social development is as follows. Monocultural societies are monocultural either because they have no contact with other societies, or because they resist the contaminating effects of such contact. If we dare to follow Gumilëv, we could even argue that such 'relicts' are only like that in the first place because they have fallen by the wayside, preferring to stagnate in isolation than to develop through cultural contacts. But as populations, technology, and commerce advance, a new kind

---

[20] 'Without scriptures or systematisation, the indigenous faith [i.e. Shinto] could not provide a philosophical challenge to Buddhism.'(Matsunaya and Matsunaya, 1974, p. 6)

of community is created: the trading centre or city. Over time, this attracts a range of people, whose cultures are brought into contact under new conditions. The city is polyglot and polycultural, compared with the monoglot, monocultural village or town. But the cultures of this new urbanised environment do not immediately creolise and mix together (although they will certainly tend to do so over time). There are a number of important isolating factors, after all: different languages, moralities, belief systems, social structures, and so on, plus the important factor that individuals and groups within the city will still be in physical or cultural contact with the monocultural societies from which they came, which may well continue to function outside the city. This creates a condition of parallel cultures. It is a very general and widespread type of social configuration.

The city (especially the pre-industrial city) is inherently in this condition, since the city represents a more developed kind of social organisation, and the city will always suck in people from less highly structured societies. But the city in this sense is really the urbanised way of life, and in the contemporary world, the urbanised way of life is provided by technology more than by physical location. From a historical point of view, though, the sociological flux can be seen in action in a number of real historical cities: Babylon, Alexandria, Rome, Constantinople and Baghdad in the past; London, Vienna, Moscow and New York more recently. The city will tolerate speakers of another language, and worshippers of another god. This is part of its function as a social structure. But whether its police authorities will be so tolerant is a question of a different kind: a question of policy.

The particular mix of cultures living in parallel in any particular place and time will be limited by some objective factors, such as ease of travel, physical distance, commercial demand, and so on. The city may simply bring together neighbouring villagers who would otherwise never meet; or at the other extreme, the city may bring all the people of the world together in a kaleidoscope of cultures and languages. But still, there will probably be one social and cultural group which is at the top of the pile. One group with the authority to make the laws. And from the point of view of this dominant group, there is a basic choice to make: inclusion or exclusion of other moralities and identities.

This choice is repeated at all levels of an urbanising system. Will strangers be allowed to do business in the market-place in the town square? Will a local language be tolerated in the state's education system? Will the state issue passports to those who claim a different nationality or religion?

We could even talk about the urbanisation of the whole planet, within this schema, and ask whether the emerging world administrative and political culture should be inclusive or exclusive. The answer that it should be inclusive seems obvious from a general moral point of view: but in fact the trend of history would seem to point in the other direction. It is the exclusivist, Western Christian, social model which provides the real international standard, it seems. The international political system (to the extent that it really exists) is a system of exclusivist nation states. For the West, this seems natural and inevitable; but for Africa, say, it is just as clear that the nation state system is highly artificial and divisive. The central paradox is still that Western European paradox mentioned above: that such an ideology seeks to promote two directly opposed ideas at the same time, namely its own local version of state morality and the idea of a universal moral order.

This, then, will be the texture of our argumentation. We will look at minority populations as components of large-scale processes of social formation, and not just as bits of nations that have got stuck on the wrong side of a border somewhere by mistake. We will look at various historical attempts to deal with this kind of social configuration, and compare these with recent policies. While trying to keep a world perspective, we will focus on post-communist Europe and the former USSR, since here the process of social regeneration is of great importance from all points of view, and some preparatory work is called for. The synthesis of nation states there is in general less advanced than in Western Europe; and it is a real question what kind of policy norm will eventually decide the fate of those people whose everyday cultural norms are not those of the dominant group in the territory where they live.

II. A Preliminary Analysis

The 'national' identity as a type of cultural identity pattern (and there are other types, of course) has a particular and characteristic texture in Europe. It is not, generally speaking, an identity based on total cultural homogeneity. Not every Frenchman or every German has identical values by any means (though the size of the state is relevant here: inhabitants of San Marino or Gibraltar are in a different kind of position). But there is an attempt at a limited kind of homogeneity. Politically, for example, every Frenchman is supposed to be equal and equivalent to every other; and we could easily find other examples of this assumption of *égalité*. This search for a common group identity is not something which has just come out of thin air. Man is both a social and a territorial creature, and if we look at technologically less developed societies, we see that it is the social unit rather than the individual which determines the ownership of territory (though this is commonly personalised through an institution such as monarchy, so that the group's territory is conventionally understood and more importantly felt to be that of a ruling individual, who acts as an emotional symbol for the whole society). Now, the nationalisms of the nineteenth century, which did so much to define the modern nation-state, were closely linked with the romanticism which lionised the noble savage and the proto-national culture he was supposed to represent. Ossian (the wholly imaginary protagonist of a falsified epic poem of the same name, which provided the authoritative image of a lost age of Germano-Celtic heroes for a generation of romantics and nationalists in Europe – the impressive figure of Johann Wolfgang von Goethe standing proudly at their head) symbolised the supposed continuity of nationalistic thinking from a supposed golden age of 'pure' culture(s). The idea is roughly that at some unspecified period in the past, there were a number of pure tribal cultures in Europe, each speaking one of the modern languages of Europe, but in an ancient, original, and pure state – undefiled, that is, by the deplorable cultural mixing of recent centuries – and in general living with the pure and therefore exemplary values of a pure national culture. This is in essence another appearance of the naive anthropological hypothesis we have identified in part one above; and the observation of technologically less developed peoples, which began in earnest during the same nineteenth-century expansive period in European history, certainly fed this kind of thinking too. In village societies we do see a high degree of cultural separation, with wide linguistic gaps, for example, opening up between neighbouring 'cultures'. In Polynesia, it seems that an original, perhaps homogeneous, population and culture has spread and diverged, so that, in the words of a nineteenth-century traveller, 'The islands of the South Seas present a spectacle of extraordinary interest to the moral and political philosopher. While certain principles of polity are common to them all, there are striking diversities everywhere apparent.' (Campbell, 1840, p. 474) In the Americas, the languages spoken before the coming of the white man display an amazing diversity, and this diversity is reflected by social structures and other cultural indicators too (though, paradoxically, there are also some unifying factors which are difficult to explain – on the one hand, some close cultural similarities between people of very different 'ethnic' identity, and on the other, phonological similarities between languages otherwise structurally very different). In Africa, in India, and elsewhere, the nineteenth-century romantic could easily find evidence to support a nationalistic anthropological hypothesis. Everywhere, it seems, man spontaneously divides himself up into cultural in-groups, where language and culture (food, dress, mythology, art...) are shared by a population within a bounded territory. Man? Well, there is a feminist angle, of course. In village societies, whether we are talking about China, the Americas or the Caucasus, women are commonly sent out to other villages to marry, and to learn another language and culture if necessary. Indeed, this exchange of women is observed among the hunting bands of peoples preserving Old Stone Age lifestyles, and we may reasonably suppose that it predates such basic-seeming institutions of social life as the family unit. This important mechanism, and the constant pressure towards cultural transmission and assimilation it represents, has been largely ignored by (male!) cultural theorists, who on the whole prefer to see the male 'culture' (the proto-nation, that is) as single and inviolate. This, it seems, corresponds with its psychic content. In the same way that a naive biology sees human reproduction in terms of the male 'seed' being transmitted from generation to generation, with the female just a passive carrier of the man's sons, a naive anthropology sees human society in terms of its own social ideology: as something bounded and whole, and as something whose essential social structure is that of its male component. This is surely instinctive (at least, it is difficult to imagine another explanation for so universal a phenomenon); but perhaps only within a male-dominated social universe. In the same way that the individual man sees himself as a single, bounded whole, he also sees himself as part of a single, bounded community. The bounds are primitively bounds of territory, it seems (although again, it is only the weight of the evidence that supports this assertion: a precise biological theory is lacking so far), and so we can call this aspect of human identity 'boundary consciousness'. Since the boundary is something over the horizon of the immediate, it can be of any size, and the Russian or the American (or the Canadian or the Algerian) is used to a huge mental territory, where the jungle villager might accept a comparatively tiny range: but some version of this boundary consciousness seems universal. Where a people lives without a fixed physical territory, then they have some other kinds of boundaries (of religion or language or social structure) to keep them apart. In the parallel culture configuration, the boundaries are internal to a single society, and are 'cultural': linguistic, religious, or involving some kind of isolating, exclusivist behaviour.

Taking the long view, and looking at the whole development of human society, we can see that what we could call the contact conditions go through a number of phases. In the first phase, humans expand into empty territory. In this phase, each little group, now physically isolated, develops its own variant of an original mother tongue and culture. Both social structure and language are surprisingly variable – but at the same time surprisingly conservative, so that some structures in language and in behaviour generally can survive through thousands of years, as we see with groups which, though originally related, have been separated for such long periods. An important thing to note is that linguistic and social diversity do not necessarily correspond, even in these early stages of social development and territorial spread. It is reasonably suggested that one way to analyse cultures as a whole is by considering the whole culture as a language – and in that sense of course a cultural boundary is a linguistic boundary. But if we look just at what we normally call 'language' – speech – then we easily find both the requisite kinds of counter-examples: speakers of the same language who have adopted separate group identities, and speakers of different languages who have identical cultural and social patterns apart from that.

In the next phase of contact we will identify, the available territory is saturated (though at a very low level of population by modern standards), and so groups must establish boundaries with their neighbours. The boundary is now not just with the wild and the unknown (with the Dreamtime, for instance, in the Australian case – the Dreamtime having a physical as well as a psychological location for the Aboriginals), but with neighbouring groups. In a hunting society, dominated by violence and ideas of bravery, the borders will in this phase be protected from invasion by organised retribution. This is the proto-national condition seen by naive nationalist theorists; the paradox being that in many cases – most cases, probably – the 'foreigners' over the border are actually close blood relatives, with a closely related culture, who just happened to separate off and take over the next valley.

So, in this phase, we have low-technology societies, in which people live in monocultural, bounded territories; and before our eyes we have the modern European nation states. The naive anthropological hypothesis is that the latter are highly-developed or evolved forms of the former: that at some remote time there were wild and noble Frenchmen and Germans and Turks and Portuguese and Serbs and whatever it might be, but speaking the pure forms of the corresponding languages, singing the ancient lays of the people, eating their traditional dishes, doing their ancient folk dances, and so on. This, the Ossian alternative, is an interpretation which is now deeply embedded in European folk-cultural (and high-cultural!) beliefs. Apart from Macpherson himself (the inventor of Ossian, and author of the spurious Celtic poems in which he made his entrance into Europe's mythological tradition), Herder and Rousseau are largely to blame for making this kind of thinking acceptable among intellectuals;[21] and especially among just the kind of intellectuals who would then set about 'reconstructing' local 'folk traditions' in conformity with this inspiring ideology. (And from the point of view of the philosophical and literary tradition of Western Europe, we also see an identification of the life of the 'noble savage' with the ideal 'state of nature' described by mainstream theorists such as Hobbes and Locke: so that the romantic nationalist could see himself as a profound moralist and philosopher as well, selflessly devoted to re-making a life of uncontaminated and natural morality. Something of the distinctive flavour of this enterprise still permeates the nationalistic ideologies of Eastern Europe today.)[22] But if we look more closely at the real situation in Europe, in the light of more detailed and careful researches into low-technology cultures in particular, we will see that a more refined kind of theory is required.

To take up our account of the phases of development in contact conditions, we see that the 'proto-national' phase, with culturally homogenous groups living on bounded territories which are defined not only by their own boundaries (and so by their own boundary consciousness), but also by those of their neighbours, is not the end of the story. We can say some interesting things about this phase, though, before we go on. From a psychological point of view, we see that the identity of the group under these conditions, expressed and preserved in the value-structures of the society, is subject to the influence of some outside factors: namely, the equivalent value-structures in the neighbouring groups. Through ritual contacts (North American 'potlatch' exchange is the classic phenomenon in the anthropological literature) and through trade, the cultures can exchange not

---

[21] 'Listen to the wailings of Ossian on the death of his little son, and you will perceive in them the bleeding wounds of the paternal heart, the saddest wounds of the manly breast.' (Herder, 1969, p. 306). Rousseau was more original: he invented a fantasy world of happy rustic primitives for himself, and succeeded in propagating this image through his elegant writings to a large and influential audience.

[22] 'The belief in a happy "state of nature" in the remote past is derived partly from the biblical narrative of the age of the patriarchs, partly from the classical myth of the golden age. The general belief in the badness of the remote past came only with the doctrine of evolution.' (Russell, 1975, p. 602)

just magical virtue – the original aim of such contact, apparently – but any and all other values too. This process, however limited it may appear at any one time, will eventually spread cultural values across subjective boundaries. These values are not necessarily marginal, either. In pre-Columbian America, we find that the Mesoamerican cultural area, though its population was differentiated into some twelve linguistic groups, had a distinctive and easily-identifiable calendar system (of a 365-day year and a 260-day almanac, which combined to form a 52-year 'calendar round'), and this system, which had an associated ritual significance and cosmological interpretation, was common to the whole region. Subjective cultural differences, in other words, were transcended by objective cultural diffusion. In general, there is no reason to suppose that the distinctive pre-literate 'cultures' reconstructed by archæologists on the basis of characteristic stylistic or technological criteria in the material culture had any particular linguistic identity; and the reverse assumption would seem just as reasonable. It is only because we work backwards from modern national cultures that we assume that linguistic and cultural boundaries coincide.

Contact with strangers is ritualised and controlled in a hunting society. After all, it threatens the whole integrity of the group. But still, it can and does take place; and the exchange of women, a ritually invisible and therefore very much under-valued mechanism of cultural exchange in my view, binds cultural exchange to the even more powerful mechanism of genetic bonding. It is this above all which gives the lie to the nationalist assumption. Descent from a common ancestor, as Freud notes, is a universal myth among self-identifying groups; but it has only a psychological reality, since it is completely sabotaged by the realisation that 50 per cent of the genetic material in this 'descent' comes from a female population which characteristically shows quite a different pattern of group identity – and this for evolutionary reasons, since any other pattern, over the tens of thousands of years during which many low-technology societies have functioned, would have led to genetic collapse through mental and physical deformity. And in more recent times, the same realisation can sabotage modern versions of what are essentially the same myths of group psychology. In the Balkans, for instance, the national identities which have arisen since the end of the Ottoman period are based on a male, warrior society ideal (Ossian again! Or at least his ghost); and I for one will be very surprised if genetic studies do not soon reveal that the exchange of genetic material between the 'nations' of the Balkans has been high enough to make them a single breeding community by purely biological standards.

The next phase, anyway, is that of the re-combination of societies. The low-technology society is ritually homogeneous on a given territory, it is true; but between this social pattern and its modern descendant there lies another long phase of development, which actually forms the bulk of recorded history: the pre-modern but post-primitive phase of the ancient civilisations. The city-based civilisations of Mesopotamia, Egypt, Greece and Rome.[23] The Roman society, as we argue here, actually forms the bridge to our modern European world, and so we should analyse it separately. But in all these city cultures of the ancient world, we see that the boundary consciousness has undergone a basic change. Cultural boundaries, it suddenly appears, are resilient enough to withstand physical proximity, under the conditions of city life. The city is depersonalising, compared with the village. In the city, you can go from place to place without speaking, or only carrying out a few elementary verbal transactions; so that you can wait until you return to your own little corner, with your own people, before you start to function again. The basic isolating mechanisms of the controlled exchange of values (and of genetic material) are in place, but the cultural boundaries no longer correspond to simple physical boundaries of territory. The territories are now bounded by social structures. In the logically simplest case, a number of participating cultures will share a single territory. This is the basic parallel cultures configuration. In time, we can see that it will also tend to produce a genetically homogeneous breeding community (through the exchange of women, typically), so that cultural differences, accompanied by myths of separate descent, will persist in a population which has slowly removed any real genetic basis for the differences that may originally have existed to justify such differentiation and myth-making. And in the extreme case, as we have also seen, the exchange of values may be so complete that there are no real cultural discrepancies left either, apart from the rituals of self-identity themselves.

'Culture' is notoriously difficult to define, but we can set up some indicators of cultural differences. Language, religion, dress, food... an obvious enough list. But whatever criteria we adopt, looking around at contemporary Europe, we see that the nationalistic assumption (of culturally homogeneous national units) is compromised in almost every real case. Iceland is the only European 'nation state' which really has a single language and culture (though we could include Armenia also, if we wanted to stretch

---

[23] Yes, it is a Eurocentric account. Elsewhere, cultural contact took place through other social structures. But let us develop a European theory first of all.

our definition of 'Europe' that far). An undivided, monolithic population. In every other European state (disregarding Monaco, the Vatican, and so on), we see a different phenomenon: the non-coincidence of borders. The populations, despite the state ideologies, are only roughly homogeneous – and the physical borders (which, after all, are in most cases military rather than cultural boundaries) are similarly approximate, if we look at other, more objective, cultural indicators. (There is another kind of non-coincidence, too: the tendency for states to fall apart, which is by no means a modern phenomenon. An important reason for the union of Poland and Lithuania in 1385 was that the provinces into which successive members of the Piast dynasty in Poland had divided their patrimony did not conform to the diocesan boundaries established by the church – which led to political instability and contributed to the extinction of the Polish state: or at least its radical reconfiguration.)

Language is a convenient marker of cultural structures of various kinds. England, for instance, speaks English. This is true in a general sort of way: but if we look at the internal linguistic situation of the British Isles, we see that this generally true characterisation needs considerable qualification. English, for one thing, is still in a dynamic relationship with the languages of the Celtic substrate of the British Isles before the coming of the Angles and the other Germanic invaders: with Welsh and Scots Gaelic (the Cornish branch of 'British' having now been eradicated by the pressure of English). The prognosis for Scots Gaelic looks bad – it is not spoken by urban populations anywhere, and actually it looks possible that this language will survive longer in Nova Scotia, Canada, where a thinly-populated and remote area still uses the language in everyday life, than in Scotland itself, where Gaelic is probably not being passed on to the next generation. But Welsh has been managed into a much stronger position. The conversion of the population to Christianity had brought with it the usual introduction of a native version of the Bible, something which eventually provoked a gloomy literature of pessimistic sermons and bleak religious tracts, which then displaced the bardic poetry of the old aristocratic courts to provide the normal written standard for the modern language. Welsh-language publishing and university teaching is now well established, and this feeds the mass media, so that almost the whole spectrum of 'national culture' is available in Welsh. This approach has also worked well in Catalunya, where the Catalan language has been rescued from the advance of Spanish (another big world language) in a roughly similar way. The strategy is clear: to establish an alternative national language, with a full range of activities (including, for instance, official forms, court procedures, and so on) conducted according to the new standard. This approach can be criticised as artificial, since it in fact represents a managed bilingualism: Welsh- and Catalan-speakers do not really live in a 'normal' national linguistic culture, and will mostly continue to use English and Spanish as well to some extent. Only time will tell if this strategy will work in the end, but so far it seems that probably it will. After a long period of increasing English use, some children now grow up using mainly Welsh, for instance. But this is not the whole story. The Welsh that they use is not in fact the Welsh of their parents and grandparents.

Welsh, despite its use as a language of religion, was systematically displaced in the few centres of learning and industry in Wales during the industrial revolution period, when much of the more populated part of Wales (the south) was industrialised and integrated into English commerce. Although the language had its ancient epic poetry and its tradition of biblical translation, one effect of the industrialisation of Welsh society was to remove the bulk of Welsh-speakers from contact with this upper register of the language. Employment was offered by English-speakers, and education was provided by the British Empire. Preserving Welsh was not high on its list of priorities. Religion, too, was increasingly taken over by English, and Welsh gradually died away among the slag-heaps of the more 'developed' parts of Wales. This meant – and it is a common enough pattern – that Welsh became the language of those untouched by official culture: the language of hill farmers and the lowest stratum of the new proletariat. The high language of the epic poetical tradition and the Bible survived, but almost independently, as the language of a Welsh middle class who still clung to the Christian ideas of the past. For reasons of general culture (rather than for narrowly linguistic reasons) the bulk of Welsh speakers lived in a condition of diglossia with this elevated language – something like that of Greek villagers listening to the elegant but largely incomprehensible periods of the Alexandrian Greek which is preserved in the liturgy of the Orthodox Church. English was the language of opportunity, and so the middle class/aspirant working class (the classical generational change being the miner to schoolteacher one: Britain is still full of Welsh schoolteachers; few of whom, however, can speak good Welsh) went along with imperial practice more generally and encouraged their children to drop Welsh in favour of English. The situation has changed dramatically, though, largely as a result of Welsh nationalist agitation in the 1970s, and radical intellectuals were able to formulate a new language policy. They were able to do this basically because the electoral system of

Britain, which is fine-tuned to ensure the survival of the status quo, was for once defeated. There are sufficient concentrations of Welsh speakers to allow (in principle) the election of Welsh Members of Parliament reflecting this local culture, and this in fact happened with the election of three *Plaid Cymru* (Welsh Nationalist) MPs in 1974. The three seats gave a disproportionate political importance to the party in 'national' British politics during the 1974-79 parliament, and the successes of political Welsh nationalism generally gave the nationalist movement enough of an edge for it to be able to make some important changes. Chief among these were the establishment of Welsh-language schooling as a normal alternative (in Welsh-speaking areas, that is; industrialised Wales already speaks English on the whole), and the establishment of Welsh-language television and radio on a large scale.

Now, the process which is being encouraged is not the spread of Welsh, but its preservation. There is some degree of outreach to English-speaking families, to encourage them to encourage their children to learn the language, but this is a difficult task, and the main challenge of the policy as a whole is to prevent the disappearance of Welsh as a normal spoken language of everyday life, and that means dealing with those sections of the population who already use it, and preventing or slowing down the generational switch to English. It is this which is killing Scots and Irish Gaelic. Television, pop music, and other low-cultural, mass-media aspects of language use are the vital factor, since the people in question, as just explained, have little contact with education, and little interest in education either. Specifically, they have little interest in the high-flown Welsh of the bardic tradition or the Bible. Now, Welsh is an ancient language, and over time the normal spoken language has fragmented into a great many local dialects. It has survived best in thinly-populated areas, where every village has its own way of speaking to some extent. It is a question of methodology and typology how many distinct 'dialects' the analyst makes out of this, but at least we can say with certainty that there are two large dialect areas, North Welsh and West Welsh, with native speakers instantly knowing which is the home of a new Welsh-speaking acquaintance. The solution that has arisen in Wales is the creation of a new, synthetic form of Welsh: a 'BBC Welsh', in unconscious imitation of the 'BBC English' which forms such an important part of the imperial culture across the border in England. 'Cymraeg Byw', or 'Living Welsh', is the result: a politically correct homogenisation of Western and Northern elements, according to modernised social standards which are closer to the urban life of the still more developed South. An unpredictable bilingualism will be the actual result, with English or Welsh predominating in a given geographical area or field of activity.

Returning to our general analysis, we see that Welsh has been transformed by its contact with English, and that a language policy has been constructed to adapt the language to the new circumstances. But in terms of frontiers, we can see that a simple map, with an English-speaking area marked in one colour, and a Welsh-speaking area marked in another, would be a misleading guide to the overall tendency of events. It is a delicate business. Irish Gaelic, despite having been adopted as an official language in the Irish Republic, where it also has an important symbolic value, is in a similar state of decline to Scots Gaelic (which is actually an isolated dialect of Irish Gaelic, transported to the Highlands and Islands of Scotland by Irish settlers from the fifth century on). The Irish language activists have succeeded in codifying and preserving it to some extent as a written and literary language, making it a compulsory school subject, for instance, but this preserves it in form only. A real language is used naturally, unthinkingly, for making the tea and for making love, and writing school text books is not enough to bring this about. There are not enough solidly Gaelic-speaking areas (in Ireland or in Scotland) to support a homogeneous regeneration of the language according to the present norms of industrial society. The language continues to function – but as the language of an older pattern of society, and therefore as an anachronism in modern Scotland and Ireland. (But since no-one really understands the dynamics of this process, which is so complicated that every case is really unique, one cannot responsibly counsel a policy of surrender. Who knows? Perhaps talking computers will provide a means of preserving even the language or dialect of the smallest village population. Anyway, apart I suppose from Hebrew, which was 'revived' by teaching it from scratch to people who originally spoke other languages, all the signs are that once a language dies, it dies forever.)

The cultural frontier of English-speaking Britain, then, roughly coincides with official boundaries; but not completely. The 'English way of life', if you like, has basically spread throughout the British Isles, and where the corresponding spread of the English language has been arrested or slowed (that is, only in some parts of Wales), this does not automatically mean that the effects of the rest of the cultural invasion and assimilation have also been reduced. Quite the reverse: language policy has been successful because it has been managed so as to conform to the requirements of the wider cultural movement, which is almost entirely one-way.

We can compare this development of the Welsh language not just with that of Scots-Irish Gaelic, but also with that of the Lallans tongue of Scotland. 'Lallans' is a conventional spelling for the dialect pronunciation of 'lowlands', and the idea is that this is the national language of the Lowlands Scots. It is interesting to note that the movement (led by intellectuals, unfortunately; for this is usually a recipe for disaster) to establish 'Lallans' as an official language of Scotland bears a close family resemblance to the efforts of Slav, Greek, and other Eastern European and Balkans nationalists to establish 'native languages' in their own countries. This process is always a bit hit and miss. In Greece, the officially-sponsored attempt to establish a 'katharevousa' or 'purified' Greek was only very partially successful. The general idea of this was to set up a new standard form which was not so self-evidently Turkish in much of its lexicon and phonology as the spoken dialects which were in use after five hundred years of Ottoman rule. The official idea of a 'return' to a classical norm was compromised by the fact that the Orthodox Church disapproves of the classical Greek religion, which it rather attractively still treats as a spiritual threat. More generally, the dynamic of social change (from Ottoman-Byzantine to state-nationalist, roughly) could not be controlled by decree, and the population (mostly illiterate) rejected the new norms in favour of what came to be called 'dimotiki' – the demotic form of Greek, based on the prosody of radio pop music as much as anything else, which has in fact become the recognised language of the modern state. There is something preposterous about the whole project of constructing 'purified' national cultures in the Balkans in the first place: it is the most creolised part of Europe, and apart from linguistic and other indications, the day to day cultural similarities between 'Serb', 'Greek' and 'Albanian' village life are immediately obvious. The thing is that these identities were as much indications of social position as of 'nationality' in the Balkans. Greeks were those people under the protection and jurisdiction of the Orthodox millet in the Ottoman Empire. Albanians, as Muslims, had a higher status; and Serbs, though infidels, were appreciated as fighters. These social indicators, then, and the corresponding social structures, have been laboriously unravelled and separated, so that people who before lived in parallel, now supposedly live in separated, state-national cultures. As with Welsh, something that was originally a hangover from an older social structure (the 'British' language and culture of pre-Roman times; the recognised religious identities of the Ottoman system) is transformed into the marker (the defining characteristic, that is) of a local, national culture, now supposed to be homogeneous on a bounded territory, on the model of the Western nation states.[24]

Now, it is no accident that the two classes of markers which are generally accepted as legitimate for a state-nationalist category (a 'nationality') are religious and linguistic identities. In the first place, these can be spread throughout a society in a way that other potential markers may not be. In what is now Poland, for instance, the Polish nationality was not consolidated until the nineteenth century, and political loyalty to the state did not include this nationalistic element. But since then a state-nationalist ideal, in which the people are glued together with the double glue of an organised national Polish language, and a nationally-organised branch of the Roman Catholic religion, has succeeded in including the overwhelming majority of the population. In the second place, national religions and national languages are, as we have already seen, closely linked in their development and history. A national religion is indeed in most cases the explicit means by which a national language is established, with translations of the Bible typically providing the field of operations for nationalistically-minded scholars wishing to separate out a standard, official strand of local language and fix it by a programme of state-sponsored and/or church-sponsored publication. This pattern, so familiar and obvious in the West that we don't even think about it any more, is not repeated in the Muslim world, though, and we see that national versions of Arabic, Turkish, Farsi and related languages have been correspondingly slow to develop. They must continue to coexist with a liturgical language – the Arabic of the Koran – the existence and special status of which in effect denies the validity of the local languages (including local standards of spoken Arabic) as potential vehicles of truth. The implied resistance to the development and differentiation of national cultures is more than imaginary, and the contradiction between being a loyal Muslim and a

---

[24] J. R. R. Tolkein, in a very learned and provocative paper, points out that Welsh too (or 'British', as it is known in an earlier, pre-Roman phase of its life) is a language of invaders, and only appears to be indigenous because we have no documents of the pre-Celtic language(s) of Britain. This gives the lie to the emotional identification of Welsh as the language of a subjugated race. '... it remains an evident conclusion from history that apart from language the inhabitants of Britain are made of the same "racial" ingredients, though the mixing of these has not been uniform. It is still patchy. The observable differences are, however, difficult or impossible to relate to language. (...) But whatever the success of the imported languages, the inhabitants of Britain, during recorded history, must have been in large part neither Celtic nor Germanic: that is, not derived physically from the original speakers of these varieties of language, nor even from the already racially more mixed invaders who planted them in Britain.' (Tolkein, 1997, pp. 170, 171) Comparisons with the Balkans, and indeed with the European situation generally, immediately present themselves.

loyal Iranian or Saudi or Turk or whatever it might be represents one of the most important stresses of cultural transfer in the world today. The world demands nation states; but Islam demands unity and the homogenisation of precisely the differences which the nation-state systems sacralises and literally graves in stone: differences of tribal affiliation, language and culture, we could say – though the concept of a 'tribe' is actually derived from a Roman political term (*tribus*),[25] so that even an analysis in terms of tribal societies and identities refers us to the complex conceptual structures of the Roman idea. But there is an underlying reality: a boundary consciousness. We are territorial creatures, after all.

This leads us to an important process: the transfer of vocabularies. This essential mechanism of cultural transfer is often overlooked, but this is because we in the West live in societies where the differences between national vocabularies have been minimised already. If we look at Africa, the Far East, or anywhere in fact outside the developed West, we see that cultural assimilation can be seen in action through the acquisition of vocabulary items relating to the conceptual and material world of the West. Where the target language has no native term for a particular vocabulary item, it may coin a new compound, or it may adopt a foreign term instead – and it is increasingly likely that it will be an English term. A striking contemporary example of this latter mechanism is the word 'disco', which has passed into Chinese. This individual example is surprising because it contradicts the received wisdom about Chinese. This says that the Chinese language 'cannot' accept loan-words, because they do not fit into the phonological scheme of Chinese, and therefore 'cannot' be pronounced. Well, 'disco' is quite definitely a non-Chinese-sounding word, which does not fit into the strict templates of Chinese phonology: and yet it has been transferred. It is apparently such an important term that nothing so trivial as phonological awkwardness is going to stop people from using it. The important thing about this kind of transfer, though, is not this or that striking feature of this or that individual example: it is the scale of the process. The whole specialised vocabulary of the industrial world has been propagated in this way, through the means of standard languages originally devised and codified for quite different purposes (in the context of quite different social

---

[25] Jean Jacques Rousseau, 1762, *The Social Contract*, Book IV, Ch. 4, *The Roman Comitia* gives an excellent treatment of the political division of the Roman population into tribes. We can note briefly a) that one of the three original tribes was made up of foreigners – *i.e.* simply of people not included in the other two, and b) that the tribal system was soon changed from a quasi-ethnic to a territorial one, and in time lost its ethnic reference entirely.

structures, that is). We have considered the case of Sanskrt already, as an example of how a different kind of social structure is encoded in the use of this standard but not really national language; and let us now take another Indian example, and compare the international penetration of a Western industrial-world vocabulary with the international penetration of the intellectual vocabulary of Buddhism.

In India, remember, texts were not primarily written, but verbal, and held in memory. This, however, relied on a pre-existing development in Hindu society, and so when Buddhism came along, it was immediately propagated by these means (though not immediately absorbed into the Sanskrt-using high culture, actually). But when Buddhism was propagated outside its Indian home, the problem of vocabulary was acute. The languages of Central Asia, Tibet, China, Japan and the Far East generally, though not entirely lacking in philosophical terms, had nothing like the degree of codification in the relevant vocabulary areas to allow the expression of Buddhist metaphysical concepts. These concepts, though, were the whole basis of the Buddhist message (and especially in the Mahayana school which was transmitted to the East, eventually forming the basis for the Chinese Chan and Japanese Zen schools), and so the only method which presented itself was the laborious creation of whole new registers of language and especially of vocabulary. It was the self-evident philosophical superiority of the Buddhist teachings which powered the spread of the religion and its doctrines; and so Buddhists everywhere saw the great importance of presenting these teachings in a correct and comprehensible form. Now, the effect of this on local languages was complex and profound. Tibetan Buddhism and its vocabulary is basically a faithful transcription of the Indian original, with the Tibetan writing system having been developed in the seventh century specifically so as to make it possible to write down Buddhist scriptures; but the Chinese civilisation had already developed its own philosophical traditions and terminologies by the time Buddhism arrived, and the philosophical language of Chinese Buddhism shows a higher degree of influence from these older terms and ideas – including the very powerful effect of the writing system itself.[26] Japanese Buddhist terminology shows yet another level of linguistic interference, as the attempt to read out Chinese

---

[26] See (Wright, 1959) for a detailed treatment of the whole process of transfer and its consequences for China. He notes (p. 36) some specific examples of the adaptation of older Chinese terms – with the Indian terms *dharma*, *bodhi*, and *yoga*, for instance, all having been translated with the Taoist term *tao* in early attempts (2nd and 3rd centuries) at rendering Buddhist texts.

texts in Japanese led to the creation of a 'native' vocabulary conforming to Japanese phonology, but actually representing a direct transliteration of the Chinese version as represented in its written texts.

Further more or less exotic examples could be presented; but the important thing to grasp is that there is a unifying philosophical vocabulary throughout the Far East, transmitted by Buddhism, and that this is not necessarily marked by direct linguistic borrowing (though such borrowing is often an immediate sign of this process having been at work). It is a special case of the general process of partial cultural transfer. Only in the most extreme kinds of invasion, annexation and subjugation is a culture completely destroyed and replaced by another. The far more widespread phenomenon is that of partial transfer. Vectors of this transfer might be words, ideas, or fashions of dress, food or music; and a single complex vector – the disco experience, say, with its special clothes, music, vocabulary, gestures and dances, etc. – might transfer many fragments at the same time; but the sociologist should be particularly interested in the transfer of values in general, since it is by changing the value-structure of a society that the most profound and far-reaching effects of cultural contact and transfer make themselves felt. The case of Buddhism just considered is supposed to illustrate exactly this: the creation not of a language area exactly, but of a value-area, under the influence of a common set of words, ideas and other factors. But the Buddhist case has an important difference from the modern case with which we compare it. While Buddhism was superior, all countries had some kind of philosophical beliefs before, which were displaced or altered; but industrialism pours in something entirely new. The vocabulary of computing, for example, does not need to displace an older computing vocabulary (though older scientific and other vocabularies will be relevant to some extent; but of course their meanings will be contaminated and altered). The disco arrives ready made.

What we have as a basic repeated pattern, then, is this not-quite national model of the modern European nation state, whose political boundaries nearly but not quite correspond to linguistic, religious and other cultural boundaries. This imprecision is repeated at any physical scale we choose. At the largest scale, the division of territory between different brands of Christianity was never completed. National languages are (still) not completely established. Everywhere, we find pockets of resistance: and inside those pockets of resistance, there are other pockets of resistance; and so on. A basic dividing line in the Balkans is between the Albanians and the South Slavs; but Yugoslavia (whose name means 'land of the South Slavs') had an Albanian population on its territory (though this was not officially recognised). The Albanians, we know, are Muslim, while the Serbs are traditionally Orthodox: but we find that this neat division is compromised by reality, since the Kosovo Albanian population includes a significant Catholic minority. For yes, we can agree with Herder that as soon as a population is enclosed, or otherwise given a distinct and distinctive identity – by which we should really understand a sense of identity – then the development of its society will begin to take a separate course. The Hungarians who live in Slovakia, Romania or Serbia, however much they might like to think of themselves as being just the same as the Hungarians living in Hungary, actually are not, since their daily lives involve dealing with Slovaks, Romanians and Serbians, something which Hungarians in Hungary are systematically less likely to do. This is mainly because the nationalising project has been successful enough in Hungary itself to have promoted the Hungarian component of the population to a condition of overall demographic and cultural predominance, with other component populations having been more or less eliminated from society by various means. To take a tragic example of this kind of multiple exclusion and separation at work, though, we can take the 'Protestants' or Scots-Irish of Northern Ireland.

Ulster had been a centre of resistance to British rule in Ireland, and was left largely depopulated by protracted British military operations to put down this resistance. These new circumstances attracted a wave of poor but determined immigrants from Scotland, and in time this population settled down as an island of Protestantism in mainly Catholic Ireland. Sadly, this original religious difference seems to have been enough to prevent the arrivals from being assimilated. Some of these new Scots-Irish, incidentally, never really established themselves, and after a pause of a generation or two, continued their westward journey by going to the American colonies; the early settlers of Pennsylvania and the Shenandoah Valley included many of these Scots-Irish – though few of their descendants, Scots-Irish-Americans, are aware of the reasons for their hybrid background. In any event, the position of the Ulster Scots-Irish today is not good. They did not participate in the nineteenth-century Highland revival in Scotland, and in fact their only real link with Scotland today is the appalling Orange Order, a religio-nationalist organisation which is a relic of British Empire ideology at its least legitimate, and whose bigoted approach ('Onward Christian Soldiers', basically), which mixes religion and nationalism to produce hatred and delusion, has long become obsolete elsewhere in Britain. It survives as a mark of backwardness in the most run-down urban areas of Scotland and Northern Ireland. Lacking a credible national identity (beyond the rather imprecise 'British'), the Ulster Scots-Irish are identified and differentiated by the marker of religion – and since the religion in question is of the militant Orange Order variety, this leads directly to confrontation.

No-one involved in the conflict in Northern Ireland has clean hands, and there is an ever-present danger of romanticising the conflict. Indeed, taking a wider cultural perspective, we can see the conflict as ultimately a product of romanticism: a product of the romantic nationalism which creates the question of who 'rightfully' owns the territory in the first place. Outside the nation-state framework, the Northern Ireland question might be a good deal less dangerous; and positive thinkers in Northern Ireland and in the Republic look to the European Union, in which the British and the Irish have equal political status, as a possible source of eventual reconciliation.

The analytical point, anyway, is that there will always be some part of the population which does not conform to the national ideal; and a characteristic feature of Europe, where the political borders have been repeatedly re-drawn, is that these discrepancies tend to appear at or near the borders, with pockets of German-speaking Frenchmen, or Catholic Albanians, or whatever it might be. Now, there is a recurrent delusion that it is just a question of approaching the political drawing board with a sharper pencil, and that a more precise division of territory will somehow fix these problems. This, after all, is the only kind of solution that is sanctioned by the nationalist hypothesis, according to which territory is naturally divided into nation-states in the first place. But the states with more mixed populations know that this is not the answer. The status of the German-speaking population of Czechoslovakia, for instance, was the most-debated political question of the inter-war years. All kinds of different compromises were suggested and rejected; for the problem would not go away. The Czechs (for it was the better-educated Czechs, and not the Slovaks, who dominated Czechoslovakia politically throughout its history) wanted to control the state which had been constructed for them, while the Germans had no real interest in this arrangement. The 'solution' they eventually adopted was that proposed by Adolf Hitler: to join the German Reich on an out-patient basis. But did this teach anyone a lesson? Of course not. Czech nationalism continued to wear the mask of 'Czechoslovakism' through the communist years, but was given the chance to express itself more fully in 1989, when huge crowds of flag-waving nationalists greeted the new national hero, Václav Havel, who would lead them into a new age of Czech greatness. The spontaneous outburst of nationalism had the immediate effect of compromising the Czechoslovak compromise that had been the basis of the state since its foundation in 1918. Czechoslovakia had been modelled on Yugoslavia, the idea being that these states reunited brother Slav nations. In Tito's Yugoslavia, the Croat and Serb linguistic identities were amalgamated into 'Serbo-Croat', said to be a single language with two scripts and a number of local dialects. In Czechoslovakia, Czech and Slovak were kept separate, the politically correct solution being to alternate their use, so that radio and television would use one or the other by turns. The rhetoric of brother nations was sustained, but as if by magic, it disappeared almost overnight when the Czechs realised that keeping their political union with the Slovaks might have some material cost. After the Velvet Revolution, what people wanted primarily was colour televisions and new cars; and it quickly became clear that Slovakia, with its Soviet pattern of heavy-industry development, coupled with the more backward, rural background conditions, would be a real drag on the advance towards consumerism, which was all the Czechs had ever wanted in the first place. After the Second World War, they had fallen under the delusion that this was going to be made available through some kind of consumer socialism; but now they realised that American-style TV capitalism offered their only hope of catching up – and so they dumped the Slovaks, to general relief. It was fortunate in a way that the Slovaks didn't seem to mind. They, too, had come under the influence of their own brand of nationalism. In every country of the former Eastern Bloc (except for strange little Albania, which had always ploughed its own furrow), the acceptable post-communist political message was that the heroic nation of [insert name here] had at last emerged from Soviet/Marxist-Leninist domination. Bizarrely, nationalism was equated with democracy – despite the fact that the nationalist alternative in every case involves suppressing the political demands of some minority population. In the Czech Republic, for instance, the transition to a nation-state ideal has led to a general acceptance of chauvinistic and racist sentiments. The Roma population, already in a difficult position under socialism, is increasingly excluded from Czech life under capitalism; and the general feeling is not just that this is a good thing, but that it is the natural and inevitable thing – just as the rejection of Slovakia and the Slovaks is seen as the natural and inevitable thing. It is ethnic cleansing by other means, and if the process looks less radical in former Czechoslovakia than in former Yugoslavia, this is largely explained by the fact that the more violent phases of the process – the

extermination of the Jews and the expulsion of the Germans, specifically –
have long since been completed there.

Now, Central European nationalism is very reasonably explained by
Ernest Gellner's theory that nationalism is part of the process of the
industrialisation of society. According to this theory, the advance of
industrial organisation requires a standardisation of language in particular
and of society more generally, and what this means in practice is the
establishment of national political cultures. This being the only way forward,
it does indeed take place as a natural-seeming process. And the sudden jump
into digital technologies and the corresponding social restructuring that is
taking place in post-communist Eastern Europe has indeed led to a particular
kind of nationalistic politics – which would seem to confirm Gellner's
theory. There is, however, another force at play, which nationalists and
theorists of nationalism alike tend to avoid in their analyses: the force of
Americanisation.

It is the standardisation of social experience which is at the heart of
the process Gellner describes. He dwells on the importance of standard
languages, especially standard written languages, and from a historical
perspective, with reference to the emergence or establishment of national
cultures in modern Europe, this seems quite correct. The standardisation of
communication is vital, since experience is shared by some technological
processes in a developed-world society, and for the establishment of print
media, it is essential to have a standard written language, as Gellner argues;
and this has indeed had the effect he describes. But we live in the age of
television; and so there is another process, which operates in the reverse
direction, and which has now taken centre stage: the propagation of a single,
global standard of communication and shared experience. The standard of
American commercial television production. Let us cast our minds back to
the work of Marcel Mauss, the great French theorist of society. He called for
a study of the 'techniques of the body', since he saw that these were being
lost: that fishermen or hunters or whatever it might be were losing the
physical skills imprinted in their bodily movements by their socialisation.
What led him to this realisation was the observation of some nurses, when he
happened to be hospitalised in America. He looked at the nurses, and realised
that there was something very familiar about the way they walked. He had
seen Parisian girls walking in just the same way; and he realised that the
French girls had learned to walk like that by watching American films. Well,
is there anyone who would like to suggest that this process has somehow
come to a halt? The propagation of American commercial films and

television programmes, including pop music and sports programmes (which seem to infiltrate the most quickly into alien cultures) is simply unstoppable. A society can resist by preventing the import of new technology (as the Iranian government has recently attempted to outlaw satellite dishes), but this is a hopeless kind of resistance, since it is evidently a policy of deliberate backwardness. Now, Gellner argues that a standard language is essential for the homogenisation of a national culture. But we can also argue that, at a higher level of technology, this need is surpassed. We can make a direct comparison between two similar artefacts: a novel and a television film. If the values of the novel are to have a significant impact on a society, then it will have to be published and read. This, as Gellner shows, requires an elaborate reorganisation of society, so that there are sufficient schools teaching a sufficiently standardised version of the local language(s) for this to be possible. If there is not some process like this at work, the novel will serve only as furniture. But a television film operates in quite a different way. All over the world, mass populations are quite happy to watch television films they cannot 'understand', from a narrowly linguistic point of view. Pornography, sports coverage and advertising are among the most international and supra-cultural genres, but ordinary mass-market violence and car-chases are very easily presented to an audience who do not know the language of the original. This first cultural impact soon brings dubbing in its wake. Has a more efficient means of cultural imperialism been devised? It rivals the introduction of literacy itself. Indeed, in a way it is a kind of literacy, making cultural artefacts – texts, in a way, but screen texts rather than page texts – legible where before they were not. In the Eastern Bloc, there was a kind of low-budget dubbing for foreign films, in which one or two actors would do all the voices, just reading them out from a script live as the film was broadcast or projected. This intermediate procedure (could we compare it with the adaptation of Taoist and Confucian terminology to the needs of Buddhism, as discussed above?) is now relegated to film festivals and other highbrow uses, since 'normal' dubbing, with the original voices replaced by those of competent native professionals, has been established everywhere. The cultural impact of this is simply devastating. The whole spoken language is re-coded: associated with the standards of emotional response of Hollywood and its imitators. Pop music has a similarly powerful effect, but for technical reasons this must preserve the original language. Native-language re-workings of pop songs will always have a certain appeal, but local industries cannot hope to compete with the production values of international superstar efforts. Paradoxically, this has the effect of removing the verbal reference from what is after all originally a poetic medium. Mass audiences have a sort of general feeling that pop music in English contains some message they ought to be interested in, but they have only their preconceptions to guide them as to the precise nature of this message, as is demonstrated by what they come up with when they attempt their own national versions. No, for the fine detail of their verbal and cultural re-programming, it is television which is king. It is television that most effectively eradicates the differences in content between supposedly national cultures, so that the different standard languages merely transpose the same messages into a different surface code. This affects the style of language as well as its 'national' character. American television does not in fact aim at the cultural purity we have discussed in relation to European nationalism. Characters speak in all kinds of dialects and sub-standard forms. There is no pretence at grammatical consistency of the type that is central to the whole project of Slav linguistic nationalism, for instance. The range of dialects presented in an evening of American television (though including a standard, news-presenter, neutral form) would be sufficiently wide to sabotage entire national cultures in Eastern Europe. The differences between the Northern and Southern dialect areas of American English, for example (and there are many other examples one could give) would definitely be sufficient grounds for the creation of new states according to the traditions of Slav nationalist ideology. But who is winning? Standardising day-to-day culture without a corresponding standardisation of language is simply a transitional phase. Everywhere where there is television, people are being prepared for English – the English of the American commercial world and its mass media information products. Even if they can't speak the language yet, they are still allowed a thousand ways into the whole general experience of this style of consumption.

III. Cults of Nationality

Let us follow the line of thought which says that nationalism is linked to religion and see where that leads us. European nationalism is our starting point, of course, since, as we have said, the state-nationalism with which we are concerned is a European phenomenon, now exported to the rest of the world, along with European music, literature, medicine and so on; and so we should consider this phenomenon in the specific context of European civilisation, which means Christianity.

We have observed that nationalism has a quasi-religious character, in the sense that it promotes a particular kind of unthinking allegiance and enthusiasm. The Crusaders went to war for Christianity; the modern state sends its citizens to war in the name of the state itself and its national symbols. The songs of Christianity are replaced with the songs of the national tradition, and pictures of Christian saints are replaced with pictures of national leaders. In Canetti's pregnant phrase, this is a question of 'Crowds and Power': the national sentiment is the sentiment of the football crowd, and should be understood not in terms of rational choice, but in terms of mass psychology. At times of crisis, a collective organism has some special mass mechanisms. Bees will swarm, a herd will stampede, and people too will obey a mass drive at certain times. Indeed, the football crowd emotions just mentioned are a way of channelling this energy and releasing it in a harmless way: without recourse to the weapons of war, that is.

Religion and nationalism share a certain quality, then: an unreasoning, blind faith quality. But what is the nature of the link between them? I would like to suggest an analysis in terms of 'cults of exclusion'. This is an idea I have developed elsewhere, but let me now reiterate briefly a few main points.

In what is called 'primitive religion' in the literature (and our starting point can be Durkheim's classic study of Australian beliefs: Durkheim, 1912), everyone is included. The religion is not a 'state' religion, since there are no states, and it is not a 'national' religion, since there are no nations. And in fact it is not really a 'religion' either, unless we work backwards from modern religion and assume that something similar must always have existed in a 'primitive' form. As much as hunting rituals, ways of preparing food, or marriage customs, the system of cult beliefs is the very fabric of society; and indeed, in a fully-developed analysis, rituals of hunting, food, marriage and so on will be included as part of the cult system of a people or society, since these all have a cult or magical aspect to them. Exclusion from society exists as a logical possibility, since a common way of dealing with crime (murder or rape, typically) is cult exclusion, with an individual being stripped of his membership in the society, and therefore being excluded from its rituals; but this punishment is so terrible just because it is so unusual. In the normal course of events, every individual is bound into society by a network of rituals. We cannot say that some of these rituals are 'rational' and some 'irrational', or that some are 'practical' and some 'magical': for there is no way of separating them out. A hunt is in a way a very practical activity, providing not just food, but fur, bones, teeth and so on – and also providing such intangible social benefits as group solidarity, the reinforcement of hierarchies of authority, the transmission of knowledge to the next generation, and so on. Now, we know that hunting is very likely to be accompanied by cult rituals. The oldest cave art seems to be associated with hunting rituals, and special dances, masks and so on have survived into modern times among the remnants of the hunting peoples. But it is wrong to think of these as magical rituals being attached arbitrarily to the practical activity of hunting. This is a modern way of thinking, projected backwards on to our predecessors. The dance held in the jungle village before going off to the hunt is not the exact equivalent of a church service held before going off to fight a modern war: for the fight itself is part of the cult ritual in early human society. The hunt is a continuation of the dance.

Bear hunting is an ancient activity, and one that survived until the twentieth century. There seems to be no reason to suppose that its basic ritual interpretation was fundamentally different in the Old Stone Age. The bear, in a bear hunt, is one of the dancers. In the Arctic, where polar bear hunts have continued longest as a basic social ritual, the hunt is an adventure, a game and a test of strength and bravery, to be carried out with a sense of style and triumph. Now, a common feature of low-technology society, and something we may reasonably envy, is an imagined continuity with the rest of nature. There is no hard line dividing the human with his mind from the rest of the world. For everywhere there are spirits, and the spirits do not differentiate between a man and a tree, rock or beast. So the bear, this great and powerful creature, is certainly animated by a great spirit. The bear hunt is so important for this reason, and not just because bear paw soup is so good to eat.[27] To conquer the bear spirit in a ritual test of strength is a great distinction for the brave hunter. And so the hunt starts with a dance, begging the bear spirit to condescend to allow the hunters to fight him. If the hunters find a bear, they are happy that their prayers have been answered, and they wait happily for the next stage of the dance, in which the bear pretends to run away. They chase merrily after him, and when he feels that they have demonstrated their bravery and skill sufficiently, he will turn at bay and pretend to fight them. They must obey all the rituals now, and above all they must show respect for

---

[27] And the evidence that this attitude was common in the remote past is compounded by observation of another low-technology culture which has survived from the earliest times. Among the Akoa and Mbuti pygmies, elephant hunts display the same spiritual dimension. (Coon, 1972, pp. 135-144)

the bear himself, for the bear spirit is their protector and their friend. This is demonstrated by the fact that he has condescended to be caught. They fight; they kill the bear; they return, exultantly, with happy memories and their heroic story of the hunt; and, almost as an afterthought, with the meat, fur, bones, teeth, claws and so on – with the dull material necessities which our mechanical age interprets as the true and real goal of their adventure.

In a hunting society, everything has a cult aspect: a cult interpretation and a cult component. This is the essence of human society – the incorporation of the irrational into the rational structures of eating, sleeping and reproducing. (Indeed, this is not something limited to low-technology societies. The modern person does not hunt the bear, but goes through a cycle of food procurement which is dominated by a different kind of magic: the magic of advertising, and the cult rituals of supermarket shopping.) So, it is a little misleading to talk about 'cult practices' or 'cult rituals' in society: everything has a cult aspect, and if we cannot see it that is because we are blind and stupid. But some practices are more readily interpreted in their cult aspect, and some are more readily interpreted from a practical, instrumental point of view; and so when we talk about cult beliefs and cult rituals, we are in general talking about those parts of a society's beliefs and practices which have no immediate practical justification – the dances and masks and not the hunt itself. To look at it from a slightly different angle, the cult or magical belief characteristically offers a reason and an explanation for some kind of structure which we could also interpret from a different, instrumental, point of view. The incest taboo, for instance, can be explained in terms of instinct and evolutionary pressure; but early man has no such categories, and accepts a ritual explanation: what Frazer calls a magical style of reasoning.

Well, the original social cult – this style of reasoning, or what we can call the cult aspect of the social structure taken as a whole – includes. That is its whole nature. It ties every individual, from birth to death, into the social structure of the group. It is the characteristic pattern of beliefs of the society living in the wild, and represents the interface of man and nature: the externalisation of the mind and the personality, both its rationality and its fantasy, into the living world outside. Its basic assumption is that the world is motivated by the same kinds of forces found in introspection: by love, hatred, kindness, malice and so on. Now, we can link this to our schematic account of the development of society, given above. The monocultural society, 'culturalised' in this way, expands into empty space in a first, very ancient, phase. The next phase is the establishment of territories, with boundaries established between neighbouring peoples who are ritually separated by language and by social structure, but with the boundaries made porous by a number of mechanisms of exchange, the most important from most points of view being the regular exchange of women. The boundary consciousness is at the same time a boundary of consciousness. People generally believe that what happens within the boundary of their group also refers to them as individuals, while what happens across the boundary has nothing to do with them at all. This is a matter of psychological necessity, I would argue, and not of rational choice.

In this phase, what we see is bounded inclusion. Everyone is included, but people over the border do not count. This is a question of degree, and will depend on the nature and extent of the social differences between neighbouring peoples, and also on the degree of hostility to outsiders which has arisen. For it is a sad truth that a natural response to having neighbours is to want to kill them. Among hunters, who have an ethic of conduct based on personal bravery, coming across a member of a neighbouring group and not killing him would require considerable explanation afterwards; and in fact such societies develop special means, such as ritual clothes and ritual locations, so that the necessary meetings (for exchanges of various kinds) can take place without the immediate necessity for bloodshed. In fact, the sharp psychological differences between peoples are largely imaginary. But the imaginary boundary is nevertheless the important thing. The anthropologist or other observer might find it difficult to tell by objective means where one society ends and another begins, so powerful is the tendency towards homogenisation and what linguists call 'arealisation' – the creation of areas of social structure (in this case of linguistic structuring), cutting across the subjective cultural, linguistic or social boundaries. In the end, if two peoples dissolve all the differences between them, so that they speak the same language, wear the same clothes, exchange their daughters, and hunt together on the same territory, then the arbitrary and now pointless-seeming division of territory may come to an end, and the two peoples may merge into one. But it is just as likely that the boundaries themselves will become part of the cult apparatus of the society, and that they will be defended to the death. After all, losing the boundary of the territory would be losing a boundary of consciousness, and would therefore already be a kind of death in a way.

A basic force in human development is population growth; and the bounded monoculture must give way before this force like the unbounded monoculture that preceded it. We have argued that the next phase of development is created by the social institution of the city: the place where cultures can meet and exchange their goods and values at a permanent physical location. We will now consider the cult aspect of this fundamental advance in human society.

The basic change which has taken place is that the inner world is no longer simply extended to the natural world outside. The life of the mind, which in the first phase sees the whole world as an extension of itself, and in the second phase sees this extension as having a territorial limit, must now accommodate a specific psychic threat: the presence of strangers. This is revolutionary. In hunting societies, as we have seen, strangers are dealt with by specific rituals, which tame them by erecting a special temporary psychological barrier around them – often by giving them a special temporary status as members of the group. (When they are not just killed out of hand, that is.) But this strategy cannot be followed in the new social circumstances. The cult of inclusion cannot systematically include whole groups of people who are living according to an alien set of rules. The existence of such people can be accommodated when they live elsewhere – even close by. As long as you never see them or speak to them: or, more subtly, as long as you never accept them emotionally as being real people; then they can basically get on with it as far as you and the values of your society are concerned. But when they are living next door and you can hear them singing to their own spirits through the wall, something has to give. And what gives is the principle of inclusion.

Faced with the psychological impossibility of adjusting to the new social circumstances, the cult and culture of inclusion transforms itself into a cult and culture of exclusion. Rather than providing a means of managing a monocultural society, it becomes the means of managing one component of a polycultural society. It therefore involves a basic change in self-image and psychological identity, and I have argued elsewhere that this produces a set of symptoms which are closely related to schizophrenia.

The cult of exclusion replaces the simple physical boundary of a territorial limit with a boundary of membership – a social structure, that is. In terms of Frazer's magical reasoning, we could say that the individual in a monocultural society accepts the beliefs of his society because they are presented to him as true and reasonable; but in the next phase, they take on an additional meaning, and must be accepted not just for this reason, but also so as to exclude other individuals who are not members of the group whose identity is now preserved by their means. The stranger's physical presence is dealt with in this manner: by excluding him from the magical reality set up by cult practices. In the cult of inclusion this is an emergency procedure; in the cult of exclusion, it is a central mechanism.

What this means in practice is that the exclusion works in two directions simultaneously. On the one hand, strangers are excluded from the group – pushed to the other side of a psychological barrier, that is, since they can no longer be kept on the other side of a simple physical barrier; and on the other hand, the group excludes itself from the too-threatening social environment, where it is now exposed to forces which could easily destroy it. The inner motivation is clear: it is an attempt to preserve the psychological integrity of the group – its boundary consciousness. But it has some immediate and far-reaching consequences.

The first thing is the demonisation of the stranger. This is a particularly tragic development. The stranger, held at arm's length before, an object of scorn and ridicule, now becomes the source of all evil. The threat has become much more real and immediate, and so the defences must be correspondingly more frightening. What is tragic about this is that the real threat is from inside: it is the threat that comes from recognising that the ancient traditional belief that the world is shaped like a crocodile is perhaps not the only possible explanation of things. The threat to magical rationality. For what is immediately presented is the possibility that the stranger is right – or anyway, no less wrong. Accepting this would be enough to destroy the old cohesion; and so it cannot be accepted.

Internally, there are also immediate consequences. The beliefs of the cult become a matter of honour in a way that was not so before. If nobody questions the crocodiliform universe, there is no reason even to put any particular emphasis on it. Once the next-door neighbours start insisting that the cosmos is really tortoise-shaped, the crocodile becomes a different kind of symbol. Indeed, observation suggests that this balance of forces produces a characteristic result: the isolation of a particular dogma, so self-evidently false that no-one else would ever have any reason to formulate it or inclination to accept it, which becomes the central badge of cult membership. An example is the belief of the Mormons that the angel Moroni appeared to their founder and told him of the location of their scriptures, engraved on gold, and relating the adventures of Jesus Christ after he was magically transported to America.[28] A more mainstream example is the virgin birth dogma of Christianity. The Rastafarian belief that the Emperor Haile Selassie, their immortal leader, is still alive and in hiding somewhere is an example I have mentioned elsewhere; and the reader will easily supply some others. These dogmas fulfill an important function, because they allow an instant test of belief: are you with us or against us? Also, they imply total subservience to the authority of the cult and therefore to that of its priests. If you will accept something which by the standards of ordinary rationality is obviously false, simply because the cult authorities have told you it is true, then you have by implication given them the authority to tell you anything else they decide as well; and this is a liberty which priesthoods of various kinds have certainly exploited to the utmost down the centuries.

These examples, though, are all from beliefs – cults – which have been revolutionised in the process of adjustment to changing social conditions. One tendency that we see is the tendency for the process of isolation and exclusion to repeat itself. Once Christianity has established an exclusion-cult habit of mind, then the way is open for the pattern to repeat itself internally – as with the Mormon and to some extent also the Rastafarian examples just given. (Rastafarianism is not formally a branch of Christianity, but its language and symbolism, as with Haitian Voodoo, shows a strong influence from Christianity.) Another tendency, which is just as important, is for the cult to reinvent itself according to the new logic. A set of beliefs which has come to serve as an insulator against rival cultures may reinforce those parts of its dogma which do this, and correspondingly weaken those parts of its dogma which are now irrelevant. This process may be gradual, but a common pattern – as with Islam and Christianity, for instance – is for there to be a sudden discontinuity, with a radical, revolutionary, and basically simple new version of a cult dogma arising: one which serves the sociological function of the exclusion cult more effectively. This internal reconfiguration often takes the form of a myth of rebirth: the coming of a prophet, or the revelation of a new scripture. Indeed, this discontinuity is commonly marked by an explicit break with the past, with the Christians

---

[28] 'The Book of Mormon is a sacred record of peoples in ancient America, and was engraved upon sheets of metal.... In or about the year A.D. 421, Moroni, the last of the [ancient American] Nephite prophet-historians, sealed the sacred record and hid it up unto the Lord, to be brought forth in the latter days, as predicted by the voice of God through his ancient prophets. In A.D. 1823, this same Moroni, then a resurrected personage, visited the prophet Joseph Smith and subsequently delivered the engraved plates to him.' (*The Book of Mormon*, The Church of Jesus Christ of Latter-day Saints, Salt Lake City, Utah, 1990, 'A brief explanation about the Book of Mormon', un-numbered pages.)

quickly coming to deny any continuity with Jewish beliefs, and Islam denying any continuity with pre-Islamic Arab cult practices. We can understand these various features in terms of the retrenchment of cults of exclusion. The most socially effective form of such a cult will be dogmatically simple, will demand the acceptance of self-evidently false beliefs by its members (by the standards of everyday rationality, that is), and will deny its own past, in order to pretend that all truth starts and finishes with its present cult dogma.

It is a curious paradox that the effect of this kind of belief can be to re-create the conditions of a monoculture. Christianity and Islam both started out as small exclusive cults within the larger environment of a polycultural urban society: and both ended up by establishing themselves so completely that all opposition was (at least locally and temporarily) silenced. The early history of Judaism is a little more complicated, since extraneous political factors also isolated the Jews from the beginning, but the broad outlines are the same: though in this case it was principally circumcision that served to mark out the exclusivist group from the surrounding society. But the cults thus established are a grotesque parody of the cult beliefs of the monocultures of early man. The unity of man and nature has been replaced by a society dependent on adherence to a cult which demonises an evil enemy world of non-believers, and which forces its own members to accept the authority of a priesthood committed to promoting dogmas which are self-evidently false. However, the formal similarity of this condition with the original monoculture of the inclusion cult does suggest that there is some kind of cycle at work: and so we could see all cult belief as oscillating between these poles.

This, anyway, is how we can think of the cults of nationality which, as we have seen, have generally replaced national religions as the basis of group identity in the West – and therefore, by extension, on a global scale. They are transformed religious cults, and they succeed in transferring the more heroic aspects of national religion to the cult of the nation itself. The cult of the prophet becomes the cult of the national leader, or even sometimes of a 'father of the nation'. The cult of the national version of the holy scripture becomes the cult of the national literature. It is easy to find examples. There are some complications, of course, since as we have noted already, the borders in Europe have been re-drawn so many times that the historical nations are themselves internally divided in a complicated way. But the same basic cult mechanism is at work everywhere. The nation has been sacralised, and at the very moment when it gives up its link with official religion it finds itself at the focus of cult worship instead.

Since we are looking at Eastern Europe, it is worth making a special analysis of the effects of communism. This provided an alternative sacralised cult structure in some countries; but in those countries this supposedly international ideology in practice still contained a large element of nationalism. Like Christianity, it was re-packaged in national versions which preserved exclusivist cult elements. Indeed, communism itself, in all its versions from the original Marxist economic analysis on, has much in common with religion. It has a prophet, a scripture, commandments, and so on. In terms of cults of exclusion, as analysed above, it presents dogmas which are plainly at variance with the truth – although this is more a feature of its hieratic, national-political variants than of its theoretical original. Albania is an advanced country! Its standard of living is the highest in Europe! As in a religion, demanding the acceptance of this kind of dogmatic but obviously false belief plays an important double role, at once separating out any potential dissidents (i.e. anyone who questions these statements) and creating the atmosphere for total semantic control (since if you can get away with these dogmatic statements, you can essentially get away with anything). It is interesting to see, following this line of reasoning through, that the Eastern Bloc was made up of a group of historically Christian states (Albania therefore being a bad example, since, like Bosnia-Hercegovina, it was and is mainly Muslim), dominated politically by the successor of the old Orthodox Russian Empire. We can therefore compare the communist revolutions and their medium-term effects with the Reformation. In this case, it was basically a question of the reformation of Orthodox Christianity, but the political effects spilled over the borders of the Orthodox world, so that Catholic and Protestant countries – Western countries – were included; and as an afterthought, a number of Muslim states were included too. Albania will always be an anomaly; but in the Caucasus and Central Asia, we see that the success of the Soviet idea – the Soviet communist ethical universe, that is – relied on replacing the traditional Islam of local populations with the neo-Orthodoxy of Soviet communism. This was done in the name of 'modernisation', and its concrete manifestation was the establishment of the Russian language, now loaded with the byzantine vocabulary of Soviet communism. However, since the Christian tradition – the Christian ethical universe – was lacking in these societies, it was only party cadres and similar elite groups who were fully Sovietised; and we see that the skin-deep

Russification and Sovietisation of such countries as Kazakstan and Tajikistan has left a deeper layer of folk-Islamic traditions and social patterns still functioning in people's minds and habits. We could make a broadly similar analysis for Georgia, which, though Christian, is neither Eastern nor Western in its traditions. Georgian Christianity is based on historical allegiance neither to Rome nor to Constantinople, but to Antioch in Syria. However, as Stalin (himself a Georgian) reminds us, in his 1914 paper 'Marxism and the National Question', the Georgian religious, linguistic and cultural unity did not automatically lead to political unification. 'Georgia came on to the scene as a nation only in the latter half of the nineteenth century, when the fall of serfdom and the growth of the economic life of the country, the development of means of communication and the rise of capitalism instituted a division of labour between the various districts of Georgia, completely shattered the economic self-sufficiency of the principalities and bound them together into a single whole. The same must be said of the other nations which have passed through the stage of feudalism and have developed capitalism.' (Stalin, 1971, p. 52) The separate religious tradition – separate ethical universe, that is – continues to give Georgia and Georgians a special identity and sense of separateness. Stalin's analysis of the nature of the nation, incidentally, is very modern-seeming; quite compatible with Gellner's analysis, for instance. It is evident, though, that his later policies were not in tune with his thoughts as an exiled revolutionary of 1912-13 (when he wrote the paper). At that time he favoured a policy of regional autonomy coupled with national minority rights, and denounced the Russian imperial policy of divide and rule; but his own nationalities policy was of the latter type on the whole, even if he did stick to the language of class struggle in formulating it. Rather than creating Soviet regions, based on a modernised and educated proletariat, he took the nation state as his basic model, superimposing Soviet ideological models on to the process of capitalist consolidation described in the analysis just quoted.

This is the whole nature of revolution: the transformation of a pre-existing pattern. Soviet 'revolution' in Kazakstan or Tajikistan was basically imperialism – as much the imperialism of the Christian tradition over Islam as the imperialism of Marxism-Leninism over capitalism. In the 'European' parts of the Soviet Empire – the traditionally Christian parts, that is – we see on the one hand that the acceptance of the new version of the creed was more complete, and on the other hand that despite this very complete success, older patterns were evidently not erased, since the post-communist societies of Europe are now reverting to their pre-communist ethical universes to some extent, with religion (Protestant, Catholic, or Orthodox Christianity, that is, but in national variants) once again taking on an emblematic role. However, this process has been compromised to a degree by the modernising function of the Soviet system and ideology. In urban Russia, religion has been pushed aside for so long that the bulk of the population has no real experience of Orthodox values or ideas. In Eastern Europe, on the other hand, renewed contact with the West tends not just to re-install local versions of Christianity, but to replace them with the gleaming new version of the (Western) Christian ethical universe represented by Americanisation and consumerism. So there are forces working in both directions; and the overall result is a tendency towards a nationalism which acknowledges local religious traditions, but which does not base its appeal on these. As in the Western Europe of a previous generation, it is the nation itself which is now supposed to be the object of worship. However, this change in the national ideologies of Eastern Europe comes at a bad time: for the nation states of Western Europe are themselves undergoing a crisis of national identity. Various forces – the homogenisation of society under the influence of international consumerism, and the political and economic integration of Europe, principally – now challenge the assumed priority of the nation state. Spain, for example, has undergone a profound reorganisation since the death of Franco, and has adopted a quasi-federal structure of autonomous provinces which may well be a pattern for the future of Europe. The result is that the iron curtain division of Europe continues, but with a transformed significance. The division is weakest in Germany, where national reunification is not opposed by a local nationalism; and in the end it is probably the German solution which will provide a model for the whole integration of the Eastern Bloc. As with the Spanish *autonomía*, the German *Land* structure provides a precedent and a base for a different kind of political organisation. For the time being, though, we see that the former East is temporarily over-Westernised, in that it has adopted a heroic brand of nationalism which went out of style in the West in the 1930s. This produces a predictable list of problems: white supremacist skinhead groups, extreme right-wing political movements, and so on. Isolated minority populations naturally bear the brunt of all this.

What we see is that all this cult of 'national reawakening', like the 'national awakening' cults in these same countries in the nineteenth century (which provide a direct precedent and model), relies on the false anthropological premise already discussed: that the proper, moral and correct organisation of humanity is into national territorial units. This idea is so wildly at variance with the truth in Eastern Europe that it has always been a major source of political problems. The Austro-Hungarian Empire managed to deal with all the nationalities and languages of the peoples under its control precisely by placing their aspirations under a larger system of control. In Hungary, this was symbolised by the choice of Latin as the official state language until the 19th century; though noblemen and others of high status were expected to know several other languages as well. The 'national' states of Czechoslovakia and Yugoslavia, both of which were attempts to reconfigure the political arrangements of this part of Europe along the supposedly scientific lines suggested by nationalist theoreticians (originally theoreticians of language, remember), relied for their whole existence on the implicit proviso that those sections of the population who did not fit into the new, majority-based national identities of these countries in the end did not matter. In the treatment of the Gypsies or Roma (who are numerous and widespread in Eastern Europe), we see that this basic attitude persists.[29] But applying these nationalistic ideas as the basis for a political ideology in Czechoslovakia left out a people with rather a different idea of social and political organisation: the Germans. Left out of Czechoslovakia's nationalistic political agenda, they turned *en masse* to Hitler.

Nationalism is the problem and not the solution. What is necessary is to expose the falsehood of the naive anthropological assumption that living in a coherent monoculture on a bounded national territory is the normal and natural condition of man. It is true that there is normally a dominant section of society, and this does create a kind of national identity, but this is certainly not simply to be equated with the national majority of the population. In the middle ages, it was an international military aristocracy that dominated the political arrangements of the European states, and princes sometimes could not even speak the local language. The normal condition of an urban population is that of parallel cultures: the simultaneous existence of several ethical universes in a single population. We see outward signs of this structure in the use of different languages, and in the practice of different cult beliefs of various kinds – including national cult beliefs. The persistence of this social pattern, in spite of modernisation, world wars, Soviet Marxism-Leninism, industrialisation, and all the other forces of history, suggests that it

---

[29] For a balanced and up-to-date treatment of the position of the Roma, see (Liebich, 1997). See index entries for specific countries. This work is a thorough survey of demographic, political, legal and other aspects of minority issues in the region, and is particularly good on the problems of the former Yugoslavia – to which this Swiss-Canadian author brings both sympathy and a thoughtful understanding.

is time we looked reality in the face and accepted that there will always be minorities of this type: minorities with an organic, permanent relationship with the majority. The social structure that makes this possible is not explicitly or necessarily one of ethnic or national stratification. The stratification of urban societies by class or caste is at root the same phenomenon. It is more visible where an ethnic element is involved, and this case has a particular importance because of the nation-state ideology which is commonly professed by governments and other official institutions. The political paradox is quite clear. Mass democracy will compound the problem by systematically tending to exclude minority groups from 'national' decision-making. As far as Eastern Europe is concerned, this produces the uncomfortable result that the recent installation of democracy has actually worsened the relative position of minority groups in many cases. The Soviet system of divide and rule was rather favourable to minority identities, and this was often mirrored in the policies of the vassal states of Eastern Europe (though not everywhere). As with the Austro-Hungarian solution just mentioned, imposing a larger system of organisation did provide one method of stabilising the inherent conflict between the real social structure and the nationalistic ideologies and projects of political leaders. Indeed, in the long term some similar imposition of a higher level of order may prove to be the only way out of the same problem in its latest incarnation. The political integration of Europe may eventually include not just Western Europe, but Eastern Europe too (though how far that will extend is anyone's guess). Under those circumstances, the minority populations might find themselves under the protection of a European political structure committed to protecting their political rights. This, however, is not likely to solve the problem of the former USSR. Global efforts, based on the United Nations, are likely to be slow-moving. But if the political question is too large and complex – and after all, it naturally fragments into a thousand local 'minority questions', each with its own specific difficulties and contradictions – we can at least attack the false intellectual base of the nationalistic interpretation of things. Forming a theory of parallel cultures will in the end lead to a politics of parallel cultures. And in this way we can defeat the nationalist cycle, which constantly tends to re-invent heroic and exclusivist self-images for the majority components of ethnically mixed populations.

IV. Historical Parallels

In this section, we will consider the dynamics of majority-minority relations by means of an analysis of some important religious minorities in mediæval Europe: the dualists (Bogomils and Cathars) and the Jews.[30] This will lead us to some general analytical points.

We have seen that the historical source of the nation state was the Western Roman Empire, and that the corresponding prototype for the status of a national citizen was Roman citizenship. We have also argued that the introduction of Christianity was a decisive factor in the process of transition from Roman Empire to nation state and from Roman citizen to national citizen. The identification of Christianity as the official religion of Rome introduced a new element into citizenship; and the new moral standard that resulted would in time produce a moral identity: that of the Christian Roman. This moral identity would develop and fragment into the moral identities associated with the national states of Western Europe – their 'nationalities'.

Christianity itself did not come ready-made. As the cult of a radical Jewish faction, it was of little interest to Rome. It was only transformed into a state ideology for the multi-cultural Empire after some significant changes in its content; and the first and most basic of these was its separation from Judaism. Judaism was not just a religious identity, and it was not simply based on territorial claims either. In its political aspect it was based on group loyalty first, and only then on physical territorial claims. This provides interesting parallels with Christianity and Islam, and raises a rather obvious question which it is nevertheless very difficult to answer. Is there some instinctive, psychological or other correlation between monotheism and some form of national consciousness and monolithic group solidarity? 'The notion of the State in Israel is in fact closer to that of the Aramaean kingdoms of Syria and Transjordania. First Israel, then Israel and Judah, were, like them, national kingdoms; like them they bore the names of peoples, and like them they did not at once accept the dynastic principle... These states emerged as the result of the solidarity of the tribes which eventually settled down in a limited territory.' (Vaux, 1961, p. 92)[31] This solidarity is basic to the Jewish

---

[30] I am grateful to Prof. Stuart A. Cohen of Bar-Ilan University, Israel, for looking at a draft of this chapter, and for his detailed and learned comments, especially concerning the questions of Jewish history and society discussed in this section.

[31] The use of the word 'national' here is a little misleading, since at this point the national territorial system was not established as a political norm. Indeed, we should note that this Jewish 'national' solidarity was not originally linked to a territorial claim. It was based on cultural factors.

identity; and the same principle of solidarity has lasted for two thousand years, regardless of physical movements and political persecution – although it seems reasonable to suppose that the Babylonian captivity, following Nebuchadrezzar's siege of Jerusalem in 597 B.C., also played a defining role in the Jewish group awareness. (Oates, 1986, pp. 128ff) Indeed, to anticipate our arguments a little, we could argue that this was a defining moment for social development generally, with Babylon's Jewish quarter becoming the first urban parallel culture location: the first ghetto. It was the need for a creed to keep the Jewish identity alive in coexistence with or as we can put it in parallel to the political order of the Persian Empire between the 6th and 4th centuries BC, and then with the Empire of Alexander (who, seeing himself as the heir to the Persian dignity, sought to continue its legal system as far as the treatment of the Jews was concerned as in other matters), and then under the Seleucids and Ptolemies (who had more or less the same idea), that established the hybrid religious nationalism of the Jews in the period before the existence of the Christian and Muslim variants of Middle Eastern monotheism.[32] Early Judaism, anyway, was not the ideology of a voluntary association of converts and believers: it was the tough-minded creed of a specific and separate social group, aimed at survival, and at preserving traditional values. This deep and structural conservatism was enough to fight off the internal threat from Christianity, when that arose. It is not entirely clear why Christianity should have spread through the Roman legions (if we accept that this was the decisive factor in its acceptance by the Empire more generally); but it is clear that it could only have done this after it lost its Jewish connotations, and became a cult of conversion, open to anyone who accepted its simplistic claims. A reading of Gibbon suggests that it was basically an underclass belief at this stage, with a crude millennarian appeal based on a superstitious conviction that the end of the world was

---

[32] And we should not forget the Captivity itself, the ultimate source of this parallel culture configuration, both in terms of the subjective cultural identity of the Jews, and in terms of the legal accommodation with this identity offered by the foreign state. 'Whilst religious conditions in Judea were on the decline, the Jews in Babylon were developing a vigorous religious life. Being without a temple and without a country, they saw themselves faced with imminent extinction as a people through absorption by the heathen, among whom they found themselves... They turned more and more to the Torah and their other sacred writings, and around these spiritual possessions they built up a new polity, stripped of all territorial limitations and political loyalties... The Babylonian authorities, for their part, perceived from the first the value of allowing the Jews to practise their own religion and develop their own institutions and of affording them opportunities for their material advancement... The same favourable conditions were enjoyed by the Babylonian Jews when they came under the rule of the Persians.' (Epstein, 1959, p. 83)

coming soon. But side by side with the popular movement there was a more organised elaboration of Christian dogma, and this quickly succeeded in bringing the folk superstition under central ideological control. This central organised ideology then remained at the centre of political life in the West for nearly two thousand years. For our present purposes, we see that specifically in their treatment of non-Christians (Jews and dualists – we could call them 'near-Christians'), the successor states of the Western Roman Empire relied on theological dogma for their ideological and legal position. This, we will argue, is the historical source and basic template for the treatment of national minority populations in Europe.

A key event in European history was the onset of the Crusades at the end of the 11th century. Urban II preached the First Crusade in 1095, and in 1096 the starving remnant of a devout but hopelessly disorganised crowd of peasants – led to its doom by a donkey-riding fanatic named Peter the Hermit – reached Constantinople; only to be wiped out by Seljuk archers when they attempted to penetrate the Holy Land.

This moment has a profound inner meaning, representing as it does a deep psychological change for Europe: a transformation in boundary consciousness.

It seems that Christianity had originally been established in Rome through a spontaneous mass movement, based on the simple appeal of a creed which promised that when the world ended, as it soon would, then only the Christians would survive this catastrophe and go on to salvation, eternal life, and so on. (This apocalyptic message, incidentally, was preserved in Gnostic sects and dogmas, and transmitted through an independent channel to the dualist tradition.) A thousand years later, the Christian population of Western, Latin Europe found a similarly appealing belief: that the time had come to rise up in arms against the forces of evil.

The more sophisticated plans of the nobility, which had commercial, diplomatic and political dimensions, were matched by popular uprisings based simply on the fanatical belief in holy war. Illiterate peasants marched happily off to places they only knew from the inspiring tales of Christian mythology: as if they had decided to go and conquer Camelot or Atlantis. Indeed, they had been displaced from their firesides in the first place by the inspiring but entirely false news that the body of Saint James had been transported by the magic of the Divine Will to the pleasant but geographically remote city of Santiago de Compostela in northern Spain: news which had provoked uncontrolled mass pilgrimages as rapturous

European Christians made their way to the site of the miracle. The Crusades harnessed this energy for other, more sinister, purposes.

When the pilgrim warriors eventually reached the Holy Land, they behaved with a savagery that beggars belief. In the words of a contemporary Frankish chronicler, Radulph of Caen, 'In Ma'arra our troops boiled pagan adults in cooking-pots; they impaled children on spits and devoured them grilled.' (Maalouf, 1985, p. 39. These events took place in December 1098) The aims of the rulers and the ruled were in harmony for once, and the keynote of this harmony was a spiritual idea – the idea of *Christianitas*: of Christianity made concrete as a bounded political, social and military unit. A territorial unit. Its boundary therefore became the imagined and indeed imaginary boundary of the Christian European's territory, whatever Christian language he spoke, and whichever Christian king he obeyed.

It could be argued that Eastern Christianity had achieved a comparable sense of unity in the 4th century, and that Islam had achieved something similar in the 8th century under the Caliphate. But the new sense of unity – of exclusion, in the sense explained in the last section – was limited to Western Christianity. When the Crusaders (the rabble armies this time led by the flower of the nobility) sacked Jerusalem in 1099, they did not limit their zeal to their Muslim enemies, but also expelled the Eastern Christian priests – Greek, Armenian, Coptic, Georgian and Syrian – from the Holy Sepulchre, where they had always been allowed to maintain a presence, and tortured them in order to force them to reveal the whereabouts of the True Cross. (Maalouf, 1985, p. 51) The new sense of international solidarity had this other meaning: it translated into a new capacity for collective violence.

In psychological terms, we can still see this as a displacement of the original boundary of the hunting band: a limit to a physical area in which the natural world is assimilated to the internal life of the mind and the emotions. A kind of horizon. As soon as the individual gives up personal control of this boundary, something which must take place at a very early level of social development, he or she is at the mercy of the social group, which will look over the horizon, and provide the individual with the content for a territorial awareness. If the individual is told that the group's territory extends to a river that is three days' march over the horizon, and if this is reinforced by songs or dances or whatever other cultural means are employed, it seems that this will satisfy the emotional need for a boundary to consciousness of this kind; but once this displacement away from direct experience has been achieved, then the boundary could equally be three weeks or three months or three years away: from now on it depends on what values the cultural factors enshrine and reinforce. In the case of the Crusades and the corresponding idea of Christian unity, we see that the long process of separation of national versions of Christianity in the West (national moralities, expressed in national languages) reached this crossroads: a point where the Western Christian world became aware of itself as a whole, and in a new, militant way.

The use of Latin among the learned provided an international cultural basis for this (which is a paradox, since European society was still mostly pre-literate), and what this unity meant in psychological terms was a new awareness of a world outside *Christianitas*: a Satanic world of evil non-believers, to be trampled underfoot, destroyed, and even eaten. Since this motivated actual physical movement of people, new settlement, and mass subjugation of new populations, it was truly revolutionary, leading for example to the large-scale assimilation of Slavs and extermination of pagan Balts in the east and north-east, and setting the stage for such world-historic processes as the centuries-long struggle of Christian Europe with the Ottoman Empire.

But the uniting ideology of the Crusaders also implied a new kind of internal culture: some important changes in cultural values, that is. The lowest common denominator of religious bigotry enabled half-nationalised Christians from different countries to march side by side. And when the threads of European culture were gathered together and pulled tight, it was discovered that some of those threads were now definitely the wrong colour.

As we have argued, urban society represents an infolding of cultural boundaries, so that the horizon of consciousness and territory need no longer be physical; and in mediæval Europe, apart from the Muslims who now became the main focus of Christian hatred (and who did live across a physical boundary), there were a number of dissenting religious groups who had lived in parallel with mainstream Christianity for centuries – and indeed, in the case of the Jews, whose religious identity sometimes actually predated Christianity. Similarly, there were still small and anomalous political formations which did not conform to the emerging norm of a large, centralised Christian/military state. The battle with the Devil and the forces of evil therefore also turned the attention of the devout to these internal enemies. But to understand the religious environment of the middle ages, we need to look at an element of the European tradition which is often left out of schematic historical accounts: dualism and its influence.

It is well known that St. Augustine, who lived through the sack of Rome, and whose voluminous theological writings provided the basic theoretical framework for mediæval Christianity, had been a Manichæan as a young man.[33] What is not so clearly appreciated is that his Christianity was still marked by Manichæan, that is dualist, ideas, to the point that we can see his writings as a kind of synthesis: the moral and political loyalty is now to Christianity, and the analysis is much marked by his reading of Plato and a few other classical philosophers, but the overall intellectual framework (specifically, the treatment of good and evil, and of the nature of physical substance compared with that of God) is largely continuous with a pre-Christian tradition of mysticism. In his treatment of angels, for instance, we find a similarity with Arab theology ('angelology', that is; which also resembles Jewish ideas on the subject) which demonstrates a common origin in pre-Islamic and pre-Christian Middle Eastern religious traditions. More specifically, in his *Confessions*, where the transition from nine years of active Manichæanism – including the writing of (long lost) philosophical works – to orthodox Roman Christianity are described in some detail, we see that the theoretical questions which mainly obsessed Augustine were various problems of dualist stamp. In a discussion of sin in the *City of God*, (Book XIV, Chapter 5) he cites and seeks to oppose the Manichæan position that the body, as a physical thing, is inherently bad. In his *Against The Epistle of Manichaeus Called Fundamental* (Contra Epistolam Manichaei Quam Vocant Fundamenti) of 397, we find him not just criticising but ridiculing dualist dogmas which the modern reader would be hard pressed to distinguish from Augustine's own mystical doctrine. Augustine, the eclectic intellectual, consciously rejected the letter of Manichæan doctrine, and as a

---

[33] This is discussed in the *Confessions*. The relevant passages for what follows are Book 3 for his period as a Manichæan; Book 4, XV for his dualist ideas at that time, and for references to his theoretical writings as a Manichæan; Book 4, XVI for his reading in rhetoric, logic, geometry, music and the liberal arts generally; Book 5, X and Book 7, I for his attempts to reconcile dualist ideas with Christianity on the one hand and classical philosophy on the other; Book 5, XIV for his rejection of Manichæan doctrines when he realised they could not answer some question raised by the pagan philosophers; Book 8, I and X for his reformulation of certain dualist conceptions in a Christianised metaphysical language borrowed from the Greek authors he read in Latin; and Book 10 passim for one interesting but typically idiosyncratic solution to the basic philosophical dilemma of how to reconcile a rationalistic and heavily dualist-influenced conception of the universe with the Christian dogma of the time. Faced with the question whether God is present in man's mind (which would lead to the conclusion that God took part in evil actions), he devises a theory of memory which allows him to say that not God himself, but the memory of God, is ever-present: which displays the same classical/dualist style of thinking as he applied to the questions raised in the *City of God*.

Christian convert that was clearly important to him; but the divided universe of the Manichæans is very close indeed to the City of God and the Earthly City of his own writings: so close that it is no distortion to say that he preserved the dualist spirit, and general intellectual approach, in his own elaborate cosmology. He constructed some novel solutions to the philosophical problems posed by Manichæanism, drawing on the various traditions and sources available to him; and as we will see, these new conceptions marked the thought of the middle ages and of Europe generally very profoundly. Augustine's theories, though couched in the language of orthodoxy, were actually quite original, both in comparison with the Latin theology of Tertullian, Cyprian and Chrysostom, and in comparison with the formulations of Origen and the Greek Fathers.

The dualist tradition strictly speaking – of Manichæanism, Catharism and so on – took an idiosyncratic position. Christian, Islamic and Jewish schools had constructed versions of a mysticism based on the identification of light and dark with good and evil, a tradition that survived in Catholic thinking for instance until the seventeenth century, and which in the Jewish tradition is at the heart of the mystical system of the thirteenth-century *Zohar* and its elaborations. The dualists added a cosmology, based on a characteristic idea of an *invisible world*: a world defined by a peculiar synthesis of ethics and ontology.

The idea of an invisible world has been absorbed so completely into the Christian tradition that we now think of it as a natural component of Christianity – the idea of a place called Heaven, inhabited by souls of the dead, angels, and God, and of other ontologically similar places such as Hell, Purgatory or Limbo. The equivalents in Greco-Roman religion (Olympus, Hades) were thought of as real physical places;[34] it was the mystical traditions of the East which were the source of the later Christian conceptions, and these were transmitted largely through the medium of the various more or less syncretic dualist beliefs, which spread from Persia into the Greek-speaking world, and which are also acknowledged to have played an important role in establishing Jewish mystical concepts (in the Kabbala).

---

[34] Although it is interesting to note that Marcus Terentius Varro (116-27 BC) attempted a rationalistic interpretation of pagan cosmology, based on what seems to have been an original personal system of etymological analysis, and according to which the gods and places of mythology corresponded to various natural phenomena and philosophical principles. Although the bulk of Varro's writing is lost, he was much admired in late antiquity, and in particular was used as an important source by Augustine. Indeed, if we are looking for the historical starting point of the rationalistic theology that differentiated the Latin West from the Greek East, the fanciful etymologies of Varro look like a good candidate.

According to the dualist conception of the universe, though, the vital feature of the parallelism was simply that the material world was bad and belonged to the Devil, and the spiritual world was good and belonged to God.

This provided a robust and convincing theory of the universe, with all good and evil neatly explained as corresponding to the same basic division between the spiritual and the material. This, as just argued, bears a strong structural similarity to Augustine's distinction between an Earthly City and the City of God: so strong, indeed, that it is difficult to believe that there is no immediate personal reason for this in the religious development of St Augustine himself. The *Confessions* are silent on this particular question; but do demonstrate a similar genealogy for Augustine's thinking in other, closely related areas of religious theory.[35]

The dualist cosmology, though, could not be accepted by any Christian writer as it stood, since it implied that the Christian churches, which were physical places, were owned and run by the Devil, who was also in control of earthly power more generally, in the form of royal courts and the establishments of the aristocracy. Kings and aristocrats were to become the most important clients of Christianity in the middle ages, and what with one thing and another a long succession of Christian writers much preferred the idea of relegating the Devil to ownership of a Christian Hell, filled with the screaming souls and tortured bodies of their enemies. So the simple and logical picture of the universe enshrined in dualist thought could under no circumstances be accepted as it stood, and this created a real ideological and theoretical discrepancy between Christians and dualists. Although later dualist sects absorbed a good deal of Christian symbolism (including the symbol of Jesus Christ himself), no amount of compromise could close this gap, and in the end the Christian church, having taken what it wanted in the form of monotheistic theological conceptions, stamped out dualism with fire and the sword.

It is a paradox of the millennium-long dualist tradition that although its strength lay in the superiority and coherence of its intellectual position, its attitude to official power was such that for the most part it could only ever appeal to the poor and illiterate masses – although there were a few outbreaks of sympathy among the upper classes from time to time.

---

[35] For instance, in the treatment of questions concerning the nature of God, the origin of evil, polygamy and murder in Book III, Chapter VII of the *Confessions*. Augustine specifically cites a Manichæan source for these questions, and for his own doubts in relation to them.

St. Augustine lifted a style of thinking from this dualist tradition for his general cosmology, then: and against this background it is instructive to consider his treatment of the Jewish question.

The Jews were a deep embarrassment to Christianity, since their mere existence called the basic dogma of Christianity – that Jesus of Nazareth was the son of God – into question. Jesus, everyone knew, had been Jewish, and yet here were the Jews themselves (who should surely know) denying his divine status, and by implication challenging the international political order based on the authority of Christian mythology. Now, the Jews were a significant element of the Roman imperial population, and some accommodation had to be made. The Empire had twice found itself at war with rebellious groups of Jews (in 66-73, when the Zealots of Judaea tried unsuccessfully to oppose Titus, and in 132-5, when Simeon ben Kocheba led a rebellion against Hadrian; both these adventures ending in disaster for the rebels – something, incidentally, which encouraged the idea of cooperation with Rome: passive obedience, that is), but this was very unsatisfactory; and when Rome decided to be Christian the Jews had to be dealt with in a different manner.

Christian writers had attempted various approaches to this difficult question, with Tertullian for instance attacking the Jews (in his *Adversus Iudaeos*) for practising carnal circumcision rather than the circumcision of the heart of the Christians, and for celebrating an earthly Sabbath rather than waiting for the Sabbath at the End of Days. This was rather similar in tone and general approach to Jewish attacks on Christians; and accusations of black magic also flew in both directions. Some third-century rabbis claimed that Jesus had been an evil magician, given power by Satan; and accusations of evil magic formed part of the basic vocabulary of anti-semitism for centuries, as did accusations of gross sexuality or 'carnality'. Tertullian and Origen accused the Jews of conducting human sacrifices to the Devil, and this traditional accusation resurfaced regularly at least until the 16th century. For Chrysostom, 'The souls of the Jews are the dwelling places of demons.' The carnality of the Jews has also been an *idée fixe* of Christian Europe in more recent times, with Nazi propaganda for instance playing on German insecurities by accusing Jews of monstrous sexual crimes. Indeed, the first attempt to force Jews to wear special clothes – a decision of the Fourth Lateran Council of 1215 – had the purpose of preventing accidental sexual contacts between unscrupulous Jewish men and innocent Christian girls.

But the central theological difficulty was not addressed by this kind of mud-slinging; and it was St. Augustine who found the answer that stuck.

In his *Adversus Iudaeos* (it was a popular genre) of 429, he formulated a theological position that was to provide the ideological basis for the relationship between Christians and Jews up until the rise of nation states and the end of the middle ages – that is, for about a thousand years (though St. Paul's position that the Jews were potential Christians, who would one day be converted, also had a long-term effect on Christian dogma).

Augustine's concept of the Jews – which was compatible with Paul's concept (Meslin, 1967, pp. 368-9, « Vision dualiste des relations judéo-chrétiennes », discusses Paul's theological position on the Jews, and its effects on the *Contra Iudaeos* of Maximin.), and which would in time be adopted in its essentials by Aquinas, and fixed in the official doctrine of the Catholic Church – was that they represented a kind of geometrical complement to the Christians: a demonstration of the ill-effects of not accepting Christian dogma. Spiritual and good Christians had been given this example in the form of the carnal, evil Jews. This not only explained why the Jews existed at all, but gave them a determined function in the divine purpose. They were a lesson to the faithful, and for that reason, despite being hateful to loyal Christians, were still to be tolerated at the heart of generally exclusivist Christian society. For the Jews, like evil itself, were to be seen as an eternal part of the human condition, and something that would endure until the End of Days, when among other impressive events the Jews would at last be banished to Hell for all eternity.

This theological position (with a style of thinking borrowed from the dualist conception of good and evil as a principle not just of ethics but of cosmology – a conception with no immediate correlate in Jewish thought, either in pre-Christian times or in the later Talmudic tradition) was enough to institutionalise qualified toleration of Jews – not, that is, actual religious toleration (for the laws and scriptures of the Jews were certainly not accepted as valid, except to the extent that they were to be allowed to continue with their own traditions within their own communities), but a particular, well-defined kind of social and political toleration.

There were also certain practical considerations affecting this development. Jewish financiers and bankers provided credit for aristocrats and monarchs, and Jewish doctors, lawyers, scholars and other professionals provided other valuable services at court. (Ancient Persia had faced this same difficulty; for the Jews even then displayed a disconcerting industry and intellectualism, coupled with a definite commercial talent.) Mediæval Christian society was certainly anti-Semitic; but still, it is remarkable that in a society which followed ideas of the most extreme and unreasoning stamp, these self-confessed enemies of the central Christian doctrines should have been tolerated at all. What we can suggest is that the theological accommodation represented by Augustine – with its partially-transferred dualism – institutionalised the principle of accepting a dissenting moral community more generally, so that while the Christians and their community formed the historical prototype of the 'national' populations of the 'national' states which eventually emerged in Western Europe, the Jews and their community formed the prototype for a different kind of structure: the parallel culture which is recognised and tolerated within the national population, despite being hateful, evil and foreign on general principles. This difficult ideological conjuring trick allows the circle to be squared, since state authorities can insist that there is one and only one national ideology, based on eternal and immutable truths, and yet at the same time accept that there are people who live on the territory of the state, but nevertheless cling to a different system of beliefs.

This, schematically, is the Western European model. The Muslim Arabs who coexisted with the Jews in Babylonia, Syria, Egypt, North Africa and then Spain from the seventh century on had a policy of toleration of the Jews based seemingly on practical considerations as much as anything else. The synthesis of Arab, Greek and Jewish cultures that resulted provides fascinating material, with such exotica as the tenth-century Arabic translation of the Bible of Saadya, or the twelfth-century *Kuzari* of Halevi, also in Arabic, and purporting to be a dialogue between a Jewish scholar and a king of the Khazars, illustrating our theme of cultural interchange in the most direct manner.

The Ottomans, whose conquests also impinged on European lands, took their legal tradition from Persia and the pre-Muslim Middle East, and had a special system for dealing with their non-Muslim populations: monotheist 'people of the Book' were given a special status, so that they could be tolerated in an organised way, according to explicit moral and legal principles. As we have argued, an urban society is driven by its parallel cultures; and so some means of ideological accommodation – some form of official toleration – must be devised. In the Ottoman state, this toleration took the form of the *millet* system, a kind of pluralistic apartheid based on simple religious distinctions, which included political oversight by religious leaders appointed to provide a link between the non-Muslim millets and the Sublime Porte. For the Jews themselves, incidentally, toleration of non-Jews and of foreigners generally is enjoined by Talmudic law for ethical reasons: again on theological grounds, then, but not on grounds of cosmology.[36] But Islamic and Jewish models are of secondary importance in terms of their influence; for in the same way that the Western Christian nation state system has succeeded in providing the basic world political model, we can see that the 'national minority' structure by which that Western Christian model is compromised or complicated has also been internationalised.

A neat illustration of this process in action is provided by the treatment of Muslims in mediæval Spain, after the retreat of the Moors left stranded pockets of Muslim groups. 'For a quarter of a millennium at the end of the Middle Ages Muslims of the Iberian Peninsula had a simple choice: either to accept subject Muslim (Mudejar) status within one of the Christian states (Aragon, Castile, Navarre) or live within the Islamic kingdom of Granada.' As with the Jews (expelled from Spain in 1492), 'The eventual outcome was the Expulsion of 1609-1611, a signal admission of total failure', (Harvey, 1990, pp. 41, 64) but on the way the Christian kingdoms had made a serious attempt to find a middle way. Specifically, in Castile, the exhortatory legal code 'Las Siete Partidas' of Alfonso X demonstrates 13th-century thinking. 'And so we say that the Moors should live among the Christians in the same manner as... the Jews, observing their own laws and causing no offence to others.' (Alfonso X, 1807, *Las Siete Partidas*, 3 vols., Madrid; Vol. III, pp. 675-76) This code was based on Roman law, and it is important to realise that the traditional authority of this body of law provided the basic legitimacy for state institutions when they began to revive in the middle ages, being the only real alternative to the canon law tradition promoted by the religious authorities; especially as an important aspect of the centralisation of Papal authority from the twelfth century on. (Much of southern Italy, though, had remained under Byzantine rule until the tenth and eleventh centuries, and so Roman law prevailed there in an unbroken tradition.) The canon law tradition, perhaps understandably, drifted more and more towards outright punitive measures against Jews, with the *Decretum* of Burchard of Worms (1012), whose measures were copied in more than thirty other canon law collections, prescribing a comprehensive Jewry law which sought to place legal restrictions both on the practice of the Jewish religion, and on contacts between Christians and Jews. But the legal tradition of the late, Christian, Western Empire, as represented in the jurisprudence of

---

[36] The principal commentator on the Talmud of the middle ages, Rabbi Solomon ben Isaac of Troyes (1040-1105), also known as Rashi, dealt with Jewish-Christian relations in his *Responsa*. He took the rather legalistic line that Christians were not to be considered as idolators, which exempted them from certain important prohibitions.

mediæval Europe, also included a treatment of the Jews (ultimately depending on the theology of the Church Fathers, and preserving the theological balance of power established in late antiquity), and since the long-term trend was still in the direction of a consolidation of state power over independent ecclesiastical power, this tradition of state law provided the base for a limited degree of toleration from the state;[37] though at the same time we should remember that this general trend often faced some pretty stiff opposition from the Church – Innocent III's codification of canon law in the 13th century representing a particularly serious attempt to provide a legal basis for an increase in the relative power of the Papacy and its representatives.

While we see that Alfonso X's suggested treatment of Muslims in Spain was not so successful in the end, the Jewish paradigm for dealing with non-Christians is clearly visible; and the paradoxical status of the Jews in the Christian Europe of the middle ages is still preserved and reflected in its modern counterpart: the paradoxical status of national minorities who live within nationally-determined state structures. And this is thrown into relief as far as our wider argument is concerned by the fact that while *Jews* were offered a degree of protection, as just described, it was the same Roman tradition of state law (and not canon law) that provided the legal means for burning *heretics*, when political and cultural developments made this an attractive policy alternative for the Dominican Inquisition.[38] The ultimately theological basis for the laws protecting the Jews meant that these laws could not necessarily be extended even to other religious minorities: for the same early Christian theology which had been forced to compromise where the Jews were concerned had been stern in its treatment of heresy.

To see the full force of this argument, it is necessary to grasp that the political structures of state sovereignty in Europe are explicitly theological in origin. It was the gradual but general recognition of the divinely-granted and

---

[37] 'The Carolingian age... continued Roman law traditions; some that had fallen into disuse in the seventh century were reinstated. No shift in the Jews' constitutional status took place; in fact, it was restabilised in the direction of the status that Jews had been assigned in the time of the late Roman Empire.' (Stow, 1992, p. 57)

[38] 'After the time of St. Augustine the idea that the secular arm might strike against heresy recurred in the writings of the Church Fathers, the decisions of oecumenical councils, and other texts going to make up the official canonical tradition. In addition to this material, the collections of ecclesiastical law also contained some imperial constitutions which, unlike canon law, established the death penalty for unrepentant heretics. These late Roman legal compilations were not unknown in the early Middle Ages, but for a long time there had been no practical opportunity to put the measures they contained into effect against heretics. The occasional aberrations in doctrine which occurred were effectively dealt with by ecclesiastical disciplinary measures, and there was no reason to call in the secular arm.' (Loos, 1974, pp. 152-153)

divinely-ordained authority of kings that led to similar claims of moral authority in state politics (the politics of the 'sovereign state', that is, which came to embody the magical virtue at first assigned by Christians to the King himself). Remembering that the Jews, too, had a theologically-conceived identity (though one with a different kind of logic), we see that the relationship between Christians and Jews did in fact contain and fix the essential ideological and political problem. The whole trajectory of the treatment of the Jews from the break-up of the Western Roman Empire to the expulsions of the Ashkenazim from Western states which took place between the end of the fifteenth and the middle of the sixteenth centuries can therefore be understood in relation to the change in the theological position of the king in the mediæval state. Indeed, we can interpret their continued toleration in Poland-Lithuania in consistent terms, since a mediæval pattern of kingship continued there until the eighteenth century.[39] At the beginning of the middle ages, the theological model of kingship was that of Protector of the Faith: protector, that is, of the imperial Roman faith, as preserved in Church structures. At the end of the period, we find that the king has become the protector of the faith in a national variant, and that he is supported in this task by a national ideology and state apparatus. The City of God of Augustine – the 'mystical' or invisible counterpart to the earthly City, with its state-run political structures – has been nationalised, so that the king rules not all Christendom, but only his own little corner of it. And since the most important political and commercial competition was now with other Christian states, the common Christian belief-structure steadily lost political value compared with the new national discrepancies, which transferred Christian messianism to national projects.

It was at this point that the Western European Jews became intolerable. Their official identity in state and canon law and in politics generally still corresponded to the old universalising dogma, in which what was at stake was not a national culture, but the general European culture of Christianity; but when Christianity was reorganised and nationalised, it was found that the Jews could not so easily be made to fit in with this project. They had a defined role within the logic of establishing a Christian community in Europe generally, that is, but had no obviously equivalent role in Christian France, England, or Spain. Since the state ideologies which

---

[39] This was somewhat complicated by the existence of a separate legal tradition in formerly pagan Lithuania, and in fact the legal position of the Jews was more consistent with mediæval Western practice in the Polish part of the dual state.

defined the place of the Jews in society were still explicitly based on the idea of a universal Christian identity, it made little immediate sense to think of 'French Jews', 'English Jews' or 'Spanish Jews'. The Jews were not Christians, and so could not be admitted as the loyal nationals of Christian nation states. No, the actual result of consolidating state identities at the expense of a pan-European Christian identity was to exclude the Jews more completely – and to remove the theological safety-net which had guaranteed them their strange position in society for so long. Physical expulsion demonstrates this new kind of exclusion in action.

We can draw a parallel with the linguistic situation. Latin, the language of dignity and power in the middle ages, was the universal language of the Western Church as well as the ancient language of the Roman state and its laws. The Christianising of Europe implied an acceptance of Latin and its authority; but just when this project was complete (and as if in a collective response to this phase of cultural development coming to an end), the practical advantages of using languages which everybody in the state could understand came to outweigh the advantages of using Latin. The universal Christian dogmas were re-packaged within national literatures, and the familiar-seeming division of territory according to linguistic boundaries acquired its concrete expression.

Now, the reader might object that the theological position of the Jews could have been re-packaged too; that French Jew and English Jew and Spanish Jew were no more contradictory as cultural and legal identities than Frenchman or Englishman or Spaniard. And indeed this is what has happened in recent times. Up until the Holocaust, anyway, it was quite natural to speak of 'Dutch Jews' or 'German Jews', for example – as we still quite naturally speak of 'Russian Jews' today. Jews, like other minority populations, have adapted to the conditions of modern society, and so of course operate with the national language, culture, bureaucracy, education system, and so on, of the country in which they live. But the fact is that the position of European Jews was changed profoundly by the late mediæval expulsions. Specifically, what had lapsed was the Europe-wide, officially-sponsored policy of compromised toleration: the development of Augustine's position, which was that the Jews were a necessary evil and a divine example to the faithful. The political result of this is conveniently fixed for us by the doctrine of Perpetual Servitude (*perpetua servitudo*), announced in Innocent III's Bull 'Etsi iudaeos' of 1205. But when monarchs discovered that they could get away with a more vigorous kind of policy (and, as Kenneth R.

Stow notes,[40] this corresponded with a process of legal development whereby Jews were increasingly placed under the formal protection of the monarch), they took advantage of this splendid opportunity to remove their creditors, along with their families and as far as possible everything to do with them. Since the Jews were universally identified as the enemies of Christianity, this won popular support, but not in the brutal way that the Crusades had won popular support. No mass killings by bloodthirsty mobs, that is. And since the expulsions were on the whole orderly and non-violent, the door was left open for Jews to find another niche in European Christian society; which they did, where possible. But from now on it was not enough to be a Jew. This no longer defined your political identity. From now on the European Jew had to learn to think of himself also as a national citizen.

It is also instructive to consider the further history of the expellees. They naturally gravitated towards places where something like the traditional protection was still on offer. One such place was the Ottoman Empire, where their religion offered them a defined legal position, but the main refuge was Poland-Lithuania, where a mediæval pattern of kingship continued. This included the traditional protection for Jews. However, the bulk of this polycultural territory was then assimilated to Russia, and as Russia modernised, the Jews (though now officially Russian) became correspondingly more foreign, with anti-semitism becoming a normal component of the Russian identity. We see that this development fits into our general account of the relationship of the Jews to modern national states; although the October Revolution created a different political environment in the twentieth century.

Let us now remind ourselves of our more general theories, and place the processes just described in a model of parallel cultures. We can make some precise suggestions.

Firstly let us tentatively state that parallel cultures are inherently unstable in their relationship. The monocultural society tends towards a certain kind of stability, and the polycultural society tends in the opposite direction. This provides for a dynamic relationship between the component cultures which, though perhaps internally very stable, make an unstable whole when put together like this. At any one time, it is the state of the

---

[40] (Stow, 1992): 'I will argue that what principally governed Jewish life in the earlier Middle Ages was a firmly defined legal and constitutional status.' (p. 4.) But 'The more Christian political thinking coalesced, the more precarious became the Jews' theoretical and constitutional hold on their right to reside in Christian kingdoms.' (p. 178.)

dynamic equilibrium between them that determines the balance of power, and the cultural balance more generally.

Secondly, let us observe that the relationship between parallel cultures is not one of political or social equality. On the contrary, one of the forces which holds this configuration together is a universalising law to which all are subject, whether they like it or not. The Jews did not choose a condition of Perpetual Servitude: but they accepted it as the best they could get, and so the society was able to function. It is an uneasy balance, though, and one effect of nationalism in recent history (the ideology of nationalism, that is) has been to convince a great many component cultures of parallel culture societies that they have a natural right to political domination – even when making such a claim directly destroys the means by which the dominant culture accepts their presence in the first place. But the unhappy conclusion that there will always be a dominant nationality or culture is softened in its impact by the observation that this is chiefly a legal and political requirement, and that this 'dominant' function can also be fulfilled by a universalising system which does not enshrine national values. There are several other alternatives available. One, naturally, is a set of religious values. Catholic countries, for instance, still to some extent conform to a trans-national ideology. In Habsburg Europe, the isolation of national cultures did not lead to the political isolation of corresponding nation states. This only took place in the twentieth century (in the case of Austria-Hungary); and we see that the tradition of political management imposed a central authority which was not crudely nationalistic. The Soviet system, though Russian-dominated, was not simply Russian-nationalist in its ideology, and indeed actively promoted identities which compromised the Russian identity: a Soviet identity on the one hand, and the synthetic nationalisms of the non-Russian components of the Soviet population on the other.[41] More positively, perhaps, we can see that European political integration is proceeding according to a logic which is not just French or German or British. It fulfills the dominant-culture function without a dominant-culture ideology; and this is necessary, since there is no dominant national culture in Europe today (unless it is the American one). And this

---

[41] For these issues, (Tishkov, 1997) is an invaluable contribution, based on a unique set of personal qualifications. Prof. Tishkov was Yeltsin's Minister of Nationalities in 1992, during a crucial period of transition and policy formulation, and as Director of the Institute of Ethnology and Anthropology of the Russian Academy of Sciences, is also well placed in the corresponding academic field. Much of what follows is informed by the very complete documentation of this impressive work where the former USSR is concerned; but the abruptly Westernised theoretical position taken by Tishkov, though well articulated, is in my view inadequate in the end.

looks like the next phase of development – driven by the advance of technology, which has led to greater physical mobility and interchange, to massively increased flows of electronic information, and to greater transparency between cultures. The overall stabilising forces are no longer provided just by national states, with their national mythologies and moral systems. These are increasingly compromised from above, by the voluntary acceptance of trans-national systems of various kinds. And the weakening of the national state's moral authority must be good news for members of parallel cultures. Again, we can look at a linguistic parallel. As the nationalistic assumption that state equals nation fades in importance, so does the relative importance of the national language. And we have seen a retreat from monolinguistic states, among the most advanced industrial economies (though not everywhere). Turkish is heard in Germany, Urdu in Britain, and in America, where the single most important badge of being American has been the use of English, the Spanish-speaking parallel culture is spreading fast.

Now, this process, and processes like it, are visible because they refer to easily-observed cultural indicators: language, primarily. But language does not just isolate by means of standardising communication. Many of the European boundaries are only there by accident, after all, and the division into national languages is in many cases entirely arbitrary. Between Dutch, Flemish and German, for instance, or at the time of their separation between Spanish and Portuguese, there is or was originally only the degree of separation that exists between neighbouring dialects of a national language. It is not the degree of difference that ultimately matters, nor even whether people can understand each other. The language has a content and not just a linguistic code of its own. Its content is what is isolated by adopting a national standard; and if this content includes some specific ideological dogmas (myths, laws, ideas...), then this will immediately lead to cultural separation. Now, we observe that this cultural separation can take place inside a national boundary as well as at that boundary. We observe furthermore that the cultural separation need not correspond to the separation of territory, and need not involve all the elements of national culture. Indeed, another general rule would seem to be that parallel cultures must have something in common: some common ground, we could say. So what is the essential aspect? What is it that marks people out as truly different? Many of the obvious-seeming answers are demonstrably wrong if we look not at Europe but at America. Differences of race, language and religion can all be accommodated, it seems, if not always easily or quickly. But what cannot be tolerated is systematic disloyalty to the state idea. Culturally-coded moral opposition, that is, to the state's single, defining morality. Un-American Activities. High Treason. Offences against Islam or Soviet Marxism-Leninism. Heresy.

This leads us to another historical interlude: an analysis of the Cathar dualists of southern France in the 13th century. This fits our purposes particularly well, because the Cathar minority or parallel culture was not configured along lines of race, language or nationality. It represented a moral rebellion against the authority of the state religion, but nothing else. It illustrates the mechanisms by which a parallel culture can arise and be maintained within the social practice of a much more powerful dominant culture. Its history also illustrates how and for what kinds of reasons such a parallel culture can be destroyed.

The reader will easily accept that religion is enough to make a minority. On the one hand, many 'national' differences today, such as the Serb/Croat/Bosnian division of the former Yugoslav population, correspond to overt religious differences (Orthodox/Catholic/Muslim); and on the other hand, we see that the modern phenomenon of the instant religion, spread internationally by high-technology communications, can also create instant religious minorities – such as the Moonies or the Scientologists. In the case of the Cathar dualists, we are dealing with a deep and enduring religious division in Europe. Like the Bogomils of Bosnia, the Paulians, Paulicians, Arians and some other sects of uncertain origin (the documentation is typically very unreliable, being in the nature of polemical tracts either for or against one particular interpretation of dogma), the Cathars or Albigensians of Languedoc believed in the version of the world already mentioned: based on the dualist conviction that the visible world was owned and run by the Devil, and that it corresponded to a spiritual world that could not be seen. It was their particular misfortune in 13th-century Languedoc to find themselves in the path not of the Devil in person, but of the political ambitions of Popes Innocent III and Gregory IX, who unleashed the power of the future to stamp them out forever, along with the rather pleasant – but equally anachronistic – Provençal society of which they formed a rustic and inoffensive part.

The dualists represented not just a different belief system, but a different social order. Like the Jews, their different theology implied a different social structure; but unlike the Jews, there was no theological accommodation with official Christianity, and so no legal accommodation with the Christian state authorities either. One can speculate that the general poverty of the ascetic dualists was also a factor. While there was some temporary sympathy for dualist beliefs in Bosnian and Provençal aristocratic circles at different times, on the whole this was a belief of the illiterate poor, and so there was no economic or political incentive to protect its adherents when they came into conflict with the officially-sanctioned versions of Christianity. In the Catholic West and in the Orthodox East alike, dualist sects were stamped out, with the Dominicans establishing burning at the stake as the most effective method. It is interesting to note that in the West, the final extermination of the dualists coincided with the establishment of a unified French religious and political identity; and so the Cathars can be seen directly as victims of a large-scale process of structural change in society. In the areas with dualist believers which fell under Ottoman domination (Bosnia, possibly Bulgaria and possibly Serbia), there are simply no surviving records to allow any reliable reconstruction of events. It is supposed that the Bogomil population of Bosnia formed the basis for the modern Muslim population there, the mechanism for this transformation having been the acceptance of these heretics by the Ottomans on the principle that the enemy of my enemy is my friend;[42] but this is not much more than a plausible speculation. What we can say with certainty is that in the East, too, dualism was successfully extirpated. One way or another, its followers were absorbed into the more successful official religions.

A look at some dualist beliefs will quickly reveal why it was that state Christianity rejected it. Dualism as a whole has its origin in a complex of ideas associated with Mazdaism, Gnosticism, and their product, Manichæanism. Its associated social structure (which was fairly consistent) relied on the separation of a class of the Elect – the *katharoi* or pure – which was present in Mazdaism; its mythology fused Mazdaist elements with the apocalyptic tradition of Christian Gnosticism; and its characteristic synthesis of Christian and non-Christian beliefs arose through the 3rd-century cult of Mani, a religious leader in Southern Babylonia who claimed to be the latest incarnation of Christ. The Paulicians, a sect of 7th-century Armenian/ Byzantine origin, preserved some Gnostic doctrines, such as the belief in two Gods, along with some folk Christianity and the characteristic dualist social structure, and this inoffensive heresy spread steadily through the Byzantine world until it was put down by a massacre in 843. The basic logic of mediæval European dualism, then, has this hybrid origin, and in very general

---

[42] (Braudel, 1993) likens this to the wholesale conversion of Buddhists to Islam in Bengal in the 12th century: both processes, he suggests, being a reaction to earlier persecution.

terms can be seen as a synthesis of cultural traditions. But as a semi-organised system of folk beliefs, the European dualist sects developed a version of the tradition which had lost its roots, and which now mirrored the main stream of European Christianity, whether in the form of a modified Christian liturgy, or in the form of a heretical version of the Christ myth, with Christ interpreted not as a historical figure but as a mythological symbol. In one document, for instance, we learn that Christ's visit to earth was actually a descent into Hell. As with West European witchcraft, or the Voodoo of Haiti, we see that the developing folk beliefs, though supposedly independent, were completely bound up with the development of the official doctrine to which they were subjectively opposed – and the reaction of official Christianity in all three cases was to see these alternatives as nothing more than Satanism. The magical figures of Christian doctrine – the saints, demons and prophets – were detached from the official Christian mythology (which was too complicated anyway), and given new values in a rough and ready peasant theology, which was not constrained by any historical, political or other intellectual considerations. But as time went by, the doctrinal opposition to official Christianity became more and more overt (expressed by a belief that the dualists were the only true Christians), until the cross was interpreted as the symbol of the Devil's victory on earth, the Temple of Jerusalem was said to have been his first headquarters, and a secret teaching grew up that the Devil was actually 'Satanael', the secret son of God, whose victory on earth was so complete that the only way out was a complete renunciation of the world. The Cathar *endura* was the practical demonstration of this belief. This is all very confused, though, and it would be a mistake to see dualism as providing a real intellectual alternative to Christian dogma. Its very nature as a cult of the uneducated and the poor precluded the development of a highly intellectualised doctrine, and its specific condemnation of the material world meant that dualists had no interest in erecting monuments or works of art. Similarly, they had no interest in attracting the learned to their cause, and they produced no distinguished authors or great artists.

Before proceeding to a look at day-to-day life among the Cathars, it is worth noting that the legal treatment of the dualist sects was quite different to that of the Jews. In the case of the Jews, theology counselled (and produced) legal toleration. No such luck for the Cathars and their colleagues. Hounded as criminals and heretics, they were eventually exterminated by the application of state rather than ecclesiastical law, following in form the norms and traditions of Roman law, as we have seen. The Holy Roman Emperor, founder of the University of Naples, sometime excommunicate,

Arabic- and Greek-speaking Crusader, and King of Sicily Frederick II –
despite having at one stage of his extraordinary career considered founding a
new religion to replace Christianity – established an additional new legal
basis for this by making heresy a crime of *laesa maiestas*, in other words a
crime against the state, still expressed according to the norms of Roman law
(especially in his generally liberal and forward-looking *Sicilian Constitution*
of 1224). This innovation was enthusiastically welcomed by the Church,
which set about promulgating this new legal doctrine across Europe; so that
the courts of the Dominican Inquisition, already employing such effective
judicial means as torture and the cutting out of the tongue, were now given a
free hand to order the burning alive of dualist heretics where necessary,
under the authority of the secular courts with whom they cooperated. This
was an important legal development for the churchmen, because the
Inquisition courts were reluctant to impose the death penalty on their own
account. After all, they were committed to a doctrine of charity, forgiveness
and universal love, and decisions based on canon law could not directly
violate these central doctrines. However, the (technically illegal) practice of
the mass burning of heretics had recently been established by the enthusiasm
of the Crusaders, and so the Church was keen to put this useful technique of
social and spiritual engineering on a more business-like basis.

We have already characterised the Crusades as a welling-up of
Christian feeling right across western Europe, and seen that a consequence of
this was a spontaneous killing of Jews. In this, Jews and dualists were more
or less in the same boat, although dualists, living mostly in remote rural
areas, were not so close at hand as the ghettoised Jews. But a look at another
little-discussed feature of mediæval life will put their relationship in a
different perspective: the slave trade.

Slavery was one of the basic social institutions of the ancient world.
Roman law dealt with it extensively: the Code of Justinian, for instance,
devoted more space to the regulation of slavery than to any other topic –
although by the sixth century, Christianity was already established, and
Justinian was a Christian Emperor. As the Western Empire decayed, though,
various changes created a new social class: the serfs, who became the chief
source of unskilled labour in mediæval Europe.[43] But it is often forgotten that
slavery nevertheless continued in Europe throughout the middle ages.[44] The

---

[43] See (Finley, 1968), for an excellent discussion of slavery under the Romans; especially
pp. 158-9 for principles of law.
[44] And in Russia, where the middle ages lasted longest, slavery was not abolished until the
18th century, when the legal status of slaves and serfs was merged. (Sumner, 1962, p. 140)

Vikings were active slavers, and it is suggested that Russia (or rather, its precursor, the *Rus'* proto-state founded by the Norsemen in the 9th century) was basically a by-product of the trade:[45] a commercial staging post for slaving raids. Similarly, it is said that the rise of the city of Prague and of a proto-Czech state (that of the Přemysl dynasty) in the 10th century was the result of the success of the slave trade there.[46] In the English Domesday Book of 1086, ten per cent of the people registered were slaves, rising to twenty per cent in some places. This, however, was well below the thirty per cent or so recorded for the late Western Roman Empire; for slavery was gradually going out of fashion in the West.

In Byzantium and in the Islamic world it still flourished, though, and it was considered legitimate for Western Christians to participate in the international trade, even if they gradually had to give up their own household slaves themselves. There are few documents, and there is no real consensus of what consitutes a slave: the legal and social status varied considerably from society to society, and slaves were defined in relation to other extinct social categories. Indeed, as Marc Bloch reminds us in a classic study, there was a general concept of *hommage* – of being the man of another man – which sanctioned a whole extinct network of social relations in the middle ages.[47] But still we learn with interest of one theological and legal debate: whether Jews should have the right to buy and sell Christian slaves. Now, from an etymological point of view, the words 'slave' and 'Slav' differ only in spelling. 'Sclavonia' was traditionally seen as a wild and primitive interior, where enterprising merchants could legitimately go and procure pagan savages for the European markets. This tradition was compromised, though, by the spread of Christianity among the Slavs, and more and more of them fell under the protection of the law as a result of their conversion. The dualist beliefs of the Bosnians, though, (along with those of the Bogomils of Bulgaria and Serbia) put them in a special category. They talked of Christ, and prayed and fasted and worshipped a God close if not identical to that Italianate version of the Deity worshipped in far-off Rome; but unfortunately for them, the nearby trading centre of Dubrovnik was an outpost of the West, and the slave markets there were still hungry for product. The general

---

[45] *Encyclopedia Britannica.*

[46] This is the hypothesis of the leading contemporary Czech mediævalist, Dušan Třeštík (in *Dějiny a součastnost* [History and the Present], 1999); his idea being that taxation on the huge slave traffic through Prague enabled the first Christian state on this territory to arm and feed a professional army, with which it established a large and prosperous realm.

[47] 'L'homme d'un autre homme... Le comte était « l'homme » du roi, comme le serf celui de son seigneur villageois.' [The man of another man... The count was 'the man' of the king, as the serf was that of his village lord.] (Bloch, 1989, p. 209)

consensus of the legal debate seems to have been that Jews could not buy and sell Christian slaves, even if those slaves simply converted after capture specifically in order to escape their servitude. This inconvenient development had the effect of isolating one reliable group: the dualist heretics, who preferred slavery to official Christianity, which in their eyes equalled damnation. And so we have a concrete image of the relationship between Christian, Jew and dualist in the middle ages: the sale of dualist slaves in Christian-run markets by Jewish middle-men. We may salve our consciences by going along with the historiographical tradition which makes the eventual customers Muslims. The delicate moral balance of this unusual system was a result of the normal working of the social mechanism, and specifically the result of its legal and theological treatment of dissenting groups, according to two basic models: the special toleration given to the Jews (both as potential Christians, and as an example to the faithful of the ill-effects of failure to accept the Christian reality), and the dehumanised, marginal status constructed for heretics. And we see that the different positions of the Jews and the dualists in this arrangement are the direct result of the intersection of two much older conceptual traditions: Roman law, and a theology based on that of St Augustine, with its Manichæan influence and general logic; and so we see that the dualist intellectual tradition, for all its faults, was in the end strong enough to provide the means of its own destruction.

We are fortunate to possess a detailed picture of dualism in its terminal phase, in the form of the Inquisition records assembled by Jacques Fournier, Bishop of Pamiers, and subsequently Pope Benedict XII of Avignon (elected in 1334). Since stamping out heresy was seen as a noble and necessary activity, the forward-looking Fournier kept a detailed record of the work of his court, including transcriptions of interrogations (which were conducted without torture, except in one case involving some lepers accused of poisoning wells). These comprehensive records form the basis of a classic historical study, *Montaillou* by Emmanuel Le Roy Ladurie, which is the most complete study of a mediæval village that we have – apart from its interest as a document of the Cathars and their culture.

For the peasant of mediæval Europe, faith was a serious matter: part of the texture of everyday life. Although certain individuals showed signs of scepticism – atheism, even – on the whole religion was ever-present, giving a basic meaning to life. In particular, it provided a basis for social solidarity, and played a role similar to that of a national ideology: an ever-present background of belief, and a reason for that sense of superiority without which, it seems, we are unable to get through the day. The nation had not yet been invented, and even its geographical reference had little meaning for people such as the inhabitants of Montaillou, whose physical movements were limited to a few villages and some sheep pastures. Without access to the mechanisms of cultural contact provided by parallel culture urbanism, they had no direct experience of people speaking other languages, or more generally of people whose knowledge of the world was not about the same as theirs. Nevertheless, the effects of urban culture – specifically, of the progress towards a unified religious and political culture in France, and indeed in Western Europe generally – were felt even in Montaillou.

The contradiction of values between official Christianity and their own predominantly Cathar beliefs – by implication a contradiction between two competing social systems – made itself felt as a conflict of loyalties between the urban reality represented by the priests and the village reality represented by their own Cathar 'perfects' (*parfaits*), as the purified stratum of believers was called in this version of dualism.[48] This was the last gasp of Catharism, by the way. The wave of repression represented by the proceedings of Fournier's court, implementing the policy of the central Church authorities, succeeded in stamping out the heresy for ever, although it took a few more massacres to complete the job.

For the purposes of our analysis, it is interesting to note that the choice between Catharism and Catholicism was not exactly a personal one. It was seen both by the peasants themselves and by the priests who fought against it as a question of the *domus*: the largish house where a family group was based. A *domus* would accept the visits of the perfects or it would not, and personal loyalty would follow this group decision: and we see immediately that there is a link between this cultural identity and social structuring. The subjective value-system does not necessarily create the social structuring, but it is still (subjectively) identified with it. This is a Christian house. This is a French house. And the battle for souls in Montaillou was fought at the micro-level of these smallest cells of society.

What, then, was altered when a *domus* went from one religious affiliation to the other? Not language, not physical location; there was not much change in economic or other relations with the rest of Languedoc society: but there was a decisive normative discrepancy, symbolised by the

---

[48] Let us note in passing that this distinctive theological gambit – the isolation of a class of perfected individuals by means of theological and spiritual differentiation – has a close parallel in the Sufi tradition of Islam. The Sufis, like the Cathar *parfaits*, do not merely transmit the teachings of the tradition they represent: they embody the perfection of its message in their own absolute personal perfection.

acceptance of certain rituals, some of them rather extreme. For the Cathars, the physical world was fundamentally evil, and they had devised a system of leaving it which demonstrated this conviction in a very direct form. The preferred death of a Cathar believer was by *endura*, or voluntary starvation. The perfects would do this to themselves, but would also encourage the imposition of the *endura* on others at times of sickness, so that the dying person could leave the world in a state of purity. Whether or not a particular sick person should receive this benefit of religion must have provoked some lively discussions.

Catharism, like all the local variants of dualism across Europe, had unconsciously adapted many of the formal features of the dominant religion against which it measured itself. The Cathars were not foreigners, and they were not treated as such. Their only conflict was with the official priests, that is, with a level of social organisation which they could not understand or aspire to. Some documents suggest that there was a sort of dualist Pope somewhere in the Balkans (See Duvernoy, 1979, p. 14, for sources and a discussion), but any contacts were very irregular. However, the liturgy did succeed in preserving the essential concepts of dualism, even where the words used were borrowed from Catholic or Orthodox texts. But their attitude to power and wealth was out of step with the needs of the centralised urban culture which was everywhere becoming dominant, and the normative discrepancy between their ideology and that of their enemies served to isolate them from the widespread social changes which we see in retrospect as 'progress'. According to Le Roy Ladurie, the concrete reason for the wave of persecution documented by Fournier's records was that the Church insisted on collecting its tithes, and the Cathars – thinking, presumably, that this would have been equivalent to financing the Devil – refused to pay up. Christianity itself was changing, and adapting to the rising urbanism and mercantilism of society generally. As political power centralised, religious power centralised too. In France, this meant that the society of Languedoc, based on a local language standard, the authority of a series of local courts, and the corresponding division of territory according to aristocratic identities, had to surrender its independence (and its whole principle of political organisation) to the new order based in Paris. The Inquisition was an instrument of this political and social change; and the heretics had to go.

Village life, though, was far removed from this kind of power politics. In Montaillou, it was said that the chief advantage of being a priest was that it gave you the opportunity to sleep with a great many women, since in the first place they could not deny you entry to their houses, and in the second place you could blackmail them with threats of eternal damnation. And some dim rumours of the Tatar invasions across the far-off Russian steppes had penetrated far enough for there to be a feeling that the end of the world, discussed with great imagination both by the priests and by the perfects, was a real event, and coming soon. With no organised high culture to speak of, the villagers could accept the most extreme-seeming versions of reality, as long as they did not interrupt the eternal daily routine of picking lice and looking after the sheep. It was the priests who wanted to make serious changes in this way of life; and a natural sense of rebellion against this take-over was the basis of peasant support for dualism everywhere, in Bosnia or Bulgaria as in Languedoc. It was, we could say, a counter-culture, based on and arising from opposition to the domination of a culture from which an isolated rural population was alienated, either for directly economic reasons, or for more general reasons of resisting the imposition of change from outside.[49] This reflex, indeed, was what sustained heretical sects from the time of the establishment of Christianity as the religion of Rome onwards. If it is true that there was a free-standing dualist church in Bosnia, its organisation was very different from the loose fraternity of perfects we find in Montaillou. A counter-culture, which rejects the dominant culture but lacks the structures to replace it, in the end lacks a basis for social cohesion on the large scale. The Jews, with their laws and ancient social practices, could function very completely in parallel with Christian society, providing an alternative to the official state-sponsored system of culture; whereas a counter-culture such as that of the Cathars (or of many disaffected urban groups today) rejects but does not build. It says, perhaps legitimately, that the dominant society is no good, but its message is not such as to create a positive alternative, since it characteristically does not deal with the problems of large-scale social organisation in its ideology. In the Cathar case, the best alternative promoted by the perfects was literally suicidal. In terms of ideology (understanding this term to refer to that part of the belief-system with a relevance for social or political structure), the counter-culture does not move from a critical phase to an active phase. (See Lord, 1999, Chapter 3,

---

[49] This schematic treatment is slightly unorthodox. (Duvernoy, 1976, pp. 262-3) agrees that the Cathar religious beliefs did not lead to a consistent political position, but says that in general the rural Cathars supported the social and political order represented by the Occitain aristocracy, who were mostly sympathetic to the dualists. Another position, defended by some scholars, is that Catharism was originally established as the religion of the provincial bourgeoisie of Languedoc, and that the documents from Montaillou are misleading because they represent a stage in the repression of the sect when it had already been displaced from the towns by official Christianity. (Nelli, 1969, pp. 137-9)

'The ideological base' for a full explanation of these terms.) It may be that the Cathar faith could have made this sort of adaptation, given the chance; but actually it did not. It did not look forward to an improved version of society, but contented itself with reiterating its criticisms of the norms of the larger society inside which it lived.

Now, it may be that this was not typical for dualism as a whole. We have no other records as complete as those of Montaillou for other periods or places, and so direct comparison is impossible, but the evidence would seem to show that the dualist faith always grew up as a counter-culture: a reaction to the growth of state Christianity. It provided an ideology of opposition to the state power, whether this was Byzantine, French or Roman Catholic, by providing a means of cultural opposition to its religious norms. The perfects were as poor as the people they lived with, and did not represent the domination of a foreign power, or the imposition of the rules of a far-off central religious organisation. But their ideology, interpreted as a political creed, was limited to the negative: to providing a means of opposition.

We see, then, that mediæval Christianity had two basic approaches to dissent. On the one hand, the Jews, following the theological tradition, were accepted as an organic part of Christian society, even if the same theological tradition that gave them this special status also suggested that they should be hated and despised. On the other hand, the various dualist heretical groups, whose beliefs had not been assimilated into the theological tradition of the church, represented a social alternative which could not be tolerated, even though the basic symbolism of mediæval dualism was Christian. Now, we have already alluded to 'progress', and if progress was definitely slow in the long dark years between the collapse of Rome and the Renaissance, it was not entirely absent. We have interpreted the Crusades as a symptom and vehicle of an important change in social awareness, for instance. At a political level, it was the Church which provided the focus for centralised organisation, both of bureaucracy and of ideology, and we have also seen that the transfer of religious authority to kings formed a bridge to a political system based on nation states, with local variants of Christianity forming the basis for national moral orders – which is still the system we are used to today (even if it is breaking down under the influence of international communications). If we consider the different reactions of Christianity to the Jews and to the dualists, we see that there are two trajectories which are possible for dissenting groups within this overall development of national moral orders.

If a minority group is organically related to the host society – culturally bound to it, and legally tolerated – then it can follow the same social development. It can develop as a sub-system of the larger society, preserving its separate traditions and culture. Even if the Jews of Western Europe themselves were not in the end made safe by this pattern of toleration, we see that the Western Christian society is still coded for this kind of toleration, accepting that a sort of compromised national identity is morally and legally acceptable. Passports are issued to people who, while probably speaking the national language, are clearly of foreign origin and culture. Since the whole basis of our civilisation is a modern urban social pattern which depends on the management of parallel cultures, it is not surprising that some such mechanism should have evolved; and if we are to understand its genesis, we must look at the theological order from which the political order we are used to has sprung.

If a minority group does not have this organic relationship with the host society, it will be left behind in the development of the social structure. This is what happened to the dualist heretics. Since the development of the urban culture was slow and at first localised – limited in its effects to the newly-developing urban centres themselves, such as Paris in the case of mediæval France – it was quite possible for rural life to continue according to a set of social norms which were incompatible with the needs of such a culture. But not forever. For a heretical attitude to centralised religious authority turns out to mean a heretical attitude towards the system of nation states, and of the corresponding national moral differentiation. And since the national state system is supposed to include literally every single individual – who is assigned a national identity not just in the form of a set of cultural values, but actually in the form of official documents issued by the central national authorities – heresy against the system of national states is difficult to sustain. In contemporary Eastern Europe, we find a direct example of this heretical pattern in the relationship of the Roma with the official structures of the national states on whose territory they live. Like the Jews, the Roma are particularly inconvenient because they are a trans-national population; but unlike the Jews, they are not integrated into the dominant ideological structures in any organised way. They consider themselves to be Christians, but it is a Roma version of Christianity, a sort of portmanteau religion which preserves many non-Christian elements within it. Cervantes, for instance, reports that the Spanish Gypsies of his day believed that they had a special dispensation from God to steal. As the modern state extends its structures through the countryside, it comes across some islands of resistance, then, and the Roma even today naturally gravitate towards these islands of freedom, where the domination of writing and the central state apparatus has not been established. But heresy of this type is not to be tolerated, and since the Roma (unlike the Jews) are not in the type of organic relationship with the state and its ideology which will allow them to develop their own segment of society according to the urban pattern, and alongside the dominant national system, they are on the one hand left behind in its 'progress', and on the other hand increasingly victimised by its policemen. Their social structures fail to modernise, and become structures of opposition to the national order. No longer providing a complete, free-standing social structure, internal coherence is lost, and the culture degenerates into a counter-culture. National state systems therefore seek to destroy these rival social structures: by immobilising the Roma, by forcing them to conform to national educational standards, or by more creative methods, such as making unemployment a crime, and imprisoning them (as in communist Czechoslovakia, which also had explicit policies of forced assimilation).[50]

This example should make it clear that the mediæval historical material just considered is not just some kind of abstract metaphor for the situation of minority populations today. The spread of urbanism is still not complete in Europe; but even in the most developed countries, the peasant way of life has only been extinct for a few generations, and so the slow spread of an urban way of life is something we can still observe. Looking at the issue from the other side, the spread of nationalised state identities is also not complete in Europe. Indeed, it seems that it will never be completed. As at the time of the crusades, Europe is at a time of crisis in its whole identity. Under the opposed forces of inward-looking political and economic integration versus an outward-looking move to connect itself with part of the former Soviet bloc, the signs are that the national system itself is breaking down, with regional devolution and minority nationalism ascendant in many countries. But there is a corresponding tendency to demonise the outsider; political 'Europe' may not think of itself as white and Christian, but the rise of its bland Euro ideal coincides suspiciously closely with the rise of anti-Muslim xenophobia.

Finally, we should be aware that television has revolutionised social structure. In particular, it has revolutionised the process of the transfer of

---

[50] Law No. 74/1958 'On the permanent settlement of nomadic persons'; and Decision of the Central Committee of the Communist Party of Czechoslovakia 'On work among the Gypsy population', 1985.

social structure, by revolutionising the transfer of mythologies, with their implicit systems of values and social norms (*mythologiques*). It also selects what kind of mythology is transferred. The boundaries of the urban culture are not territorial, but technological, and the most isolated peasant community is permanently transformed into a loyal outpost of international consumerism after a few years of exposure to television advertising. All the intermediate stages are jumped over, for Montaillou can resist the Catholic Church, but has no means of resisting *Dallas*. But here we find that we must return to the present, since an important technological boundary that ran across Europe – the Iron Curtain – has recently been lifted, and the technological discrepancy between East and West in Europe was certainly significant for society, since the two generations of insulation between the two population groups were the time of the fastest technological advances ever; and so our analysis should now at last turn to the present rather disturbed configuration in the less technologically developed component of the new Europe.

V. Some Conclusions

Firstly, let us summarise our arguments so far. We have suggested that modern society – that is, the urban, nationalised society which has become the global norm – has its origin in the system of nation states which developed in Christian Western Europe. From a sociological point of view, the establishment of this type of society has involved some important changes in the patterns of 'boundary consciousness' of the Western European populations. One of these, which we suggest began in the 11th century, was the establishment of the idea of a Christian territorial unit – actually including only Western Christianity. Another significant change was the establishment of a pattern of parallel culture urbanism in the large cities which came to dominate Western Europe. The city, we say, can be viewed as a mechanism for managing parallel cultures. It is a place where more than one set of cultural standards can coexist, and where commercial and cultural exchange between cultural groups can take place in a regular, daily manner. However, this social pattern is directly opposed to the pattern of society suggested by nation state ideology, which supposes that these same cities are really *national* capitals – the centres of states in which one single nationality predominates. Looking for an explanation for this discrepancy, we find that the same theological arguments which promoted the centralisation of power in nation states in the first place also provided a means of compromise as far as national identity went: although the theological arguments originally dealt with Christian identity, rather than its nationalised local variants. The compromise was represented by the treatment of the Jews in the middle ages. They were seen as the enemies of Christianity, and yet they were tolerated as inhabitants of Christian states. This paradox is resolved by two connected bodies of concepts: theology and law. Once a theological accommodation had been made (and we find it in St. Augustine), this was connected with the legal tradition based on Roman Law, so that the Jews were able to live in parallel with the proto-national citizens of the mediæval European states. This balance, between alienation on the one hand and organised toleration on the other, provides the basic pattern and prototype for the 'national minority' of recent history. The nation state model, we suggest, is coded by this history for the acceptance of the parallel cultural pattern which is implicit in the growth of urban society. However, a look at the history of the dualist sects of the middle ages shows that not everyone qualified for this kind of treatment. The crucial factors here are not to do with general structural features of society, but with the specific features of Christian ideology, and its impact on the development of national political institutions. The dualist heretics had beliefs which were so deeply opposed to the development of a centralised political-religious state that official Christianity could not tolerate them, and in fact they were hounded out of existence by the Inquisition. Comparing them with the Jews, we see that their culture was only ever able to function as a negative complement (a counter-culture) to the Christianity of the dominant culture. Without the legal acceptance that was granted to the Jews, they could only develop a counter-cultural identity: a partial and negative ideology and practice of opposition, rather than a complete and separate identity of their own. Disregarding the other obvious differences between Jews and dualist heretics for the sake of argument, we see that two roughly equivalent groups – groups identified by their dissent from the official Christian religion – were treated in two quite different ways. This, we suggest, is a demonstration of the two paths open to the nation state in its management of parallel cultures.

The twentieth century has seen the transfer of the Western European nation state type of society to most of the world's population, at least as far as the large-scale organisation of state political structures is concerned. In fact, in the many cases where there is a basic conflict between this vision of society and the real social structuring of the population, it is the nation state model which has won. Perhaps we could imagine that the advance of technology could have taken place in a similar way under the sponsorship of the Chinese or another branch of civilisation, but actually it did not, and since no-one can reject the fruits of Western science and technology, it appears that no-one can reject the Western Christian nation state model of society either. But the acceptance of a nation state idea has some real consequences. It involves setting up the idea of a corresponding nationality, and the only way you can decide who should qualify as a co-national is by designating some people who should be left out. Since human society is not in fact organised according to the naive vision suggested by nation state ideologues – that is, in neat territorial blocks corresponding to unified, homogeneous nations – the establishment of political nations immediately produces 'minorities' of various kinds. One imaginative approach (which we have not so far taken into account) is simply to deny that they exist. This, for instance, is basically the approach of the Greek state towards the Albanians, Turks, Slavs and other Ottoman remnant populations living on its territory today. They are simply Greeks. Hungary in the 19th century was similarly declared to be populated entirely by Hungarians. But less imaginative people than the Greeks and Hungarians are left with two alternatives: tolerate the other culture or destroy it. Now, Western Europe has taken many centuries to reach its present cultural configuration. In the twentieth century, many societies had to go through a formally equivalent development in a highly-accelerated form, and the results are still not clear in many regions of the world.

The largest 'nation' of the world today is China, which also had the most highly-developed alternative social and cultural pattern. But China, too, had to modernise and nationalise itself, and if we want an outward manifestation of the deep social and cultural change this has involved, we will find it in the establishment of a different approach to language. The standard form of Chinese before this century was not a national spoken standard, but an imperial written standard, which corresponded to many local variations of pronunciation and even of grammar. But Mao's revolution also produced a revolution in language use, with the illiterate majority being taught not just to read and write, but also to use a new spoken standard, Mandarin, or Standard Modern Chinese as linguists call it, which is arbitrarily based on the speech of educated people in Beijing. The establishment of a standard form of spoken Chinese has had the unexpected result of isolating the speakers of the Southern Chinese dialects, a large group of whom have discovered to their surprise that they are not after all speakers of Chinese but of 'Cantonese'. This dialect group is sufficiently different from the North Chinese standard (with a more elaborate tone system, for instance), and sufficiently coherent internally, to qualify as a different language (if the analysis of Chinese language use is to be organised in this way). So the attempt to turn China into a modern nation, with a corresponding national culture, has had the unexpected result of creating the linguistic basis for a Cantonese proto-nation. There is no telling what the eventual result of this will be. One might expect that the larger and dominant cultural group, the North Chinese, would just absorb the smaller group, but the evidence is that this is not happening. For the Cantonese dialect area includes some of the most prosperous and dynamic regions of China; and Cantonese speakers have been successful outside China too, so that in Hong Kong, and in many Chinatowns around the world, it is Cantonese and not Mandarin which provides the linguistic norm. And the use of Cantonese, which is perceived as the language of business and wealth, is actually increasing, even in the highly-centralised People's Republic.

Will 'Cantonese' one day become a nationality too? We can only speculate. But what is important for our analysis is to understand that this dynamic of social and cultural development has been set in motion by the need to conform to the Western Christian social pattern. In imperial times, the Chinese scholars knew that there were a great many local dialects among the uneducated masses, but paid no particular attention to this marginal phenomenon. The only thing that mattered was the literary standard of the educated elite. But mass communications require mass standards, and the only model of society which has developed in such a way as to accommodate this technological revolution is the Western one.

Although the overall cultural conditions are very different, we can see a structurally similar case to the Chinese/Cantonese one just discussed in another very large country, the United States of America. This is one of the most advanced countries in the world by technological standards, and also conforms very closely in its official ideology to the nation state ideal, despite the immediately obvious fact that its population is not culturally homogeneous. 'American' is a different kind of nationality to 'French' or 'Italian', but there has been little deviation from the idea that all Americans share a national ideal and identity. However, as in China, there are some unexpected results of social and political development. For while all the immigrant groups from elsewhere in the world can be assimilated into the American way of life, more or less conforming in their expectations to the White Anglo-Saxon Protestant ideal of North America, it seems that the

Spanish-speaking Latino culture of the rest of the Americas (treating the Portuguese-speakers of Brazil as a sub-system of this Latino identity, for simplicity) is deeply-rooted enough to survive physical relocation to the United States. As in China, we see in language use an outward manifestation of complex changes in cultural patterns: and the incontrovertible fact is that the use of English, which is the immediate sign of an American identity for immigrants, is not automatically establishing itself as the natural choice for Latino immigrant communities. Instead, Spanish-language television, radio and publishing is becoming more and more normal in the centres of Latino population. The Anglo establishment can do little about this beyond talking about it. English has not been imposed exactly as the natural choice of immigrants; it has just always been obvious that it is the language of a unified American culture. So will the Latinos establish a fully-developed alternative American identity? Americano? It has happened to some extent already, but now there is a question of state policy. Should the legal system recognise this alternative? Should schools accept that some Americans should be educated primarily in Spanish? Should Spanish-speaking citizens be able to deal with the Federal Government in Spanish? And if we think back to the European origins of the nation state system, we can see the choice before the state institutions in these terms: should the Latinos be treated as Jews or as heretics? Should their emerging identity be tolerated or destroyed? There are arguments on both sides, and a real debate is under way, especially in the area of education policy. With its immigrant-based history and culture, and its technologically advanced urbanism, the USA is the perfect example both of the parallel culture configuration of society and of the strain it is under today; but its political identity has always been monolithic and culturally unified. This case has a particular importance for the world for the reason that the nation state ideal is now mainly promoted at the international level by the United States, which sees itself as the undisputed leader of world affairs. In the twentieth century, it was American policy to promote national states which imitated, on however tiny a scale, the American idea: a moral, democratic state of equal co-nationals, founded on national pride and the worship of national symbols. And in American policy in Latin America, for instance, we see that promoting nationalism has conformed more immediately to the American project than promoting democracy; since American foreign policy has had no problem with supporting explicitly anti-democratic states – while the anti-nationalistic ideology of world communism was immediately (and plausibly) interpreted as the enemy of the American nationalist ideal. This ideal, which is the successor of late mediæval European proto-national projects, does not in itself preclude the existence of national minorities; as we have suggested, its moral universalism also includes the cultural memory of the alienated but tolerated minority: but it does not directly promote such minorities either. They are supposed to sit quietly and behave. But if America itself accepts not just its traditionally fragmented culture and society (with Afro-Americans for instance largely excluded from positions of power), but a compromised national identity, then this will have a global effect. In the same way that the world was forced to conform to American ideas of nationality in the twentieth century, perhaps in the twenty-first century we will be forced to conform to a non-national American social ideal. For instance, an America that accepted the reality of its Spanish-speaking population and their partially separated society would be the natural sponsor for non-dominant cultural groups in Europe: for the Welsh and the Basques and the displaced Turks and Bangla Deshis and so on. For America itself, the means by which this ideological transformation can take place will be the same kind of surrender to a higher authority: the surrender to the idea of the Americas as a single economic unit. White, Anglo America will still be the winner, of course (for why should the establishment accept any other outcome?), but the absorption of Latin America into the dollar economy coincidentally consolidates the 'Latino' identity: an identity, that is, of a transnational or partially transnational parallel cultural group which defines itself in opposition to the dominant Anglo identity and its power-structures. The international standard of the nation state model is the American standard; and if that changes in the manner suggested, accepting a bilingual, two-cultural model of nationality, this model will also become a global standard. In view of the glaring discrepancy between the monocultural nation-state ideology and the polycultural reality of modern urban society, this would probably be a move in the right direction.

For the time being, though, the international standard of nation-state ideology is monolingual and one-cultural. We see the result of the sudden impact of this standard on a society configured according to a different kind of ideal in contemporary Russia, which has abruptly and unexpectedly been Westernised, becoming, in its own imagination and self-image, a nation state according to the international standards set by the American-dominated West, which from a cultural and political point of view is still an extension of Christian Western Europe.

At the time of the 1917 Revolution, Russia was still only very partially urbanised, even if it was the urban part of society which was important from the point of view of political organisation. A convenient scheme for understanding Russian history is to view it as the geographical spread of the power and influence of Moscow: the establishment of a Moscow standard, in politics, society, and culture. Leaving aside the most remote past, the withdrawal of the Tatars coincided with the spread of the power of the Grand Duchy of Muscovy as the overlord of what we now call European Russia; and the consolidation of Russian society according to this standard created a more or less unified Russian state and culture, even if other local standards of language in particular (Ukrainian and Byelorussian, for instance) did survive in places. In the Imperial period of Russian development, the new, Westernised capital at St. Petersburg, with its German clothes and its French manners, created a significant counterweight to the traditional values of Moscow, seat of the Patriarch and enemy of progress; but at the time of the 1917 Revolution, there were still some fundamental differences in social structure between Russia and the West.

Since the 18th century, there had been some attempts to provide education for the masses, at least to the extent of elementary arithmetic, but these attempts had basically failed, and society at large was not 'modernised'. Although aristocratic circles had access to all the latest things from Paris and London, and although a system of specialised technical education was little by little introduced for military and industrial purposes, very little of this had penetrated to the mass culture, which was close to the mediæval pattern by Western European standards.

The October Revolution, anyway, removed power from the aristocracy and put it in the hands of a modernising elite of intellectuals and professional revolutionaries. The Russian Empire was transformed into the Soviet Union, and not just Russia itself, but its vast territories to the south and east, were dragged screaming into the twentieth century. But it was a version of the twentieth century created and controlled by the ideologues of the state apparatus, and subsequent events demonstrated that their view of things was incorrect from a factual point of view. Society failed to obey the objective economic laws they claimed to understand, and the pattern of scientific development they promoted could not (in direct contradiction of the claims they made for it) provide a faster rate of technological advance than that of the West. Since admitting this failure would have destroyed the legitimacy of the whole system, successive leaders decided that the best alternative was to promote a deliberately falsified and heroic view of things, according to which the progress they promised was being triumphantly realised, while the decadent West continued its inevitable decline. This technique of semantic control, though, became progressively more difficult to sustain, and in the end *glasnost* and *perestroika* made it possible for a more accurate view of things to prevail, both in elite circles and in the population at large. The legitimacy of the whole system was indeed destroyed, and the Soviet system immediately collapsed.

Now, the USSR was not just Russia. Even though it was dominated by Russians and administered by means of the Russian language, Soviet ideology embraced two interlocked concepts of nationality: that of a brotherhood of nations, and that of a projected synthetic Soviet nationality, representing a more advanced stage of internationalism and socialist development. Both of these concepts had complex practical effects. The whole vast Soviet political and administrative system ran according to this dual standard; so that passports, for instance, were issued by the USSR, but also recorded nationality. This was partly a consequence of the ideological commitments of the Bolsheviks (which in this area followed an Austro-Marxist pattern, and therefore preserved some important 19th-century Central European nationalist preconceptions), and indeed of an effort to avoid total Russian domination of the USSR; and partly a political strategy to defeat the threat of regionalism and secession from Moscow rule by the supposedly free and equal Union Republics: but the idea that the Soviet population was made up of a collection of national groups was evidently very problematic in the first place. At the time of the Revolution, if Russia itself was largely mediæval in its level of social development, the Eastern possessions of the Empire still included populations living according to an Iron Age pattern (among the nomads of the steppes, and the Finno-Ugrian pastoral peoples), and even some isolated groups living according to the cultural norms of the Stone Age, such as those among the Arctic peoples of Siberia who were still apparently living without fire. The introduction of the Soviet system in these regions was at the same time the introduction of modernity, although typically some isolated imperial Russian military outposts had already been established in Tsarist times, which now served as political and economic centres for the Soviet re-organisation.[51] This was self-consciously a modernising activity, and in its political aspect involved the

---

[51] Such as Grozny (*Terrible*, like Ivan) in the Northern Caucasus; and Vernyi (*Faithful*: this is now Alma-Ata or Almaty, depending on who you listen to) in Turkestan (but now in Kazakstan).

creation of a sort of commonwealth of equal nations. Kazakhstan, Uzbekistan, and the other Union Republics were therefore created in the image of the new Russia. It was a complex policy area, though, and for reasons of large-scale strategy, the borders, which were from an ideological perspective supposed to reflect the natural boundaries of the national populations (and here we see the influence of Herder once again, though indirectly), were in some cases deliberately drawn so as to divide populations which might one day pose a threat to Soviet rule; and the inconvenient fact that the pre-modern populations were not settled on nice neat national territories in the first place was simply ignored. There were still some nomadic populations, for instance, in Turkestan, while in the Caucasus there was an unusual interpenetration of cultures, so that neighbouring villages would use different languages, but exchange women and therefore cultural patterns to create an arealised configuration of languages and social patterns generally: almost the direct opposite of the picture suggested by nationalistic anthropology. Anyway, the political doctrine called for the creation of a mosaic of national units, and although in many cases there were some appropriate boundaries and population groups for this purpose, in many other cases there were not. The doctrine could not be adjusted, though, for such a trivial reason as this, and so the blank spaces on the map were filled in by a variety of means – such as inventing new nationalities, in extreme cases (Moldova), or more commonly, by separating or amalgamating existing population groups to make a more convenient fit. The political identities corresponding to the political organisation of the state were established by Moscow dictate, and in the name of socialist internationalism.

This led to the strange fetishism of titular nationalities. Emerging gradually from the Tsarist middle ages into the brave new world of Socialism, the Sovietised non-Russians, especially in more culturally mixed areas, were faced with the fact that the USSR systematically favoured this or that cultural group by naming a political unit in its honour. This can be explained by the fact that holy Moscow, seat of the Tsars and the Patriarchs, now promoted itself as the guardian both of Soviet and of Russian honour simultaneously. This characteristically Russian emotional role – which we should see in terms of Orthodox Christian tradition as much as anything else, despite the official atheism of the Soviet state, and also of course in terms of the Tsarist tradition which was connected with Russian Orthodoxy – was the immediate basis of its legitimacy as political centre. Other nations, therefore, though now relying on Moscow for the preservation of the Soviet segment of their honour, still had some residual honour left over for themselves, which allowed them to form corresponding administrative structures in its name. In the absence of elections, this mechanism did have a psychological reality, in that people naturally and correctly felt that this type of representation gave them a collective voice in all-Union decision-making. Russia itself was naturally the model – and the idea that Russia was inhabited by a single, homogeneous people, called Russians. Once this had been swallowed, it was easy to accept that the whole hierarchy of republics, oblasts and okrugs held in the obscure magic of its litany of ethnonyms the final truth about the happy family of Soviet nationalities. Whether it was in a large chunk of crucial Soviet territory like Kazakhstan, or in an obscure corner of the Northern Caucasus like the Kabardino-Balkaria Autonomous Republic (one of the dual nationality units, where two groups were recognised together as joint owners – at the expense of other candidates, of course), the Soviet system, seeking to legitimise itself, created an official hierarchy of nationalities, whose right to the territory where they lived was proved by official documents, and celebrated in a thousand statues, films, novels and academic ballet performances. The 1936 Soviet Constitution recognised 11 Union Republics and 20 Autonomous Republics. By 1991 this had grown to 15 Union Republics, 20 Autonomous Republics, 8 Autonomous Oblasts and 10 Autonomous Okrugs.

Census data, in particular, were used to demonstrate the truth and justice of this system, and this produced an extraordinary and as far as I know unique phenomenon: the spontaneous nationalism of official forms. Since it was evident that political decisions would be made on the basis of census returns, sociological surveys, and information gathered at workplaces and educational institutions, it became a matter not just of national pride but of simple prudence and family duty to give the most appropriate answers on all official forms – especially in the 1960s and 1970s, when there was an attempt to redress the balance for the crimes of the Stalinist era, during which time particular nationalities had been officially eradicated by a stroke of the pen for reasons of state. Despite the rhetoric of brotherhood and cooperation, the system was highly competitive, and especially where there might be some doubt about which nation had the best right to political power in a particular administrative unit, elites which did achieve official political recognition for their efforts would do all they could do prevent their local rivals from challenging this success; and the populations they officially represented were recruited to assist in this struggle for superiority. People would proudly identify themselves with ethnonyms which now referred to official Moscow-sanctioned Soviet nationalities, even where they must surely have realised that for one reason or another the Soviet authorities had got it wrong. In extreme cases, people would routinely claim that languages they could not speak were their mother tongue, spoken daily at home with their children;[52] for the fetishism of nationalities could not stop the spread of the Soviet/urban/modern complex in society at large, the main vector of which was the Russian language. Indeed, especially in the Caucasus and Central Asia, the spread of nationalisms which ultimately relied on the bourgeois intellectual models of European nationalist movements – resting on history, linguistics, Herder and so on – was only possible in the first place for people who had been Russified to the extent of having learned to read and write. In the 1920s, for instance, literacy among the Chechens is estimated at 1 per cent; and of course no nationalistic literary movements could have much of a mass appeal under these circumstances.

The Soviet component of the national honour needs careful analysis. At first sight, a putative Soviet nationality looks like a civic nationality – like the British, say – which provides an artificial administrative shell for a number of component national groups. However, Soviet and Russian thinking never in fact went in this direction. The Soviet Union was the successor state not of Russia itself, but of the Russian Empire, and it had a different psychological function to start with. There is clearly some root psychological mechanism in the individual's identification with a group or collective symbol. Freud, discussing African examples, supposed that it involved a transfer of emotion to a collective father figure: and in Russia, this looks like a good explanation of the traditional role of the Tsar as the 'little father' of the Russian people. A definitive psychological explanation of these social reflexes is not available; but as with Mao in China, a succession of Soviet leaders found themselves acting as all-powerful father-figures for the Soviet people as far as the social awareness was concerned. In spite of this personalisation of political consciousness, though, Bolshevik and Communist Party ideology still played the defining role in defining the terms and techniques of Russian and Soviet political discourse. Although at a mass-psychological level, they were evidently still empowered by the glory of the Tsars of All the Russias, the official idea of the central authorities was that in

---

[52] (Tishkov, 1997, p. 88) gives two striking examples of this, referring to one large and one small population. Looking at the 1989 census figures, he estimates that about one third of Kazaks cannot speak Kazak, although 99 per cent of those identifying themselves as Kazaks also identified Kazak as their native language; and while 90 per cent of registered Buryats in Ust'-Ordynsky Buryat Autonomous Okrug said that Buryat was their native language, in fact Russian has almost completely replaced spoken Buryat.

the course of building socialism (their world-historic task), an entirely new nationality would be created – Soviet Man. This would actually be the creation of a new type of human being, and building this Superman was something that could only take place in the Soviet Union, thanks in the end to a more advanced understanding of science. To accept the authority of the central Soviet institutions, then, was to glory in the success of this splendid project: and this was the source of the Soviet component of national honour just discussed. It was a society which was not quite ready yet, but which nevertheless, for reasons of loyalty, should be accepted on a provisional basis. It had one peculiar formal feature which was common to Soviet and Soviet-bloc ideology after Stalin: it preserved the language of revolution and change in order to administer a system which was as static as possible. In terms of nationalism, this compromise meant that two apparently antithetical ideas – the nationalism of the future, expressed by Soviet thinking and symbols, and the ethnonationalism of titular nations and ethnic minorities, which was configured on lines familiar from 19th century European national awakenings, especially in central Europe – could both be nourished simultaneously by the same political and ideological system. This aspect of the Soviet project was part of the Never-Never Land of Party thinking generally: a dream world in which people of a radically different type would live together in a radically different society. The nationalist project, embraced from the beginning by Lenin and especially Stalin, had a much more immediate logic, since it provided a direct political legitimacy for the intellectual elites who were the only ones educated enough to be able to understand the advances in scholarship and culture through which the nationalist stream of thought had become available in the first place – both in its 'European' and 'Soviet' variants.

The USSR, then, apart from this half-built and somewhat ill-conceived Soviet nationality, recognised a number of large and largely artificial national groups at Union Republic and Autonomous Republic level, on the model of the Russian nationality, which is itself highly artificial from a historical or ethnological point of view, and which was now also re-invented, being described and defined in the terms of the Soviet theory of nations. Smaller national groups were given oblasts or okrugs. Within this basic structure, though, a variety of other minority groups were also encouraged to preserve their language and culture, but according to a modernised, Soviet, pattern. An Institute would be established, and Soviet scholars (the effort was naturally coordinated from Moscow) would establish a written form of the language, where necessary (about 50 languages having acquired a written form during the existence of the USSR), and go on to organise a folk literature, a canonical body of folk music and dance, and so on. This meant that many small populations were taken from a pre-modern way of life and 'modernised' into the peculiar half-way house of a Soviet minority.[53] It is difficult to make overall judgments about the effects of this. On the one hand, we can see that a basic aim of this activity was ideological: to indoctrinate these populations, and at the same time to promote the idea that the Soviet philosophy was one of brotherhood and equality. But on the other hand, many of the Soviet scholars who worked on this large and decades-long project of social engineering were certainly well-meaning in their attitude to the populations they dealt with, and did their best to protect their cultures, and to equip them for the modern world. Indeed, the brutal truth is that these fragile relics from a previous age would not have survived nearly so well in the West. This is demonstrated by the fact that this Soviet programme of cultural management has now largely collapsed, as a result of the partial adjustment of the former USSR to Western standards, and some of the partially modernised minority cultures which were protected and preserved by the Soviet system now face extinction. This, after all, has been the result of contact between the technologically advanced Western system and pre-modern societies elsewhere in the world.

Apart from these less developed peoples, there was an important group of Soviet populations whose social pattern, though relatively advanced in terms of technology and general development, was not configured according to the Western European Christian model. The Georgians, for instance, had a well-established identity and culture, as did the Armenians. Once again, we see that the Soviet system was relatively tolerant. Russian was certainly promoted everywhere, but this was a natural process, comparable with the spread of French in West Africa, or of English everywhere: a reflection of the political reality of Moscow centralism on the one hand and of Soviet urbanisation and modernisation on the other. Other languages were tolerated, and national cultures were allowed to function, once their institutions had been adjusted in the direction of Soviet Marxism-

---

[53] (Tishkov, 1997) speaks of *ethnographic processing*: something carried out mainly by Moscow-based scholars and then recognised by political structures. Different populations would acquire different levels of recognition, depending mainly on the size of the population involved, but also on the local balance of political forces. The relatively stable ideological conditions allowed a list of some 190 nationalities to be constructed on this basis; but the delicate balance of power established between them as part of the same process could not survive the collapse of the Soviet system.

Leninism. In the terms of our larger analysis of the European tradition, the USSR preferred to treat non-Russian peoples as Jews rather than as heretics where possible, and expressed this preference in real legal and constitutional arrangements. But if a particular group proved inconvenient or troublesome, then they could suddenly find themselves in the position of heretics all the same, and therefore as traitors to the state idea. Under Stalin, for instance, the Chechens were effectively declared enemies of the state, and mass deportations and killings were the result. But after Stalin it was unusual for people to be treated in this way on the basis of nationality alone. After all, accepting a nationality within the Soviet framework meant accepting the legitimacy of the system as a whole. The state was organised according to a different kind of ideology, and so the heresy that really counted was heresy against Soviet political dogma. As in Western Europe in an earlier age, the heretics against Soviet Marxism-Leninism formed a sort of disorganised, non-national counter-culture, and the Inquisition, with its torture-chambers and its burnings at the stake, found a parallel in the show trials and labour camps of the 1950s. This rough parallel should not be pushed too far; but it can remind us that there was a basic continuity between the state nationalism of the West and that of the USSR. Both had a common origin in the Western European Christian idea,[54] and both preserved the internal, historically-determined structures of this idea to some extent.

It is worth making some remarks about the unusual Russian and Soviet social structure. While the pattern of urbanisation – basically, the migration of peasants to cities, and their change of role to industrial workers – is clearly similar to that in the West in a general way, from another point of view it has a specifically Russian character. To put the matter carefully, the establishment of parallel culture urbanism has taken place in a number of waves, so that the urbanising populations have represented different stages of social development, reflecting the overall dynamics of the imperial society. The social development in question has two aspects which are unique to Russia. The first is related to the process of the emancipation of the peasants. Imperial Russia, in a movement which was markedly different from that in Western Europe, preserved a serf society alongside its modernised service aristocracy, so that the relations between landlords and serfs in 18th and even 19th century Russia were comparable to those in England, say, four or five

---

[54] In Russia this was in fact opposed to Orthodox/Tsarist traditions, and could therefore be interpreted in terms of the world-historic tensions created by the division of the Roman Empire into Greek and Latin parts.

hundred years earlier (although the 'bondsmen' of Scotland's salt and coal mines lived in similar conditions of slavery – in a different, proto-industrial context – until the end of the eighteenth century). Descriptions of Russian peasant rebellions from this period, with the startled gentry being chased into the woods by exalted but aimless gangs of peasants, read just like descriptions of the English uprisings of 1381; and the revolution of dress, with the home-made mediæval clothes of immemorial tradition being replaced by manufactured items, was part of Peter the Great's programme of reform in Russia, but was similarly related to the fourteenth century in England. This change was a direct and visible sign of the shift to capitalist production methods. (Trevelyan, 1944) In terms of social development, Russia may even be said to have moved backwards, since neither the gradual regulation of the 'state peasants', nor the continuing serfdom of the private estates of the aristocracy, did anything to promote education or the modernisation of life for the masses, whose material conditions actually worsened as independent farming became more and more difficult to sustain. Nevertheless, the inevitable modernisation of industry, commerce and military affairs was consistently resisted by conservative elements in society, including many of the clergy, but also the bulk of the peasantry themselves. As with the Old Believers in religious matters, there was a widespread reflex among the peasants and serfs generally that anything new was foreign and bad.

Living in almost total ignorance of the world outside Russia, the peasants had developed a quasi-religious belief in the Tsar, who was their loyal Russian defender against the evil foreigners who were blamed for everything that went wrong. This faith is illustrated by the series of rebellions which took place from the Time of Troubles[55] on, in each of which the rebel leader either claimed to be acting in the name of a true Tsar (usually a recently dead one, said to have been miraculously saved for the purpose of leading the poor people to freedom), or, more imaginatively, actually to be such a Tsar in person. The rebel Pugachev, for instance, claimed to be Peter III, despite the fact that he could not write his name, was the wrong age by fourteen years, looked nothing like him, and was well-known both to many of his followers and to his enemies under his real name. Just as confusing is the fact that the real Peter III, like his wife and successor, the Empress Catherine, against whom Pugachev was rebelling, was a German by birth and culture, who disliked both the Orthodox Church and Russian tradition in general. He

---

[55] A period of social and political unrest triggered by the death without issue of Tsar Fyodor, son of Ivan the Terrible, in 1598, and aggravated by widespread famine.

had become a hero to the peasants by accident, his policies having been misunderstood. He had freed the nobility from some of their obligations (in 1762), for political reasons, and this had been misinterpreted by the masses as an act of kindness by the beloved 'little father'. General emancipation and freedom was sure to follow. The Tsar was assassinated in the same year, though, and the peasants put this down to the foreign-inspired machinations of his wife and her followers. This belief was immediately confirmed by Catherine's more active policies of modernisation, and so Pugachev's message – that the true Tsar had come back to rid Moscow of the foreigners and thieves who had brought the present misery on holy Russia – was attractive enough for thousands to flock to his banners. They kissed the cross to him, and rejoiced that he let them wear beards, which were seen by the state as a symbol of backwardness, but by their wearers as an important symbol of godliness, since everyone knew that God himself wore a good Russian beard.

Pugachev's rebellion also reminds us of the second unique feature of Russian social development. Pugachev, like a string of similar rebel leaders, was a Cossack, and despite his ultra-Russian language and imagery, his rebellion should be seen in the framework of the long-term process of the Russification of other populations in imperial times. It is a process which also continued through the Soviet period, though on a slightly different basis.

By the 18th century, the Cossacks were a Russian group, living, though, outside the physical and legal borders of the state in their own society, which was organised on the lines of a warrior Horde; and it is generally supposed that they were originally a Turkic outlaw population, who had absorbed Russian-speaking runaways and prisoners to the point that the Russian language, religion and culture had taken over.[56] The Cossacks were fighting for their independence, which they indeed lost as a consequence of the failure of their various rebellions. Another part of the clientele of these anti-state rebellions consisted of Bashkirs, Chuvash, and other non-Russian populations, who also saw the encroachment of the new model of state power – after Peter the Great's reforms, that is – as impending doom for their independent existence.[57] Russification, like Sinification in imperial China, is

---

[56] There is a formal similarity with the Bulgarian identity and ethnonym: these were also originally attached to a non-Slav ('Turkic') group, but through centuries of assimilation, became attached to a different, Slavic population, which also adopted a local variant of Byzantine Orthodox Christianity.

[57] (Avrich, 1976), drawing on Russian and Western materials, gives a detailed account of the rebellions of Bolotnikov, Razin, Bulavin and Pugachev, and this provides the framework for a valuable essay in Russian social history.

a basic element of the social history of Russia, and this cultural development is not simply to be seen as an aspect of modernisation. It is a specifically Russian factor.

In Soviet times, the picture was complicated still further by the fact that the old, simple division into rich and poor was suddenly abandoned in 1917. The state from now on categorised people according to Marxist class divisions, with most people categorised as 'working class'. But the Soviet working class, too, consisted of several historical layers, depending on how recently they had been proletarianised, and whether this was done willingly or not. The bulk of the working class in Stalin's USSR was made up of a large wave of recently proletarianised peasants, who contrasted sharply both with their predecessors and their successors. (Deutscher, 1967, Chapter III, 'The Social Structure', esp. p. 47 for the internal structuring of the working class.) What this illustrates is that the parallel cultures pattern of urbanisation need not follow national, ethnic, religious or other traditional lines. In this case, the most important distinguishing factor is the degree of modernisation of the urbanising populations: but the effect of group isolation and the resulting cultural stratification is the same. Still, given the suddenness of the introduction of a quasi-Western industrial idea in Soviet times, we should see this against the background of the two longer-term processes just described: the enserfment and gradual emancipation of the peasantry, and the Russification of most of the Empire's population. This complex of factors meant that the drift to an industrial, urban way of life was at the same time the completion of Russification for many, and also the final stage in the development over many generations from peasant to slave or serf to 'state peasant' to proletarian. This spiral of development – if that is not too optimistic a name for it – produced a population stratified in a complicated way, not just by its degree of modernisation and education, but also by its degree of Russification, and by its status within the Soviet class structure and planned economy.

A specific mechanism of social stratification which has played a decisive role in the politics of the former USSR since the collapse of the Soviet system is also worth mentioning here: the distribution of state patronage in the form of academic degrees. Apart from the official structures of the Communist Party and the Army, which awarded visible official ranks and decorations, academic degrees created a less visible but pervasive and highly influential social structure, by deciding who would be given access to different administrative grades. As far as non-Russians were concerned, being given a Soviet academic degree was like being made an honorary

Russian (in terms of access to Russian-dominated structures of all-Union power); and the essentially bourgeois[58] Communist Party ideology succeeded in creating a new all-Union crypto-bourgeoisie of officially-stamped Soviet intellectuals on this basis. This group, however, has been the pool from which the anti-Moscow and anti-Russian political reaction since the fall of the USSR has drawn the bulk of its personnel. Equipped with the standard Soviet idea that national honour confers the right to political power, and educated in an official version of history and ethnography that explained the basis of their own national honour in fairly convincing terms, these Sovietised and Russified intellectuals have now been able to turn to their compatriots with an almost ready-made set of arguments and facts explaining exactly why it is that Moscow has no further right to rule over them – the Soviet component of the national honour having suddenly evaporated. But since these same intellectuals were the element of their societies who lived according to the most explicitly Russian and Soviet patterns, it may reasonably be questioned how legitimate they are as representatives and upholders of their national traditions. It may also be whispered that an ideology of national renewal will favour national intellectual elites disproportionately: to the extent, indeed, of placing them permanently in positions of political power and social control. In the former USSR, though, the alternative to rule by intellectuals and bureaucrats is apparently rule by criminals, and so for the time being it looks as though the strand of Soviet ideology following Stalin's formulations on nationality (learned in Vienna, and closely related to the nationalistic central European literary movements of the nineteenth century) will continue to provide an important polarising force not just in Russia, but in all the post-Soviet societies.

Parenthetically, it is interesting to note that there is one large-scale process of social and cultural synthesis in the populations formerly brought under Soviet control that cannot be explained with reference to the urban model of parallel culture development developed as the main thesis of this

---

[58] Not in a Marxist sense. The CPSU preserved the values of the European intelligentsia of the early twentieth century, and was therefore inextricably linked to the ideology of the bourgeoisie. It championed the proletariat; but preserved Marx's supposition that the proletariat would advance in the direction of a middle class set of values – such as respect for the state and its officials. Sovietisation, paradoxically, brought with it the rapid embourgeoisement of a selected stratum of loyal apparatchiks: the *New Class* of Djilas' classic exposition.

essay. This is the centuries-long contact between Mongols and Turks,[59] a truly non-European factor, which illustrates that the urban model just mentioned is not a universal sociological phenomenon, but something specific to Europe. Elsewhere – in Africa, say, where watercourses have provided important sites for cultural contact – other characteristic patterns have emerged.

Turning back to Europe, though, we see that the USSR and its system of political organisation had a ragged border with the West. The Baltic states could easily have become independent Western countries (although Lithuania is from a historical point of view a much reduced entity, having at one time, in partnership with Poland, possessed a sizeable empire in its own right), and are now partially-Russified, partly-Sovietised countries, clinging to a Western orientation in the face of a rather callous lack of interest from Western political structures. Their specific problem is the influx of Russian-speakers during the Soviet period, which on the one hand compromises their own nation-state identities, and on the other hand creates islands of Russian/post-Soviet culture. In Estonia, for example, attempts to encourage Russian-speakers to learn Estonian have failed. Estonian is just too difficult. From an objective point of view, there is a parallel culture configuration of society in the Baltics, but the problem is that there are two rival types of urbanism being promoted in different urban centres: the old Soviet pattern, based on industrial centres, and a more conventional Western pattern, based on political and historical centres. The difficulty is that the national governments do not want to recognise anything but the most exclusivist type of national identity, which means that they must promote a

---

[59] Lev Gumilëv's extraordinary *Ethnogenesis and the Biosphere* (Moscow, 1990), contains (along with a wealth of similarly interesting and exotic material) a profound analysis of the peoples of the Steppe. For instance (pp. 291ff), Gumilëv suggests that the Tatars of the Golden Horde represented a new kind of social unit and 'stereotype of behaviour', and this argument is supported with detailed observations about such peoples as the Oirats, the Nogai and the Berguts, based on years of original work. A profound study of the Byzantine world also provides much food for thought. This dense book is well worth reading for this kind of information alone; but the real purpose of the work is to develop a philosophical position which it is difficult to evaluate fairly. In some passages Gumilëv seems anxious to adopt a Soviet Marxist-Leninist position: but this rather unconvincing and now cruelly dated show of dialectical materialism is extraneous to his main arguments – which, however, suffer from other defects, such as a peculiar 'scientific' Russian nationalism that seems in places to include a nasty dash of anti-Semitism. But it is a shame that Gumilëv did not wait another five years to finish a work that is obviously a labour of love that took decades to complete. His laboured support for Soviet science and thinking sometimes makes him appear ludicrous; but he was clearly a scholar and thinker of the first rank. His work is enjoying a certain vogue among Russian nationalists today, but this is a sad development, which we could compare with the Nazi enthusiasm for Spengler. Gumilëv does not deserve to be written off as a right-wing clown.

self-image which is basically false. After two generations of Russian domination, they see this as their right; but from the point of view of dealing with the real problems of social reconstruction, this is not a very positive attitude to take. Apart from the Baltic states, anyway, and a few marginal areas like Moldova (where the USSR promoted a synthetic national culture, based on writing the Romanian dialects of the local population in Cyrillic, so as to make an appropriate national language for a Soviet nationality) and Karelia (where a supposedly autonomous Karelian ASSR was actually a means to ensure the detachment of this area from Europe and its absorption into the USSR, with a corresponding Russification of its cultural institutions), Soviet domination in Eastern Europe was limited to political hegemony over formally independent states; although in the framework of international Marxism-Leninism and its associated pro-Russian reflex, some transfer of Soviet cultural models more generally was inevitable. As far as the nationalities policy was concerned, though, the formal independence was real, and although in the long run the promotion of the Russian language in all the school systems of the Eastern Bloc might have led to Sovietisation, there was no direct attempt to absorb the Eastern European nationalities into the Soviet family in the short term. Since these national identities were actually older and more deeply-rooted than the Russian identity on which the Soviet system was ultimately based, any such effort would probably have failed, as it failed in the Baltics; but who knows? It is reported, for instance, that a small Czech minority in Kazakstan has more or less switched nationality and become Russian, the reason for this being that the most important cultural division of society in Soviet Kazakhstan[60] was between Kazaks and Slavs, and the Czechs therefore identified with the Russians, and adopted their language.

For political reasons, Yugoslavia (and Albania, with which it is historically and culturally connected, despite the isolation of Albania under Enver Hoxha) forms a special case; and it is particularly interesting for our present analysis, since in the wars of secession from Belgrade rule we see a conflict between the old and the new visions of society in microcosm. Yugoslavia has often been compared to the USSR by scholars, and in its close political union between somewhat artificial ethnically-based states, each with a mixed population, there is a genuine structural similarity. Each of the component states of Tito's Yugoslavia was different, though, and without

---

[60] Kazakhstan is now Kazakstan. The change is supposed to reflect the switch of national language from Russian to Kazak.

looking at these differences, it is not possible to go beyond a very superficial analysis of the Yugoslav tensions. The easiest component state to analyse is Slovenia. This is more or less a small nation state on the Western model, and its cultural separateness was demonstrated by the fact that it did not get involved in the protracted ethnic conflict that attended the break-up of the federal Yugoslav state. The Slovene language is not part of the South Slav dialect spread: it is a West Slav language, related to Czech, Slovak and Polish. Ljubljana is not really a Balkans capital; its cultural mix is basically Austro-Hungarian/Italian – or Alpine/Mediterranean, looked at in another way. Although members of other Yugoslav ethnic groups lived there, there were no ethnic enclaves, and this is what made the rapid political separation from the dissolving Yugoslavia possible. As far as the rest of the former country is concerned, though, there are three basic problems. The first is the variety of the cultural mix. The Yugoslav population did not just consist of Serbs, Croats, Albanians and Bosnians. Every nationality of the Balkans was represented, and this at the same time represented a spectrum of political development, with the Albanians of Kosovo, for instance, naturally feeling some connection with the Albanian nation-state, and the Hungarians of the Vojvodina looking to Hungary, whereas such people as the Vlachs and Roma had no independent kin state institutions to look towards. The second problem is the fact that any attempt to divide the territory up into national units is doomed to failure. Neither ethnic nor religious boundaries will produce viable state formations, and this is because the historical state formations that existed among the South Slavs and their neighbours were not constructed in this way. Even the simple-seeming Orthodox-Catholic division that is supposed to follow an ethnic boundary between Serbs and Croats actually superimposes an ideological separation on a population which is culturally continuous, speaking what could easily be considered the same language under different political circumstances. As with the Islam of the Bosnians, South Slav Orthodoxy and Catholicism serve as markers of submerged historical fault lines, indicating not primæval differences between the populations, but the extent of foreign cultural inroads on their social institutions. This, though, is connected with the third problem, which is the imposition of false interpretations of local history, in particular by political elites seeking to promote a simplistic nationalistic view of the past. In many countries of the region – Romania and Hungary, for instance – this approach has been so successful that the idea that political borders correspond to the territorial borders of homogeneous national groups now seems broadly reasonable and correct; whereas in fact there has been a radical reorganisation of the facts so as to make them conform to a programme of semantic and political reconstruction in the direction of a nationalism informed by the naive anthropological hypothesis we have discussed.[61] According to this kind of view, the South Slav population of former Yugoslavia consists of a small number (five, if we count them as Serb, Croat, Bosnian, Montenegrin and Macedonian; or four, if we count Serbs and Montenegrins together) of independent national cultures, marked by linguistic differentiation and separate cultural traditions. Since the Western European system of national states actively promotes such a view of political development, this interpretation is sanctioned by the international background conditions, and indeed, the political recognition of self-proclaimed ethnic leaders by the international community during the wars of secession has demonstrated that this interpretation was more or less what the rest of the world wants to hear too. Now, science counsels extreme caution about this thesis. From a philological point of view, any definitive separation of the South Slav area into national languages must be very contentious. As with the mediæval French or English we have discussed above, there were as many local standards as there were population centres in the Balkans, and this situation is still preserved in the South Slav area, since the regeneration and division of society according to a centralised urban model has still to be completed there. It is proceeding, though, and the two main urban standards which have emerged – Zagreb 'Croatian' and Belgrade 'Serbian' – provide two centres of gravity for corresponding national projects. However, the pattern of linguistic differentiation revealed by analysis of isoglosses and other dialectological methods does not correspond to the Serb / Croat distinction. The recent attempt to create a corresponding 'Bosnian' standard demonstrates the artificiality of the whole exercise. There are real dialectical variations: but not according to a Serbian / Croatian / Bosnian / Montenegrin / Macedonian pattern. Montenegro has no separate language, Bosnia had more or less forgotten it had ever had one, and Macedonia, while linguistically varied, is a kind of microcosm of the whole Balkans cultural mix, and has no 'national culture' at the day-to-day level – although there is an attempt to connect the state ideology with a reconstructed Slav Macedonian historical identity, and to claim that the local version of South Slav (Macedonian; which is a dialect of Bulgarian which has absorbed some

---

[61] Although another important factor is mere ignorance of the true facts, due to the practical impossibility of reconstructing crucial matter: *cf.* the English/Welsh distinction as discussed by Tolkein – see note 24 above.

Serbian elements) is therefore the legitimate national and state language. There are serious political problems with international recognition for this idea, though, since the Bulgarians claim the 'Macedonian language' for themselves, while the Greeks say that the name Macedonia refers to somewhere else entirely. Whether the Macedonian national project will succeed is anyone's guess. And if we look at the Serb / Croat distinction, we find (to our surprise?) that even this is not based on a clear territorial division, but is actually the result of trying to promote two rather similar projects of homogenisation. This is demonstrated by an elegant study of heraldry by Ivo Banac, now a professor at Yale (Banac, 1993). This approach to the question – the analysis of the establishment of heraldic identities – succeeds in illustrating the complexities of the situation, not with nationalistic mythologising, but with real documents. The complexity of the material makes summary difficult, but it is worth giving an illustrative quotation, to show the texture of the argumentation.

> The initiator of the modern idea of Slavic integration among the Croats was Vinko Pribojević, a learned Dominican from Hvar. In 1525 he delivered his famous oration *De origine successibusque Slavorum* (On the Origin and Advance of the Slavs) to the nobility of his native island. This unprecedented glorification of the Slavic peoples blended scriptural testimony, ancient myth, and learned sources to derive the Slavs from Noah's grandson Thyras, from whom stemmed the Illyrian forefathers of all the Slavs. That meant that all the non-Hellenic notables of Balkan antiquity were Slavs. Macedonians Philip, Alexander, and Aristotle were Slavs. So were twenty-four Roman emperors and Saint Jerome. Moreover, three Dalmatian noble brothers – Czech, Lech and Rus – were the forefathers of the Czechs, Poles, and Russians. From these in turn rose mighty kings, such as Pribojević's contemporary Sigismund I of Poland whose sword brought low the Tatars, Livonian knights, and the Wallachian vassals of the Turks. The Slavic nation, whose further task was to rule the world (*ut totius orbis habenas regeret*), clearly had the wherewithal to loose the Ottoman bonds that shackled the Croats of Pribojević's generation. (p. 221)

This tangled web of distortions and fantasies, then, is the origin of the nationalising project in Croatia, and the other local traditions are no more accurate or convincing. The ideological elements include religious factionalism, the aggrandisement of the local nobility, anti-Ottoman solidarity, and the attempt to identify with the Roman Empire. This last is particularly important, since Banac's exposition shows that the political identities of modern Serbia and Croatia are both based on similar attempts to reconstruct the Roman province of Illyria, as a historical justification for local aristocratic hegemony. This is a good illustration of the fact that the ultimate political basis for the state formations of modern Europe generally, and therefore of the whole world, is the historical memory of the institutions of the Roman Empire. But if, as we have also argued, European nationalisms generally rely for their ideology on the acceptance of a naive anthropological hypothesis, exemplified by Herder's ideas, according to which the natural condition of the population is a division into ethno-territorial units, the naive anthropological theory of history that results is presented in an extremely complicated form in these Balkans ideologies. Pribojević and his colleagues succeeded in weaving religion and local cultural and political factors together into a heroic tradition of ethnic politics which is unfortunately based on lies so huge that it is difficult to stand back far enough to comprehend their significance. If there is a common thread running through it all, it is ethnic hatred; and if we look for the real origin of this, we find it in the Christian cult of exclusion, with its demonisation of the infidel. In the Balkans, this reserve of antagonism was originally directed against the Ottoman Turks, and provided a means of uniting local populations, somewhat in the manner in which Western Europe had been united against the Muslims during the Crusades, several hundred years previously. For instance, what we think of as historical Hungary – a Latin-based administrative unit bringing many nationalities and intermediate groups under a single system of land ownership and state organisation, that is – had been reduced by Ottoman incursion to a small region which is now mostly in Slovakia; and the sacred duty of taking back the bulk of the Hungarian territory from the evil infidels at the same time provided the basis for creating a corresponding Hungarian nationality, complete with national language, national mythology, songs, dances and all the rest of it – the idea now being that these had really been there all along, representing the true culture of the land and its people. Religious solidarity is used as a bridge to a national solidarity based at first on an appeal to loyalty to the national cult of exclusion, re-directed from state loyalty in the direction of ethnonationalism and a monolithic idea of national culture. But this style of ideology turned in on itself in the Balkans, and the lack of any other real internal cohesion among the artificial ethnic units created by the projects of the nationalisers and awakeners made opposition to each other the most important badge of identity. This refusal to see the neighbouring society as anything but hateful and foreign is a pattern observed in the most technologically primitive hunting societies, and has a social validity that cannot just be wished away. It does, however, rely on the existence of psychologically plausible boundaries. Under the psychological stress of the wars of Yugoslav secession, it seems that individuals have reverted to this primitive group defence mechanism *en masse*, despite the fact that the implicit nationalisation of territory according to group identities could self-evidently not be achieved without large-scale killing and forcible expulsion. However, the group identities, as we have said, are cultural artefacts, created or at least managed by ideologues and intellectuals in modern societies, but largely outside the control of individuals. Since there is a constant need to justify the massacres and inhumanities of the past, which were mostly conducted according to the most stirring slogans of national glory and honour, nationalistic myth-making is everywhere triumphant – and this is encouraged by the so-called international community, which seems to demand a nationalistic political project of some kind as a badge of membership; but the only intellectually honest course for the analyst and observer is to deny that this type of account of the development of society is valid from a scientific point of view; and to insist on this, supplying better, more complete and more consistent arguments.

Let us therefore develop a strong version of our position. The European civilisation – which is the most important defining element of the emerging world civilisation today – is perceived from inside as consisting of national cultures, and these have a basically competitive relationship. But it is manifestly absurd to believe that any of them are really as exclusive as they claim. A glance at the shelves of any European bookshop or library will show that the magic of translation has spread Europe's ideas across its national boundaries on an industrial scale; and a glance at the television should convince even the most hardened nationalist that it is culture itself which is the enemy of the nationalist project. At both ends of the cultural scale – both in the low culture that is globalising faster than we can imagine, and in the high culture that corresponds to what the snob and the aesthete usually think of as 'culture' – the best and most successful achievements are precisely those that have a reference to an identity – a human identity – that goes beyond the merely national. People spontaneously recognise that quality of universality which great art and great thought provides, whether it is in Indian Buddhism, German symphonic music, or the works of a Shakespeare, Tagore or Picasso; and modern Europe has been eminently successful in managing its inherent cultural variety so as to produce this kind of result – but has sometimes also displayed an infantile insistence that nothing of this kind has any value at all: that the finest flower of its art is the *Epic Of Kosovo Field* or the *Horst Wessel Lied*.

What linguists call 'arealisation' is an ever-present phenomenon where cultures are in contact: the creation of a cultural area, with the ritual differentiation of languages and peoples masking the steady osmotic pressure by which their cultures are actually mixed permanently together. Not everything is mixed, of course, and the differences between the component cultures are real; and so the strength of the European civilisation comes from these two opposed structural trends – the creation of a European cultural area on the one hand, and the preservation of subjectively independent national traditions on the other. It is a scheme, indeed, which seems to provide the most viable available cultural model for the whole world. But there is a danger here: namely that the nationalistic mythologising which allows this differentiation of national cultures to be preserved should convince people that its claims are literally true. For what is at the heart of the European diversity is not the greatness of this or that independent national variant of European civilisation: it is the interlocked system of city cultures which arose in imitation of the imperial Roman original across Christian Western Europe; and these city cultures succeeded so brilliantly not exactly because of the greatness of the related national cultures, but rather because they provided locations and mechanisms by which this particular European cultural pluralism could flourish. They provided the organisational means by which the cultural exchanges which have produced the European arealisation of culture could take place, in opposition to the political nationalisation of religion and culture which, left to its own devices, would turn all of Europe into a series of little Albanias, deliberately isolated, and pursuing some mad dream of superiority and inherent national virtue.

We have argued that the historical source for the European Christian toleration of non-national population elements, in morality and in law, was the treatment of the Jews in the middle ages; and the Jews will also provide us with the perfect image of the process of cultural enrichment just described. The Jews have certainly benefited from their access to the various European national cultural traditions; and Europe has benefited from their presence too. In medicine, art, literature and science, the contribution of Jews to modern European and world civilisation is beyond comparison with that of any other population group of similar size. The twentieth century is imaginatively said to have been the century of Freud, Marx and Einstein, and it is not so unreasonable a characterisation. Nazi Germany set out to re-create its culture with the Jewish element removed, and this project is a terrible reminder of the dangers of romantic nationalism. The speeches of Dr Goebbels and of Hitler himself on this subject were models of nationalistic moralising: freeing the German people from the corruption of this foreign element in their midst and so on. And what was the result of this purifying drive? The collapse of the moral order of German society to the point of deliberate genocide, accompanied by the simultaneous suicide of the German high culture. In retrospect, it is easy to see the writings of such men as Herder and Nietzsche as being implicated in some way in the German cultural disaster, and it is a matter of historical record that Hitler was particularly inspired by the operas and the vision of German greatness of Wagner: but these are as much symptoms as causes. It is the principle of nationalism, in culture as much as in politics, that is to blame. It is at root a gang instinct which tells people 'We are in the majority, and therefore everything we do at the expense of others is OK.' Christianity learned to tolerate the Jews, admittedly not from any fine motives, but even so, the result of establishing the Jewries and the ghettoes was (unconsciously) the establishment of the parallel culture mechanism as an integral part of mediæval European urbanism. This encouraged systematic cultural exchanges, and also established the principle of such exchange. It is not automatically guaranteed that city life will work in this way, though. Alexandria, the most successful international centre of the Mediterranean world of late antiquity, where Greeks, Arabs and Jews produced the scientific synthesis which distilled and preserved the thinking of the ancient world for later civilisation, has been transformed by nationalist thinking and practice into a dreary national city, whose contribution to contemporary world culture is virtually nil; and the same is true of Rome and Athens. Vienna and Budapest, only a hundred years ago centres of a polycultural civilisation generally assumed to be the most successful and advanced anywhere, have become sleepy national capitals, where the parallel culture dynamic that made them great has been carefully and completely destroyed. Where are the most important scientific and artistic centres in the world today? Which are the great cities in world-cultural terms? Obviously, they are the locations where the processes of the greatest international cultural exchange can take place: New York, Paris, London... and Moscow still has the potential for greatness. It is still an international capital, in its way.

There is a question of choice. Of policy. Nationalism produces narrow-mindedness and cultural stagnation; internationalism produces exchange and mutual cultural enrichment. But European internationalism cannot exist without the component national traditions of Europe, and so there is the question of how to find a balance between the two. The general cultural trend towards internationalisation of the low culture is clear everywhere; but it is still opposed by a trend in the opposite direction: a trend which sees exclusive national values as the highest, noblest and purest. It is not difficult to understand the reasons for this kind of psychological development; but that does not mean that we have to go along with it. The concrete symbol of this basic choice at a political level is the protection of minority rights, and the promotion of minority cultures. This, we say, is the mark of civilisation. The smaller and more foreign a cultural minority, the more it needs protection against the vandalism of the majority. The nationalist demagogue will try to enlist the support of that majority for the project of erasing minority cultures from the collective awareness. It is a project which goes in small incremental steps, each of which individually may be easy to take, but let us have no illusions: it is the road that leads to Auschwitz. And it has led us more recently to the torture of Sarajevo – whose crime was precisely that of providing a location for a type of parallel culture urbanism which contradicted the nationalising ideas of militant Serb and Croat ideology – and to the 1994 genocide in Rwanda, a country which now suffers from the same political disease which has so wounded Europe itself, but in a more virulent, African form. Perhaps there will be another Balkans act in this tragedy too, with the status of Kosovo, Macedonia and Montenegro still unclear.

Mythology is a potent kind of fantasy, made more potent by the admixture of nationalistic traditions of historiography, but the introduction of this fantasy into politics is potentially lethal. It can kill not just people, but their culture too. In the former Eastern Bloc, where the older political models (Ottoman, Austro-Hungarian, and Russian/Soviet) are poly-cultural, the basic choice about the role of nationalism in politics and culture generally is still not clear. Much depends on what will happen in Russia, because Russia is still potentially so powerful – for good or for evil – that the smaller nations of Eastern Europe must still live in its shadow, as must the Turkic, Armenian, Georgian and other non-European peoples of the former USSR. It is still a time of insecurity, and the appeal of romantic nationalism, which offers the talisman of self-aggrandisement as a cure for this insecurity, is still potent. Also, there is a kind of tolerance for the idea of re-writing the past for ideological purposes, that comes from the prevalence of this method during the years of communist rule and before. But to continue with the creation of supposedly monocultural nation states – to promote this as the only politically correct solution in the eyes of the international community – is to surrender to the lies of the past. The Slavs are not descended from Noah's grandson. The brothers Czech, Lech and Rus never existed. And the exclusivist national ideologies attached to the state formations of modern society do not correspond to the underlying social structuring of the population.

References

Amselle, Jean-Loup (1985), 'Ethnies et espaces: Pour une anthropologie topologique' [Ethnies and Spaces: For a topological anthropology], in Jean-Loup Amselle and Elikia M'Bokolo, eds., *Au coeur de l'ethnie: Ethnies, tribalisme et état en Afrique*, Paris, La Découverte.

Avrich, Paul (1976), *Russian Rebels 1600-1800*, Norton, New York.

Banac, Ivo (1993), 'The Insignia of Identity: Heraldry and the Growth of National Ideologies Among the South Slavs', in *Ethnic Studies*, Vol. 10, pp. 215-237.

Bloch, Marc (1989), *La Société Feodale* [Feudal Society] (originally 1939), Albin Michel, Paris.

Bradley, John F. N. (1984), *Czech Nationalism in the Nineteenth Century*, Eastern European Monographs No. CLVII, Boulder.

Braudel, Fernand (1993), *A History of Civilizations*, tr. Richard Mayne, Penguin, Harmondsworth.

Brühl, Carlrichard (1994), *Naissance de deux peuples, Français et Allemands* [Birth of Two Peoples, French and Germans], tr. Gaston Duchet-Suchaux, Fayard, Paris.

Campbell, John (1840), *Maritime Exploration and Christian Missions*, John Snow, London.

Coon, Carleton S. (1972), *The Hunting Peoples*, Penguin, Harmondsworth.

Deutscher, Isaac (1967), *The Unfinished Revolution*, Russia 1917-1967, OUP.

Durkheim, Emile (1912), *Les Formes Elémentaires De La Vie Religieuse* [The Elementary Forms of Religious Life], Paris.

Duvernoy, Jean (1976), *La Religion des Cathares* [The Religion of the Cathars], Privat, Toulouse.

Duvernoy, Jean (1979), *L'histoire des Cathares* [The History of the Cathars], Privat, Toulouse.

Epstein, Isidore (1959), *Judaism*, Pelican, Harmondsworth.

Finley, M. I. (1968), 'Aulos Kapreilios Timotheos, Slave Trader,' in *Aspects of Antiquity*, Pelican, Harmondsworth.

Gumilëv, L. *Ethnogenesis and the Biosphere* (tr. Vadim Novikov), Progress, Moscow, 1990.

Harvey, L. P. (1990), *Islamic Spain, 1250 to 1500*, University of Chicago Press.

von Herder, Johann Gottfried (1969), 'Ideas For A Philosophy Of The History Of Mankind' (1784-91), Book VII, in *Herder On Social And Political Culture*, translated, edited and with an introduction by F. M. Barnard, Cambridge University Press.

Horowitz, Irving Louis (1991), 'Anti-Modernisation, National Character and Social Structures', in *The Impact of Western Nationalisms*, ed. Jehuda Reinharz and George L. Mosse, Sage, London.

Hroch, Miroslav (2000), 'Central Europe: the rise and fall of an historical idea', in *Central Europe, Core or Periphery?*, ed. Christopher Lord, CBS Press, Copenhagen.

Ibrahim, Taufic and Sagadeev, Arthur (1990), *Classical Islamic Philosophy*, Progress, Moscow.

Kalomiros, Alexander (1996), 'The River Of Fire', cited in *Parish Life*, March/April 1996, Russian Orthodox Cathedral of St. John the Baptist, Washington, D.C.

Krejčí, Jaroslav (1996), 'State versus Nation' in *Human Rights and Responsibilities in a Divided World*, ed. Jaroslav Krejčí, Filosofia, Prague.

Le Roy Ladurie, Emmanuel (1979), *Montaillou: The Promised Land of Error*, translated by Barbara Bray, Vintage, New York.

Liebich, André (1997), *Les Minorités Nationales en Europe Centrale et Orientale* [National Minorities in Central and Eastern Europe], Georg, Geneva.

Lilie, Ralph-Johannes (1993), *Byzantium and the Crusader States 1096-1204*, OUP.

Lodyzhensky, M. V. (1915), *Mystical Trilogy*, Vol. 2. 'Light Unseen', Petrograd (in Russian).

Loos, Milan (1974), *Dualist Heresy in the Middle Ages*, Academia, Prague.

Lord, Christopher (1994), 'Cults of Exclusion', in *Christianity-Judaism-Islam; Europe at the Close of the 20th Century*, papers from an international symposium, European Culture Club, Prague, pp. 162-169.

Lord, Christopher (1999) *Politics: An Essay Concerning The General Nature Of Political Discourse (with some remarks on power, rationality and consciousness)*, Karolinum (Charles University Press), Prague.

Maalouf, Amin (1985), *The Crusades Through Arab Eyes*, tr. Jon Rothschild, Schocken, New York.

Matsunaya, Daigon and Alice (1974), *Foundations of Japanese Buddhism*, Buddhist Books International, Tokyo, 2 volumes.

Meslin, Michel (1967), *Les Ariens d'Occident 335-430* [The Arians of the West 335-430], Seuil, Paris.

Nelli, René (1969), *La Vie Quotidienne des Cathares du Languedoc au XIIIe Siècle* [Daily Life of the Cathars in Languedoc in the XIIIth Century], Hachette, Paris.

Oates, John (1986), *Babylon*, Revised Edition, Thames and Hudson, London.

Patočka, Jan (1969), 'Dilema v našem národním programu – Jungmann a Bolzano' [The dilemma in our national programme – Jungmann and Bolzano], first published in *O smysl dneška*, Mladá fronta, Praha, pp. 87-104. Reprinted in *Náš národní program*, Evropský kulturní klub, Praha, 1990, pp. 41-56.

Rieff, David (1996), *Rwanda: The Big Risk*, New York Review of Books, October 31, 1996, pp. 70-76.

Russell, Bertrand (1975), *History of Western Philosophy*, Unwin, London.

Sen, K. M. (1961), *Hinduism*, Pelican, Harmondsworth.

Stalin, J. V. (1971), *Selected Works*, Cardinal Publishers, Davis, California.

Stow, Kenneth R. (1992), *Alienated Minority; The Jews Of Medieval Latin Europe*, Harvard University Press, Cambridge, Mass. and London.

Sumner, B. H. (1962), *Peter the Great and the Emergence of Russia*, Collier, New York.

Tishkov, Valery (1997), *Ethnicity, Nationalism and Conflict In And After The Soviet Union: The Mind Aflame*, Sage, London.

Tolkein, J. R. R. (1997), 'English and Welsh' (first published 1955) in *The Monsters And The Critics and other essays*, Harper Collins, London.

Trevelyan, G. M. (1944), *English Social History*, Longmans, London, Chapters I and II, 'Chaucer's England'.

de Vaux, Roland (1961), *Ancient Israel, Its Life And Institutions*, McGraw-Hill, London.

Weber, Max (1958), *The Protestant Ethic And The Spirit Of Capitalism*, tr. Talcott Parsons, Scribner's, New York.

Wright, Arthur F. (1959), *Buddhism in Chinese History*, Stanford.

2 Competing Cultures, Conflicting Identities: the Case of Transylvania

GAVRIL FLORA

Any effective approach to the study of inter-ethnic relations in Central-Eastern Europe should consider ethnic and national communities in their mutual interaction, rather than seeing them as isolated and self-sufficient entities. Due to the specificities of nation- and state-building in this part of Europe, the various national self-images have been developed to such an extent (generally as a reaction to policies and images promoted by the 'other side'), that it would be extremely counterproductive for researchers to ignore this fundamental fact of ethnic co-existence.

In this regard, the term 'parallel cultures' will prove effective as a key concept if it is interpreted from a sociological, rather than a purely 'geometrical' perspective, so as to include the relationship between cultures as an essential component of social relations. According to this vision, interaction is in itself a driving force: both a cause and an effect. It constantly creates and recreates the interethnic context, but at the same time is significantly affected and influenced by it, thus acting both as a factor of stability, and as a motive power of change. The case of Transylvania, a multi-cultural region in the Central and North-Western part of Romania, is particularly relevant in this regard.

From Parallel Cultures to Rival Nations

Historically, Transylvania has been regarded as a homeland by its Romanian, Hungarian and German (Saxon) inhabitants equally. The area has had a distinct path of development, which produced its own specific cultural environment and identity. During the middle ages, 'Transylvania was an integral part of the mediæval Kingdom of Hungary, but owing to its remote situation, enjoyed a certain autonomy.' (Seton-Watson, 1943, pp.

2-3) After the collapse of independent Hungary in 1541 it became a separate principality under Turkish Ottoman rule, and maintained this status for more than 150 years, until the beginning of 18th century, when it was integrated into the Habsburg Empire as a self-governing unit. From 1867 the province belonged to Hungary within the framework of the Austro-Hungarian Monarchy, and only became part of Romania after the dissolution of the Dualist State at the end of the First World War.

Several centuries of co-existence created in this region a space of cultural diversity and ethnic and religious tolerance, including a very specific institutional system, aimed at preserving the very delicate balance of power, which recognised and reflected the plurality of cultures within the territory. It is worth recalling in this connection that the political structure of mediæval Transylvania was based on the shared dominance of the three recognised 'political nations': the Hungarian nobility (which included the feudal leaders of the Romanians), the Szekels and the Saxons. At the same time, Transylvania was the first country in Europe to codify religious pluralism – by the so-called Edict of Toleration of 1571, which institutionalised full equality for the four recognised churches (*recepta religio*): the Catholic, Calvinist, Lutheran and Unitarian denominations.[1]

Although the term *natio* in its mediæval sense should be understood primarily as expressing a community of legal rights and privileges, including the *'libertas'* enjoyed by the individuals who belonged to it, the Transylvanian system of three political nations should by no means be considered empty of ethno-cultural significance. Two of the three 'nations' (the Szekels and the Saxons) were ethnically homogeneous, while the third – the 'county-based' nobility, although including individuals of various ethnic backgrounds, was Hungarian in its spirit, mentality and style of life: thus, if not originally homogeneous, in effect homogenised. The reasons that laid down the fundamentals of the system were evidently connected with the necessity to provide

---

[1] The only important exception was the Romanians, who could not be integrated into the system due to the socio-economic and cultural discrepancy between them and the rest of the population. At the same time, the Orthodox faith, though it had been granted complete freedom, nevertheless had not been accepted as having equal status. These facts of exclusion had long term consequences for the characteristics of nation-building deveopment in the region, which I shall discuss later.

participation in the power structures and thus ensure the loyalty of the ethno-regional groups concerned.[2]

It is important to note here that each *natio* had its own autonomous territorial basis; and that the rights of the three recognised estates could be exercised only collectively by political-territorial communities, rather than by individuals. The Saxons held the southern areas granted to them by a special charter, the *Andrenaum* of 1224, where they formed their *universitas*. (Müller, 1928; Müller, 1941) The Szekels, a group closely related to Hungarians, but often regarded as ethnically separate during the middle ages, had been settled as border guards, with their own autonomous lands in the eastern regions. (Bodor, 1983, pp. 281-305) The rest of the country was administered by the 'county-based' nobility. One can identify in the territorial individuality of the various ethnic communities the early roots of subsequent strong autonomist tendencies, something which has deeply influenced the modern political process and also the mentalities of the people in the region.

In spite of all these favorable preconditions for the development of a culturally pluralistic and tolerant society, Transylvania did not become an 'eastern Switzerland'. It entered the age of nation-building facing the consequences of competition between two parallel discourses of legitimacy – the Hungarian and Romanian ones – both of which claimed state-building rights for their own nation. The long-term results have been the sacralisation of 'national territory' as an essential element of cultural identity, and a predominant, mutually exclusive perception of national interests, which has led to the polarisation of society along ethno-national lines.

Why did it happen so? The only answer which seems credible points to the lack of a real alternative. Basically there was no qualitatively different path of development available. Ethnic nationalism was in fact the only effective means available to build up a satisfactory level of legitimacy, and the only efficient tool of political mobilisation in the region. Two major factors contributed to this:

1. *Lack of territorial-political continuity* The period of the autonomous Principality was, by all accounts, too brief to produce a solid basis for a

---

[2] We can see a parallel with the division of the population of ancient Rome into three parts, one of which was also ethnically mixed; the reason for the division also being political. This division into three is of course the origin of the modern term 'tribe' (Latin *tribus*).

distinct Transylvanian national identity. In fact, Transylvania has always been a 'borderland country',[3] standing at the fringes of large empires, and it entered the era of modernity as a remote province of Austria. Within the territory of the Austrian Empire, the alternatives to the creation of nation-states had been limited from the start by certain characteristics with constraining effects: the multi-ethnic character of both the imperial state and its constitutive parts, and the low level of continuity with mediæval political and territorial entities.

2. *Weak civil society institutions* Historically a lack of balance between the ethnic and civil dimensions of national identity determined the crucial role of ethnic affiliation throughout the process of nation-building. The weak supraethnic civil bonds within society made the creation of a citizenship-based identity particularly difficult. Socio-economic backwardness was of course a key factor in producing such an outcome. The institutionalisation of the so called 'second serfdom' in the XVI-XIII centuries has to be regarded as a particularly unfavourable development in this respect. The consolidation of feudal-type relationships, at a time when the Western part of continent was preparing to open a free path for modernisation, to a large extent prevented the creation of strong civil society institutions and therefore of a sense of civil nationality in this part of Europe.

While in the West modern national identities have developed as a definite rejection of feudal privileges, and have symbolically expressed the rule of the 'people' as well as the equality of all citizens, in Central-Eastern Europe, as a consequence of weak urban and bourgeois development in the first stage of national movements, the nobility largely took over the role of 'national awakener', paradoxically using the modern idea of nationality for the preservation of its old power positions.

In Transylvania, instead of the liberation of serfs from feudal ties and the proclamation of full equality, in the beginning the opposite trend manifested itself: the traditionally free, and socially and ethnically homogenous communities (such as the Szekels, but also including free Romanian villages) started to lose their privileges due to an internal

---

[3] This expression was used by George Cushing in a lecture entitled *Hungarian Cultural Traditions in Transylvania,* first delivered at the School of Slavonic Studies, University of London, on 7 December 1982, and subsequently published by the School in 1984.

differentiation process, which gradually led to the creation of a unitary ruling stratum, joined only by wealthy members of the previous ruling *nationes*. The nobility was not only not excluded from the nation (as happened during the French revolution), but on the contrary, the past and present dominant position of the elites aspiring to nationalist legitimacy had become the most effective argument: their fight, that is, for higher status and more privileges for themselves and by extension for the 'nations' they were claiming to represent.

As a result, although a comparative analysis of differentiating factors during the process of nation building should involve a series of other economic, social, political and cultural causes as well, the main factor in shaping the separate modern national consciousness of Hungarians, Romanians and Germans in Transylvania seems to be related to the *unequal power positions of their respective leading political strata.*

According to this criterion, the Hungarian elite was evidently in the most favoured position. After all, two of the three ruling 'political nations' of Transylvania, the county-based nobles and the Szekels, were Hungarian by culture, mentality and language. As Transylvania had belonged to the mediæval kingdom of Hungary, a traditional link also existed between the Transylvanian and Hungarian nobility. Thus, the appeal to the tradition of the mediæval state provided them with a shared ground of legitimacy.

In addition, Hungarians – both those inside and outside Transylvania – could argue that the Transylvanian Principality was in a sense the continuation of historical Hungary. Consequently, the core principle of Hungarian nationalism (which had been embraced by Transylvania's Hungarians too) became the idea of establishing – or, in their vision, of re-establishing – a Hungarian nation state within the historical borders of Hungary. This aspiration became to a large extent a reality as the result of the 1867 Compromise, when the Austro-Hungarian Monarchy came into being. The Hungarian nation received equal status with Austria within the central government, and full self-governing power in the areas belonging to the territory of their historic kingdom, including Transylvania.

In the case of the Romanians, by contrast, the most important determinants had been the lack of past political participation, their exclusion from the status of a recognised *natio*, and the almost complete absorbtion of their privileged members into the Hungarian nobility. As a consequence, the leading role in the creation of a Romanian national identity had to be assumed by the intelligentsia, and especially by the clergy of the Uniate

(Greek-Catholic) Church. There were no traditions of independent statehood to be invoked in support of national claims, and, in their absence, only some (controversial) arguments of historical ancestry and continuity as well as demographic arguments had been put forward. It was claimed that Romanians were both the oldest inhabitants of the country (allegedly being the offspring of Roman colonists) and the most numerous. Indeed, by the end of 18th century, the Romanian population did achieve a numerical majority in the region, partly as the result of higher birthrates and partly by immigration from the Danubian Principalities.

At first, Transylvanian Romanians did not demand a state exclusively of their own, but the autonomy of Transylvania and shared power with the other nations within the region. This claim was in fact in line with the traditional Transylvanian constitutional principles, which were based on the plurality of territorial community rights. These Transylvanian institutions, however, were at variance with the legal tradition of Hungary proper, where only one political nation existed, the *natio hungarica*. The difficulty of resolving this contradiction might partly explain why leading Hungarian national thinkers and political leaders in the 19th century, though to some extent in favour of cultural pluralism, were nevertheless not able to accept a multinational model in the *political* sense, and as a consequence, ultimately failed in their attempt to integrate Transylvania into the Hungarian nation state.

The idea of a 'Hungarian political nation', supposed to include all citizens regardless of their ethnic belonging, can be seen as an unsuccessful attempt of Hungarian leading circles to reconcile the need to assert an ethnonationalist rhetoric of legitimacy with the practical political necessity to recognise ethnic diversity within the state (since ethnic Hungarians amounted to less than half of the total population). This task was intended to be fulfilled by the 1868 Law of Nationalities. While granting, in a liberal spirit, the possibility for all non-Hungarians to use their own mother tongue in their contact with authorities, and also their right of association 'for the development of language, arts, sciences, industry and trade', the law stated that 'all citizens of the country, in the political sense, are members of one nation, the unitary and indivisible Hungarian nation, which includes with equal rights all citizens of the fatherland, to whatever nationality they belong'. (Péter (ed.), 1992, p. 34)

The reaction of Romanian representatives to the idea of their being included into the 'Hungarian political nation' was sharply negative, as they saw it as a step towards ethnic homogenisation, and an attempt to separate and alienate the national elites from their own communities. The fact that the proposed unitary political community was designated 'the Hungarian political nation' rather than 'the political nation of Hungary' was regarded by Transylvanian Romanian leaders as a proof in itself of the real intentions of successive Hungarian governments.

Echoing this position, the Romanian National Party of Transylvania considered the proposed replacement of the ethnic principle with a 'modern', 'civil' one as a tactical move only, aimed to conceal and at the same time to legitimise the real dominance of the Hungarian element and its envisaged plans for the ethnic assimilation of non-Hungarians. Making the Hungarian language a compulsory subject in the mainly church-owned Romanian schools and in the kindergartens, and the fact that the state-owned educational institutions used Hungarian almost exclusively as the language of instruction only underlined such suspicions.

The language issue indeed created a delicate problem. Hungarian nationalism itself had started mainly as a struggle for linguistic rights: specifically, for the recognition of Hungarian as an official language within the Austrian Empire. This 'birth certificate' had long-term consequences. As the Hungarian national movement began to take shape, it became more and more important for the leading nobility to enlarge the popular base for their nationalistic claims.

The appeal to language – and to folk culture – as essential symbolic bonds linking all Magyars regardless of their socio-economic status fulfilled an important role in this legitimising strategy. Proclaiming Hungarian as the only official language, beyond the instrumental advantage it provided to Hungarian speakers, also offered them an additional sense of privilege and dignity compared to the rest of the population, thus enhancing their legitimacy still further. This had an exclusionary effect on non-Hungarian speakers, and prompted their elites to follow the same model in order to gain popular acceptance, that is, by emphasising the nation-building virtues of their respective languages. This created an inevitable political and social pressure which would bring its consequences in time.

Denying national entities the status of political subjects, and the increasingly strong dissatisfaction of non-Hungarian political leaders, particularly of Romanians, concerning the perceived dominance of an ethnic Hungarian element within a state which pretended to be equal towards all citizens regardless of their ethnicity, encouraged the development of alternative nationalist rhetorics, which eventually led to the challenging of the existing political-territorial arrangements.

'Greater Romania'

On the 4th of June, 1920, the peace treaty signed at Trianon between the victorious allied and associated powers on one side and Hungary on the other, along with the other treaties signed at the conclusion of the First World War, put the seal of international recognition on a new territorial division of East-Central Europe. As part of the territorial transfers which resulted from the peace process, 37· 5 per cent of the territory belonging to the semi-independent Hungary within the framework of the Austria-Hungarian Monarchy, an area of 103,093 km, which included historical Transylvania, Partium and a segment of the Banat of Timişoara, with a population of 5,565,000 (of which 1,651,000 were Hungarians and 565,000 Germans), was incorporated into the Romanian state. (Takács, 1992)

Transylvania was the most important, but not the only acquisition. 'Greater Romania' also included Bessarabia, taken over from Russia, Bukovina from old Austria, and the south of Dobrogea, obtained from Bulgaria: territories with large numbers of Russians, Ukrainians and Bulgarians, respectively. As a result, the Kingdom more than doubled its territory, and a basically one-nation society was transformed into a multi-national one. According to the 1930 census, the proportion of ethnic Romanians in the total population was no more than 71· 9 per cent, but within Transylvania their share was only 57· 8 per cent.[4] Thus a major problem emerged: whether, and if so, to what extent the state should now change its structures, so as to provide a model of integration for its numerous ethnically non-Romanian citizens.

However, the difficulties that Romania had to face in integrating Transylvania after 1918 were much harder than those encountered by Hungary a few decades earlier, since the contradiction between the state-building models of Transylvania and Old Romania was much more striking. The early modern political identity of the Old Romanian Kingdom – deeply influenced by the Byzantine mentality on one hand and by Turkish rule on

---

[4] *Recensamintul populatiei si locuintelor din 7 ianuarie 1992. Structura etnica si confesionala a populatiei* [The census of 7 January 1992. Ethnic and confessional structure of the population], Bucharest, 1995.

the other – was based on the idea of cultural homogeneity, to the extent that inhabitants who did not belong to the Orthodox faith were for a long time even denied citizenship, being merely regarded as aliens. Thus the problem faced by the ruling elite consisted not only in how to accommodate a multi-cultural society under the roof of one state – a difficult task in itself – but also, how to reconcile through this process two rather different political cultures and historically- and regionally-determined state-building traditions.

During the first few months, shortly before and after the extension of Romanian sovereignty over Transylvania, it seemed that Greater Romania might be built to some extent on the foundation of shared power between the Romanians and the other numerically and politically important nationalities. The Proclamation of Alba Iulia, which expressed the initial view of the Transylvanian Romanians, embodied the following principles on the nationality question, which were favourably received by minorities:

> *Art. 3* The National Assembly declares as fundamental principles of the Romanian State the following:
>
> (1) Complete national liberty for all the peoples inhabiting Romania. Each people to educate, administer and judge itself through the medium of persons from its own midst. Each people to have the right to administrative legislation and of taking part in the administration of the country in proportion to the number of individuals of which it is composed.
>
> (2) Equality and complete autonomous religious liberty for every denomination of the state.[5]

It was on the basis of this programme that Saxons had voted in favor of unification, and in the decades of the interwar period the political organisations both of the Hungarian and German populations had insistently demanded a solution of the nationality problem on the basis of the principles put forward at Alba Iulia. Within the Hungarian community of Transylvania a new ideological trend developed, suggestively called *transylvanianism*, which expressed the renunciation of irredentism, and envisaged the life of ethnic Hungarians within the territorial framework of the Romanian state. The proclamation entitled 'Cry!', issued by transylvanianist leaders in 1921,

---

[5] 'A Gyulafehérvári egyesülés' [The Alba Iulia Unification], in *Háromszék*, 1 December 1994.

expressed in this respect a clear break with the exclusiveness of traditional Hungarian nationalism, promising as it did the faithfullness of Hungarians to Romania with the condition that 'national autonomy' be granted to them. (Kós *et al.*, 1921, p. 4) This proposal was aimed at preventing the creation of an ethnic division line between the two main national communities of Transylvania, by trying to overcome Romanian fears concerning the territorial integrity of the enlarged state.

However, frequent political signals indicated from the beginning that the ruling circles of Old Romania would favour a unitary centralist state, and nationalistic models of legitimacy, instead of federalist or even autonomist solutions. The policy of ethnic mobilisation and homogenisation was in conformity with the interest of the centralist bureaucracy and was perceived as a political priority and even as a matter of urgency by the Bucharest elite. Transylvanian Romanians too very soon abandoned more or less explicitly the model proposed at Alba Iulia and in the following period fully supported the intensive centralising and homogenising efforts initiated by the political elite of the Old Kingdom.

This became evident when the Constitution of 1923 was adopted in a form which embodied exclusively the conceptions of the ethnic majority. Romania was defined as a 'national, unitary and indivisible state'. (Balázs, 1993) No provisions had been included for the protection of the identities of national minorities, except for the principle of full citizenship and equality. A unitary administrative territorial system was established, without special status being offered to those areas mainly inhabited by minorities. No institutions of political or cultural self-government were established for the needs of national minority populations. The Romanian language was declared 'the language of the state', and the use of languages other than Romanian in the political life and state administration was declared illegal. Citizens were allowed to communicate with the administrative authorities, including those at local level, and regardless of the ethnic composition of local populations, exclusively in the official language. Furthermore, the Constitution proclaimed that 'the nation' is the only legitimate source of power, stating as follows: 'All the power in the state is originated in the nation, and may only be exercised by delegation, in accordance with the principles and rules stated in the present Constitution'. (Balázs, 1993)

Transylvanian Romanian leaders felt that their national interests could be protected more effectively if they assumed a privileged power position, instead of sharing power with Hungarians and Germans within the framework of autonomous Transylvanian institutions. Their choice should also be interpreted in the context of the social structure of interwar Transylvania. Due to historical peculiarities, the social set-up in this region had strong ethnic connotations. Hungarians and Germans (together with Jews, who underwent a quick process of magyarisation) were predominant within the urban population (in the ranks of industrial and commercial enterpreneurs and of the working class), while Romanians had been very much under-represented in these social categories. (Glatz, 1995, pp. 105-109) Thus one of the important aims promoted by Bucharest governments was to change this distribution – regarded as inequitable – by promoting the upward mobility of ethnic Romanians to the detriment of other nations. Hungarians, as the formerly dominant nation, who were considered mostly responsible for 'the past injustices', were the principal negative target of such policies.

Through the decades following the creation of Romania's national, unitary and 'indivisible' state, a series of administrative, political, cultural and economic pressures were applied to minority groups, often clashing, both in principle and in practice, with the general democratic requirement to ensure equality of citizenship regardless of ethnic belonging. Such was the case, for instance, of the intensive campaigns of 're-Romanianisation' (Vécsey, 1992) initiated by interwar governments, which, on the basis of 'etymological analysis' required minority citizens whose family name was found to be of Romanian origin to take up an obligatory Romanian identity and to belong to the Orthodox Church, while their children were only permitted to attend schools using Romanian as the teaching language.

The Romanian majority has from the beginning taken it for granted that its own national interests are identical with those of the state. According to the logic of such an assumption, the minorities have been expected either to adhere fully and unconditionally to the view of the majority, or face accusations of disloyalty. The major problem faced by Romanian governments after 1918 was how to build up nation state legitimacy in a territory which included historically diverse and ethnically mixed regions. In such conditions, the urgent political need to forcefully assert 'the national idea' often conflicted with the general democratic requirement to create a citizenship-based state. Although declaratively affirmed from time to time, the political and cultural rights of those belonging to minorities were in many respects dependent on the shorter- or longer-term interests and calculations of those in power.

The preferential socio-economic mobilisation of the ethnic Romanian population was most attractive to the Transylvanian Romanian middle class: the very social stratum which, due to its education received under the Austro-Hungarian Monarchy, had otherwise assimilated fairly well the culturally pluralistic and tolerant mentality specific to the region. In other conditions this economic and cultural elite could have been much more open towards the idea of an autonomous Transylvania. But its immediate interests, and particularly the way these interests were perceived in the years of euphoria and enthusiasm after the creation of 'Greater Romania', ultimately prevailed.

To the political, economic and social causes outlined above, one should add the peculiarities of cultural development. Until the 18th century, which marked the start of Romanian nation-building, the high culture of Transylvania developed mainly as the result of the Hungarian and German contributions, the result being perceived by Romanian inhabitants of the area largely as a foreign culture. (Macartney, 1937, p. 280) The historical frustrations, which deeply affected Romanian national ideology, prompted an important segment of Transylvanian Romanian intellectuals and political leaders to look for support beyond the Carpathians, and join the ethnic homogenisation policies of the central government.

In 1924, in order to promote Romanianisation, now regarded as a 'national mission', so-called 'cultural areas' came into being in the nine Transylvanian counties with the largest Hungarian population. As part of the special provisions implemented in this area, ethnic Romanian teachers, who did not know the language of their pupils, were sent to overwhelmingly Hungarian localities, being offered special economic incentives such as higher salary, quicker advancement, and 10ha of land in the case of definitive resettlement. It was intended to create, in the first stage, small but spiritually and politically active 'islands', with the task of preparing the ground for a subsequent, larger-scale colonisation.

Although regionalist tendencies did exist in interwar Transylvanian Romanian political life (Romul, 1995, pp. 25-27), this orientation, even if somewhat more generous in its formulation of political offers to minorities (compared to the terms of the 1923 Constitution, that is), nevertheless did not agree with any form of power-sharing with the other Transylvanian nations, regarding the Romanian supremacy within the region as a political axiom. Even put in such a mild form, the regional idea never succeeded in aquiring majority support within the Transylvanian Romanian political class, being advocated mainly by some leaders of the older generation who were discontented with their own loss of position in favor of the administrative and political bureaucracy from the Old Kingdom.

In contrast, younger Transylvanian Romanian ideologists, socialised intellectually and politically in the years following the territorial shift, formulated the aspiration of a 'pure Romanianism',[6] free of regional connotations and nostalgia. Their desideratum was complete integration into Romanian society, by the disappearance of any differences between Transylvanian Romanians and 'Regaters'. The social model envisaged by these intellectuals was conceived on an *ethnocratic* basis, proposing economic, political and cultural privileges to be granted to the ethnic Romanian population.

Communism and After

If in the interwar era citizenship rights frequently entered in conflict with the national principle, but were nevertheless legally affirmed and could be openly claimed and defended by the representatives of the individuals or groups concerned, under communism the leading role of the party nullified any practical significance for minority rights. (Schöpflin and Poulton, 1990, p. 10) The extent and the limitations of these 'rights' depended exclusively on the arbitrary will of the political leadership, and provisions could be offered as well as withdrawn according to tactical moves and calculations by those holding power. Thus, paradoxically, even the existence in certain periods of facilities created specially for minorities, such as a state-controlled minority language education system, newspapers, broadcasting programmes, etc., could also serve as a façade to hide the absence of real rights. (Glatz, 1992, p. 47) The situation of national minorities was made even more difficult by the fact that, like all other social groups, they did not have any real possibilities for independent representation of their interests.

Compared with the interwar period, two additional motives played an important role in the intensification of ethnonationalist homogenisation policies. First, this was the period when the society of Romania entered the phase of economic mass mobilisation and large scale rural-to-urban

---

[6] See the review of the book by Nichifor Crainic, 'Az etnokrata állam' [The Ethnocratic State], in (Gaál, 1986, p. 132).

migration – a process which was planned and implemented from above by the communist leadership, and under strict government control, which included the smallest details. Ethnonationalist rhetoric played the leading ideological role throughout this period, in an attempt to offer a surrogate sense of identity to the uprooted population, in order to integrate them into the new environment as fast a possible. While temporarily 'efficient' in that regard, its 'socialist patriotic education' implied at the same time the inculcation of a false sense of superiority in ethnic Romanians, with disastrous consequences for the climate of interethnic relations.

The second important motive force in the Romanian version of co-habitation between communism and nationalism, particularly under Ceausescu, was the regime's desperate search for a traditional type of legitimation in order to enlarge the power basis and consolidate the stability of communist rule. Appealing to the widespread nationalistic sentiments of the population attracted part of the intelligentsia and gained popular support, or at least a silent acceptance of repressive totalitarian measures, by obsessively invoking the argument of a 'threat to the territorial integrity' of the country. Though Romanian communist minority policies did occasionally include short periods of relaxation (as in 1945-47 and again in 1968-70), during times when the regime needed to make some concessions in order to consolidate power, the general trend was an ever more intensive use of ethnonationalism as a political tool of mass mobilisation, a tougher limitation of the cultural space available for minorities, and the use of more complex and effective strategies and methods in order to achieve higher degrees of ethnic homogeneity.

By the second half of the eighties, education in the Hungarian and German languages had shrunk drastically. While in 1976 only 37 per cent of Hungarian pupils were required to attend Romanian schools, in 1986 the proportion of those forced to do so rose to 77 per cent. In December 1984 the central television and local radio stations ceased broadcasting in Hungarian. Ethnic Hungarians' ties with neighbouring Hungary were restricted, and travel abroad reduced to a minimum. Non-Romanian versions of geographical names were forbidden to appear in publications, and the use of personal names without a Romanian equivalent was also banned. (Schöpflin and Poulton, 1990, p. 17)

Unlike the interwar governments, which could rely only on limited means, mainly of an administrative nature, in their policies of Romanianisation, and which consequently could not bring about a major change in ethnoterritorial distribution, the socialist state disposed in addition of a wide range of economic, demographic, political and cultural resources and instruments, which were often used in combination, according to specifically drawn designs, so as to provide maximum benefits as far as furthering the regime's nationalist aims was concerned. The steps taken by the party leadership in this respect included: merging of Romanian and minority schools, with the aim of subsequently reducing the share of classes and subjects using a non-Romanian teaching language, up to their complete closure; dismissal of most minority functionaries from such institutions of the central apparatus as were regarded of vital importance, like the Ministry of Foreign Affairs, Ministry of Interior and the Army, and a severe reduction of their number in other administrative fields; and establishing a system of compulsory assignment for university and high school graduates, with the aim of preventing specialists belonging to minorities from returning to their home regions.

To reinforce the effect of such measures, a system of 'closed cities' was institutionalised, which included several heavily Hungarian- and German-populated localities, with the undeclared task of barring the settlement of minority inhabitants, while at the same time offering financial, housing and other incentives for ethnic Romanians to come to those cities, often from remote areas. In 1930, out of the eight most important cities of the province, four (Satu Mare, Cluj, Oradea and Tirgu Mures) were overwhelmingly Hungarian-inhabited, while the other four had a balanced Romanian-Hungarian-German population, without any particular group holding an absolute preponderance. By 1992, however, only two urban localities of this category (Satu Mare and Tirgu Mures) preserved a very narrow and vulnerable majority; all the other six cities had become predominantly Romanian-populated.[7]

The Hungarian community living in Transylvania, unlike the Roma or other smaller ethnic groups, but similarly to the Transylvanian Saxons, does have a strongly developed and fully integrated sense of regional national identity connected to this region, which includes the perception of its own historically constituted territorial basis. That is the main reason why the demographic advancement of ethnic Romanians, and the concomitant reduction of Hungarians' share in state and national activities, partly as a result of nation-state-conducted homogenisation policies, has always been perceived by the Hungarian population as a painful loss, and as a continous

---

[7] *Recensamintul populatiei si locuintelor...* Bucharest, 1995.

threat to the preservation of its culture and identity. The arguments in this regard are indeed numerous. The diminution of the demographic importance of ethnic Hungarians over the past 75 years has usually meant a dramatic loss of their previously dominant positions in the economic, political and cultural life of Transylvania. Moreover, these changes have been implemented with the help of state-conducted measures aimed at encouraging the dissolution of the traditional ethno-demographic composition of the predominantly minority-inhabited regions by means of migration and assimilation.

This was also the period when the Romanian government 'successfully' negotiated with the West German and Israeli governments to allow the emigration of ethnic Germans and Jews. As a result, populations of several hundreds of thousands, which for centuries had made an important contribution to the economy and culture of the country, almost completely disappeared from the life of the country, a loss which it is still very hard to evaluate. According to official census data, in 1930 ethnic Romanians formed some 71· 9 per cent of the total population, and in the interval 1930-1992 this share increased to 89· 5 per cent. During the same period, as the result of assimilation and resettlement, the proportion of ethnic Hungarians dropped from 10 per cent to 7· 1 per cent, that of Germans from 4· 4 to 0· 5 per cent, and that of Jews from 3· 2 per cent to 0· 1 per cent: mainly due to extermination and emigration.[8] As emigration affected German and Jewish populations much more than Hungarians, one long-term consequence in the field of ethnic co-existence was a diminishing of Transylvania's traditional multi-cultural profile, and an increasing Romanian-Hungarian bipolarity within that region.

After the collapse of the communist system, nationalism very quickly and effectively filled the vacuum of legitimacy; the more so as members of the political elite left over from the old system acutely perceived an urgent need for sudden 'conversion': and, given the preconditions, they could hardly find a more convenient and suitable solution than becoming fervent promoters and defenders of the 'national cause'. At the same time, the appeal to nationalism probably also addressed a psychological need, offering some reassurance to people who felt insecure that not everything had changed and that there were some values – such as the national ones – which remained the same. On the other hand, such concepts as 'democracy' or 'freedom', which were to play a key role in the post-communist period, had been emptied of their real content under communism to such an extent that

---

[8] *ibidem.*

an urgent political necessity emerged to overemphasise 'national values', the only ones which seemed to preserve a clear and unaltered meaning to the population.

The negative memory of past homogenisation policies, shared by all the national minorities, concerning especially the last years of Ceausescu's dictatorship, when they indeed had to face a not very remote prospect of complete annihilation as separate ethnocultural entities, led to a rapid political mobilisation of minority groups. This was particularly the case of the ethnic Hungarian organisation, the Hungarian Democratic Union of Romania (UDMR), which was already functioning at the end of 1989. Almost at the same time, however, an intense ethnic Romanian nationalist political activism manifested itself, with a virulent and occasionally aggressive anti-minority discourse, claiming to defend the rights of Romanians in their own country against revisionist threats, and particularly against Hungarian irredentism.

In January 1990, the organisation *Vatra Romaneasca* [Romanian Cradle] (Deletant, 1991, pp. 38-40) was founded. This firmly rejected Hungarian demands for the restoration of past cultural and educational rights, and accused UDMR of an attempt to force the 'enclavisation' of ethnic Hungarians, in order to create a state within the state with the ultimate aim of secession and eventual reunification with Hungary. In a few months, the organisation also formed a political arm – the Party of Romanian National Unity (PUNR), which was intended to serve as a counterbalance to the Hungarian Union. Under the effect of conflicting positions concerning the ethnic issue, particularly on the emotionally charged problem of separating Romanian and Hungarian schools, demonstrations and counter-demonstrations followed, and the situation degenerated into ethnic clashes in March 1990 in the city of Tirgu Mures, with a population almost equally divided between the two ethnic communities. Although a certain degree of stability has been achieved since then, and further violent events have been avoided, the polarisation of society and political life along ethnic lines has remained, since the country's minority problem is still basically unsettled, and the main sources of the tension which generated the Tirgu Mures conflict have not yet been extinguished.

The articles concerning minorities of the 1991 Constitution were adopted in a form which basically reflected a consensus of political forces representing the 'state building' majority population only, rather than being the outcome of a political process based on the equal participation and shared views of all the various ethnic communities. The Constitution approved in November 1991 defined Romania as a 'national state, sovereign, unitary and indivisible' (art.1), where 'the official language is the Romanian language'. (art.13).[9]

The principle of a 'national unitary state', as has been the case in the past, is still regarded as an essential guarantee of stability and territorial integrity. Both the population and the political parties share the concern that the implementation of collective rights on an ethnic basis might be a starting point for further steps towards some kind of territorial autonomy or other form of self-determination, and might lead ultimately to secession. It is worth mentioning in this respect that even ethnic Romanian politicians and analysts who are generally regarded as having a genuinly 'liberal' and 'democratic' outlook on ethnic issues insist on making a firm distinction between those minority rights which can be regarded as rights 'in themselves' and those which might induce further political action (i.e secession). (Mungiu, 1996) Collective rights and territorial autonomy are almost unanimously seen by ethnic Romanian political actors as falling into the latter category.

One of the hardest obstacles to overcome in this respect is the negative psychological effect of the way past historical events are perceived. By far the most important instrument in creating both the Romanian and the Hungarian national identity has been modern historiography. The two nations' rights over Transylvania were characteristically legitimised by arguments which described the other nation as the 'eternal enemy'. Nationalist historians took nations as the unchanging elements of world history, seen in the light of a continuous struggle for liberation from foreign rule, the creation of the modern nation state being viewed as the culmination of this historical process. While rather succesful in mobilising and integrating the members of the titular nation (the 'state-building majority') this strategy excluded minorities – both in real terms and symbolically – from this integration, constantly creating and recreating the image of the minority as the enemy: and thus ensuring political instability and a constant crisis of legitimacy.

Changes in territorial status have appeared for the members of the two communities either as an apotheosis or a tragedy (with the two sides naturally adopting contradictory interpretations). The memory of these shifts produces a sense of insecurity, and is only likely to increase the lack of confidence. As long as history still provides important raw material for

---

[9] 'Constitutia Romaniei' [The Constitution of Romania], in *Adevarul*, 23 Nov 1991.

national political legitimacy it is very hard to make any significant step forward in this highly sensitive field. The transformation of the way history is written should involve a metamorphosis of national self images, as well as of the mutual (and now overwhelmingly negative) perceptions of the 'other'. This should probably mean in essence a gradual reversal of the traditional relationship between present and past, when history has seemed to dominate (at an illusional-ideological level of course) the way of thinking and action of the people.

Secondly, there is an important argument of a pragmatic political nature, shared by part of Romania's political and administrative elite, especially by those who represent the interests of the central bureaucracy: namely, that recognising collective rights and guarantees for the protection of minority identities would diminish their chances to justify state centralism by invoking the 'political necessity' to exercise tight control of minority populated areas; the available means of furthering assimilation policies would diminish, and the current ethnic balance would probably be frozen; there would be much less of a possibility to make non-Romanians a convenient scapegoat for the country's difficulties – as has frequently happened in the past: and it would become more difficult to gain or retain power or political capital by exploiting the ethnic agenda.

Finally, there are also ideological-cultural reasons connected with the historical path of nation-building, which in Romania has resulted in an ethnocentrist, organicist vision of the nation, something now profoundly entrenched in the minds of an overwhelming majority of the population, particularly of the ethnic majority. How deeply seated this way of thinking about the nation is, not just in the mentality of ordinary people, but also in that of a significant part of political and intellectual elite, can be seen by the way members of Romanian majority usually refer to the country's Hungarians. While strongly rejecting any form of collective minority rights, they still often speak of and treat Hungarians as a block, a collective homogeneous entitity, sometimes even invoking the supposed collective responsibility of the Hungarian community for certain events and facts of the past or present. Within the specific logical structure of the traditional nationalist mode of reasoning, the refusal of collective rights and a strong affirmation of collective guilt of the very same minority community seem to complement and reinforce each other. The most extreme version of this type of political discourse even proclaims that in Romania there are only Romanians. Therefore, in accordance with this vision, those who pretend they are Hungarians can enjoy rights like any other Romanians, but only *as* Romanians.

The gap between Romanian and Hungarian views on the relationship between minority and majority, so evident in the debate on individual versus collective rights, manifests itself with the same clarity in the rather different interpretations of the two groups concerning the issue of loyalty to the state. In the Hungarian minority vision loyalty is, above all, a relationship between citizen and state, and therefore it can only belong to the individual, it being absurd to demand it from a whole collectivity. Secondly, loyalty is seen as being conditional on the fulfilment of rights; as the expression of a mutual relationship in which both the state and its citizens have certain obligations and responsibilities to each other. By contrast, the Romanian nation-state's attitude to minorities has always demanded unconditional loyalty. According to this view, while the loyalty of ethnic Romanians is regarded as self-evident, minority citizens, and the minority community as a whole, must demonstrate again and again through the way they act that they are faithful to the state.

What appears at the surface as an opposition of the contractualist vision shared by Hungarian minority representatives and the paternalist conception of Romanian politicians has in fact far deeper roots. According to the East European model of nation building, primary loyalty must always belong to one's own ethnic group, rather than to the state. To Romanians living in Romania this reality is somehow hidden, since to them the relationship between ethnic loyalty and faithfulness to the state 'of their own' is non-problematic (at least as long as the state preserves a biased attitude in favor of the majority ethnic group). However, for minority members the same preconditions might produce a rather different effect. In certain circumstances a dilemma of loyalty might appear, which might implicitly lead to a hierarchisation of loyalties. This is one of the main potential sources which might generate suspicion and produce situations where the minority is denied collective rights, but at the same time is insistently commanded to display collective loyalty.

The split between the Romanian and Hungarian positions concerning ethnic issues and the envisaged status of minorities is widely regarded in influential political circles of both sides as being too deep to be overcome in the foreseeable future; the more so as even 'moderate' leaders of the two communities are inclined to be more sceptical than optimistic about their partners' readiness and real political will to agree on mutually acceptable compromises over questions of principle. Both Romanians and Hungarians regard certain issues as non-negotiable. For Romanians the 'national and unitary character of the state' is sacrosant, while Hungarians cannot conceive any long-term solution without their acceptance as a separate national community, with the right of self-government – which is obviously irreconcilable with the Romanian position. Even those Hungarian ethnic representatives who are considered by their Romanian counterparts as adepts of a more gradual approach maintain that the 'step by step' strategy followed by them does not affect in any sense the basic goals of the Hungarian community, and does not mean a renunciation in any sense, but rather refers only to an optimisation of the available political means.

In spite of the progress which has been achieved in recent years, as a result of the democratisation process and of the participation of ethnic Hungarian political organisation in the government coalition, many deep-rooted historical problems still affect the climate and general state of inter-ethnic relations in Romania today. A civil society able to facilitate the integration of citizens of different ethnic belonging into the political community still needs to be created; the terms of a mutually acceptable compromise between the main national communities have yet to be worked out and agreed upon; and the polarisation of society along nationality lines, with exclusive perceptions of interests and incompatible interpretations of history, still hinder the process of reconciliation and form a serious obstacle in the way of democratic transition and the European integration of the country. For a more encouraging positive development it would be important if the population could experience in everyday life a completely new pattern of interethnic relations, based on equality, partnership and mutual respect. This alone would have an effective chance to succeed, and to bring stability to Romania.

References

Balázs, S. (1993), 'A politikai-jogi viszonyok alakulása' [The evolution of political-legal conditions] in *A Hét*, 17 September.

Bodor, György (1983), *Az 1562 előtti székely nemzetségi szervezetről* [The organisation of the Szekel clans before 1562], Történelmi Szemle.

Boila, Romul (1995), 'A kiegészitett állam átszervezéséről' [On the reorganisation of the enlarged state], in *Szövetség*, 7 January.

Deletant, D. (1991), 'The Role of Vatra Romaneasca in Transylvania', *RFE-RL Research Report*, 1 February.

Gaál, Gábor (ed.) (1986), *Szerkesztette Gaál Gábor*, Korunk Antológia, Magvető Kiadó, Budapest.

Glatz, Ferenc (1992), 'Kisebbségek Romániában', in *História Plusz*.

Glatz, Ferenc (1995), 'Data on Trianon Hungary', in Ferenc Glatz (ed.), *Hungarians and their Neighbours in Modern Times*, Columbia University Press, New York.

Kós, Károly, Zágoni István dr., Paál Árpád dr. (1921), *Kiáltó Szó. A magyarság útja – A politikai aktivitás rendszere* [Cry! The road of the Hungarians – the system of political activity], Cluj-Kolozsvár, Lapkiadó és Nyomdai műintézet R.T.

Macartney, C. A. (1937), *Hungary and Its Successors*, Oxford University Press.

Müller, Georg Eduard (1928), *Die sächsische Nationsuniversität* [The Saxon National Assembly], Hermannstadt.

Müller, Georg Eduard (1941), *Stühle und Distrikte als Unterteilung der siebenbürgisch-deutschen Nationsuniversität, 1141-1876* [Chairs and districts as subdivisions of the Transylvanian German university of nations], Hermannstadt.

Mungiu, Alina (1996), 'Problema democratiei transetnice' [The problem of transethnic democracy], in *Sfera Politicii*, March-April.

Péter, László (ed.) (1992), *Historians and the History of Transylvania*, Columbia University Press, New York.

Schöpflin, G. and Poulton, H. (1990), *Romania's Ethnic Hungarians*, Minority Rights Group Publication, London.

Seton-Watson, R. W. (1943), *Transylvania: a Key-Problem*, Oxford.

Takács, F. (1992), 'A romániai népszámlálás' [The Romanian census], in *Heti Magyarország 7*.

Vécsey, K. (1992), 'Asszimiláció és kivándorlás' [Assimilation and emigration], in *Romániai Magyar Szó*, August 1-2.

3 Transformations of Ethnic Identity: the Case of the Bulgarian Pomaks

MADELEINE DANOVA

Introduction

The research carried out on the Pomak group in Bulgaria has aimed to shed new light on the identification processes among one of the most controversial minority groups in Bulgarian history.[1] The controversy is primarily due to the unresolved issue of their ethnic origin: there exist at least two theories of how the group has come into existence. Some scholars claim that the Pomaks are descendants of Christians once forced into converting to Islam; others insist on their Asian origin, or on their gradual conversion to Islam. Therefore, in order to proceed further with the research, it was necessary to collect enough empirical material to have serious grounds for discussing the issues, before making any theoretical conclusions and before suggesting a possible model of identity construction within the group.

The research can be formally divided into four stages. The first stage involved the process of collecting historical and sociological data concerning the origin and the present state (both economic and cultural) of the Pomaks. It turned out that due to the enormous quantity of literature on that subject,[2] this stage took most of the research time. The second stage was mainly given up to the location of the different Pomak communities inside and outside Bulgaria and their investigation. The third stage (which in some sense was carried out as a preliminary stage as well) was mainly devoted to building up a theoretical framework within which to analyse the concept of identity and in particular the concept of ethnic identity. The

---

[1] It is interesting to look at the other Balkan countries as well, where the Pomaks, as they are known in Greece too, and the Bosniaks (the Muslims in Bosnia) have always appeared to be among the most 'troublesome' groups in Balkan history. (For a more detailed account of the attitude of the Balkans historians to these groups see (Желязкова, 1997).

[2] See the references at the end of this paper.

147

fourth and final stage saw the putting down in writing of all the facts gathered, their analysis and interpretation, and the formulation of final conclusions. It will be difficult to follow these stages of research in this exact sequence in what follows, but it is inevitable that they will determine to a large extent the structure of the present chapter, even though in many places the research findings from the first stage will be intermingled with some later theoretical conclusions or constructs.

Historical, Socio-economic and Cultural Description of the Pomaks

The Bulgarian-born Nobel Prize winner Elias Canetti, in his book *The Human Province,* wrote about national history as consisting of 'walls in the wrong places' and 'heroes who died for them, and their posterity, who pull the borders away from under their graves' (p. 20). This seems to describe Bulgarian history very well, especially in relation to the situation of the Pomak group. No other group in Bulgarian history has been so diversely treated by historians, ethnographers, social anthropologists and (a typically Bulgarian or Balkan phenomenon?) politicians as this group of people speaking Bulgarian as their mother tongue and of Islamic confession, living in the high-mountain regions of the Rhodope mountains and in some of the central regions of the Balkan range. Their language and religion seem to have built these 'wrong walls', hampering both their self-identification and their inclusion in the 'national' history of Bulgaria.

Giving an explanation of the question why it is that in modern society, which is expected to present, more or less, an entropic picture, some nations are still not unified, homogeneous and centred, Ernest Gellner points out two basic reasons, namely 'barriers to communication', and the presence of factors that he calls 'inhibitors to social entropy' (Gellner, 1990, pp. 63-87). An attempt will be made to explain the existence of the Pomaks in Bulgaria first of all in these terms.

As has already been mentioned, the Pomaks live predominately in isolated, island-like communities either in the higher regions of the Rhodopes and of the Balkan range or in some mixed communities in the lower parts of these mountains. Due to internal migration in Bulgaria there are also members of the group who have settled in some of the big cities throughout the country; but these are exceptions. Especially interesting is the region of the Rhodopes, which has traditionally attracted a lot of researchers, both in the past and the present. That is why the literature on this part of the Pomak group is so vast and so controversial. There is no doubt, however, that the group has always been viewed as largely predetermined by its geographical isolation, one of the several 'barriers to communication' Gellner speaks about. An interesting hypothesis has been developed recently by some of the scholars studying this group, namely that the mountains/plains dichotomy can be seen as a local variant of the primitive society/civilization dichotomy, and thus can be used in the explanation of the ethnocultural processes affecting the Pomaks.[3]

Another 'barrier to communication' can be found in the fact that the people from this group have been primarily engaged in agricultural activities, the growing of tobacco being their main occupation in the Rhodope mountains, as well as mining and construction. Due to their geo-cultural situation they have had a lower standard of living than the rest of the population, and a marginal social status. This is clearly shown in the last census, from the end of 1992, which gives some of the highest percentages of people with primary education only in the regions where the Pomaks live.[4]

Pursuing the argument as put by Gellner we can look at the 'inhibitors to social entropy', which have played a decisive role in the constitution of the Pomak community. For Gellner these inhibitors are either genetic features (which are not of any significance in the case of the Pomaks); or religious and cultural habits of population groups, which, as in our case, are as powerful as the genetic ones; or language, which also matters, but which, as Gellner says, 'can be easily shed off'. This seems to be exactly the case of the Pomaks. What has formed and preserved the group as a separate one throughout history has been their distinctive religious and cultural habits, together with the ambiguous status of their language.

In order to understand the exact meaning of this we have to look into the history of this community, so that a fuller understanding of these religious and cultural habits can be achieved. Due to political circumstances and pressures, the origin of the Pomak group has been defined in different ways. We can group the hypotheses in two large groups. The first group is made up of scholars who put the stress on the

[3] For the development of this thesis see (Алексиев, 1994).
[4] In the Kirdjali region, for example, where 65·7 per cent of the population are Turks and Pomaks, the percentage of the people with primary education only is the highest in the country: 37·1 per cent.

forced mass Islamisation of large groups of Bulgarians. This process started, they claim, with the colonisation of the Bulgarian lands by the Ottomans at the end of the 14th century, and continued with great vigour through the 15th, 16th and especially 17th centuries.[5] That was the chief force in the creation of a separate community within the boundaries of the Ottoman Empire, which would become known as the Pomaks. This group of scholars use as their sources official Ottoman documents as well as local chronicles.[6] This was a very popular thesis during the 1980s, and it saw its culmination in the so-called 'returning to the origins' [възродителен процес] process instigated by the communist regime in the mid- and late 1980s: it was used as the scientific rationale behind the forced change of identity of the Muslims in Bulgaria.

Though this theory was based on substantial empirical research, which helped to reveal a lot of unknown sources concerning the process of Islamisation throughout the Bulgarian lands[7] during the five centuries of Ottoman domination, the fact that the conclusions were phrased in such a way as to serve the communist regime made many of them come under severe attack immediately after the socio-political changes of 1989. The conclusions drawn on the basis of the local chronicles about the forced mass Islamisation of the population of the Rodophe mountains have come under particularly critical scrutiny.[8] The most often cited and discussed chronicle among the three main local chronicles used as sources, the Chronicle of Metodi Draginov, an Orthodox priest from Chepino,[9] has been called a fake in an extensive linguistic study by I. Todorov. He claims that it was a literary mystification executed by Stoyan Zahariev on the basis of the really existing chronicle of Gorno Belovo. The motivation for one of the most renowned 19th century researchers of the Rhodope area, Stoyan Zahariev,[10] to invent a whole chronicle could be explained by the

---

[5] Cf. the official History of Bulgaria (История на България, 1983-5).

[6] See the whole collection of articles of the Bulgarian Academy of Sciences. (Янков, 1988)

[7] Due to the zeal of these scholars to prove the correctness of the official doctrine of the 'loss' of Bulgarian identity as a result of mass Islamisation, a lot of new documents, such as official registers, and documents connected with the collection of taxes and property rights issued by Ottoman authorities, have been made available to the scholarly public. (Велков и Радушев, 1988, p. 57)

[8] (Zhelyazkova, 1990)

[9] The others are another chronicle from the village of Gorno Belovo, and another one known as the Batkuninskiya Chronicle.

[10] His most famous work is Географико-историко-статистическо описание на Татар-Пазарджишката кааза. [Geographical, historical and statistical survey of Tatar-Pazardjik kaaza]. (Захариев, 1870)

nationalist movement gathering momentum at that time in Bulgarian lands, and by the need to consolidate all the different regional groups into what Anderson would term a century later 'an imagined community', (Anderson, 1991) by asserting their common origin.

The group of scholars who do not accept the theory of the forceful mass Islamisation of Bulgarians through the centuries would see the process of the formation of the Pomak group as a very long process of identity formation, which started with isolated cases during the 16th century, and continued through the whole of the 17th century, with a certain speeding-up of the process during the second half of the century. This is evident from the official tax registers from that time. All the Christian households were listed in these registers, so that the number of households who had to pay the tax known as *ciziye* could be assessed. Whenever a household became Muslim it was erased from these registers, and the tax was re-distributed among the other Christian households from the village or the town. In the second half of the 17th century the number of Christian households decreased dramatically (in some regions by 50, 60, and even 70 per cent) (Христов, 1989, p. 31). But this need not signal a direct and forceful mass Islamisation, as authors engaged in communist policies tried to conclude. The reasons were political as well as economic, and this change of confession was either the individual choice of a person or a family, or of a whole village – especially in the case of the so-called *vakif* villages, which were part of the system of *Yuruk* settlements (Желязкова, 1997).

My own conclusion, very close to that of B. Alexiev (Алексиев, 1994, p. 235), is that economic factors were the main reason for the turning of these people to Islam. What explains the fact that it was these regions in particular (the Rhodope mountains, the Lovetch region in the Balkan mountains, etc.) where the percentage of the converts was so high, is both the daily co-existence with other Muslims, and the great difficulty these people experienced in earning their living in these mountainous regions. Most of them were seasonal workers or shepherds who had to seek work far from their homes, in the affluent towns and plains of Thrace.[11] So it was impossible for them to pay any increased taxes, and conversion to Islam may have been the only way out for them.

That all these people acted out of necessity rather than out of religious fervour is confirmed also by the phenomenon known as crypto-

---

[11] (Георгиева, 1994, p. 216)

Christianity which is observed among some of the Pomaks (Желязкова, 1997, p. 33). This phenomenon characterised some of the Greek Pomaks at first, and then it became common among Albanian converts and Bulgarian Pomaks too. It is associated with the secret practice of many Christian customs and traditions in the everyday life of newly-converted Muslims. This was helped by the predominance of unofficial syncretic religious cults, retaining elements from old pagan traditions, among the local Muslims (Желязкова, 1997, p. 39). A very interesting phenomenon in that respect is the secret cross which can be found on many of the tombstones of the Pomaks, and which cannot be seen because it is under the ground.

Even if we assume that the problem of the origin of the Pomaks can be settled in a more balanced way nowadays, there are a lot of other issues which remain problematic. First there is the name of the group. The name 'Pomaks' is often considered both by members of the group and by members of other ethnic groups to have a pejorative connotation. It is derived from Bulgarian words which are associated with the conversion of these people to Islam, which was an abandonment of the 'true faith': 'helper' of the Turks [помагач - помак], or people who were 'lured' by the new regime [помамвам, помамил се] or have renounced their faith [пометнал се], or 'imitate', 'follow' [мъкна се, помъкнал се по чужда вяра] the other Muslims. On the other hand, the Turks called them 'half-faithful' [*yarim dinly*] or simply 'traitors to their religion and country' [*donme*] (Панайотова, 1994, p. 274). That is why another name has emerged, and the group quite often identifies itself as 'Bulgarian-Mohammedan' (which has remained as a kind of official name for the group throughout the years), as if in an attempt to stress the two-sidedness of its identification: Bulgarian because of the language they speak and Mohammedan because they are Muslims.[12]

Another aspect of the question of names is the fact that within the group, especially in the Rhodope region, there are many other names given to some of the smaller Pomak communities [ахряни - *Ahrids*, рупци, казълбаши - *kazilbas*]. This uncertainty as far as one of the basic components of one's identity is concerned, the name, is not accidental. It is present in the many aspects of their group history and everyday lives. One of the most telling examples is the way this group has been treated in

---

[12] It is curious to note the opinion of one of the young scholars working on these questions, B. Alexiev, who insists on calling them 'Bulgarian Muslims' because the other name sounds inferior: derived as it is from the name of just one of the prophets and not from the name of God's son as is the case with Christianity. (Алексиев, 1994, p. 64)

official censuses after 1878. In the 1880, 1885, and 1888 censuses they were included under the heading 'Turks'. After the inclusion of the variable 'nationality'[13] in the census of 1900, in 1905 they were differentiated from other Muslims under the heading 'Pomaks'. During the first Balkan War, in 1912 and 1913, the government tried to force them into converting to Christianity and changing their Islamic names, which was undone in the following year. During the 1930s there was a revival of the attempts to make the Pomaks feel like a part of the Bulgarian nation, or in other words to make them drop the second part of their official name. The most active organisation during this period was the voluntary organisation of the Pomaks in the Rhodope mountain, 'Motherland' [„Родина"]. The Koran was translated into Bulgarian, the religious organisations of the Pomaks were separated from the main religious body of the Bulgarian Turks, and new-born Pomaks were given Bulgarian but non-Christian names during the seven years of the existence of this organization. Up to 1944 about two-thirds of the Pomaks had changed their names.[14]

This ambiguity has continued, and it is very clearly expressed in the fact that though the census of 1992 included the three variables of *ethnicity* (or 'nationality', as the older term went), *mother tongue* and *religion*, once again there was no separate heading for the Pomaks. The ethnic groups mentioned in the census were Bulgarians, Turks, Gypsies and Others. Under 'others' the people identified themselves as either *Pomaks, Bulgarian-Mohammedans* or *Bulgarian Muslims*. A representative sample published in 1993 gave the following figures: total number of people 8,472,724; of whom 7,206,062 (85· 1 per cent) identified themselves as Bulgarians, 822,253 as Turks, 287,732 as Gypsies and 91,131 as 'Others'. In the last group we can probably include the Pomaks as well, the uncertainty coming from the fact that while some of them did identify themselves as Turks, from cross-comparison with the language variable it is evident that they did not speak Turkish. What is strange, however, is that in the Statistical Yearbook for 1995 in the chart of the 'population by ethnic group', once again we find that there is no such

---

[13] The other two variables used were mother tongue and religion. All three categories continued to be used until 1934. After the 1946 census religion was not used till 1992. The other two continued to be used till 1975. (Национален статистически институт, 1993)

[14] For more details concerning the work of this organization see (Панайотова, 1994, pp. 276-7).

ethnic group as the Pomaks. The groups listed, beside the three major ethnic groups in Bulgaria already mentioned are: Tatar, Jewish, Armenian, Circassian, and Gagauz. The total number of these, 70,499, however, is less than the number of the people in the group of the 'Other'.

Other Bulgarian scholars, such as Mihail Ivanov and Ilona Tomova, have tried to give a somewhat clearer picture of how these people have identified themselves. According to them, from the group of Bulgarian Muslims (distinguished from the other ethnic groups by its Bulgarian language and its Muslim religion) 70,251 identified themselves as Bulgarians. Another group of people, 65,546, identified themselves as Bulgarian-Mohammedans, Pomaks, or Muslims, and were put down under the general name of Bulgarian-Mohammedans (but, as we have seen, appeared as 'others' in the Statistical Yearbook for 1995). Still another group of people, 25,540, identified themselves as Turks. Thus, according to Ivanov and Tomova, we should include in this group another 35,000 people who had identified themselves as Turks and Muslims but for whom, without asking them, the interviewers had put down Turkish as their mother tongue. So very roughly speaking we can say that 60,000 of the Muslims speaking Bulgarian as their mother tongue have been identified as Turks in the census (Иванов, Томова, 1994, p. 23).

If we assume that these figures can be accepted, we can say that the Pomaks would emerge as the fourth largest ethnic group in Bulgaria, with about 200,000 people. On the other hand accepting this figure involves an element of speculation, since unless they were openly asked to identify themselves as Pomaks, the group could well also include some Gypsies who for one reason or another have renounced their real mother tongue and have declared Bulgarian as their mother tongue, although they are Muslims and therefore identify themselves as Turks (and are for that reason also less likely to identify themselves as Bulgarians).

Another important aspect of this group which should be mentioned is the fact that even their monolinguality has recently been challenged. One of the 'firm' distinguishing features of the group has always been the fact that they have remained monolingual throughout their history.[15] Nowadays, however, we observe the phenomenon of some Pomaks claiming Turkish

---

[15] Cf., for example (Шишков, 1936, p. 11).

as the 'forgotten' mother-tongue of the group, something which is also clearly expressed in the census.[16]

B. Aleksiev also talks about bilingualism among the Pomaks, but his idea is different. For him the fact that all the local toponyms are of Turkish origin, that the family relations are described with Turkish words, and that there is a marked uncertainty in the use of gender in the Pomak dialects, speaks of a latent bilingualism (Алексиев, 1994, p. 232.). In my opinion this is pushing things too far, since the very definition of bilingualism is the ability of individuals to *speak* two languages, and obviously the concept does not lend itself to such a stretching of its boundaries. Probably if the phenomenon is considered under a broader definition, as a *bilinguality* or *diglossia* which can accomodate different linguistic and non-linguistic levels, such as different relative competence in both languages, complex cognitive organisation, different ages of acquisition, the presence of different language communities speaking the languages used to different degrees of competence by an individual, as well as different social-cultural status and cultural identity for the languages in question (Hamers and Blanc, 1992), then we can understand it better.

The last problem to be dealt with in this section is the cultural heritage of the Pomaks. One of the reason for the constant preoccupation of Bulgarian scholars with this group is their unique place in the folk tradition, both as a rich reservoir of authentic and extremely colourful folklore, and as one of the main 'heroes' (or rather 'anti-heroes') in folklore tales and songs. Their archaic rituals and life-style also make them very attractive for ethnographers and anthropologists.[17] The problem with many of these scholars who have worked among the Pomaks is their attempt to see only the features which can be related to some pre-historic

---

[16] There is a vast quantity of press materials I have collected in recent years concerning this phenomenon. For example, in an interview with Ibrahim Kadri, one of the co-ordinators of the Turkish political party in Bulgaria (The Movement for Rights and Freedoms), Slavcho Vodenicharov, a journalist from Radio Blagoevgrad, was told the same thing - that all these people are just Rhodope Turks. His interview with two Bulgarian-Mohammedans and two Turkish children from the village of Dabnitza after that seem to refute this (в-к „Дума" , бр. 114, 19. 05. 1993, p. 12). A similar article appeared in the opposition newspaper, *Democratzia*, from about the same time, under the title *The Towns of Gotze Delchev and Yakoruda are being Turkified* (в-к „Демокрация", бр. 117, 22. 05. 1993, p. 1).

[17] I use these two terms, which for such practical matters as the collecting of foklore materials and recording of customs and traditions may not seem to differ much, for the sake of scholarly precision, since there is a great difference between the way that 'ethnographers' from Eastern Europe and Russia will analyse and interpret their findings and the way this will be done by Western 'anthropologists'.

or Christian folk past and not to push to the foreground such elements as could speak directly for the group's different religious identity. Thus the fate of the Pomaks, in history and in the present, has always been to provide a means of mobilising national myths for the Bulgarians.

This is very clearly expressed in the mythological paradigms which the Pomaks usually provide in Bulgarian folklore. There are at least two such mythological paradigms. One is the mythic event of not renouncing one's Christian faith even if that means death, and the other is connected with the legendary heroes who heroically tried to fight the Ottoman conquerors. In the former case there appear quite often people who have renounced their faith and become Muslims. In many of these cases they are called not just Muslims or Pomaks but 'Turkified' [„потурчили се"]. This is true for all folklore songs, chronicles and legends, even articles from the 19th century and later. Thus their conversion is assumed to have automatically led to the loss of their 'nationality', or at least of their Bulgarian ethnic identity. To this most pitiful state is opposed the heroic example of the 'martyrs' of Christianity ready to die for the 'righteousness' of their faith.[18]

The other paradigm is even more interesting. It includes the so-called heroic ballads and legends in which there are historical figures who have acquired mythic qualities in their fight against the Ottoman conquerors. Why I find them relevant is because in the most famous cycle of these ballads the hero has the name of a feudal lord from one of the mediæval kingdoms in the Balkans who became a subject of the Sultan after the Ottoman conquest and died in a battle between the Christians and the Muslims, fighting on the side of the latter. But in the folk ballads he is

---

[18] There are a lot of examples of such songs and legends, but probably one of the most widespread variants recorded in the Western parts of the Rhodope mountains starts with a conversation between the Ottoman Muslim Turks and the Bulgarian hero about whether he is ready to give his sister into Islam. Here is the text:

> - Море, даваш ли, даваш, Никола,
> хубава Яна на турцка вера?
> - Море, глава си давам, войводо,
> Яна не давам на турцка вера! -
> Та му отсекоха едната ръка,
> море, та па го питат и го разпитват.

The 'conversation' ends with the maiming of the Bulgarian, who says farewell to his sister, who will become a Muslim, without being able to walk her away, to hug her or to see her for the last time. There are other variants of the same story, the most famous being a literary version by one of the great Bulgarian poets from the first decades of the newly formed Bulgarian kingdom, Pencho Slaveikov.

the hero [*юнак*] who takes care of the conquered and maltreated Christians, and frees them from Ottoman slavery (one of the most famous motifs in these ballads is the setting free of 'three chains of Christian slaves' [*три синджира роби*]) by using his super-human skills and attributes. There is more than mere curiosity involved in the attempt to explain such a transformation. For me one of the possible explanations is the fact that for the folk consciousness it was impossible to associate heroic behaviour with the denial of one's religion, which was always assumed to be the most degrading act in human life. This myth could be also taken as one of the heroic myths which every *ethnie*, to use Anthony Smith's term (Smith, 1991), needs in order to constitute its heroic past, which can then be used in the constitution of the national consciousness. This also gives us basis for the subsequent understanding of the processes of identification within the Pomak group.

As far as other aspects of the traditional culture of this group are concerned, there is a predominant view that most of the traditions and customs of the Pomaks, though based on the canons of Islam, share many features in common with the traditional Christian culture (Благоев, 1994; Кальонски, 1994).[19] Most of the studies are devoted primarily to these common features, and distinctions are found mainly in the way of dressing, and in the organisation of the architectural space as a socio-cultural space (Алексиев, 1994, p. 92; Стоилов, 1994). In Bulgarian *belles lettres*, the image of this region is mainly built up in a picturesque tradition as archaic and very isolated from modern times. One of the explanations offered in regard to the conservatism and the closeness of the traditional way of life of the Pomaks, both in the Rhodope mountains and in the Balkan mountains, is that it is primarily connected with their economic status[20] and their geographic situation.

---

[19] Another very interesting collection is the recently published ethnographic history of the Rhodope mountains: (Родопи. Традиционна народна духовна и социо-нормативна култура, София, 1994). Some important aspects of the Pomak culture are also discussed in (Родопа и Родопска област. [Rodopa and Rodopska oblast]. В чест на Ст. Н. Шишков за 70г. от рождението му и полувинвековната му културна дейност, София, 1935).

[20] Cf. the whole chapter „Етнически отношения и икономика" [Ethnic relationships and economy] in (Аспекти…1994, pp. 59-111).

Locating Pomak Communities and Field Work Among Them

Before any field work begins there should be some hypotheses formulated which are to be tested during this stage of the research work. Also it is very important to choose research methods which could provide the best answer to the determined tasks, and the circumstances of the conducting of the field work: such as the fact that it had to be conducted by a single researcher, interviewing people who might be unwilling or not sufficiently experienced to answer any pre-determined set of questions. Thus, it seemed that the quantitative methods of sociological research could be more of an obstacle than an advantage. The limited time was also a hindrance, since it did not allow for the employment of the very successful and much used nowadays qualitative method of the life-history interview. So the main method chosen was the free conversation, during which some questions prepared in advanced could be slipped in.

Limitations like this demanded that there should be some preliminary elucidation of the situation to be investigated. That was why all the questions and interview tactics were prepared on the basis of a survey carried out in 1992, the aim of which was to clarify the ethnocultural situation in Bulgaria (Георгиев *et al.*, 1993). This survey was carried out among 3,227 people, of whom 765 were Christian Bulgarians, 826 Turks, 797 Pomaks and 777 Gypsies. The survey is very detailed, with more than 50 questions, which provide enough basis both for some conclusions and for further analysis.

I was mainly interested in questions aimed either directly at the Pomak respondents, or asking for the attitudes of the other three groups towards them. The conclusion of the research team in respect to the Pomak community is that it is subjected to complex processes of seeking their own ethnic identity. According to the survey, one sixth of the Pomaks interviewed (who lived in the municipalities of Gotze Delchev, Yakoruda, Satovcha, Velingrad, Garmen and Madan) were in the process of renouncing their ethnic identity and of acquiring a new, Turkish, identity. The way to do that was to claim Turkish as their mother tongue. Though only 6 per cent of them would claim to know it, 18 per cent said that Turkish was their mother tongue, a language they had forgotten because of the acculturation policies of the Bulgarian governments after 1912. Another small part of this group were in the process of coining a new identity as belonging to a specific ethnic group – Muslims, Aryans, Pomaks

– as distinctly different from the Bulgarian and Turkish ones. The chief differentiating characteristics in this case was their religion.

The survey also concluded that the largest part of the Pomaks had a firm Bulgarian national consciousness, were proud of their unique Bulgarian language, which had preserved archaic grammatical and lexical forms, boasted of their carefully observed traditions in dress and handcrafts and, moreover, quite often talked about themselves as the 'purest Bulgarians'. Conversion to Christianity was seen as a way to enhance this identification and that is why another six percent of the Pomaks, mainly from the Central and Eastern Rhodopes, declared their choice to return to the Christian religion of their ancestors.

A last, very important conclusion from the survey is the fact that the Pomaks were the group towards which the other three ethnic groups were least biased and most tolerant. In their turn, the Pomaks shared the extremely negative attitude of the other two groups towards the Gypsies, and displayed a negative attitude towards the majority group of the Bulgarians.

Thus the primary goal of the field work was formulated as the testing of these attitudes among the people three years later in order to see if the situation had changed, especially in respect to the ethnic identification of the group.

It is clear from all the material collected and presented here that one of the most interesting places to investigate in respect to the Pomak group is the Rhodope region. As has already been pointed out it was impossible for a lone researcher to cover a very great area in her field work, so I chose the town of Velingrad as one of the places where all the aspects of the life of this community meet: namely, the interplay between high mountain regions and river valleys, between villages and towns, and the tensions in the ethnic identification which the survey suggested. Moreover, Velingrad is a town which was formed in 1948 out of three Pomak villages: Kamenitsa, Lazhdane and Chepino.

An important aspect of the region is not only that there are a lot of Pomak villages near Velingrad but also the fact that only 26 km away is the town of Batak, a place which saw a most atrocious bloodbath resulting in the massacre of almost the whole Christian population of the town by

Pomak and bashibazouk hordes during the April Uprising of 1876.[21] Though a century and more has passed I was interested in possible distant echoes of this event.[22]

Trying to avoid possible limitations arising from the preoccupation of scholars with this particular region, and also in search of more facts and new data, I decided to visit some of the Balkan villages near the town of Troyan and near Lovetch, which are known to have been Pomak settlements for many centuries. In this way it seemed to me that some useful correctives could be found and a new, comparative perspective introduced.

Through the course of doing the research an interesting problem emerged. There started appearing in the press a lot of articles on 'the insistence of the Greek authorities' (as the Bulgarian media said) on the existence of one distinctive Pomak 'nation' in both the Greek and Bulgarian parts of the Rhodopes. These articles began to appear during the spring of 1997. This led me to a re-adjustment of the schedule of my field work in order to take into consideration this new issue.

All the conversations, most of which were quite informal, which I had mainly with early-middle-aged people from Velingrad confirmed the conclusions of the previous research. First, the majority of the people did not want to appear different from the rest, either in their language or in their names, customs and traditions. Some of them took great pains to explain the origin of their names, which were in most cases non-Christian Bulgarian. Somehow they did not want to leave any doubt in their listener's mind that they were just ordinary Bulgarian people.[23] When finally some were provoked to reveal their ethnic background they would tend to start boasting of some of the unique aspects of their culture. All of them showed great tolerance as far as the customs and traditions of the other ethnic groups were concerned, and said they would never object to intermarriages. In one of them there was felt a sort of 'imagined' link with

---

[21] The massacre caused a great reverberation throughout Europe and eventually led to the Russian-Turkish War of 1878, which saw the Liberation of the Bulgarian lands; it is, in fact, an indispensable part of the national discourse in Bulgaria.

[22] This can be assumed to be a somewhat exaggerated expectation, since just a few years after the massacre the leader of the hordes took part in one of the common religious festivals in the region. Moreover there are many examples of Pomaks who helped the Bulgarians in their struggle against the Ottoman Empire.

[23] A very telling example was with a woman who insisted on being called by her pet name which, being derived from the Bulgarian word for 'lamb', sounded much more Bulgarian than her full, Muslim name.

the Pomaks from the Greek regions expressed in the sentence: 'Yes, there are a lot of us!'[24] but the others just talked about the many similarities in their folk costumes and customs, as well as about the isolation and backwardness of the Pomak villages on both sides of the border. It should be stressed that among the people I met the folk traditions both in dress and everyday life have become a museum artefact. There was a woman who showed me how she would dress on some of the big traditional holidays including St. George's Day (which both Muslims and Christians in this area celebrate) but that was felt as a ritual, sacred act meant as a way of reaching out for another not profane but sacred area of human life.

There were, however, a lot of women from the nearby Pomak villages who wore their 'shalvars', the traditional part of the everyday clothing of Muslim women, and their scarves covered their faces almost completely. This suggests that the globalisation of modern life, which takes place mainly in the towns and cities, is one of the decisive factors for the loss of some deeply rooted customs and traditions.

It is important that most of the people were *offended* when they were directly asked if they were Pomaks. They themselves considered it a very pejorative term, and they would only admit the fact that they were Muslims but not Turks. There was in some cases strong antipathy against the Turks, who were blamed for some of the recent misfortunes of the people from the region: but none of the grievances seemed to have any bearing on the historical facts. I did not come across any respondent who would claim a Turkish identity, but some of the people pointed out to some of the young women in the streets dressed in the traditional Muslim way as belonging to the Pomak group. As a whole the attitude towards them was negative. It is important to say that all the people I talked to in Velingrad had graduated from high school.

The situation in the villages from the Troyan region was quite different. Not only were the people there dressed as Muslims, but their first answer to the question about their ethnic identity was that they were Turks. In some cases these people would never admit to having anything in common with the Pomaks. They seemed to be more zealous in their religious activities than the Turks themselves, and only the fact that they did not know the dialect of Turkish used by the local Turks revealed their

---

[24] Some other researchers, like Tz. Georgieva (op.cit.) have recorded a similar phrase in other regions, which makes one take this for a cliché rather than for a genuine product of a chauvinist ideology.

ethnic origin. Two things should be taken into consideration here. Firstly, that there were a lot of young people among them, and secondly that not all of the people I talked to had graduated from high school. They insisted on their Turkish names as well as on their archaic traditions. As a whole they felt somehow betrayed by the state, at least economically, and they considered their new identity as a way to escape their sordid economic conditions. However, there seemed to have occurred a certain 'retreat' from any ethnic identification in some of them because the only answer they would give was that being one or another would not help them find money for their daily bread. There is nothing about these people in the media and they are right to view themselves as totally neglected by society. This makes them cling to their traditional culture, and highlight any elements in it which express their difference, as a symbolic protest against the neglect of the official authorities.

This seems to be the case with the Greek Pomaks as well, who seem to have been used as a political trump card to be produced at the right moment. The villages I visited in the region of Xanthi looked very much like the villages of the Bulgarian Pomaks, with the exception that in some respects they seemed even poorer. The people there have preserved their traditional culture, which is a curious mixture of Christian and Islamic elements. The language they speak is very much like the language of the Bulgarian Pomaks from the other side of the mountain, but with a lot of Greek and Turkish words in it. According to different researchers the Greek Pomaks number around 34 978, which is 33· 5 per cent of the Muslims in Greece, or under 30 000 (Христакудис, 1992, p. 52).[25]

Unfortunately, I did not manage to talk to these people much. One of the reasons was their deep suspicion and even fear, which would need a longer time to overcome. Another reason was their inability to understand my Bulgarian (though this could have been a pretext for not answering the questions). Thus the time spent there left an impression of some very archaic past which refuses to be modernised or is deliberately kept in a kind of pre-capitalist economy. One of the reasons could be the system of 'vakifs', which does not allow the Muslim population to sell or buy land

---

[25] It is interesting that this article gives only the official point of view for the situation of the Greek Pomaks: which could be partly due to the fact of their predominant part being of Bulgarian origin; while Hugh Poulton gives a very interesting account of the situation of the Greek Pomaks and the way they have been treated as second-class citizens, having no right of free movement or of free buying and selling of their lands. (Poulton, 1991, p. 183).

out of this system. Though there has been a lot of research done on this subject, as my studies at Thessaloniki University suggested, Hugh Poulton is right in claiming that there is an official reticence about giving figures for ethnic minorities. Quite often 'official Greek sources tend to claim that the Turks are Pomaks or Muslim Greeks while conversely the Turks claim the Pomaks as Turks' (Poulton, 1991, pp.182-183).

All this very much reminds me of the situation in Bulgaria where there were moments, as has already been described, when the Pomaks seemed to present a threat both to the communists and to their opponents in 1993 and to the state and the people in 1996.[26]

Theoretical Framework

It is clear from all the gathered empirical facts that the most ambiguous question in relation to the Pomak community in Bulgaria is the one concerning their group and individual identity. 'Identity' has quite often been viewed as one of the 'eternal' human needs. This is so partly because one of the most secure places has always seemed to be the reassuring 'we' as opposed to the threatening otherness of 'they'. But as Zygmunt Bauman says, this 'we' 'must be powerful or it won't be gratifying.' Thus the personal identity tends to depend greatly on a powerful 'we' identity. The experience of identity, however, is not always universal, and it becomes more intense with the increase of competition.

Competitive challenge makes any identity seem precarious; and the one comfort identity is expected to offer is self-confidence, certainty, 'knowing where one stands'. One would expect, therefore, the *search* for identity to be at its most intense when identity is not to be taken placidly, as a gift of blood and soil; when it appears instead fluid, pliable, located in the not-yet-accomplished future instead of in the already-too-late-to-be-tinkered-with past. By and large, this is what happens at a time of rapid change – when new forms of life emerge too fast to be absorbed and domesticated by the old mechanisms of control and ancient mental frames (Bauman, 1992, pp. 679-80).

---

[26] A recent example is the sensation that some articles in the press caused by claiming that one of ex-President Zhelyo Zhelev's advisers, Kamen Burov, after attending a seminar on ethnicity in the USA, was 'instructed' by the Americans to prepare a map of the Pomak 'nationality' which has been kept secret since then. Mr. Zhelev later denied having known anything whatsoever about such a map.

This seems especially relevant for the Pomak group. It supplies the necessary focus in the otherwise eclectic attempts to explain the identification processes within the group. It is exactly because their identity is not only one of 'blood and soil' that the fluctuations in it are so great. And it is an identity which should be considered not as 'given' or primordial (which has been the attempt of many scholars so far)[27] but as one in the process of formation, very much like the identity of modernity which is evasive, melting down the solidity of the old[28] stable world of moral judgements and attitudes.

Therefore, this last part of the chapter will try to look at ethnic identity both as *ethnic change* – to use Donald Horowitz's term (in Glazer and Moynihan, 1975, p. 114) – and as *maintenance of a boundary* as Frederik Barth defines it (Barth, 1969). This will help us understand the ethnic identity of the Bulgarian Pomaks in a more subtle way, as part of the postmodern world of de-centred identities, as filling in the 'in-betweens' of culture, which in its turn is a necessary condition for 'narrating the nation' as Homi Bhabha defines it (Bhabha, 1994). Thus the term 'ethnic identity' will come closer to 'cultural identity' and to Stuart Hall's understanding of the way modern group identities are constructed, de-constructed and re-constructed (in Rutherford, 1990). Moreover, it is very important in the age of multiculturalism to be able to look at identity construction from the point of view of the minority group as well, and not only to use discourses belonging to the dominant groups in society, as Charles Taylor suggests (Taylor, 1994).

There is, however, still another problem when we come to the theoretical aspect of the Pomaks' identity. Scholars studying the group seem to have been engaged in a constant play with terms they consider to be interchangeable: nation, nationality, national identity, ethnicity, ethnic identity, and cultural identity. In the process of doing this research it became more and more clear that the only way to understand what was going on within the community itself as well as outside it was to look 'behind' these terms and 'unveil' their meaning. This, of course, is a

---

[27] I have already mentioned some of the theories of the origin of the Pomaks as the central question in all of the discussions of the group within the national discourse in Bulgaria, but especially telling are such examples as Kemal Karpat's hypothesis of their Turkic origins ('blood' as the common denominator) (Karpat, 1990) and all the theories which stress primarily the Islamisation of a native Bulgarian populace as the chief factor in the genealogy of the group ('soil' as the common denominator).

[28] I use the very powerful methaphor of Marshall Berman, from his book *All That Is Solid Melts into Air*, based on Marx's image of modern times (Berman, 1992).

problem encountered by scholars in all fields who 'face mounting ambiguity in their use of keywords because new meanings are continuously stipulated for them by scholars unwilling to coin new terms and face resulting criticism'. (Riggs, 1992, p. 281)

The first to open a wide debate on ethnicity were Glazer and Moynihan. The contributors to their collection of essays, *Ethnicity*, discussed a great variety of topics, but of special interest for the present study has been Horowitz's essay on 'Ethnic Identity'. He concentrated on the processes of ethnic fusion and fission rather than on ethnic identity as a stable, solid category within a community. He identified four major processes: of amalgamation and incorporation, both part of the broader process of assimilation, and of division and proliferation as part of differentiation. I am very much inclined to view the Pomaks as now being entangled in a very complex process of such changes of identity, and their whole group history as a constant 'trying-out' of different models. Thus they came into existence as a result of two different processes: division and amalgamation. On the one hand we had a splitting of the group of 'Bulgarians' throughout the 16th, 17th, and 18th centuries into two parts – the Bulgarians who remained Orthodox Christians and the Bulgarians who turned to Islam. On the other hand, historically there was a process of amalgamation going on at the same time. The several different groups who came to these parts of the Balkan peninsula with the Ottoman conquerors, or were transferred from other parts of the Empire,[29] together with part of the Bulgarian population, united to form a new, larger group. It is very interesting that the processes of division and amalgamation, according to Horowitz, 'tend to involve a multiplication of identities, rather than a mere exchange of one identity for another. This may leave [these] processes more flexible for a potential revision downward or upward as new contexts impinge on perceptions'. (Horowitz, 1975, p. 138) This can explain the internal fluidity of Pomak identity described in the previous part of the chapter.

The other two processes, of incorporation and proliferation, seem to involve, once they are accomplished, a rejection of earlier identities; and in contrast to the other two, which are usually results of sudden and abrupt changes of political boundaries, these two are usually associated with 'specific collective goals such as economic or prestige goals'. This seems exactly to be the case, as is reflected in the survey from 1992 and in the

---

[29] See the case of the Yuruks described in the previous part of this paper.

1991 census. As has already been mentioned, a large group of Pomaks have now assumed the identity of Bulgarians, and thus have become part of the process of incorporation while, at the same time, the possibilities of group identity have proliferated, as the Pomaks have become divided into people who identify themselves not only as Bulgarians or Pomaks, but now as Turks, too.

Despite these possibilities for changes in identity within a group, this does not mean that there are no groups which are able to sustain their traditional identity over time. What is even more important than the different processes of identification which Horowitz describes is the distinction he offers between '*criteria* of identity' and operational *indicia*. The latter are evidence of identity, but unlike the former they do not define it. (Horowitz, 1975, p. 120) This distinction is very important because what we have in the case of the Pomaks, in my opinion, is a total mixing up of these two on the part of most of the researchers who have considered the group. Surnames, for example, are quite often employed as an indicium of membership, but they are taken as a criterion in the case of the Pomaks (as well as in the case of the Turks) in Bulgaria. But the indicia depend on the criteria, since they are the visible signs for determining the individual membership, while criteria form the subjective bases on which collective identity is determined. (Horowitz, 1975, p. 119) Thus Horowitz defines two criteria for shaping and altering group boundaries: contact with ethnic strangers and the size and importance of the political unit within which groups find themselves. It is clear that in the case of the Pomaks both factors have played a great role in their identity formation.

This points to significant differences in the processes of fusion or incorporation and amalgamation, especially in reference to the relation between cultural change and identity change. For Horowitz incorporation seems to involve at least some form of acculturation, while with amalgamation there exist centripetal forces which bring cultural variations into a basic harmony. What seems to emerge is the 'least common denominator' culture of the amalgam. The Pomaks present this in a very interesting form. On the one hand we have an amalgam of Sunni Islam, Alevi Islam, and other local and sectarian practices among them, and on the other, we have the crypto-Christianity described in the first part of the chapter.

Among the other factors which influence the enlargement of groups, Horowitz singles out the 'towns as the crucibles of group enlargement'. (Horowitz, 1975, p. 127) This explains the results of my field work in Velingrad where the people I met tended to identify themselves as Bulgarians, thus enlarging the boundaries of the Bulgarian ethnic group. This is very strongly determined by the interaction of self- and other-definitions of group identity, too, as the results of the field work have shown.[30]

The conclusions that can be drawn in light of Horowitz's model of ethnic identity are primarily tied to the view of this identity as determined by the shifting boundaries of the group. Thus, it is 'the ethnic *boundary* that defines the group, not the cultural stuff it encloses' as Frederik Barth has put it, (Barth, 1969, p. 211) and thus an ethnic group depends for its existence on the maintenance of a boundary. To my mind this serves as an explanation of the uncertainty in the identification of the Pomaks, i.e. their inability to maintain clear-cut boundaries differentiating them from other ethnic groups. It is enough to mention the fact of their acceptance of intermarriages both with Bulgarians and Turks and the fact that they are the most tolerated group by the other ethnic groups in support of this statement.[31]

Following this argument, it should be stressed that the fluctuations in the Pomaks' ethnic identity have been largely determined by the uneasy relationships among the Balkan communities. The total collapse of the communist regime in Bulgaria, and the deep economic as well as social and spiritual crisis of Bulgarian society, have turned the polity into a weak, ineffective and unattractive one for the self-realisation of its people. As a result a massive exodus from the country has started, and the numbers, especially among the Muslims, have been steadily rising.[32] Being unable to cope with its own problems, the Bulgarian state has also totally forgotten the Pomaks living in Greece. That is the reason for their unwillingness to maintain the ethnic boundary which separates them from the other 'Turks', including some Bulgarian Pomaks, who are their only link with a polity, Turkey, which is not only doing better economically but which is also

---

[30] There were people who said that they were ready to change their names, or had done so, only because they did not want to be different from the others at their workplace, school, or university.

[31] Another example in support of this is provided by the non-acceptance of Bulgarians of intermarriages with the Gypsies, which signals a very rigidly maintained ethnic boundary between the two groups, and also a strong sense of ethnic identity, something which is clear from all surveys.

[32] The number of Muslims who have left the country in the last seven years has allegedly reached 500,000.

showing considerable interest in their lives.[33] This, of course, is valid for the Bulgarian Pomaks as well.

The phenomenon of the great instability of the Pomaks' ethnic identity, however, is not fully explained by these models, since the group identity itself remains undefined. That is why I have turned to Stuart Hall's concept of cultural identity. The terms 'ethnic identity' and 'national identity', when used in reference to the Pomak group, seem either to be too politically loaded or to be taken, unreasonably, to mean something firm and unchangeable.[34]

Stuart Hall talks about two different understandings of cultural identity. The first sees it as 'one shared culture, a sort of collective "one true self", hiding inside the many other, more superficially imposed "selves", which people with a shared history and ancestry hold in common'. This is more or less synonymous with ethnic or national identity, and it provides us 'as "one people", with stable, unchanging and continuous frames of reference and meaning'. (Hall, 1990, p. 223) This seems exactly what is lacking in the case of the Pomaks.

The second definition speaks of cultural identity as a 'matter of "becoming" as well as of "being". It belongs to the future as much as to the past. It is not something which already exists, transcending place, time, history and culture. Cultural identities come from somewhere, they have histories. But, like everything which is historical, they undergo constant transformations. Far from being eternally fixed in some essentialist past, they are subject to the continuous 'play' of history, culture and power.' (Hall, 1990, p. 225)

This understanding is a way of accounting for what we have observed in the case of the Pomaks. The perspective suggested diminishes the role of the past, thus making unimportant the question which has been the main stumbling block in the debate on the Pomaks – the question of their past – and shifting the attention to the self- and other-positioning of the group within different historical discourses. But then, together with Stuart Hall, we should ask how, if identity does not proceed in a straight, unbroken line from some fixed origin, we are to understand its formation. (Hall, 1990, p. 226) It can be described as 'framed' by two vectors which

---

[33] Most of the people I was able to talk to in Komotini region were ready to go to Turkey if the borders would be open, but not to Bulgaria.

[34] Cf. the discussion on ethnicity in Аспекти ... where the idea that the Pomaks have a stable ethnic identity, whenever expressed, is met with vehement opposition, wrongly assuming that this would mean that the group has a separate national identity as well.

operate simultaneously: the vector of similarity and continuity and the vector of difference and rupture.

Thus the Pomaks and the Bulgarians or the Pomaks and the Turks are simultaneously both the same and different, as the whole previous part of this chapter has shown. But the Pomaks present this very interesting phenomenon of having their identity as if for ever 'deferred', 'postponed' in the sense of Derrida's *différance*. This will allow for a re-thinking of their identity in terms of different 'presences' whose interplay is responsible for the deferring of their group identity, which can never crystallise into anything solid. If we use Stuart Hall's terminology[35] then we can talk about *Présence Bulgare* and *Présence Turque*. These are even more complex than the 'presences' Stuart Hall talks about. *Présence Bulgare* is at once dominant and repressed, in the language these people speak and in the past they want to forget but which comes out again and again. It is there in the pain they feel that the other Bulgarians would not accept them or have totally forgotten their existence, and in the sudden burst of ethnic pride contained in the exclamation 'We're the purest Bulgarians'.

This presence, of course, is the one of power as well, constantly speaking the language of dominance, haughtily asking these people to leave aside all their differentiating features and join the main discourse of the nation. It is the presence which is remembered for its brutality in trying to change some of the indicia of ethnicity, and so making these people live their 'double' lives under their two names. Bringing in the question of the brutality in the present life of these people, this presence denies them the rational choice to 'become' somebody and leaves open only the choice 'to be' somebody, to be Bulgarian or to be a traitor.[36] Their 'otherness' as 'seen' by the Other in their religion and way of dressing serves as the scene for the re-framing of their identity, for the profound splitting and doubling of the self. But as M. Bakhtin has suggested, the self can never be realised without the Other, and only in the never ceasing dialogue between the two it is possible to constitute a self. In this sense it is impossible to think of any kind of identity as being constituted without the 'gaze of the other'. What is important for us in this 'heteroglossia' (to use another of Bakhtin's

---

[35] This is based on Aimée Cesaire and Leopold Senghor's metaphor. (Hall, 1990, p. 230)

[36] This can explain the hysteria about the possible identification of the Pomak group in numerous publications in the press, especially in reference to their turning to the Turks for securing a new identity, and being influenced by the Greek idea about the existence of a separate Pomak nation on the Balkans.

terms) of group identities is what kind of a 'gaze' this is and in what way it can affect the identification of the group. So, in this sense we can say that the *présence Bulgare* is one both of exclusion and expropriation, asking the group to join at the expense of its shedding most of its differentiating features and unconditionally joining the Bulgarian nationality.[37]

The *Présence Turque* is even more ambivalent in the re-framing of the group identity of the Pomaks. It is what constitutes the other side in the dialogue of power and resistance, of refusal and recognition. The ambivalence comes from the fact that this presence was once itself associated with power and dominance. As distant memory tells the story it was one of terror and blood. But it was one of worldly success and prominence for the Muslims as well. And nowadays it can be one of success once again if the ambiguity of Pomak identification is lifted by a gesture of allegiance to the group of the Turks.[38] And the question is the same one Stuart Hall asks: How can the dialogue be staged in such a way that it will finally be positioned by the Pomaks and not they by it? And as in the case of the Caribbean identity, it is impossible to answer it for the time being. The only thing that can be done is to recognise the necessary heterogeneity, diversity and heteroglossia of the group, to acknowledge 'a conception of "identity" which lives with and through, not despite, difference', in a permanent state of *hybridity*. (Hall, 1990, p. 235) This type of identity Stuart Hall calls 'diaspora identities', identities which are constantly producing and reproducing themselves anew, through transformation and difference. In my opinion this is exactly the case with the Pomaks. This definition can explain not only the fact that we have such groups of people, in Bulgaria as well as in Greece, Macedonia, Bosnia and Turkey, but also the fact that nothing like a firm, solid identity can be defined in regard to this group.

Probably it is time to put aside the limited discourse on the Pomaks, which identifies only the stereotypes (the Pomaks as 'guilty' of giving up their faith, as uneducated, backward, etc.) and other such images in order easily 'to elaborate them in a moralistic or nationalistic discourse that affirms the *origin* and *unity* of national identity'. (Bhabha, 1994, p. 68) We should be able to look at cultural otherness, as part of a process in

---

[37] Especially important in this sense is the fact of 6 per cent of the members of the group converting to Christianity, a process which is very intense at present, with Pastor Boyan Saraev acting as a new Apostle among the Pomaks from the Rhodope region.

[38] The explicitly expressed preference of the Greek Pomaks for Turkey if the borders would be opened is a very clear example of this.

which the borders of the nation, as Julia Kristeva claims, are constantly faced with a double temporality: the process of identity constituted by historical sedimentation (the pedagogical); and the loss of identity in the signifying process of cultural identification (the performative). (Kristeva, 1986, p. 189) Thus the difference could return as the same in the national sign and the minority discourse can emerge in the antagonistic *in-betweens* of national culture which is represented by it as a contentious, performative space within the pedagogical representations of national life. (Bhabha, 1994, p. 157) In this sense the minority discourse of the Pomaks should be seen not as threatening the national discourse but as 'doubling' it, supplying for it the sign that is missing.[39]

Conclusion

The gathered material and the analysis of this material have undoubtedly suggested that a new interpretation of the group identity of the Pomaks in Bulgaria has been due for a long time. The interpretation offered here has been worked out from the perspective of the post-modern understanding of the subject as de-centred, unable to be defined by the grand narratives of modernity, one of which is the national narrative. The 'death' of these narratives has determined the 'death' of the unified, linear subject, functioning in the empty homogeneous time of Benedict Anderson's imagined community. The subject or subjects who have emerged are to be determined within the 'liminal space' of the national culture, which should begin from the supplementary writing of minority discourses. (Bhabha, 1994, p. 154) Thus the ethnic identity of the Pomaks, being in constant transformation, should not be viewed as confronting the national discourse with a contradictory or negative referent, as all attempts of the group to claim an identity different from the dominant national one have in fact been viewed. As Homi Bhabha argues, its force lies in the renegotiation of the historic times, terms and traditions through which we turn our uncertain, passing contemporaneity into the signs of history.

Another very important result from the present research is that it has shown that the ethnic identity of the Pomaks can only be understood in

---

[39] Cf. Homi Bhabha's metaphor of the supplement whose strategy 'interrupts the successive seriality of the narrative of plurals and pluralism by radically changing their mode of articulation' (Bhabha, 1994, p. 155).

terms of ethnic change and boundary maintenance and not as a stable, unchangeable entity, a view which is bound to be defeated by the reality of their lives. Only when it is thought of as being in the process of formation, as fluid and as formed 'in-between' the official identities prescribed to them by the pedagogy of the national discourse, as full of gaps and silences which should be viewed as a significant part of it, can we understand what is really going on among members of the group.

This way of discussing the identity formation processes in reference to the Pomaks can ensure the overcoming of the schizophrenic fear ripping through the Bulgarian national consciousness and instituting a discourse which views the Pomaks either as one of the most important parts of the nation or, in their attempt to find their own identity, as the arch-enemies of the nation, and a Trojan horse for Bulgarian national identity.

There are, of course, other paths open as far as the constitution of ethnic and national identities in Bulgaria and in the Balkans is concerned. As a possible different way of looking at these problems I can suggest the 'constitutional patriotism' of Jürgen Habermas. (Habermas, 1992) From this perspective, the Balkan drama can be viewed not as caused by the 'loss of national identity' due to the resurgence of ethnicity, but as the inability of the post-Communist societies to build a civil society out of which a new politics of recognition could have emerged. But the model offered by the Pomak group in Bulgaria could serve as an example how to make the 'ethnic stranger' our guest and thus to be ready to re-negotiate the boundaries dividing us. This seems to be the only common-sense route available for the future – as V. Gradev suggests. (Градев, 1997)

References

Anderson, B. (1991), *Imagined Communities: Reflections on the Origin and Spread of Nationalism*, Verso, London, New York.

Barth, F. (1969), *Ethnic Groups and Boundaries. The Social Organisation of Cultural Difference*, Universitetsforlag, Bergen and Little, Brown & Co, Boston.

Bauman, Z. (1992), 'Soil, Blood and Identity', in *The Sociological Review*, vol. 40 (4), pp. 675-701.

Berman, M. (1991), *All That Is Solid Melts into Air: The Experience of Modernity*, Verso, London.

Bhabha, H. (1994), *The Location of Culture*, Routledge, London.

Canetti, E. (1985), *The Human Province*, trans. Joachim Neugroschel, Deutsch, London.

Eminov, A. (1997), *Turkish and Other Muslim Minorities in Bulgaria*, Hurst & Co., London.

Gellner, E. (1990), *Nations and Nationalism*, Basil Blackwell, Oxford.

Glazer, N. and Moynihan, D. P. (eds) (1975), *Ethnicity: Theory and Experience*, Harvard University Press, Cambridge, Mass.

Habermas, J. (1992), 'Citizenship and National Identity', in *Praxis International*, vol. 11, No. 12.

Hall, S. (1990), 'Cultural Identity and Diaspora' in Rutherford, J. (ed)., *Identity: Community, Culture, Difference*, Lawrence & Wishart, London.

Hamers, J. F. and Blanc M. H. A. (1992), *Bilinguality and Bilingualism*, rev. ed., Cambridge University Press, Cambridge.

Horowitz, D. (1975), 'Ethnic Identity' in Glazer, N. and Moynihan, D. P. (eds), in *Ethnicity: Theory and Experience*, Harvard University Press, Cambridge, Mass.

Ilchev, I. and Perry, D. (1993), 'Bulgarian Ethnic Groups: Politics and Perceptions', in *RFE/RL Research report*, vol. 2, No. 12.

Jeliaskova, A., Gueorguieva, Tz. (1994), 'L'Identité en Periode de Changement' [Identity in a Period of Change], in *Cahiers internationaux de Sociologie*, Vol. XCVI.

Karpat, K. A. (1973), *An Inquiry into the Social Foundations of Nationalism in the Ottoman State: From Social Estates to Classes, from Milets to Nations*, Center for International Studies, Princeton University, New Jersey.

Karpat, K. A., (ed) (1990), *The Turks of Bulgaria: The History, Culture and Political Fate of a Minority*, The ISIS Press, Istanbul.

Konstantinov, Y. (1992), 'Nation-State' and 'Minority' Types of Discourse-Problems of Communication between the Majority and the Islamic Minorities in Contemporary Bulgaria', in *Innovation*, 5, 3, pp. 75-89.

Konstantinov, Y. (1990), *Minority Name Studies in the Balkans – The Pomaks of Hadjiska*, The Final Report of the Field Study 'Hadjiska'90', unpublished.

Kristeva, J. (1986), 'Women's Time', in Moi, T. (ed), *The Kristeva Reader*, Blackwell, Oxford.

Lyotard, J.-F. (1991), *The Postmodern Condition: A Report on Knowledge*, transl. Geoff Bennington and Brian Massumi, Manchester University Press, Manchester.

Memisoglu, H. (1989), *Bulgarian Oppression in Historical Perspective*, Ankara.

Poulton, H. (1989), *Minorities in the Balkans*, Minority Rights Group.

Poulton, H. (1991), *The Balkans: Minorities and States in Conflict*, Minority Rights Publication.

Poulton, H. and Pettifer, J. (1994), *The Southern Balkans*, Minority Rights Group.

Poulton, H. (1995), *Who Are the Macedonians*, Ithaca University Press, Ithaca.

Poulton, H. and Taji-Farouki, S. (eds) (1996), *Muslim Identity and the Balkan State*, Hurst & Co., London.

Relations of Compatibility and Incompatibility between Christians and Muslims in Bulgaria, (1994), draft report, International Centre for Minority Studies and Intercultural Relations, Sofia.

Rex, J. and Mason, D. (1986), *Theories of Race and Ethnic Relations*, Cambridge University Press, Cambridge.

Riggs, F. W. (1991), 'Ethnicity, Nationalism, Race, Minority: A Semantic/Onomantic Exercise', in *International Sociology*, Vol. 6, No. 3.

Rutherford, J. (ed) (1990), *Identity: Community, Culture, Difference*, Lawrence & Wishart, London.

Smith, A. D. (1991), *National Identity*, Penguin Books, London.

Smith, A. D. (1991), *The Ethnic Origins of Nations*, Basil Blackwell, London.

Taylor, Ch. 'The Politics of Recognition' in *Multiculturalism: Examining the Politics of Recognition*, ed. Amy Gutmann, Princeton University Press, Princeton, New Jersey, 1994.

Zhelyskova, A. 'The Problem of Authenticity of Some Domestic Sources on the Rhodopes, deeply Rooted in Bulgarian Historiography' in *Etudes Balkanique*, 4, 1990.

Аспекти на етнокултурната ситуация в България [Aspects of the ethno-cultural situation in Bulgaria] (1992), съст. В. Русанов, Център за изследване на демокрацията и Фондация Фридрих Науман, Sofia.

Аспекти на етнокултурната ситуация в България [Aspects of the ethno-cultural situation in Bulgaria, revised edition] (1994), преработено и допълнено издание, съст. В. Русанов, Асоциация АКСЕС, Sofia.

Алексиев, Б. (1994), 'Екологична среда – историческа традиция – мюсюлманска общност в Източните Родопи' [Ecological milieu – historical traditions: the Muslim community in the Eastern Rhodopes], in *Аспекти на етнокултурната ситуация в България*, Асоциация АКСЕС, Sofia, pp. 231-239.

Алексиев, Б. (1992), *Родопското население в българската хуманитаристика* [The Rhodope population in the humanities in Bulgaria], Sofia.

Благоев, Г. (1994), 'Съвременното състояние на традиционната празнично-обредна система на мюсюлманското население от Източните Родопи' [The contemporary state of the traditional ritual system of the Muslim community in the Eastern Rhodopes] in *Аспекти на етнокултурната ситуация в България*, Асоциация АКСЕС, Sofia, pp. 224-231.

Велков, А. и Радушев, Е. (1988), 'Османски архивни държавни документи за ислямизационните процеси на Балканите' [Ottoman archival documents for the islamization processes in the Balkans], in Янков, Г., Стр. Димитров, Орлин Загоров (eds.), *Проблеми на развитието на българската народност и нация*, Българска академия на науките, Sofia, pp. 57-74.

Георгиев, Ж., Томова, И., Грекова, М., Кънев, К. (1993), 'Етнокултурната ситуация в България - 1992' [The ethno-cultural situation in Bulgaria in 1992], in *Социологически преглед*, vol. 3.

Георгиева, Цв. (1994), 'Връзки на съвместимост и несъвместимост в ежедневието на християни и мюсюлмани в българските земи' [Relations of compatibility and incompatibility in the everyday life of Bulgarian Christians and Muslims], in *Аспекти на етнокултурната ситуация в България*, Sofia, pp. 212-224.

Градев, В. (1997), 'Политиката на признаване преди разсъмване' [The politics of acknowlegement before dawn], in *Демократически преглед*, summer, 435-507.

Желязкова., А., Ракова, Сн., Йовевска, М. (1995), *Босна и Херцеговина през 19-20 век. Нации и национални взаимоотношения* [Bosnia and Herzegovina in the 19th and 20th centuries. Nations and national relations], Veliko Tyrnovo.

Желязкова, А. (ed.) (1997), *Мюсюлманските общности на Балканите и в България* [Muslim communities in the Balkans and Bulgaria], Sofia.

Желязкова, А. (1997), 'Формиране на мюсюлманските общности и комплексите на балканските историографии' [Formation of the Muslim communities and the complexes of Balkan historiography], in *Мюсюлманските общности на Балканите и в България*, Sofia.

Захариев, Ст. (1870), *Географико-историко-статистическо описание на Татар-Пазарджишката кааза* [Geographical, historical and statistical survey of Tatar-Pazardjik kaaza], Vienna.

Иванов, М., Томова, Ил. (1994), 'Етнически групи и междуетнически отношения в България' [Ethnic groups and inter-ethnic relations in Bulgaria], in *Аспекти на етнокултурната ситуация в Българияя*, Асоциация АКСЕС, Sofia, 21-33.

История на България (1983-85) [History of Bulgaria], Българска академия на науките, Sofia, vol. 4, 5.

Кальонски, А. (1994), 'Поглед върху етнорелигиозното съжителство в Средните Родопи' [A survey of ethno-religious co-existence in the Middle Rhodopes], in *Аспекти на етнокултурната ситуация в България*, Асоциация АКСЕС, Sofia, pp. 282-293.

Кирил, Патриарх български, (1960), *Българомохамедански селища в Южни Родопи (Ксантийско, Гюмюрджинско)* [Bulgarian-Mohammedan villages in the Southern Rhodopes], Sofia.

Кънчев, А., Христов, Б. (1997), *От изник слонце до заник* [From dawn to sunset], Sofia.

Национален статистически институт (1993), *Анализ на резултатите от преброяването на населението към 4. 12. 1992* [National Statistical Institute. Analysis of the census from 4 Dec. 1992], Sofia.

Панайотова, Б. (1994), 'Българи-мохамедани и християни в Централните Родопи – поглед върху техните взаимоотношения' [Bulgarian Mohammedans and Christians in the Central Rhodopes – a look at their relations], in *Аспекти на етнокултурната ситуация в България*, Асоциация АКСЕС, Sofia, pp. 273-282.

Попконстантинов, Хр. (1970), *Спомени, пътеписи и писма* [Memoirs, Travel Writings, Letters], Хр. Г. Данов, Plovdiv.

'Родопа и Родопска област' [The Rhodope mountain and the Rhodope region], in *В чест на Ст. Н. Шишков за 70 г. от рождението му и полувинвековната му културна дейност* (1935), Sofia.

Родопи. Традиционна народна духовна и соционормативна култура [The Rhodopes: Traditional folk culture and socio-normative culture] (1994), София.

Родопа [The Rhodopes] (1922-1947), София.

Статистически годишник [Statistical Yearbook] (1995), София.

Стоилов, К. (1994), 'С отворени врати към света и хората' [With open doors for the world and the people], in *Аспекти на етнокултурната ситуация в Българияя*, Асоциация АКСЕС, Sofia, pp. 239-243.

Тодоров, Ил. (1984), 'Летописният разказ на поп Методи Драгинов' [The chronicle of Rev. Metodii Draginov], in *Старобългарска литература*, vol. 16, Sofia.

Хайтов, Н. (1981), *Шумки от габър* [Twigs of Elm], Хр. Г. Данов, Plovdiv.

Христов, Хр. ред. (1989), *Страници от българската история. Очерк за ислямизираните българи и националновъзродителния процес* [An essay on the Islamised Bulgarians and the process of national re-birth], Наука и изкуство, Sofia.

Христакудис, А. (1992), 'Положението и правата на мюсюлманите в Гърция – съвременни аспекти' [The condition and the rights of the Muslims in Greece – contemporary aspects], in *Аспекти на етнокултурната ситуация в България*, съст. В. Русанов, Център за изследване на демокрацията и Фондация Фридрих Науман, Sofia.

Шишков, Ст. Н. (1914), *Помаците в трите български области: Тракия, Македония и Мизия* [The Pomaks in the three Bulgarian regions: Thrace, Macedonia and Misia], Plovdiv.

Шишков, Ст. Н. (1936), *Българо-мохомеданите (помаци)* [Bulgarian Mohammedans – Pomaks], Plovdiv.

Янков, Г., Стр. Димитров, Орлин Загоров (eds.) (1988), *Проблеми на развитието на българската народност и нация* [Problems in the development of the Bulgarian nationality and nation], Българска академия на науките, Sofia.

4 The Identity Crisis and Emergence of Alternative Ethnic Identities among the Eastern Slavs: the Case of the Poleshuks

KIRILL SHEVCHENKO

Introduction

Contemporary ethnic processes in post-communist Central-Eastern Europe have once more revealed the unsoundness of both Marxist and Liberal long-term expectations that modern technology, urbanisation, mass-media, and growing interaction between different cultures would lead to a decrease in cultural differences and finally remove ethnic distinctions. It has turned out that 'Ethnicity has not only proved resilient in situations of change; it has also often emerged in forceful ways during the very processes of change which many believed would do away with it.' (Eriksen, 1993, p. 33)

The most general definition of identity, as formulated by P. Weinreich, holds that 'One's identity is defined as the totality of one's self-construal, in which how one construes oneself in the present expresses the continuity between how one construes oneself as one was in the past and how one construes oneself as one aspires to be in the future.' (Weinreich, 1989, p. 72) Ethnic identity is viewed by researchers as a part of the totality of one's identities. Ancestry, a sense of peoplehood, and folklore constitute core components of *ethnicity* – which, in turn, is defined as 'a shared sense of peoplehood based on presumed shared socio-cultural experiences representing a part of an ethnic group's collective experience.' (Weinreich, 1989, *ibid.*) Alongside with these rather static characteristics, ethnic identity is also described in more dynamic terms as a 'complex of processes by means of which people construct and reconstruct their ethnicity'; in other words, 'ethnic identities are not natural facts but cultural constructions which are liable to be reconstructed...' (Weinreich, 1989, pp. 45-57)

The ethnic revival in contemporary Europe has been explained mainly in terms of economic and ideological transformations inherent to post-industrial society, the peculiarities of which caused a substantially different sort of expression of immediate cultural needs. However, most of the attention in this field has been devoted firstly to the traditional ethno-regional minorities in Western Europe, and secondly to the immigrant ethnicities in Western European countries – which, however, are quite different from those of the indigenous ethnic communities.

Contemporary ethnic processes in post-communist Central-Eastern Europe provide an example of a very specific phenomenon which is obviously different from similar processes in Western Europe. The nature of the ethnic revival in Eastern Europe represents the result of the coincidence and interaction of the peculiarities of the post-communist period with the special character of Eastern-type nationalism (a term of John Plamenatz), which, unlike Western nationalism ('acting on behalf of well-developed high cultures') 'was active on behalf of a high culture not as yet properly crystallised... It presided, or strove to preside, in ferocious rivalry with similar competitors, over a chaotic ethnographic map of many dialects, with ambiguous historical or linguo-genetic allegiances, and containing populations which had only just begun to identify with these emergent national high cultures...' (Gellner, 1990, p. 100)

The crucial importance of social factors in the process of creating ethnicity is stressed by many scholars. (Roosens, 1989) Thus, T. H. Eriksen points out that 'cultural difference between two groups is not the decisive feature of ethnicity... Only in so far as cultural differences are perceived as being important, and are made socially relevant, do social relationships have an ethnic element.' (Eriksen, 1993, pp. 11-12) This remark has a direct bearing to the current situation in Eastern Europe, where some manifestations of ethnicity rest on already more or less socially 'acknowledged' cultural differences while some embryonic manifestations of ethnicity are only trying to impose a social context on a cultural diversity which may be real or which may be little more than imaginary.

The ethnic map of post-communist Central-Eastern Europe, where the influence of alternative types of ethnic identities is growing, testifies to the fact that a significant number of the previous ethnic divisions in Central and Eastern Europe, the validity of which was taken for granted during socialism, have now proved to be unreliable and questionable. It appears that there exist certain cultural regions inhabited by groups of population with a vague identity and only an obscure concept of their own ethnic belongingness. These 'ethnically indifferent groups' (Lozoviuk, 1994, p. 21) can serve as an illustration to Ernest Gellner's remark on the existence of a great number of potential nations in the world. (Gellner, 1990) As he says, 'Before the event, we can only identify countless cultural differentiations, and we can not tell just which turn into "nations".' (Геллнер, 1992, p. 59) Moravians in the Czech Republic, Kashubs in Poland, Rusyns (Ruthenians) in Slovakia, Ukraine and Poland, and Poleshuks in Belarus provide concrete cases of such situations.

When, after the final collapse of the communist system, the official ethnic self-identification imposed from above ceased to be the only option, numerous Belarusians and Ukrainians voted for another ethnic self-identification, although it would appear that by doing so they were giving up their 'own' traditional ethnic niche. Thus, more than 50 per cent of the Ukrainians living in Eastern Slovakia now identify themselves as Rusyns, reviving their traditional ethnic name and set of values. The data from March 1991 demonstrate that at that time 17,197 inhabitants of North-Eastern Slovakia identified themselves as Rusyns, while only 13,281 persons indicated themselves as Ukrainians. (The Rusyn or Ruthenian identity which prevailed in Eastern Slovakia in the interwar period was prohibited by the Czechoslovak communist authorities at the beginning of the 1950s, and the local Eastern Slavic population was officially proclaimed to consist of Ukrainians.) The most interesting fact is that at the same time 49,099 persons considered the Rusyn dialect as their mother tongue (Among these people 27,868 persons identified themselves as Slovaks, which testifies to the large-scale process of Slovakisation). The Ukrainian language was indicated as their mother tongue only by 9,480 persons, which is even less than the overall number of those who considered themselves to be Ukrainians (13,281). (Paukovič, 1994)

A similar process is going on in Belarusia's *Palesse* (that is, the South-Western part of Belarus) where, according to local Poleshuk activists, approximately 1 million of the local population declare themselves as members of the independent Poleshuk ethnie, rejecting their traditional and generally accepted Belarusian or Ukrainian ethnic belonging. This tendency was clearly manifested during the last census of the population conducted in the USSR in 1989. A considerable part of the local population preferred to identify themselves as 'Poleshuks' or 'Yatvyags' (that is, the second ethnic name of the Poleshuks); but, as this ethnic category was not included in the census, all those who chose the alternative version of self-identification were simply designated as Belarusians if they lived on the territory of Belarus, and as Ukrainians if they lived on the territory of Ukraine. This, incidentally, provides an additional illustration to Karl Deutsch's observation that the long-term tendency consists in 'slow but widespread shifts in emphasis... to regional development'. (Deutsch, 1969, p. 78)

There are certain substantial differences within these movements. Thus, unlike the present Rusyn (Ruthenian) movement, which to a major extent bases its current activity on reviving and rectifying an already created national ideology (the key elements of Rusyn national ideology were elaborated in the 19th and early 20th centuries, and then prohibited by both Czechoslovak and Soviet communist authorities), the Poleshuk movement apparently does not possess any deep-rooted or stable cultural tradition. Therefore, Poleshuk ideologists had to start the selective cultural work essential for the process of shaping a new ethnic identity from the very beginning, without any clear and visible model from the past.

The emergence of new ethnic identities should be viewed in terms of the contextual character of any identity, keeping in mind the existence of a 'hierarchy of identities' for each person which 'can be inverted or change in time, or one social identity can simply be more relevant than others in a given context...' (Roosens, 1989, p. 16) The question here is, as Donald L. Horowitz put it, 'What... determines which are the most significant membership or... which of many potential identities will be activated most frequently?' Horowitz connects the shifts in the 'centre of gravity' of ethnic identity with the influence of 'certain external stimuli. As the stimuli at a certain level persist and outweigh those at other levels, one can begin to think of himself a primarily as an Ibo but also as an Onitsha Ibo and also a Nigerian.' (Both citations from Horowitz, 1975, p. 118) The notion of an external stimulus capable of moving ethnic identity within a certain hierarchy of identities is particularly important in our case. An attempt will be undertaken to reveal the tendencies and processes which potentially could have played the specific role of such 'external stimuli' in the case of the alternative ethnic identities among the Eastern Slavs.

According to the Russian liberal historian Milyukov, 'nationality' has its roots in the phenomenon of '...collective consciousness', and to be a nation means 'to elaborate a special device of social memory and to self-determine consciously through it.' (Милюков, 1925, pp. 77-78) This mechanism of social memory has a direct relation to Deutsch's definition of a people as 'a larger group of persons linked by complementary habits and facilities of communication.' (Deutsch, 1969, p. 96) The basic criterion of membership in a people, as Deutsch puts it, 'consists in the ability to communicate more effectively ... with members of one large group than with outsiders.' The notion of a 'mechanism of social memory' is in fact specified by communicative facilities which include '...a socially standardised system of symbols which is language, and any number of auxiliary codes, such as alphabets, system of writing, painting, calculating, etc. They include information stored in the living memories, associations, habits, and preferences of its members, and in its material facilities for the storage of information, such as libraries.' (Deutsch, 1969, p. 97)

The processes aiming to construct new ethnic identities and national ideologies presuppose the creation and further development of the communicative facilities just mentioned. The question of the reasons and characteristic features of this process as well as its social context remains open.

The nature of the contemporary movements aimed at creating new ethnic identities calls to mind Hugh Seton-Watson's comments on the existence of 'old' and 'new' nations. According to Seton-Watson, 'in the case of the new nations of nineteenth and early twentieth century Europe, the main factor in the creation of national consciousness was language... A fundamental feature of all these movements is that the nationalist elites were only able to mobilise support from peasants, merchants, artisans or factory workers because many persons in these various classes were discontented with political and social conditions. One may... argue that the foundations of their discontent were economic. Nevertheless, the discontent was directed by the nationalist elites into nationalist movements rather than towards economic change.' (Seton-Watson, 1977, p. 9) Contemporary ethnic processes, as manifested in the emergence of new ethnic identities, could be viewed as the continuation of the case of the 'new nations' under the concrete mental, social and political conditions of post-communist Central-Eastern Europe. Such key questions as the role of national elites and how they create these new 'communicative facilities', as well as correlations between social, political, economic and purely cultural factors as reasons why public discontent was transformed precisely into the form of ethnic movements are still extremely important.

One of the most important traits of these processes within ethnically indifferent communities is the long-term parallel development of several models of identification. For instance, the evolution of the Rusyn national identity was marked by a bitter rivalry between Russophiles, Ukrainophiles and those who considered Rusyns to be a separate people. We will concentrate predominantly on one of the existing competitive models, that is, on the model which treats a given ethnically indifferent community as a distinctive ethnic group, differentiated from its ethnic surroundings. A general comparative view of some manifestations of the Rusyn and Poleshuk movements would also seem to be fruitful. The emergence of a new ethnic identity for the Poleshuks in the South-Western part of Belarus can be traced in the activity of the civic and cultural society 'Polisse', which has a decisive influence on the whole process of shaping the Poleshuk ethnic identity.

The first section deals with the linguistic activities of the Poleshuk elite and the most characteristic features of their language-making policy. The second section is devoted to the problem of history-making, which is a commonplace element in the activities of national elites. The third chapter traces the political evolution of the Poleshuk movement in the wider context of the current political processes in Belarus.

1. Creation of a Literary Language

Language, and corresponding auxiliary codes such as alphabets, systems of writing, etc. were mentioned by Deutsch as one of the main elements of communicative facilities. Language provides 'a bond of unity among its speakers and defines a line of separation marking off one speech community from another.' (Jyotirindra Das Gupta, 1975, p. 470) In the case of Slavs, language has traditionally played a crucial role in the maintenance of boundaries between ethnic groups. According to Roman Jakobson, language has always had a central place in the numerous political ideologies of the Slavs. The Poleshuk movement does not seem to be an exception from this general rule.

When answering the key question, 'Why do we need a literary Poleshuk language?', the founding fathers of the Poleshuk movement stress first of all the possibility to solve in a 'correct' way the endless and fruitless dispute over whether the Poleshuk vernacular is a part of the Ukrainian or Belarusian languages. Secondly, they argue that the availability of a standardised literary language is the most convincing evidence of the general cultural maturity and achievements of a people. (*Збудінне*, 1991, No. 7) These arguments basically follow the logic of other Slavic 'awakeners', for whom the existence of a literary language was a kind of a sacred matter and the most important proof of a given people's right to exist.

The whole idea of creating something like a Poleshuk literary language seems to be rather new. It is not linked with any previous stable tradition, with the exception of several isolated attempts to represent local dialects in writing, which will be mentioned below. It is worth noting that the most competent authority in the field of 'Slavonic microlanguages', the Soviet scholar A. Dulichenko, did not mention any Poleshuk language in his monograph published in 1981. The Carpatho-Rusyn (Ruthenian) language was indicated as the only such phenomenon among the Eastern Slavs. According to Dulichenko, literary microlanguages are a much more characteristic phenomenon for the Southern and Western Slavs than for the Eastern Slavs. (Дуличенко, 1981)

The problem of codification of all the numerous local dialects (which are still viewed by many Belarusian and Ukrainian scholars as mere transitional dialects from Ukrainian to Belarusian), and the creation and dissemination of the final version of a standardised literary language is one of the most urgent matters in the Poleshuk movement. The necessity of elaborating a literary Poleshuk language is also motivated by referring to mediæval times, when the local vernacular was widely used in the administrative sphere. Some scholars argue that during the early period of existence of the Grand Duchy of Lithuania, namely at the end of 14th to the first half of the 15th centuries, official documents of the Grand Duchy of Lithuania were written in the dialects of what is now called Ukrainian and Belarusian Palesse. (Stang, 1935) Poleshuk supporters of this point of view stress the urgent necessity to re-evaluate the still influential theory about the Old-Belarusian language as having been an official language in The Grand Duchy of Lithuania. They say it is necessary to distinguish between proper Old-Belarusian, which finally became an official language of the Principality only in the middle of the 15th century, and the Poleshuk language, which, they argue, was initially an official language of the state, but has been mistakenly confused with Old-Belarusian.

In spite of the allegedly long duration and glorious past of the Poleshuk language, the first ABC-book in Poleshuk dialect was prepared only in 1812, and published in 'Gazeta Polska' in 1861 – an event which did not have any important consequences. The next ABC-book was created in 1907 by the prominent Poleshuk awakener Roman Skirmunt, from the Pinsk region. His ABC-book proved to be much more influential. Nevertheless, the main work connected with the elaboration of literary norms and the creation of a complete Poleshuk Grammar was initiated only in the mid-1980s.

Although Poleshuk activists state that the norms of the Poleshuk literary language, as well as the main rules of Poleshuk grammar, were definitively stated in 1984 (the author of the modern officially accepted Poleshuk grammar is the present Chairman of the 'Polisse' society, M. Shelyahovych), this procedure seems to be far from complete. Indeed, as a result of the still serious terminological gap, the Poleshuk official organ, the monthly 'Zbudinne' ('Awakening') quite often resorts to Russian (in the majority of cases), Ukrainian or Belarusian when special terminology is required. It looks significant that in many of its issues 'Zbudinne' has published a special 'key' for reading the Poleshuk literary language, together with a brief clarification of the phonetic peculiarities of various Poleshuk dialects, indicating particular letters, and the sounds which are designated by these letters. Special attention is paid to those signs and letters which are different from both Ukrainian and Belarusian orthographic norms, and which might therefore look strange for the potential reader of the Poleshuk press.

One of the most important factors which to a certain extent influences the linguistic policy of the Poleshuk elite is Poleshuk intellectuals' perception of the indigenous local population in Palesse as direct descendants of the former Old-Lithuanian-speaking tribe of *Yatvyagi*, which inhabited this territory during the early middle ages, in the time of Kievan Rus'. In the course of time, the Yatvyags were gradually assimilated by Slavs. Indeed, some linguists and folklore-enthusiasts from Lithuania consider certain phonetic peculiarities of the local dialects as traces of the former Yatvyagian language, which belonged to the Baltic group of languages, and was particularly close to some dialects of present-day Lithuanian. Moreover, one folklorist from Vilnius, E. Trynkunas, argues that even in the middle of the 19th century some populations in the forests of the Brest region in Western Palesse spoke a language very close to present-day Lithuanian, while the names of many villages and numerous local peculiarities in clothing, folk songs, etc. are also similar to those which are characteristic for the Southern part of present Lithuania. (*Збудінне*, 1990, Nos. 10-15) All these circumstances are being stressed very vigorously, and used by Poleshuk 'awakeners' as an additional argument to select for literary norms such particular dialectisms which are recognisably different from both Ukrainian and Belarusian literary norms, and which may therefore be treated as remnants of the 'true Yatvyagian legacy'.

It should be noted that there are some serious objective problems in the elaboration of common norms for a literary language. A common feature of such 'microlanguages' (the term preferred by Dulichenko), which include apart from Poleshuk also Rusyn, Kashubian and other local standards, is 'the actual absence of any common norms' and as a result, the formation of supradialectical norms is very much handicapped by the 'extreme diversity of numerous spoken dialects'. (Дуличенко, 1994, pp. 17-20)

The most striking trait of Poleshuk ideologists' linguistic policy is their persistent fostering of even the most insignificant differences between Poleshuk dialects and neighboring languages – in the first place, Ukrainian, which is lexically and phonetically the closest to the Poleshuk vernacular. This principle of language-making was clearly formulated by Poleshuk intellectuals themselves as 'using particularly those peculiarities which make our language *distinctive* in the first place from Ukrainian and Belarusian'. This was officially proclaimed in the Poleshuk monthly 'Zbudinne', along with such principles as using all existing Poleshuk dialects, and faithfulness to the peculiar Poleshuk linguistic past, which, in turn, presupposes the fostering of local dialectisms and anachronisms, in preference to the many Polish and Russian loan-words which are commonly used at present. (*Збудінне*, 1991, No. 7)

The aspiration to make the literary version of the Poleshuk language as far from Ukrainian and Belarusian as possible often produces rather curious results. Thus, in several issues of 'Zbudinne' there was published a special short dictionary with the basic aim 'to introduce readers to the literary language'. An interesting thing was that the authors of this dictionary had to resort to a mostly Ukrainian, Russian and Belarusian vocabulary in order to clarify to their public the lexical meanings of the words of their literary Poleshuk language. (*Збудінне*, 1991, No. 4 (22))

The somewhat artificial appearance of the present literary version of the Poleshuk language is quite often criticised by some members of the Poleshuk intelligentsia. Thus, one of the Poleshuk poets, commenting on the present version of literary Poleshuk, proposed his own system of graphs, and expressed the idea that literary Poleshuk should be closer to the real spoken dialects of various regions of Palesse. At the same time, he had to acknowledge that in this case 'The literary Poleshuk language would resemble literary Ukrainian to a much greater extent. But there is still a sufficient number of local peculiarities which would legitimise the existence of literary Poleshuk...' (*Збудінне*, 1993, No. 7 (69))

Another clear manifestation of the desire to be as different from the surroundings as possible is connected with Poleshuk intellectuals' attempts to use the Latin script together with the Cyrillic alphabet. As a formal reason for this was given one of the first Poleshuk ABC-books, from 1907, the author of which, Roman Skirmunt, recommended the use of both alphabets for a practical reason: a considerable part of the local population, being under Polish cultural influence, was much more familiar with the Latin script. However, the peculiarities of the current situation have determined the final choice of the script: having proclaimed in 1991 the intention to use both scripts, Poleshuk activists now resort mostly to the Cyrillic alphabet.

Poleshuk ideologists' methods of standardisation, and for the elaboration of literary norms, clearly indicate some obvious parallels with the Rusyn situation. The most important common features characteristic for both cases are the consistent promotion of all the numerous dialect forms which clearly differ from literary Ukrainian to the official literary level, and a simultaneous desire to strengthen the existing differences between Ukrainian and the new literary languages in grammar, phonetics, etc., too.

The only serious difference when we consider the Rusyn case is the fact that due to some historical circumstances (in the first place an extremely intricate interplay of various identification models), the Rusyn movement for quite a long period of time identified itself with Russia and, as a result, tried to impose both Old Church Slavonic and the Russian literary language on the local population. These attempts resulted in an intricate mixture of the local dialects, Old Church Slavonic and literary Russian – so called 'yazychie', which became quite an influential element in the Rusyn cultural legacy. Rusyn ideologists' orientation towards local dialects should therefore be viewed as the final product of the long-term interplay of some rather contradictory tendencies. It is the result, first of all, of the long but unsuccessful attempts of the pro-Russian Rusyn intelligentsia to impose the Russian literary language on the local population, and, secondly, of their resistance to the similar attempts of the local Ukrainophiles to introduce the Ukrainian literary language. Finally, the Rusyns started to pay even more attention to various local dialects in the process of language-making, which in fact was a kind of compromise between the programmes of Rusyn Russophiles and Rusyn Ukrainophiles. Whereas the Poleshuk linguists are constructing a single literary version of the Poleshuk language based on a mixture of several main dialects, Rusyn scholars came to the conclusion that the 'Rusyn language should be codified on the basis of the spoken vernacular in each of the regions where Rusyns live (Subcarpathia, Lemko Region, Presov Region, Vojevodina) and that... the codification of a Rusyn literary language will be a long process whose success will be determined by usage in daily life.' (Magocsi, 1993, pp. 550-552)

Officially, the process of codifying the Rusyn dialects in the Presov region of Eastern Slovakia was completed only at the end of January 1995 and was celebrated by an official ceremony in Bratislava. (*Narodny Novynky,* 27. 01. 1995) This event is considered as only an initial step in a more global process of the general codification of the Rusyn language, which will be continued by the codification of the other existing Rusyn dialects. Unexpectedly, in spite of the much more developed and deep-rooted cultural tradition of the Rusyn movement, the formation of a Rusyn literary language on the basis of spoken vernaculars is taking place more slowly and in a much more complicated way than is case with the Poleshuk language – which was codified during the 1980s. At the same time, it is possible to argue that this attentive and delicate approach of Rusyn language-makers towards existing dialectical diversity could provide a more solid and reliable basis for the stability of the future literary Rusyn.

Overall, the linguistic policy of Poleshuk nation-makers resembles in many aspects the linguistic 'purism' of the Slavic 'awakeners' during the national revivals in the 19th century. The only difference – but it is a serious one – is that while Czech or Lusatian-Sorbian 'awakeners' attacked and extirpated numerous Germanisms in their languages, modern Poleshuk ideologists have a much more complicated task, because of the very close similarity between Poleshuk and Ukrainian. This requires a much more inventive approach. The natural aspiration to assert a new literary language assumes different forms among the general public and often follows the examples of the other Slavonic 'revivals' from the 19th century. Thus, several festivals of Poleshuk songs have been already organised, under the characteristic title 'Etvyz'. The main precondition for participation in these festivals has been the demand that all potential participants sing their songs only in the Poleshuk language. The organisers of the festivals have not restricted the programmes by any formal demand to sing only traditional folklore songs. On the contrary, they have actively promoted new, non-traditional modern compositions, which they judge might be capable of attracting the attention of young people, who are the most important targets of their propagandistic work. The final stage of one important recent festival was broadcast by Belarusian state TV, and obviously had a big influence on the legitimisation of the 'Poleshuk idea' at an all-Belarusian level.

One of the most urgent tasks for those promoting the new literary language is the search for a corresponding literary tradition. While there is already some quite advanced modern literature in the Poleshuk vernacular, the lack of 'true' Poleshuk literary works, sanctified by the authority of the past, is becoming more and more uncomfortable for Poleshuk ideologists. Trying to fill this gap, some popular writers who are officially considered as Belarusian are now treated by Poleshuk activists as in fact Poleshuk. Thus, a classic author from the Belarusian literature of the 19th century, V. Dunin-Martynkevich, is now characterised by them as not just a Belarusian but in the first place a Poleshuk writer who, being a native of Palesse, reflected in his literary works the mode of life and peculiar mentality of the Poleshuks. Criticising the Soviet period, Poleshuk intellectuals stress that up to the present time official Belarusian literary scholars have paid more attention to the 'Belarusian' part of Dunin-Martynkevich's literary legacy than to 'Poleshuk' one. To correct the previous 'mistakes', they proclaim the urgent need to rectify the traditional approach towards Dunin-Martynkevich's literary legacy, and to re-evaluate his literary belonging. (*Збудінне*, 1994, Nos. 5-6)

The present state of the Poleshuk literary language, its place in the self-consciousness of the local population, and its further prospects were comprehensively characterised in the conclusion of the Western Poleshuk Scientific and Practical Conference, which was held in April 1990 in Minsk. Participants in this conference came to the conclusion that 'in spite of considerable microareal differences, the indigenous population of the Western Palesse possesses a sufficient level of specificity and closeness of language and culture as to create the conditions for the formation of an independent ethnic unit. The consolidation of the literary norms and ethnic name can take place as a result of the free will of the people, within the process of the further consolidation of the Poleshuk ethnie' (*Збудінне*, 1991, No. 10 (28)). The academic results of this conference became an additional important tool in the cultural work of the Poleshuk awakeners. The question of whether the efforts of Poleshuk nation-makers will be finally successful or not is still open.

The fact that this ethnic fragmentation and atomisation has affected exclusively Ukrainian and Belarusian linguistic and cultural areas, which have proved to be quite vulnerable to such dangers as ethnic and linguistic separatism, raises the question of the specific cultural and historical roots of this phenomenon. Since the representatives of the new ethnic movements manifest themselves culturally by challenging the Ukrainian and Belarusian literary languages, a more detailed look at the history of the literary versions of these languages could also be fruitful.

Analysing the problem of the interrelation of the spoken dialects and literary languages within the Eastern Slavonic area, Nikolai Trubetzkoy stressed that

> there is no reason to believe... that two dialects, even strongly differentiated, must necessarily develop two distinct literary languages... Each of the great literary languages of Europe (French, Italian, English, German) prevails in a territory linguistically much less homogeneous than that of the Eastern Slavic ethnic group. The differences between Low German and High German or the differences between the dialects of Northern France and of Provence are not only stronger, but also considerably older than those between Ukrainian, Byelo-Russian, and Great Russian... (Trubetzkoy, 1952, p. 22)

Clear evidence of this relatively high level of homogeneity within the Eastern Slavonic area can be also traced in the fact that modern Russian,

Ukrainian and Belarusian still preserve quite visible features of other, older linguistic divisions among the Eastern Slavs which existed before the emergence of these languages. Many of the linguistic similarities and differences simply do not coincide with the present formal borders between those languages. Thus, for instance, 'there is a wide zone of transitional spoken dialects between Russian and Belarusian. There is no strict border separating these languages... Linguists stress certain resemblance between Belarusian and Southern Russian spoken dialects...' (Филин, 1972, p. 636) Trubetzkoy argues that the Russian literary language was created through the organic, natural historical process of the gradual Russification of Old Church Slavonic, representing a kind of organic symbiosis of Old Church Slavonic and local vernaculars. Representatives of all 'principal Eastern Slavic dialects took part in the development of this common Russian literary language.' Moreover, since Old Church Slavonic came to Muscovite Russia during the late middle ages predominantly from Kiev, and through the mediation of some famous Ukrainian scholars (M. Smotritskii, E. Slavinetskii, etc.), which had a decisive influence on the formation of literary Russian and Russian high culture in general, '...in its Church Slavonic element, the Russian literary language belongs to the Ukrainian domain even more than it does to the Great Russian.' (Trubetzkoy, 1952, p. 24)

The formation of the modern Ukrainian and Belarusian literary languages during the 19th century, on the other hand, was based on the absolute repudiation of the Old Church Slavonic heritage, which automatically meant an abandonment of the entire previous cultural tradition, at least within the Orthodox cultural area.

> The Ukrainian intelligentsia... broke away... from the Church Slavonic literary tradition and undertook to develop a literary language based entirely on the popular vernacular and resembling Russian as little as possible...' The result of this turning point in the language-making tradition was that '...connection with the age-old tradition of a literary language lends many advantages to the Russian language. The first of this is that external uniformity and stability... rest upon a long established tradition and are not dependent on popular dialects. This becomes evident if one compares these languages with languages which had no such tradition and developed from popular dialects. This is even more striking in the case of literary Ukrainian [and Belarusian – K. S.] where the instability is so great and the variances so important that under the general name of Ukrainian

there practically exist several languages quite distinct from one another – Galician, Bukovinian, Carpatho-Russian, Eastern Ukrainian...

(Trubetzkoy, 1952, p. 29)

Trubetzkoy's characteristisations might nowadays seem somewhat biased and not particularly relevant to the current situation – since he was referring to a state of affairs which prevailed on the very eve of the creation of modern literary Ukrainian. But if one follows his logic then it seems clear that the current situation within the Ukrainian and Belarusian cultural space could stem from just those peculiarities of literary Ukrainian and Belarusian he discusses. Indeed, by stressing the crucial importance of the spoken vernaculars in the process of language-making, the present ethnic movements are in fact following the same rules as their Ukrainian and Belarusian predecessors. Challenges to the Ukrainian and Belarusian literary languages from new ethnic movements looks just as logical and natural now as did the analogous steps undertaken by Ukrainian and Belarusian national movements in the 19th century, when they challenged literary Russian in a similar manner. Of course, the internal instability of Ukrainian and Belarusian mentioned by Trubetzkoy decreased considerably during the period of their official existence and functioning; but still, unlike literary Russian with its Old Church Slavonic background, modern literary Ukrainian and Belarusian do not possess a stable and long-term historical tradition, sanctified by the historical past and by the authority of the Old Church Slavonic legacy which is common to all Eastern and to a majority of Southern Slavs. Moreover, during the Soviet time these languages had a rather ambiguous status, surviving under the conditions of a real diglossia (with Russian), something which could not help them to acquire social prestige, to homogenise what was supposedly their 'own' linguistic space, or to establish sufficiently stable and viable cultural traditions in the territory where they were officially in use. All these factors made the Ukrainian and Belarusian literary languages extremely vulnerable to the danger of linguistic and ethnic separatism.

Commenting on this problem, Filin has emphasised that:

There are no precise criteria for differentiating between closely related languages on the one hand and remote dialects of the same language on the other, if we are taking only purely linguistic matters into consideration. There are many examples where dialects of the same language differ from each other to a much greater extent than the present Eastern Slavonic languages.... To resolve the question of the independence of these related languages it is necessary to take into account not only linguistic but also historical and cultural peculiarities... It is possible to assert that unless certain dramatic events of the 13th-15th centuries had happened, the ethnic and linguistic picture of the Eastern Slavs would have been different.

(Филин, 1972, p. 637)

The ambiguous position of present literary Ukrainian and Belarusian, which have proved to be the hostages of History, has resulted in the current wave of linguistic separatism. This phenomenon could now become a serious test for the real maturity of these languages.

2. Rewriting History

The notion of shared culture and ancestry, tied to myths of common origin, seems to be one of the most universal elements in ethnic ideologies, and provides the crucial criterion for the ethnic group membership. Reinterpretations of the past, and the selection of cultural signs and symbols related to the past, were always highly politically motivated, and dependent on the historical and social context which presupposes choices in such an important sphere as relations to Others. As Miroslav Hroch has noted, 'Historical consciousness has accumulated rich and diverse material which could be used by various classes, social groups and groups of interests in different historical situations as a building material for their ideologies...' At the same time, however, the possibilities for the conscious construction of new traditions were substantially restricted because they 'were dependent not only on the intensity of the ideological interest, but also on the capacity of the historical consciousness itself.' (Hroch, 1976, pp. 7-8)

The case of the Poleshuk movement, which does not possess any serious tradition or previous experience of constructing its own ethnic ideology, presents a sort of 'tabula rasa', where the nation-building capacity of the existing historical consciousness is now being put to the test by modern ideology-makers, and where the additional weight of political and social factors seems to be quite obvious.

This distinctive feature of the emergening Poleshuk identity was recognised by one of the leading Poleshuk intellectuals, who depicted the present Poleshuk national self-consciousness as something vague, obscure, indefinite and still marked by the absolute lack of any clear idea about common ethnic ancestors – and which does not reflect 'correctly' the historical past of the natives in Palesse. Criticising modern Poleshuk self-consciousness for its narrowness, its pragmatic commitment to the present time, and its lack of spiritual continuity with the past, the same Poleshuk ideologist proclaims that all these weaknesses are also characteristic for the modern Poleshuk literature which 'should effectively promote the process of the formation of full-blooded, active and aggressive self-consciousness.' (Антонюк, 1994) The practical attempts of the Poleshuk activists to 'correct and improve' this still 'wrong' ethnic self-consciousness presuppose the reinterpretation of history.

The emerging Poleshuk ethnic identity manifests itself in the persistent attempts of Poleshuk ideologists to acquire sufficient and reliable historical material for legitimising the Poleshuk's alleged ethnic peculiarity and distinctiveness from their surroundings. The alternative scheme of history which is actively being created at present pretends to cover the whole period of the Poleshuks' existence from the early middle ages up to modern and contemporary history, and to present the new and only correct version of the history of this region by adjusting the principal events in the past of Palesse to the emerging national ideology. In the majority of cases, this specific Poleshuk standpoint does not correspond to, or even directly contradicts, the traditional and generally accepted clichés of Soviet historiography. The ideological clash between this new Poleshuk historical outlook and the national histories adopted by the independent Ukrainian and Belarusian states is at times even more irreconcilable.

The natives of Belarusian Palesse are considered by the Poleshuk intelligentsia as the direct descendants of a mixed Slavonic-Lithuanian population which inhabited this region during the early middle ages, at the time of Kievan Rus'. This population consisted of local Eastern-Slavonic tribes, and the old-Lithuanian tribe of 'Yatvyagi', who were indigenous, pre-Slavonic inhabitants of this region and who were partly exterminated and partly assimilated over time by the Slavs. Thus, for a first mention of these 'Yatvyags' is cited the information from the Kievan 'Chronicle of Bygone Years' that among the ambassadors to Byzantium in 944 there was also the Yatvyagian prince Gunar. Poleshuk history-makers stress the fact that at that time the Yatvyags had their own statehood, and were completely independent from Kievan Rus'. According to them, the Kievan prince Vladimir managed to conquer Palesse only in 983, but already in

1015, after Vladimir's death, the population inhabiting the territory of Palesse became free once more. The further attempts of Vladimir's son, the Kievan prince Yaroslav, to conquer Palesse again in 1038-1044 failed due to the 'heroic resistance' of the local population. Generally, the period from 944 till 1319 is considered as a time of independence of the various state formations in Palesse. This period, however, was marked by numerous wars between the Yatvyags and the Galich Principality. The Galician prince Daniil defeated the Yatvyags in 1227 near Brest; and after this the Yatvyags became Daniil's allies in his wars against Poland. (*Балесы Полісся*, 1989, Nos. 1-2 (5-6)) After 1319 the whole territory of Palesse became an integral part of the Grand Duchy of Lithuania. In the framework of this state formation, numerous local principalities enjoyed a high degree of autonomy and the possibility to develop their culture (the first written documents of the Grand Duchy of Lithuania were in the Poleshuk vernacular). The most tragic date for the territory of Palesse within the Great Lithuanian Principality was 1569, when, as a result of the Polish-Lithuanian Union treaty signed in Lublin, part of South-Western Palesse was added to the Polish kingdom. In the view of today's Poleshuk ideologists, this act had twofold negative consequences for the historical destiny of Palesse: first, it separated the previously unified Palesse region between Poland and Lithuania, which undermined the cultural unity of the local population; and secondly, it exposed the southern part of Palesse to the harsh discriminatory policy of the Polish authorities. (*Балесы Полісся*, 1989, Nos. 1-2 (5-6))

It is worth noting that all the above-mentioned Poleshuk reflections on the ethnic history of Palesse and the ethnic roots of its population do not repudiate completely the main propositions of existing historiography. Russian and Polish historians, on the basis of Russian manuscripts, Polish chronicles and local geographical names, had already in the 19th century come to the conclusion that up to the 13th century the whole enormous area of present-day Western Belarus and North-Eastern Poland was populated by Yatvyagian tribes. (Барсов, 1885)

These conclusions were further corroborated and expanded by Soviet scholars. Thus, anthropological study of the contemporary population of Belarus has demonstrated that during the middle ages the river Pripyat (South-Western Belarus) was the Southern border-line of the Baltic anthropological zone. (Бунак, 1956) Accumulated archaeological material has made the picture of Poleshuk ethnic history more precise.

Sedov argues that 'Analysis of the relevant archaeological material from the 11th-13th centuries demonstrates that it belonged not to the Yatvyags themselves but rather to their Slavonised descendants. Hence, the population of this region already at this time was predominantly Slavonic. There remained islands of Yatvyagian population in the middle part of the Neman basin until the 17th-19th centuries, but they already spoke Lithuanian...' (Седов, 1982, p. 120) The historical arguments of Poleshuk ideologists might therefore seem fairly persuasive and academically proved. A quite discouraging fact here, however, is that the population of almost every historical region within the Eastern-Slavonic area can doubt its sense of belonging to the three supposed main nationalities of Russians, Ukrainians or Belarusians on the basis of similar or even more persuasive arguments. There is a great number of potential 'Yatvyagian situations' among the Eastern Slavs. As far as Belarus is concerned, for example, the population of the other parts of Belarus (apart from Palesse, that is) was formed as a result of the gradual Slavonisation of the local indigenous Eastern Baltic tribes, which were very close ethnically to the Yatvyags. Moreover, modern archaeology considers the cultural peculiarities of one of the biggest Eastern Slavonic tribes, the Krivichians (who played an active part in the ethnogenesis of both Belarusians and Russians) to be the result of the 'gradual Slavonisation of Balts – representatives of the Dnepro-Dvin archaeological culture.' (Седов, 1982, p. 164) The role of the Balts in the ethnogenesis of the Eastern Slavs is stressed still more by some other scholars. Thus, according to Tretyakov, '...the mixture of Slavs with Eastern Balts led to the formation of the Eastern Slavs themselves and... the Slavonic colonists from the basin of the Middle Dnieper were in fact not "pure" Slavs, but a population with considerable elements of assimilated Eastern Balts.' (Третьяков, 1970, p. 153) This theory, however, is criticised by other specialists as exaggerating the importance of the role of the Balts. (Седов, 1982, p. 272)

Another important example in this almost countless tally of cases is the Slavonic population of Russia's Novgorod region, which was formed as a direct result of the Slavonic assimilation of the local Finnish tribe of Vod'. Sedov stresses that as a result of this ethnic mixing there was formed an original cultural symbiosis of Slavs, Finns and Balts in the region. Similarly, the population of the modern Central Russia resulted from the 'mixture and gradual absorption of the local Finnish population (tribe of Merya) by Slavs... Anthropological peculiarities of the local Slavonic population in the 11th-14th centuries (the forms of skulls) demonstrate the obvious resemblance between them and Finnish tribes of this part of Eastern Europe.' (Седов, 1982, p. 194) All these examples prove once more that real cultural differences do not play any independent role, and are often used merely as a plausible excuse by nationalist movements.

A clearer discrepancy between the Poleshuks and proponents of traditional historiography arises about the question of Yatvyagian statehood. Apart from proclaiming the legendary prince Gunar the head of a Yatvyagian state independent from Kiev (which looks quite obscure, as the manuscript only enumerates some names, among them Gunar, of people to whom it refers as 'messengers and merchants of the Russian kin'),[1] Poleshuk historians insist on the predominantly Yatvyagian character of the local mediæval principalities of the 12th-13th centuries. Although Poleshuk history-makers are doing their best to present Yatvyagian Palesse in the middle ages as a more or less unified entity in a political sense, it is obvious that the term 'Palesse' on its own reflects just a geographical reality, designating a certain territory (which was covered by similar Slavic dialects).

Such towns as Pinsk, Turov and Berestye (Brest) are referred by them as political and cultural centres of the ancient Yatvyags-Poleshuks. The above-mentioned towns, however, are considered by Soviet and post-Soviet historiography as the centres of Eastern Slavonic principalities of the same names which were closely connected with Kievan Rus'. The Vladimir-Volyn' and Turov-Pinsk principalities were the most famous and influential among those on the territory of Palesse. Pinsk and Turov are considered as centres of the Eastern Slavonic tribe of the Drehovichians, who colonised Western Palesse during the 6th-8th centuries. Brest was founded later, by colonists from the Drehovichian tribe, and initially belonged to Turov-Pinsk principality. (Лысенко, 1974, p. 153)

At the very beginning of the Poleshuk movement, Poleshuk historians tended to doubt the Slavonic character of these state formations in Palesse. Nevertheless, they reluctantly recognised the influence of Eastern Slavs by admitting that 'from the 10th century, Slavonic crusaders started to spread Slavonic speech and culture... and finally succeeded in Slavonising the land of the Yatvyags.' (*Балесы Полісся*, 1989, Nos. 1-2 (5-6)) At that time, the idea of a non-Slavonic, particularly Baltic ethnic

---

[1] *Памятники литературы древней Руси* [Literary Works of Ancient Rus'], Moscow, 1978, vol. 1, p. 60.

origin for the Yatvyags was vigorously propagated by the Poleshuk intelligentsia. Some Poleshuk enthusiasts tried to prove that the true forebears of the Poleshuks were not only the Baltic peoples (Lithuanians and Latvians) but even the Celts.

The most traditional, and still very influential, hypothesis about the Yatvyags says that the local Yatvyagian population, who were close to Lithuanians, was mainly assimilated by Eastern Slavs and absorbed by the Slavonic, Orthodox culture, which was more developed and therefore more attractive for the pagan Yatvyags than their own traditions. Another interesting hypothesis interprets the Yatvyags as not an ethnic but rather a religious community, with militant paganism as the most distinctive feature. The name 'Yatvyag' itself was according to this view the title of the pagan priests, a meaning which was forgotten after the conversion of the people of the region to Orthodox Christianity. Nevertheless, the term 'Yatvyag' as a mean of ethnic self-identification survived up to the middle of the 19th century. Thus, according to the census conducted in the Western parts of the Russian Empire in 1857, on the territories of the Belsk, Brest, Volkovysk and Kobrin regions of Palesse, 3,741, 1,616, 2,843 and 22,725 persons respectively identified themselves as Yatvyags. (Шелягович, 1990)

More recently there has appeared a more realistic tendency to consider the Yatvyags as only one of the founding elements of the present Poleshuks, who were also greatly influenced by the Belarusian, Russian and Ukrainian languages and cultures during later centuries. By contrast, at the beginning of the modern Poleshuk movement at the end of the 1980s the main accent was placed firmly on the 'Yatvyagian idea', and on the non-Slavonic roots of the local inhabitants. The first version of the ethnic name of the present population in Palesse was indeed 'Yatvyags', rather than the generally accepted and now widely used 'Poleshuks'. The popular image of the ethnic ancestors of the present-day Poleshuks was clearly expressed by one popular Poleshuk poet who proclaimed that 'we are Slavs and we are Balts...' (*Збудінне*, 1994, Nos. 11-12) Later on, a somewhat more balanced view of Poleshuk mediæval history was expressed. Thus, one of the most crucial questions on the relationship of the Poleshuks with Kievan Rus' found a new interpretation according to which 'Kievan Rus' was a federal state of the emerging Russian, Belarusian, Ukrainian and Western Poleshuk ethnic units...' (Антонюк, 1993)

The present reinterpretation of Poleshuk modern and contemporary history also demonstrates the intention to remove the historical past of Palesse from the states which include the territory of Palesse today. Thus, Poleshuk intellectuals criticise the political arrangements between Germany and Ukraine in 1918, when Germany handed all ethnic Poleshuk territories to the Ukrainian People's Republic (UNR), as a result of the Brest Peace Treaty between Soviet Russia and Germany. All Poleshuk attempts to acquire autonomy within Ukraine were met with a cold reaction from Kiev. Poleshuk intellectuals say that the leaders of the Belarusian People's Republic (BNR) which was established in 1918 under German control considered the possibility of 'restoring' Poleshuk statehood. This seems quite possible, taking into account that R. Skirmunt, the prominent Poleshuk awakener, was one of the leading figures in the Belarusian political leadership at that time.

The interwar period when Palesse was a part of Poland is referred to as a time of the further development of Poleshuk ethnic self-consciousness. In the mean time, Poleshuk historians criticise the assimilative centralist policy of the interwar Poland. The Polish census from 1931 shows that about 62 per cent of the local population in Palesse identified themselves as Poleshuks. The course of events in Palesse during the Second World War is described in a similar way. Poleshuk representatives stress that the activity of M. Borovets, the famous leader of the local guerrilla movement Bul'ba, had in fact a Poleshuk-nationalist character. Poleshuk intellectuals argue that Bul'ba fought not only against Germans and Soviet partisan troops, but also against Ukrainian supporters of Bandera. He also published a local newspaper, 'Gaidamak', not in literary Ukrainian, but in Poleshuk vernacular. The principal contradiction between Bul'ba and Bandera was that Bandera, as a representative of Ukrainian national radicals, did not acknowledge the special ethnic peculiarities of the Poleshuks, or their right to a wide autonomy – which was the idea represented and defended by Bul'ba and his army. The present Ukrainian vision of Bul'ba as a representative of one of the streams within the purely Ukrainian movement for independence is seen by the Poleshuks as nothing more than a misrepresentation.

In general, both the prewar and post-war periods present even more favourable objects for clashes of opinion than do the mediæval times. While some Poleshuk radicals proclaim that there were neither historical nor ethnic reasons for making Palesse a part of Ukraine or Belarus, on the ground that territories inhabited by Poleshuks had never been an integral part of purely Belarusian or Ukrainian states previously, some Ukrainian representatives argue that 'making Palesse a part of Belarus' in 1939 could be explained by the anti-Ukrainian policy of Stalin's regime, which in this way succeeded in solving several problems: to punish Ukraine in the territorial question, to compensate Belarus for the loss of Smolensk region and, finally, to create preconditions for a conflict between Belorussians and Ukrainians...' (*За вільну Україну*, 21. 11. 1990, No. 99) The enormous interest which is displayed in some Ukrainian circles towards Palesse and its population can provide us with an explanation of a further characteristic feature of Poleshuk ideology, namely, its absolute disinterest in the Greek-Catholic confession, which was the main confession among the local population till 1830s, when it was prohibited by the authorities of the Russian Empire. Indeed, the Greek Catholicism which is being especially fostered in Western Ukraine as a 'pure' national Ukrainian confession can be used (and is being used) as an additional argument by those who support a pro-Ukrainian orientation in Palesse. Trying to avoid this, Poleshuk ideologists prefer not to touch upon the confessional question at all.

As A. D. Smith has mentioned, 'divergent readings of "History", and the chance of multiple histories can only weaken... a sense of identity..., [while] a unified History and a single account can 'make sense' and 'direct' that aroused consciousness.' The dispute for the right to determine the only 'correct' version of this 'unified History' is actively going on. It is worth noting that the youngest, Poleshuk actor in this dispute has already elaborated almost a whole series of the necessary motifs which we find in any national mythology, including 1. a myth of origin in time, 2. a myth of origin in space, 3. a myth of ancestry, 4. a myth of migration, 5. a myth of liberation, 6. a myth of the golden age, 7. a myth of decline, and 8. a myth of rebirth. (Smith, 1986, p. 192)

As we can see, two elements in this general scheme of History are stressed by Poleshuk ideologists. First, they emphasise the 'Yatvyagian', that is, old-Lithuanian roots in the Poleshuk spiritual legacy and mentality, which enable them to legitimise the idea of Poleshuk distinctiveness from their Belarusian and Ukrainian surroundings. This academically somewhat elusive thesis about the old-Lithuanian element as one of the main pillars of the present Poleshuk culture is embodied in the second official name of the Poleshuks and their language – 'Yatvyags'. Second, the Poleshuk intelligentsia tends to view the mere fact of Poleshuk existence as the 'miraculous phenomenon of a living relic of the formerly existing all-

Russian superethnic community and of Poleshuk Rus', which has survived to the end of 20th century'. (*Збудінне*, 1994, Nos. 5-6) This thesis has become a particularly frequent and popular one in the Poleshuk movement during recent times. It obviously contradicts many previously proclaimed axioms of Poleshuk history. Without doubt, such a radical alteration of accents reflects a certain evolution within the emerging Poleshuk system of values, which was tremendously affected by the changing political and social reality in Belarus and throughout the CIS. It is quite clear now that the starting point of this rapid evolution was connected with the emergence of the independent Belarusian state, and with its internal and foreign policy. All these questions will be touched upon in the next section.

In fact, the 'pure' Poleshuk history is so little documented that the imaginative nationalist can construct almost any fantastic past for his people that he wishes. Like the Rusyn ideologists formerly, Poleshuk activists tend to support the old idea of all-Russian unity, treating Russians, Ukrainians and Belarusians as mere branches of one indivisible organism. It is worth noting that the Poleshuks in their vernacular often refer to themselves as 'local', 'Russian', or 'Poleshuk' simultaneously, and to their speech as 'Russian' or 'Poleshuk', treating these words as synonyms – a usage which is reflected in modern Poleshuk literature. It looks symbolic that the time of Kievan Rus', which is considered as a common cradle of Russians, Ukrainians and Belarusians, is particularly eulogised by the Poleshuk ideologists. Unlike early stages of national propaganda, when Poleshuk separateness and distinguishing features were emphasised, there is a clear tendency now to stress the supreme unity of all Eastern Slavs, and to present it as the only natural state of affairs and a universal key to all problems. The only new element in this scheme is that Poleshuk ideologists insist on the existence of a Poleshuk unit as a fourth and separate element of the Eastern Slavonic ethnic community – together with Russians, Ukrainians and Belarusians.

All this provides an illustration of Gellner's idea that nationalism can use an already existing cultural legacy, even though in reality all the cultures supposedly defended and represented by this nationalism are its own artificial inventions, and nothing more than products of nationalism itself. (Gellner, 1990) The ideology chosen by Poleshuk intellectuals does not seem to be easily accessible for the general public, which may have rather negative consequences for their propagandistic efforts. As T. H. Eriksen has noted, 'Ethnic identities must seem convincing to their members in order to function, and they must also be acknowledged as legitimate by non-members of the group.' (Eriksen, 1993, p. 69) Both the above-mentioned conditions are still in question. At the same time, however, Poleshuk leaders demonstrate sufficient flexibility in constructing their own history, by keeping in mind all current social changes, and instantly reacting to new tendencies in the public sphere, with results which are being applied in their selective ideological work.

3. Public and Political Activity

From the very beginning of its formation, the Poleshuk national movement has demonstrated an obvious commitment to practical politics. Political activity is still one of the most important goals of the public and cultural society 'Polisse', in spite of numerous declarations of its leaders about the cultural priorities of their movement and their complete lack of interest in politics.

Substantial changes which have occured in the course of the political and ideological evolution of the Poleshuk movement clearly reflect all the shifts in its historical and ideological priorities. It has already been mentioned that the initial stage of the Poleshuk movement was marked by strong romanticism and by vigorous attempts to find evidence of the Baltic ethnic roots of the Poleshuks. The Yatvyagian, that is, Baltic ethnic origin of the local population in Palesse was actively stressed at that time. At the same time, this tendency went hand in hand with overt attempts to deny the Slavonic ethnic belongingness of the local population: and so 'Yatvyags' was the main and preferable ethnic name vigorously propagated by Poleshuk intellectuals at that time. This initial period of the Poleshuk movement in the political sphere manifested itself in supporting all radical democratic anticommunist movements in the Baltic Republics, Belarus and Ukraine, in demonstrations of solidarity with their political programmes, and in propagating market reforms and real sovereignty for the national republics of the former USSR. During this period, the public and cultural society 'Polisse' had close relations with the Baltic Republics, in the first place with Lithuania. Thus, the main organ of the Poleshuk movement, the monthly 'Zbudinne', was published in Vilnius, Lithuania, during the late 1980s, because of the negative attitude of the conservative Belarusian authorities towards the 'Polisse' society, which made it impossible to publish 'Zbudinne' in Belarus. Sympathetic responses towards anticommunist Popular Fronts in Latvia and Estonia, and the Lithuanian 'Sajudis', and at times very explicit suggestions about following their examples, were quite often presented in the pages of Poleshuk periodicals. (*Збудінне*, 1989-1991)

A high level of mutual understanding, and ideological closeness, were at that time also characteristic for the relations between the Ukrainian 'Rukh' and 'Polisse', although Poleshuk leaders emphasised that the best possible territorial and political arrangement of the Ukrainian state for Poleshuks would be a Federation with a high degree of decentralisation.

Total misunderstanding and tense contradictions characterised the relations between the Belarusian national intelligentsia (the most radical part of which formed the Belarusian Popular Front – BNF) and the Poleshuk movement. The Belarusian intelligentsia was (and still is) quite reluctant to recognise the existence of an independent Poleshuk *ethnie*. Belarusian national radicals accused Poleshuk leaders of 'threatening the unity of the Belarusian nation, and the Belarusian cultural and historical legacy' and even of creating an anti-Belarusian 'diversion'. (*Літаратура i мастацтва*, 3. 3. 1989) Representatives of the anticommunist BNF viewed the position of the Poleshuks as making a split in the Belarusian democratic movement, which could slow down the struggle against the communist system. (*Збудінне*, 1991, No. 2 (20))

Poleshuk-Ukrainian relations have undergone radical changes during recent years. At the end of the 1980s, Poleshuk leaders proclaimed that 'there were no contradictions between *Polisse* and the Ukrainian *Rukh*'. (*Збудінне*, 1990, No. 8 (13)) Now the situation has been reversed. The paternalist approach demonstrated by *Rukh*, and its treatment of the local population in Palesse as Ukrainians, finally aroused a negative reaction from the Poleshuk intelligentsia. These contradictions culminated in an official declaration released by the Poleshuk leadership which was caused by an interview of *Rukh*'s leader Vyacheslav Chornovil in the Belarusian daily *Zvyazda*. In his interview, Chornovil labelled all attempts to prove the existence of 'so-called Yatvyags' as a mere fiction, pointing out that 'there was no necessity to invent any fantastic Yatvyags... What is necessary in fact is just to guarantee all the national and cultural needs of the Ukrainian minority living compactly in Brest region.' (*Звязда*, 17. 2. 1994) In their declarations, Poleshuk leaders have condemned 'Ukrainian national philosophy' and all the attempts to impose Ukrainian self-identification on Poleshuks. It looks quite interesting that the interview given by Chornovil was criticised in a Poleshuk declaration as 'ignoring the right of the local population for national self-identification and at the same time interference in the internal affairs of the sovereign Belarusian state...' (*Збудінне*, 1994, Nos. 5-6)

The standpoint of Poleshuk intellectuals has undergone substantial changes during the existence of independent Belarus. Even the relatively moderate policy aimed at Belarusisation which was pursued by the Belarusian government during the first few years of Belarusian independence caused very strong criticism from the Poleshuk side. The Poleshuk elite accused the Belarusian authorities of substituting the previous policy of Russification with a policy of forced Belarusisation. The devastating social consequences which followed the disintegration of the USSR, and the tremendous decrease in the standards of living in Belarus, also had a considerable impact on the viewpoint of Poleshuk leaders. As a result, the Poleshuk movement shifted left, and to a somewhat pro-Russian direction. Such slogans as Eastern-Slavonic brotherhood, integration within the CIS, and official status for the Russian language alongside with Belarusian, have become quite popular in everyday Poleshuk political rhetoric since the end of 1993. Thus, commenting on the Congress of the Peoples of Belarus which took place in September, 1993, and which united leftist and pro-union forces in Belarus, 'Zbudinne' stressed the fruitfulness of CIS integration and even proclaimed that 'the Eastern-Slavonic superethnic community based on the brotherhood of Russians, Belarusians, Ukrainians and Poleshuks... would not survive under the conditions of being separated into independent sovereign pieces...' (*Збудінне*, 1993, No. 7 (69))

One of the most radical demands of Poleshuk leadership towards the Belarusian authorities is determined by the special status of the Poleshuks as an indigenous population in South-Western Belarus which, unlike other minorities (Russians, Poles), does not have their own mother state outside Belarus. According to M. Shelyahovych, the chairman of the 'Polisse' society, this circumstance dictates the urgent need for constitutional guarantees of equal cultural and linguistic rights for all ethnic communities in Belarus, including Poleshuks as an inseparable element of a Belarusian multicultural state. (*Збудінне*, 1994, Nos. 7-8) An even more negative attitude is demonstrated by Poleshuk activists towards Ukrainian authorities, and particularly towards Ukrainian nationalistic organisations, for their official interpretation of the local population in Palesse as Ukrainians, the linguistic similarity between Poleshuks and Ukrainians being much more obvious than that between Poleshuks and Belarusians. Ukrainian cultural organisations, which are many in the region, are accused of attempting to 'Ukrainise' Belarusian Palesse. The Belarusian authorities, in turn, are criticised for their passive reaction to the policy of Ukrainisation, and are warned of a 'Ukrainian danger' to the sovereign Belarusian state. As a result, Poleshuks now tend to support pro-Russian unionist forces, which are quite influential in Belarus. Thus, during the first presidential elections in Belarus in July, 1994, the leadership of 'Polisse' supported Alexandr Lukashenko, one of the most pro-Russian and pro-Union-oriented politicians in Belarus. It is worth noting that during the parliamentary elections in Belarus in May, 1995 all the candidates of the public and cultural society 'Polisse' alongside their special Poleshuk demands (establishment of a Poleshuk university and a Poleshuk bank in Pinsk) also included in their election programme the demand to grant Russian the status of the second official language of Belarus. (*Збудінне*, 1995, No. 1)

Conclusion

This fragmentary general picture of the most striking features of the emerging Poleshuk identity in the years after the collapse of the USSR confirms Deutsch's thesis that within the history of all societies and cultures there 'may stand out certain decisive periods of particularly large and rapid change in the course of which technologies, social and economic institutions, and the patterns of culture are reshaped, dissolved or newly combined. There are periods of "incubation" when elements of a new pattern are assembled...' (Deutsch, 1969, p. 38) The quite logical question about why this process of 'incubation' for Poleshuks should have developed exactly at the beginning of the 1990s can be partly elucidated in terms of the theory of the Russian sociolinguist A. Dulichenko. In his study of sociolinguistic strategies among the Slavs in the 19th century, Dulichenko found that they were manifested in 3 levels: regional literary languages, national literary languages and, finally, projects of all-Slavonic languages. He came to the conclusion that every ethnic consciousness shapes and preserves itself, and in certain periods activates its own ethnolinguistic space. Dulichenko argues that ethnic consciousness, in turn, is divided into 3 basic levels:

1. A geographical region covered by one homogeneous dialect;
2. A group of regions inhabited by a population speaking related and close dialects which are easily mutually understandable;
3. A wider self-perception in terms of the closeness among Slavonic nations and languages, which is sometimes manifested only at the theoretical level. (The numerous projects for all-Slavonic literary languages which appeared regularly from the 16th century on provide examples.)

The first level of ethnic consciousness engenders regional literary languages, the second level produces national literary languages, while the third level is connected with the projects of artificial all-Slavonic languages. (Дуличенко, 1993)

The viability of the regional literary languages which existed among the Slavs from the middle ages until the 20th century (for example, regional literary languages in Croatia, Slovenia and Eastern Slovakia, which even co-existed during a long historical period with the corresponding national literary languages) is explained by Dulichenko firstly by the general weakness of national literary languages in remote rural districts, and secondly by the 3-level structure of ethnic self-consciousness, which in certain periods of time resorts to such of the various possible forms of self-expression as is the most appropriate for the given ethnic community under their specific historical circumstances.

This scheme could be applied in our particular case. The weakness of the national literary language (that is, Belarusian) in the Palesse region of Belarus manifested itself even more clearly when Belarus became independent, and Belarusian was constitutionally proclaimed as the state language. Initiated by the central authorities in Minsk, the official campaign of Belarusisation deepened the tension between weak literary Belarusian and local dialects. The dissolution of the USSR and the emergence of the sovereign Belarusian state forced the local population to face the necessity to be Belarusians not just formally (as in the former USSR) but in reality. In response to these external factors, a considerable part of the natives of Palesse moved to a regional level of self-consciousness, which proved to be a more relevant and adequate means of expression of their thoughts and feelings, and simultaneously something closer to their ethnic and linguistic 'roots'.

The coincidence of the emergence of independent Belarus from one side, and active work on the creation of a Poleshuk ethnic identity from the other, quite convincingly testifies to the fact that a considerable part of the local population in Palesse proved to be unprepared for Belarusian national ideology as embodied in the mere existence of independent Belarus, which in fact played the role of external catalyst, accelerating the transition of the local population to the regional level of ethnic self-consciousness. The mutual interdependence between the emergence of independent Belarus and the Poleshuk movement is obvious. It represents one form of public discontent with the current state of affairs. Poleshuk local peculiarities just provided suitable and attractive cultural decorations, which proved the most relevant qualities for the needs of the local elite.

The majority of the Belarussian population, however, preferred a much simpler and more traditional way of expressing public discontent. Results of the national referendum in Belarus in May 14, 1995, when an overwhelming majority of Belarusians voted for Russian as a second official language in the country, for the preservation of the state symbols of Soviet Byelorussia, and for closer integration with Russia, say a lot about the real attitudes of the Belarusian population towards the present form of Belarusian statehood. The outcome of the referendum seems to be quite natural, if we take into consideration the fact that an absolute majority of the Belarusian population stood for the preservation of the USSR during the referendum in March 17, 1991. The present state of ethnic self-consciousness of a considerable part of Belarusian population obviously does not correspond to the existing form of Belarusian statehood. The Poleshuk movement is just one manifestation of this general contradiction. The same could be said about the Rusyns in Transcarpathian Ukraine and Eastern Slovakia.

The prospects of the Poleshuk movement are obscure. It seems that the latest changes in Belarus – in the first place the declaration of the official status of Russian, and the more constructive approach of the Belarusian central authorities towards minority issues and the creation of a Union with Russia – were perceived positively by the Poleshuk elite. The deviation of the Belarusian leadership from the building of the ethnic Belarusian state and from forced Belarusisation meant the disappearance of external danger for Poleshuks. Moreover, the latest trends in Belarusian political life show that the Belarusian leadership applies more and more frequently the same rhetoric on Eastern Slavonic superethnic unity and brotherhood which has been propagated by Poleshuk intellectuals. As a result, during the last few years the Poleshuk movement has lost its dynamism, and become less visible on the public and political scene.

Under the present conditions, the Poleshuk movement will probably grind to a halt somewhere in between phase A (which has been defined by Miroslav Hroch as a period of initial academic interest) and phase B (the period of patriotic propaganda) of national movements. (Hroch, 1971, p. 36)

References

Deutsch, K. W. (1969), *Nationalism and Social Communication*, Cambridge, Massachusetts.

Eriksen, T. H. (1993), *Ethnicity and Nationalism. Anthropological Perspectives*, Pluto Press, London.

Gellner, E. (1990), *Nations and Nationalism*, Oxford.

Horowitz, D. L. (1975), 'Ethnic Identity', in N. Glazer and D. P. Moynihan (eds), *Ethnicity. Theory and Experience*, Harvard University.

Hroch, M. (1971), *Obrození malých evropských národů* [The Revival of Small European Nations], Praha.

Hroch, M. (1976), *Úloha historického povědomí v evropském národním hnutí v 19 století* [The Role of Historical Consciousness in European National Movements in the 19th Century], Praha.

Jyotirindra Das Gupta (1975), 'Ethnicity in India', in N. Glazer and D. P. Moynihan (eds), *Ethnicity: Theory and Experience*, Harvard University, p. 470.

Lozoviuk, P. (1994), 'Etnicky indiferentní skupiny – obohacení, nebo hrozba?' [Ethnically indifferent groups – enrichment, or threat?], *Střední Evropa*, 43/1994.

Magocsi, P. R. (1993), 'Scholarly Seminar on the Codification of the Rusyn Language', *SLAVIA*, Ročnik 62, pp. 550-552.

Paukovič, V. (1994), 'Etnicka štruktura Slovenska, jej vyvoj, demograficke a socialne charakteristiky' [Ethnic Structure of Slovakia, its Development and Demographic and Social Characteristics], *Sociologia*, Bratislava, Ročnik 26, č.5-6, pp. 425-431.

Roosens, E. E. (1989), *Creating Ethnicity. The Process of Ethnogenesis*, SAGE Publications, London.

Seton-Watson, H. (1977), *Nations and States*, Methuen, London.

Smith, A.D. (1986), *The Ethnic Origins of Nations*, Oxford.

Stang, X. S. (1935), *Die Westrussische Kanzleisprache des Grossturstentums* [Evolution of West-Russian Clerical Language], Oslo.

Trubetzkoy, N. (1952), *The Common Slavic Element in Russian Culture*, Columbia University.

Weinreich, P. (1989), 'Variations in Ethnic Identity: Identity Structure Analysis', in K. Liebkind (ed.), *New Identities in Europe*, Gower, Vermont.

Антонюк, Г. (1993), 'Западные полешуки: их путь во всемирной истории' [Western Poleshuks: Their Way in World History], in *Збудінне*, No. 7 (69).

Антонюк, Г. (1994), 'Западные полешуки: их путь во всемирной истории' [Western Poleshuks: Their Way in World History], in *Збудінне*, Nos. 5-6.

Барсов, Н.П. (1885), *Очерки русской исторической географии* [Studies in Russian Historical Geography], Warsaw.

Любавский, М.К. (1909), *Историческая география России в связи с колонизацией* [Historical Geography of Russia in Relation to Colonisation], Moscow.

Бунак, В. (1956), 'Антропологические исследования' [Studies in Anthropology], in *Антропологический сборник*, Moscow, vol. 1.

Седов, В. В. (1982), *Восточные славяне в 6-7 вв.* [The Eastern Slavs in the 6th-7th Centuries], Moscow.

Геллнер, Э. (1992), 'Пришествие национализма. Мифы нации и класса' [The Coming of Nationalism. Myths of Nation and Class], in *Путь*, 1992, #1.

Дуличенко, А. Д. (1981), *Славянские литературные микроязыки* [Slavonic Literary Micro-Languages], Tallinn.

Дуличенко, А. Д. (1993), 'К типологии социолингвистических стратегий в эпоху национального возрождения' [Towards a Typology of Socio-Linguistic Strategies in the Epoch of National Revival], in *Историко-культурные и социолингв-истические аспекты изучения славянских литературных языков эпохи национального возрождения*, Moscow.

Дуличенко, А. Д. (1994), 'Славянские литературные микроязыки: проблема нормы' [Slavonic Literary Micro-Languages: Problems of the Norm], in *Традиция и новые тенденции в развитии славянских литературных языков*, Moscow, pp. 17-20.

Милюков, П. (1925), *Национальный вопрос* [The National Question], Berlin.

Лысенко, П. (1974), *Города Туровской земли* [The Towns of the Turov Region], Minsk.

Третьяков, П. (1970), *У истоков древнерусской народности* [The Origins of the Old Russian Nationality], Leningrad.

Филин, Ф. П. (1972), *Происхождение русского, украинского и белорусского языков* [The Origin of the Russian, Ukrainian and Belarusian Languages], Leningrad.

Шелягович, М. (1990), 'Ятвяги – были, но кем они были?' [The Yatvags Did Exist, But Who Were They?], in *Збудінне*, No. 12 (17).

5 Inter-Ethnic Coexistence and Cultural Autonomy in Ukraine: the Case of the Donetsk Region

KATERYNA STADNIK

When an immense construction is seen destroying itself before one's eyes, and simply collapsing like a house of cards, it is probably best understood as the work of immutable laws of nature. Those laws seem to be equally applicable to all the creations of human hands, minds and imaginations individually, as well as to the human world itself, taken as a whole. The fall of empires and the birth of new ones may usually be subsumed under certain social, economic, historical or other similar principles, which appear to be perfectly rational and completely consistent. Some of those principles, dealing with general theory, are well known, and some are still to be examined, as when a newly appeared historical phenomenon is in question. Communal awareness in its various forms, including that of a nation, ethnic group or region, as an ambiguous force able both to consolidate and to destroy, is a relatively novel case for study. So far, transitions in ethnic intercourse seem to be volatile and hardly predictable. And so, newly established and independent states seem often to bear a strong resemblance to houses built of cards...

Introduction

The call for national self-determination became the universal catchword on the eve of independence as the USSR dissolved. The forces calling for independence believed (or pretended to believe when seeking political power) that some Nations, as distinct from the *Sovetskiy narod,* had their own visions of future development and were theoretically ready and practically able to implement them in accordance with their social, economic, cultural, etc. *national* demands. How have they succeeded? It is not yet time to make a definitive assessment. However, a preliminary review is not only feasible but also timely.

When looking at the development of any young independent states, among the matters of special concern is the problem of the relationship between integration processes and the in-depth development of particular ethnic groups and regions. In staking out its claim of sovereignty and at the same time insisting on getting its own way, the multi-ethnic National State places itself in an embarrassing realm of double standards and therefore often becomes susceptible to quite a distressing level of internal torment. And yet some of the governments in question endeavour to implement liberal approaches, founded on the principle of preserving a balance between the prerogatives of the State and the priorities of the regions; and between the Nation's codes and the interests of the various ethnic groups in the population. Since this task is curiously demanding, those manoeuvres are not all plain sailing. However, against the predominantly negative background of contemporary inter-ethnic relations in the greater part of the post-Soviet area, the attempts to reconcile contradictory views and to balance the conflicting claims seem to have been quite generous on the whole.

Ukraine is one of those countries which are considered to have a liberal approach to the treatment of their ethnic groups (inter-ethnic peaceful coexistence in the country is a favourite 'hobby-horse' of the ruling elites, and is mounted particularly frequently during pre-election periods). However, as Ukraine develops as an independent unit, and as its state structure matures and its institutions take shape, questions of the correlation between national vs. ethnic, and social vs. individual factors have arisen more and more frequently. Having promised a wide spectrum of possibilities for political, economic and cultural development for all the citizens of Ukraine (It could not help promising such things, after all. *Noblesse oblige!*), the Government ran straight into a dispute with all those who felt able to formulate their demands. Among the most ambiguous and oft-discussed issues affecting the rights of ethnic groups in one way or another were questions of local self-government, regional national-cultural autonomies and majority/minority language status. The interim results of those discussions proved that Ukraine, though having constitutionally committed itself to the way of unitary Nation-State building (Article 2 of the Constitution of Ukraine), is striving to maintain the peaceful coexistence of ethnic minorities on its territory, and to support their development – on condition they do not act counter to the interests of the State (Articles 11, 24, 36 of the Constitution of Ukraine). However, implementing this fair-minded aim could run into difficulties for some important reasons.

Among the temporary 'risk factors', the most dangerous and the least resolvable in the near future is the lack of finance, which impedes many of the Government's progressive initiatives, including support of ethnic groups' development. Economic problems affect the majority and the minorities equally, though the situation could be interpreted as involving some neglect of non-Ukrainian citizens by the State.

Also, during the strenuous pre-election struggles of the various diverse political forces, including those calling for regional autonomy, ethnic claims could be manipulated for purposes separate from the common good. However, if we take into account that the majority of the population is endowed with a deep (*acquired rather than inborn*) scepticism towards any political parties or movements whatsoever, and is therefore experiencing an ever-increasing estrangement from political games, we see that those manoeuvres are not likely to achieve their goals effortlessly.

Next, one can speculate on the growing cultural schism between the regions, which differ not only by their locations, natural and geopolitical environments, and economic potentials but also by their ethnic compositions. The problem of regionalism is one of the most challenging issues when thinking about the present stage of Ukrainian Nation-State building. Besides the Crimean Autonomous Republic which, by the way, was autonomous before it became a part of Soviet Ukraine in 1954 as 'a gift of the fraternal Russian People', the Eastern areas, with the biggest proportion of Russians in the population of the whole country, often alarm new policy-makers by their increasingly 'alien' collective attitude. The most problematic spot in this issue is the Donbass area, known as the centre of coal-mining industry in the region. It is a territory where Ukrainians make up only 51 per cent of the whole population, while the average for Ukraine is 72· 2 per cent. (Материалы Всесоюзной..., 1989) Moreover, the coal-mining industry is currently experiencing considerable economic troubles, something that affects the majority of the employed population, representing many different nationalities. This could lead to quite biased public attitudes, and cause serious social, political and ethnic problems.

In spite of the fact that the population of Donbass is multi-ethnic, this has never been commonly considered as a cause for any considerable national conflicts in the region. However, a wide range of questions, directly or indirectly dealing with the problems of ethnic self-determination, have occasionally come up in the mass media, and during seminars and meetings organized by local and all-Ukrainian ethnic groups – even if the majority of these problems were not regarded very seriously within the circles of those who were connected with the decision-making process. And yet, the results of numerous sociological studies prove the phenomenon of ever-increasing mass anxiety over inter-ethnic coexistence in Ukraine and in Donbass[1] – see Figure 5.1.

Figure 5.1 'Do You Think Inter-ethnic Relations in the Region and in the Country are Troublesome?' (in % of the total number of respondents)

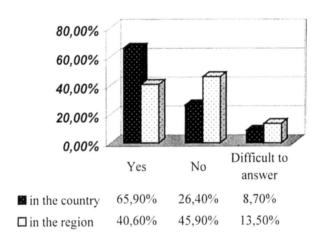

	Yes	No	Difficult to answer
■ in the country	65,90%	26,40%	8,70%
□ in the region	40,60%	45,90%	13,50%

Source: Изучение общественного мнения как социального фактора развития Донецкой области, Материалы социологических опросов за 1997, Социологическая служба Донецкого Центра политологических исследований.

---

[1] Figures are based on the results of two public opinion surveys. The data were collected in Donetsk by the Sociological Service of the Donetsk Centre for Political Studies in January-February and May-June 1997. Random samples of 539 and 530 respondents correspondingly were stratified by the city's list of districts. The socio-demographic and ethnic representativeness of the samples was verified by comparing this with compatible Census data. The method of data collection was defined as the standardised, formal interview.

In fact, although distinct from the other regions of Ukraine, Donbass could not be portrayed as a homogeneous area. There are some questionable issues, and one of those is the problem of the region's integration into the Ukrainian national-cultural framework: something which could perhaps be resolved if a proper relationship between independent ethnic-cultural autonomies, and the complementary coexistence of these in one State, was properly regulated.

As a foreign observer acutely noted, 'piecing together a Ukrainian inter-ethnic picture out of one set of all-Ukraine data is somewhat like taking an average temperature reading in a hospital, where the mean hides the extremes.' (Bremmer, 1994, p.281) Economic, geopolitical and cultural differences between regions definitely matter in the country, and some very diverse areas do exist. In order to draft impartial ethnic profiles of those distinct territories, and come closer to the formulation of an objective approach to the problem of regionalism, one should analyse a wide complex of historical, social and political questions.

In this paper, an endeavour will be made to take a retrospective look at those aspects. Firstly, we will try to reconstruct the historical picture of the major ethnic groups living in Donbass, in order to examine what social, political and cultural experiences they have gained during the centuries of their habitation in the area of modern Ukraine. We will try to look at the process through which the ethnic make-up of the area was determined, focusing on the delineation of particular groups' histories, and to trace the evolution of the minority issue under Soviet rule, as a factor that influenced the levels of their self-assertiveness which obviously matters under the new political conditions. In the main part of the article we will analyse major questions applied to the problem of inter-ethnic co-existence and cultural autonomy, on the level of state politics and mass public perception, with special attention to such aspects as *National Minority Group Definition; Language Status; Inter-Ethnic Toleration; National-Cultural Autonomy Implementation;* and *Political Priorities and Means.*

Settlement and Ethnic Make-up of the Donetsk Region[2]

The territory of Donbass has been inhabited since ancient times. Massive settlement of Donbass began in the epoch of the great Movement of Peoples. The first nomadic tribesmen known so far to have arrived were Cimmerians, who moved from the Don river in the 10th century B.C. and roamed around the Kalmius and the Seversky Donets, which was consequently established as the toponym of the region. (*Донбасс...*, 1996, pp. 5-20; *Неизвестное...*, 1978; Лаврів, 1992; Пірко, 1991) In the 7th century B.C. they were driven away by numerous bellicose Scythian tribes belonging to the Indo-European ethnic group, who founded a Scythian kingdom. In the 2nd century B.C. a wave of Sarmatians came from the Volga region and assimilated with the Scythians. In the 4th century B.C. Turkic tribes of Hunnish cattle-breeding nomads came to the Sea of Azov region from the Asian steppes. In the 5th century the region was captured by Avars who, in their turn, were pushed away by Bulgars, having surrendered to the attacks of the Khazars, who included this territory in the Khazar Khanate. In the first half of the 9th century, Turks and at the same time Polovets came to these territories. Russian princes of the growing Ancient Russian State took the field against them many times. One of the great battles with the Polovets Khan Konchak, depicted in the famous Russian chronicle 'The Lay of the Warfare Waged by Igor', took place at this time. A tributary of the Kalmius, the river which actually flows through Donetsk city, became the scene of the battle of the Old Kiev Princes against the Tatar-Mongol invaders. Zaporozhye and Don Cossacks

---

[2] During the numerous administrative re-divisions of Soviet Ukraine, the borders and the names of the region were changed many times. The first appearance of a Donetsk administrative unit was in 1919, when it was named as a *gubernia*. At that time it included the territories of Taganrog and Shakhty, which six years later would be annexed to the Russian Federation. In 1925, the name *gubernia* was abolished as obsolete, and *okrugs* came in to take their place. In 1930 these suffered the same fate, and a new administrative system with cities and districts was invented. A Stalin region, made up of Stalin, Mariupol, Artemovsk, Starobelsk and Lugansk (which six years later formed a separate region), was created in 1932. In 1961 it was re-named as Donetsk region. For years the informal name of 'Donbass' (an abbreviated form of *Don*etsk Coal *Bas*in) has been used to refer to the area. However, this place-name originally referred to a much wider territory, including three regions of Ukraine and one of Russia (respectively, Dnepropetrovk, Lugansk, Donetsk and Rostov regions). Thus, the more closely-specified designation of 'Donetsk region' should be used when speaking of this geographical area. However, the name 'Donbass', as a denotation of an industrial area endowed with distinct socio-demographic features, could still be applied to the Donetsk region, but with the implication that it is only a part of a larger unit.

played the major role in defending the Donetsk steppes. They also founded a lot of villages, which marks the dawn of urban settlements in the area. In 1762 Catherine the Second issued a manifesto inviting foreign colonists to the country. It served as a powerful spur to the development of migration to the territory. The beginning of the industrial exploration of Donbass also made for an increase in the influx of newcomers, particularly from Russian areas. By the end of the 18th century there were about 500 settlements, with nearly 200,000 inhabitants, representing 30 ethnic groups. 19th century capitalist development intensified the processes of migration and urbanisation. In the 20th century, especially after 1917, when the Donbass was named 'a region of utmost industrial importance', specialists from all over the USSR came to get involved in the so-called Building of Socialism. (Зиза, 1990) The long-term co-existence of these many ethnic groups in industrial Donbass has predetermined their active intercourse on an economic and, consequently, cultural and everyday life level, which has resulted in the emergence of a regional collectivity having its own sub-culture and sub-language and, consequently, its own distinct vision of reality and its own peculiar priorities for development. However, the histories of each of the ethnic groups show that they have each had different ways and patterns of merging into this local community. When speaking of the population of the Donetsk region as made up of about 110 nationalities, one should note that the terms of their habitation, and the numbers of compact settlements, vary widely among different ethnic groups – see Figure 5.2. Russians, Greeks, Jews and Germans have lived there for long historical periods, and have had a considerable influence on the ethnological profile of the region. The majority of the members of other ethnic groups have appeared in the region much later than those mentioned above, predominantly since the end of the 19th and the beginning of the 20th centuries, when the industrial development of the region conditioned ever greater demands for manpower.

We will briefly outline the pre-revolutionary and early Soviet historical experience of the most numerous and long-lived ethnic groups in the area, and estimate the conditions of their merging into the local community.

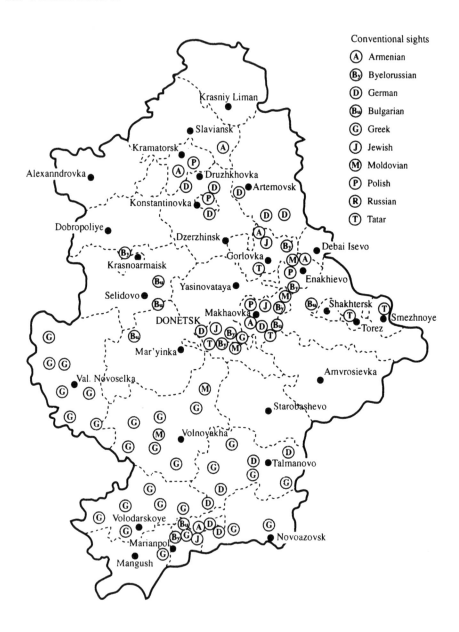

Conventional sights

(A) Armenian
(By) Byelorussian
(D) German
(Bџ) Bulgarian
(G) Greek
(J) Jewish
(M) Moldovian
(P) Polish
(R) Russian
(T) Tatar

Source: *Національний склад населення Донецької області за 1996/1997*, Донецкая областная государственная администрация, Отдел по делам национальностей.

RUSSIANS (*Національні меншини...*, 1996, pp. 14-40) Russian settlement in the lands of modern Ukraine traces its origin to the 15th century, when the opening up of the 'Wild Country' began. After the Pereyaslavl' Agreement of 1654, which unified Left Bank Ukraine and Russia, the migration of the Russian ethnic element to those territories acquired a mass scale. Many of the settlements were founded by representatives of both Russian and Ukrainian ethnic groups, and this facilitated the growth of homogeneous features in their cultures. Military and strategic priorities induced Russia to maintain a military presence in newly-assembled Novorossia, which included the Donbass area. Thus, many Russian soldiers did army service in Ukrainian lands, and then settled there forever.

The number of Russians living in Ukraine increased dramatically in the late 18th and early 19th centuries through the so-called Landowners' Colonisation, when Russian nobles, merchants and *raznochinetses* were given land allotments in this area. There was also a reasonable number of people who had suffered religious discrimination, and tried to escape persecution by coming to Ukrainian lands. Mainly, they represented Old Believers, Dukhobors and Moloccans.

As we have already mentioned, in the late 19th century, with the rise of capitalism, Russian migration to urban and industrial areas increased. It is important to note that belonging to the dominant ethnic group did not unconditionally determine their relative living conditions. The Great-Power approach of the Russian government favoured rather social than ethnic priorities, and though the Tsarist state did rigorously defend those Russians who belonged to certain social classes, this did not include serfs, state peasants and soldiers. Thus, the majority of Russians had the same civil rights as their Ukrainian compatriots.

By the 1920s the Russians had become the biggest ethnic minority group in Ukraine. According to the Census of 1926 there were approximately 2,677,000 Russians (9·2 per cent of the whole population of Ukraine). The majority of these lived in industrial centres, and many of them worked for State and Party establishments or were employed in institutions of science and culture. From that period Russian gradually spread as a language of instruction and communication all over the Eastern Ukraine and specifically in Donbass, where the proportion of the Russian ethnic group was the largest in the country. In fact, from those days up to the beginning of Ukrainian Independence the Russians were to some extent a privileged group of the population, and were never regarded as a minority. It is important to know that the number of people who received higher education up to this time was significantly higher among Russians than among other ethnic groups. (Bremmer, 1994, p. 266) This circumstance created some ambiguous issues concerning the transformation of the status of Russians in Ukraine. (Bremmer, 1994, p. 266)

According to the last Census, 11· 4 million Russians live in Ukraine, 2· 3 million (about 20 per cent) of those being settled in Donetsk region.

GREEKS (*Національні меншини...*, 1996, pp. 90-96) Greeks appeared on the territory of modern Ukraine in the 6th century B.C. Greek City States founded in the Southern Black Sea area contributed greatly to the social and economic development of the local tribes, promoting trade relations with settlements in the Dniepr area. This resulted in a process of mutual cultural enrichment between Greek and Slavonic ethnic groups and to a certain extent influenced the political development of Ancient Russia. The adoption of Orthodox or Eastern Rite Christianity in Russia strengthened contacts between Russians and Greeks and initiated further historic developments. Under the Crimean Khanate, though, the Greek population suffered from rigorous linguistic, cultural and religious discrimination. In 1779 the Greek Metropolitan Ignatiy applied to the Russian government, asking them to save their 'co-religionists' and let the Greeks of the Black Sea area settle in some other place. But in the same year these Greeks were 'naturalised for good', and 18,000 of them were the first to settle in the area of the Sea of Azov. Shortly after this, the Crimean Greeks founded a Greek community, with its centre in the city of Mariupol.

The earliest type of Greek ethnic organisation was made up of so called *bratstva* (communities of brotherhood), which incorporated craftsmen, merchants, and secular and clerical intelligentsia. *Bratstva* favoured the development of culture and education, organising schools and founding printing-houses. Those activities encouraged the growth of national self-identification: during the Census of 1897, 186,900 respondents defined Greek as their native tongue. In 1918, the Greek Diaspora in Ukraine increased considerably, owing to the influx of refugees from the Southern Turkish Black Sea area.

By the beginning of the 1920s, the Greeks had founded compact settlements in Southern Ukrainian territories: namely, in Donetsk *gubernia*. According to the Census of 1926, 104,000 Greeks were living in Ukraine (0· 36 per cent of the whole population). 89· 2 per cent of those lived in rural areas. In 1925/1926 Greek National Administrative-Territorial units were created in the places of compact Greek settlements. These included 85· 8 per cent of the Ukrainian Greeks (nearly 90,000 people). In 1928, three Greek National Regions existed in Ukraine, and all of them were located in Donetsk *okrug*. Every Region was made up of Rural Soviets, which, having been organised on the territorial principle, included all the people who lived in the area at that time. For instance, the Greek National Regions contained also some German and Ukrainian Rural Soviets. 14 Greek Rural Soviets were included in Ukrainian National Regions and one was a member of a German National Region. The Rural Soviets which were organised as ethnically Greek had some peculiarities in terms of the languages their inhabitants actually spoke. Thus, there were 16 Rural areas defined as Greek-Hellene (based on the use of the traditional Greek language) and 14 defined as a Greek-Tatar (using spoken Crimean-Tatar, enriched by some words and expressions of Greek origin). It was only in the 1920s that the first steps were taken in creating a written language on the basis of existing Crimean-Rumey dialects. A script for the local version of the Greek language had been constructed on the basis of the traditional Greek alphabet. For the Greek-Tatar language, the Latin alphabet was used.

Concerning the educational and cultural network that existed for Greeks in Ukraine, there was a noticeable decrease in the number of national schools through the period of 1920-1930. Simultaneously to the *Ukrainianisation* process, the cultural development of non-dominant ethnic groups was given the utmost encouragement. For example, by the middle of the 20th century 22 Greek national schools had been organised in the Mariupol area alone. Since there were no such institutions before the Revolution, the problem of creating these schools was accompanied with those of training pedagogical staff and of creating new textbooks. A number of National Departments were opened for these purposes in the Institutes of Civic Education all over the Ukrainian Soviet Republic. Mariupol has its own Pedagogical College. A Greek National Publishing House, *'Communistis'*, edited a number of books on society and politics, as well as textbooks in all the usual academic subjects and belles-lettres.

Amateur talent activities, singing circles and musical groups enjoyed wide popularity in all the places of compact Greek settlement. The *Sartana* Greek Ensemble of folk singing and dancing took part in the All-Union Festival of Amateur and Folk Arts of national minorities and was highly praised by the famous Russian theatrical producers V. Meyerkhold and A. Tairov.

Thus, by the 1930s, the Greeks had become one of the most self-organised and conscious ethnic communities in the region, focusing on the development of national education and culture. The traces of this experience have somehow been sustained, in spite of the persecutions that fell to the lot of all the non-dominant ethnic groups under Stalin's totalitarian regime. However, in urban areas of Donbass, as a result of cultural assimilation, the level of Russified Greeks was particularly high.

According to the Census of 1989 there were 98,000 Greeks in Ukraine, 86 per cent of those living in Donetsk region.[3]

JEWS (*Національні меншини...*, 1996, pp. 40-52) Jews came to Ukrainian lands from Crimean Greek Colonies and Khazar areas. In the 10th-11th centuries communities of Khenaanims (Jews speaking Slavic languages) are claimed to have appeared in Kievan Rus. In the 12th century, some Ashkenazi, Yiddish-speaking Jews from Southern Germany and the Czech lands also migrated to Western Ukrainian areas. Yiddish was developed from Middle High German and written in Hebrew, but soon came to be strongly influenced by Slavic languages. The three Partitions of Poland of 1772, 1793 and 1795 had resulted in mass Jewish migration from Byelorussian lands to Novorossia. In 1796 the Tsarist Government of Russia established the Pale of Settlement in order to prevent Jewish expansion to the cultural centres of the Russian Orthodox Church. Jews were allowed to settle in 13 *gubernias* of the Russian Empire, including Southern and Eastern Ukrainian lands. The first attempt to settle Jews there was made in 1807, when a number of agricultural Jewish Communities were founded. During World War I and the Civil War in Russia those settlements suffered serious damage. The restoration of these, along with the creation of new settlements, became one of the main procedures of the Soviet Government for dealing with the Jewish minority. During the period

---

[3] In the data of the Donetsk regional Census of 1989 a different number is presented. According to this, about 17 per cent of Ukrainian Greeks live in Donetsk region. The mentioned, updated figure is given in (*Національні меншини...*, 1996, p. 92).

1923-1927 the number of Jews living in Ukrainian rural areas doubled (from 56,000 to 107,000). At that time it is said that Ukraine had the biggest concentration of agricultural Jewish population in Europe. It is important to note that agriculture had not been considered as a traditional occupation for the Jewish population. They had more usually practised money-lending, which was officially forbidden for Christians, and crafts and retail trades. But during periods of drastic political and social changes, accompanied by economic decline, these kinds of work were no longer stable, and the majority of Jews lived in poverty. Many Jews were still reluctant to take up farming as their occupation, though, and large-scale Soviet political action to encourage Jewish involvement in agriculture failed in the end.

In 1925, 102 National Rural Soviets were organised in places of compact Jewish settlement. Ukraine had three Jewish National Regions (one is in Donetsk *okrug*), where a number of national schools functioned. Moreover, according to the statistical data of 1931, there were 20 technical, 5 agricultural and 3 pedagogical Jewish colleges in Ukraine, where all subjects were taught in Yiddish. In 1926, the All-Ukrainian Academy of Science founded a Department of Jewish Culture (later an Institute of Jewish Culture). A well-organised cultural network (including 7 Jewish theatres and a number of mass media institutions) conditioned a high level of national self- identification. However, in the Donbass area the majority of the Jewish population had adopted Russian as a native language, since then there was a chance to be educated in institutions of higher education, and to gain positions in Soviet political and cultural institutions.

However, along with the Greeks, Ukrainian Jews present an example of a relatively high level of ethnic consciousness – having managed to keep some remnants of their original ethnic culture, and now being engaged in actively regenerating these remnants.

According to the last Census, out of 486,000 Jews living in Ukraine, 28,135 settled in Donetsk region.

GERMANS The first references to Germans in Ukrainian lands go back to the 10th century, when representatives of the German ethnic group founded trade colonies in Kiev, Lutsk and other places. After the Mongol-Tatar invasion, skilled Germans were invited by the Galician-Volhynian Grand Dukes to restore cities and to develop trade and handicrafts. A new age of

German colonisation was initiated in 1762 by Catherine the Great, who issued an order that aimed to stimulate the settlement of German grain-growers in the Russian Empire. New German colonies were founded on the territories of modern Zaporizhya, Kherson, Dnipropetrovsk, Donetsk, Mickolayiv, the Odessa regions and in Crimea. German colonists were officially granted some considerable privileges: set free of taxes, conscription and army service. Those conditions facilitated mass German migration to fertile Ukrainian lands. By the beginning of the 20th century there were 400,000 Germans living in Ukraine. During World War I many of those were resettled from zones of military operations to Siberia and the Volga area. Deported Germans started to return home not earlier than in 1918 and by the end of 1920 the majority of them had returned to their former, abandoned settlements. In 1923 there were 147 German villages in Donetsk *gubernia* alone. According to the Census of 1926 there were 393,924 Germans in Ukraine, and 93· 2 per cent of those lived in rural areas. From 1924, when the National Rural Soviets were founded, up to 1931, Ukrainian Germans formed more than 250 of those national units. Only 7 German Rural Soviets were contained in their own semi-national regions; all the rest were contained in other National Regions: 151 in Ukrainian, 3 in Jewish, 2 in Greek, 2 in Polish, and 1 in Bolgar regions. In turn, the German National Regions also included Russian, Ukrainian, Jewish and Greek Rural Soviets. In these, the system of German educational and cultural institutions existed alongside with those of the other ethnic groups. In 1929-1930 there were 628 German schools, where 89· 3 per cent of the whole number of German pupils were taught in German. Moreover, 9 German colleges, 1 German Pedagogical Institute and a number of professional schools were organised in Ukraine.

However, there were some waves of German re-migration. For instance in the period 1922-1924, 20,000 Ukrainian German families applied to state institutions for emigration to the USA and Canada, and 8,000 of those succeeded in leaving. Among the circumstances that encouraged that process were the unequal allotment of assets, an arbitrary tax policy, and the suppression of religion. An administrative system based on command, accompanied with forced collectivisation and imposed industrialisation, was pushed on with informing and the denunciation of enemies. During 1933-1937 the National Security Services denounced and destroyed 124 'Nazi', 'spy', 'diversion' and 'revolt' groups. During the summer of 1937 alone more than 500 people of German nationality living in German National Administrative regions were arrested. According to the reports of the Regional Communist Committees about 60-70 per cent of the whole adult German population were involved in 'anti-Soviet' organisations. Without a doubt, under those circumstances, national cultural and educational institutions had no chance to survive. In 1939 all the National Administrative units were dissolved. Those Ukrainian Germans who wished to go to their historical homeland from the newly established Soviet areas of Western Ukraine after 1939 and were not likely to be accepted by the German government were resettled to the eastern part of the USSR, namely to the Central Asian Soviet Republics, Kazakhstan, and the Autonomous Soviet Republic of Komi.

According to the Census of 1989 there were 37,849 Germans in Ukraine, with 6,323 (about 17 per cent of the whole number) living in Donetsk region.

Thus, we see that the distinct historical development of the territory, which is known know as the Donetsk region, within different administrative frameworks, its particular geo-political environment and its economic characteristics together resulted in a unique ethno-demographic profile for the area. The fact that Donetsk region has a large proportion of Russian population and at the same time considerable numbers of non-Slavic groups, which have compact settlements all over the region, has brought about a phenomenon of long-term inter-ethnic coexistence and interaction. Under the conditions of intensive urbanisation and rapid industrial development, cultural gaps between the distinct groups have naturally narrowed. However, some efforts were made to manipulate ethnic processes in order to contrive a secure basis for Ukrainian nation-building. The elaboration of official approaches to the treatment of nationalities has its observed history, and quite extensive consequences remained to be seen even after the break-up of the old political infrastructure. This was particularly important for those regions whose economic and cultural development were indissolubly connected with Soviet Restructuring. Donbass has often been blamed by so-called Ukrainian patriots for its 'rich Soviet past'. For the sake of justice it should be noted that in spite of all the disadvantages of Soviet policies there were some patterns of dramatic cultural improvement among certain ethnic groups, particularly where the model of creating national-cultural autonomies was applied. Unfortunately, that progressive practice was not been implemented for long. But still, an analysis of the evolution of policy towards the Minorities Issue under

Soviet rule will certainly be instructive, since this allows an attempt at creating a typology of the issue and at introducing some practical recommendations for further solutions.

The Evolution of the Minority Issue During the Soviet Era: a Historical Retrospective

Thinking of the spectrum of policies on minorities set out in a UN Special Study on Racial discrimination in the Political, Economic, Social and Cultural Spheres,[4] and looking at this in relation to the Soviet approach to the treatment of non-dominant ethnic groups, it is obvious that, however accurately one outlines the main features of the phenomenon, no definition could be completely adequate or fully exhaustive. Through the whole period of the existence of the multi-national Soviet State, various forms of political standards have been put into practice. Resolving the Nationality question, together with those of Peace and Land, was stressed as a key objective of the Socialist Revolution. Though a 'Declaration of the Rights of Peoples living in Russia'[5] assured national equality in all its forms as the basis for a Soviet nationalities Policy, Soviet officials in particular were quite aware of the ambiguity and provocative nature of the declared principle given the internal situation in the USSR. As far as the exercise of various ethnic self-determinations would have led to counter-revolutionary consequences and would have caused damage to the very essence of the multi-national state, the political strategy was to implement the major goals, sifting out the 'questions of minor importance'. A paradox of Soviet national history consisted of the fact that against a background of mass repressions, deportations and humiliations both of individuals and of whole ethnic groups (*Материалы конференции...*, 1993, pp. 4-12), one fairly homogenous nationality, known as the *Sovetskiy narod* (Soviet Nation) did in fact emerge. How was it drawn together? Was it a process of assimilation, segregation or integration? Probably, one could find sufficient evidence for of all of these elements. One explanation of this phenomenon could be discovered by taking a retrospective look at different periods of

---

[4] Minorities and Human Rights Law (1991), *A Minority Rights Group Report*, pp. 8, 9.
[5] *Победа Великой Октябрьской социалистической революции и установление советской власти на Украине: сборник документов и маетриалов* (1951), Киев, С. 59, 60.

Soviet history, each of which was endowed with specific political strategies. The aim of building Soviet statehood was approached in different manners by those in power. For instance, during the period of February-October 1917, being involved in a sharp struggle with Provisional Government, the Bolshevik leaders formulated their view of the national question as quite favourable to the creation of sovereign autonomies. (Вінниченко, 1920, pp. 113-114) When they came to power, though, their tactics changed. As Lenin argued, 'we are to support only those bourgeois movements of national liberation which are revolutionary by their nature, and which will not create obstacles for the revolutionary education and organisation of the peasantry and the wide masses of exploited people'. (Ленин, 1956, p. 525) Stalin in his time shifted the emphasis to the inherently counter-revolutionary nature of these 'bourgeois movements of liberation'. On these grounds, such movements were not only to be refused support, but were to be mercilessly fought against. While not denying the right to 'self-determination', even up to secession from the Union, the Bolsheviks rigorously controlled all attempts to implement this right. Ukrainian independence, in the form of the Ukrainian People's Republic, was formally recognised on December 16, 1917, and this illustrates the official and declarative quality of Soviet policy on the nationality issue. Another part of this same policy, less apparent but more pragmatic, was characterised by Stalin as the policy of 'division for unification', (Костюк, 1995, p. 67) and this was realised through a series of military putsches and the establishment of new independent units within Ukraine. These units were established in areas where the majority of the population had vigorously shown their support for Soviet power, namely, in South-Eastern Ukraine. One of these was the Donetsko-Krivorozhskaya Republic, founded in February 1918[6] (it included the territory of Donetsk region) which was annexed, if only for a short period, to the Russian Soviet Republic. All these actions brought about a situation where political disorder and ideological confusion in the Ukrainian Republic could hardly be overcome without the intervention of Russian Soviet military forces. During the four years of the Civil War[7] the central Soviet power asserted her right over Ukraine and finally succeeded. The following years, from the creation of the USSR in 1922 till the eve of the 'New Stalin's Course'

---

[6] Abolished in May 1918 when the German invasion began.
[7] Some modern Ukrainian historians fix upon the term 'Russian-Ukrainian' rather than 'Civil' War.

in 1929, is characterised as an age of compromise tactics in nationality policy. (Костюк, 1995, pp. 68,69; Резник, 1990, pp. 31-34; Чірко, 1990, pp. 51-62) During those years, as we have seen in the examples of the stories of particular ethnic groups, the idea of national cultural autonomy was perfectly implemented in practice. However short the period of compromise, and however many difficulties it entailed, it was an example of pluralism in national policy, facilitating the development of 'diversities within unity'.[8] It proved cultural autonomies to be completely acceptable inside a single national State. It should be noted, though, that this was only true as long as purely cultural and educational goals were pursued. For those years when the majority of the population, and particularly members of non-Russian ethnic groups, were illiterate, fulfilling such purely educational tasks was considered as a revolutionary matter of top priority. When the period of 'global fight with mass illiteracy' was past, though, and other goals were being pursued, the development of distinctive cultures for the various non-Russian ethnic groups became something that was no longer possible.

In fact, the current renaissance in minority ethnic cultures has only recently begun, starting this development again after a half-a-century break. How will events develop? Obviously, it depends on several factors. At the present stage of things, one of the most crucial tasks is the elaboration of the general approach of the independent Ukrainian State to the treatment of nationalities, including working out decision-making schemes for the Ethnic Regional Autonomies. Any ambiguities and double meanings in official declarations of the State's approach to this matter could lead to inadequate perceptions and consequent false steps by public groups and movements. We will look at the present state of affairs, trying to analyse some important State regulations as applied to the particular region in question.

Ethnic Co-existence and Cultural Autonomy in Ukraine: the State Approach and Regional Public Attitudes

On the eve of Ukrainian independence in 1990, the intention to facilitate cultural advance for the ethnic groups living in Ukraine was straightforwardly expressed in the Declaration on the State Sovereignty of

---

[8] See Minorities and Human Rights Law (1991), *A Minority Rights Group Report*, p. 8.

Ukraine 'guaranteeing all the nationalities that reside on the territory of the country the right to national-cultural development'. Some time earlier, in October 1989, the Law of Languages, containing a provision allowing 'an other than Ukrainian language to function alongside the official language in areas where non-Ukrainian ethnic groups constitutes the majority' (Закон про мови, 1989) was passed. The legal provisions for the new approach to the minority issue in Ukraine were supplemented with the Law on Citizenship, passed in October 1991, which set up a so-called 'zero-option', whereby anyone who was living in Ukraine at the time of passage of the Law 'automatically acquired Ukrainian citizenship'. (Закон про громадянство України, 1991) These documents, along with the Declaration of the Rights of Nationalities, the first government paper fully devoted to the treatment of ethnic groups, and passed on November 1991, are commonly considered as having 'payed off the debt of the State for the almost unanimously favourable attitude of the multi-ethnic population towards independent Ukrainian sovereignty'. (Stewart, 1993, p. 55) However, while approving Ukrainian independence, many of the ethnic minority groups first of all stressed the feasibility of their own plans to gain a certain level of cultural independence and regional self-government. It is noteworthy that the question of national-cultural autonomy, however acute it is considered to be, for a long time had no corresponding legal provisions in Ukrainian legislation. Thus, since the expectations for a major reconstruction of ethnic processes still had no immediate official confirmation, they should have been considered as no more than hopes in advance of action. The first document containing an article on the right to national-cultural autonomy for ethnic minority groups was adopted by the Ukrainian Supreme Soviet on 25 June 1992 as a National Minorities Law. Having systematised the approach proclaimed in the Declaration of the Rights of Nationalities, it also contained some new principal provisions, demonstrating quite a liberal approach from the State to inter-ethnic relations. Still, the regulation that finally dotted the i's and crossed the t's was only passed some considerable time later. The long-expected outcome of the Ukrainian Supreme Soviet's deliberations was matured for several years, as if they wished to stave off the crucial moment of achieving adulthood. The first Constitution of Independent Ukraine was adopted on 28 June 1996. The period of delusions and innuendoes, if there were any, seemed to be over. Ukraine has officially declared itself as a fully-fledged independent state, with its own approach to nation-building. Hence, all the regional issues are to be treated in accordance with the established State regulation, and any representative of a distinct area or particular ethnic group is still, in the first place, a member of the Ukrainian nation and a citizen of the Ukrainian State, which is one and indivisible.

We will now move on to focus specifically on how the most crucial aspects of the Nationalities issue are treated by the legal code of the State, including all the mentioned provisions on the Ethnic Minorities agenda, and the corresponding articles of the Constitution of Ukraine. It is also worth considering how the official State concept affects local political and cultural processes, and how public opinion reflects the contemporary state of inter-ethnic affairs. Looking at the texts of the laws, and trying to estimate their outcome as applied to Donbass region, one can determine some important points, which should be thoughtfully analysed.

> **Definition of the National Minority Group** (National Minorities Law, Article 3): *'National minority groups include those citizens who are not Ukrainian by their nationality and who express feelings of ethnic consciousness and togetherness with other members of their ethnic community'.*
>
> (Про національні меншини в Україні, 1992)

This seems to imply that those who do not feel unity with other members of their nationality, and don't want to maintain themselves as representatives of that ethnic minority group, could merge with the majority. It should be up to the individual whether to take part in national cultural movements or not. Applying this issue to the case of Donbass, and analysing some results of public opinion survey data, one can see that some ambiguous factors, relating to the problem of national self-identification, remain.

There is no record of nationality in the new form of the Ukrainian passport. Officers of the Nationalities Committee of the Donetsk Regional Administration note that many people come and ask them if it is possible to put somehow in their personal documents that they are Greeks, Germans or Jews.[9] However, some years ago, when the so-called 'sixth column' in Soviet passports was required, a lot of representatives of non-Russian ethnic groups, including sometimes even Ukrainians, preferred to identify themselves officially as Russians. This indeed made some sense when it

---

[9] Author's interview with Svetlana Kuznetsova, head of the Nationalities Committee of Donetsk Regional Administration, June 1997.

came to entering prestigious metropolitan universities, getting leading official positions, or applying for trips abroad. The times and the regulations change rather frequently, and recent fashions in ethnicity are to some extent more pluralistic – belonging to the Russian nationality in countries outside Russia itself no longer strengthens the social impeccability of the person, or gives any other immediate advantage. As a result, the numbers of members of national minority groups has dramatically increased all over the former USSR. This contention, though, could not yet be proved statistically, since the last Census was held in 1989. However, sufficient justifications of its truthfulness are available. Throughout the independence period since 1989, the number of those who left former Soviet territories for their 'historical motherland' has in some cases surpassed the number of those who could have been regarded as people of 'foreign' nationality according to official statistics.[10] If an official declaration of nationality can not be trusted as an adequate index of national self-identification, then probably a better confirmation of a person's (perhaps concealed) ethnicity could be found through a consideration of what national traditions they commonly observe.

According to the results of the survey conducted by the Donetsk Center for Political Studies in 1997, when answering the question what national traditions they keep, respondents are obviously influenced by their own perception of ethnicity. For instance, Ukrainians do not tend to estimate speaking their mother tongue as the keeping of a national tradition. But members of other ethnic groups, including both those who know a national language but do not consider it as their first language, and those who speak it as a mother tongue, are more likely to classify language as a national attribute. Comparing Russian respondents' responses with those of other ethnic groups, one could describe them as being close to minority-like self-recognition, but still preserving strong remnants of their once-dominant position. Thus, even in that part of the territory where the majority of the population is Russian-speaking (see Figure 5.3) there are some indications of a transformation of ethnic prerogatives.

---

[10] Author's interview with Alexander Dinghes, Head of the German Society 'Wiedergeburt', June 1997.

Figure 5.3 'What is Your Mother Tongue'? (in % of the total number of respondents)

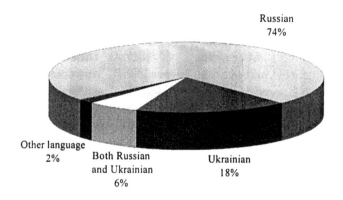

Russian
74%

Other language
2%

Both Russian
and Ukrainian
6%

Ukrainian
18%

Source: *Изучение общественного мнения как социального фактора развития Донецкой области,* Материалы социологических опросов за 1997, Социологическая служба Донецкого Центра политологических исследований.

Among other national traditions respondents almost unanimously name 'cooking national dishes' and 'celebrating national holidays'. However, only 29.1 per cent of respondents regularly keep even those customs (and only 19.1 per cent 'speak a national language'). Those numbers are practically the same for the different ethnic groups, as are the numbers of those who indicate that they observe no national customs at all. This situation should be considered a result of national integration and ethnic assimilation, facilitated by the industrial-urban development of the area. This brought about the phenomenon that intrinsic ethnic cultural habits and linguistic preferences have merged, and are no longer perceived as separate or 'national'. And yet, particular elements of the different ethnic cultures have not only been preserved, but may also be observed in the present mass culture.[11] In rural area, particularly at the sites of compact settlements of different ethnic groups, where their national customs had scarcely been affected by other cultures, they consequently remain to be seen today in their original form. However, the younger people increasingly tend to be

---

[11] This phenomenon has been delineated in many works of Ukrainian ethnologists. See Сорока, 1973, pp. 42-51.

involved in modern economic infrastructure, which, on the one hand, promises higher level of social assurance and prestige, and, on the other hand, being extremely standardised and homogeneous, demands a certain conformity. Consequently, under the conditions of industrial society, national customs have sometimes been considered as some kind of relic. Hence, as society has developed, the levels of ethnic consciousness have tended to vary along generational lines. Under the conditions of mass Russification in which the majority of the older people of today were brought up, the Russian language became widespread in every sphere of social, political and cultural life. As a result of this long-run and gradual process, one can observe that the younger the age group the larger the number of Russian-speaking people. The numbers of those who speak languages other than Russian and Ukrainian are roughly the same among different age groups. However, one can expect an increase in those numbers soon, particularly owing to the young people who are at the focus of the ongoing, predominantly non-governmental, programmes of ethnic education.[12] Taking into account the diversity of financial capabilities of various ethnic groups, and their different degrees of success in applying for support from their 'historical motherlands', the level of growth in ethnic consciousness might be not equal among all groups. Now, the problem that arises for the fervent supporters of Ukrainianisation under the new political conditions is how to run the process of national education, in order to make all citizens consciously Ukrainian. It is up to the policy makers to decide

---

[12] According to the Report of the Donetsk Regional State Administration of 1996, out of 2040 pre-school institutions of the Donetsk region, in 263 (8883 children) Ukrainian was used as a language of instruction and 226 (8258 children) were bi-lingual (Russian/Ukrainian). In 8 pre-school institutions children have lessons in Greek language and traditions and in 1, in Jewish language and tradition. All the other pre-school institutions have Russian as the language of instruction. Among the secondary schools (total number is 1262, 649,052 pupils) 267 schools are bi-lingual (Russian/ Ukrainian). Also, 492 pupils of the secondary schools study Modern Greek as an obligatory subject and 1547 as an optional course. In 5 Sunday schools pupils have lessons in Hebrew (293 pupils), Greek (240 pupils), German (67 pupils), Armenian (40 pupils) and Arabic (23 pupils). As to the library funds (the total number of libraries in Donetsk region is 3002, among which 844 are State Libraries), literature in Russian makes up 70· 2 per cent of the whole library collection, in Ukrainian 20· 8 per cent. Six regional libraries have national language sections: 3 of Greek culture and language, 2 of Jewish literature and 1 of inter-ethnic literary heritage. Only one radio station (in Mariupol) broadcasts in Hebrew (20 minutes on air a month, 4 hours a year) and in Greek (2 hours a month, 24 hours a year).

whether this is required and, if so, how such a policy could be implemented.

> **Confirmation of the Legal Provision and Verification of the Supervisory Commission** (*National Minorities Law, Article 4*): 'All questions concerning the provision of rights and freedoms of citizens which refer to their belonging to national minorities are regulated according to the Constitution of Ukraine, this Law, all the consequent legislative edicts adopted on the basis of these, and the International Agreements of Ukraine'. (*National Minorities Law, Article 19*): 'If an international agreement concluded by Ukraine contains different provisions than those declared in Ukrainian legal acts on national minorities, then the provisions of the international agreement are applied'. (*National Minorities Law, Article 5*): 'In the Supreme Soviet of Ukraine there functions a permanent Commission on Inter-Ethnic Relations. Corresponding commissions, if necessary, function in the local Soviets of People's Deputies and in the Executives of these. The Central Governing Body on inter-ethnic relations is the Ministry of Nationalities of Ukraine (State Committee of Nationalities). The Council of the Representatives of National Societies acts as an Advisory Body.'

No provision is made on the mechanisms or validity of any local statutes adopted in the regions. The inferior status of such local decisions could be illustrated by the situation regarding the language issue in Donetsk region.

> **Status of Languages** (*Constitution of Ukraine, Article 10*): 'The State language in Ukraine is Ukrainian. ...Russian, and other languages of the national minorities of Ukraine, are guaranteed free development, use and protection'.

The status of languages is the most provoking issue, especially when applied to areas with a majority of Russian-speaking population. Considering the heated discussions which have accompanied the adoption of all the statutes related to this question (and particularly the preparation of the draft versions of the Ukrainian Constitution), it is noteworthy that a number of persistent suggestions have been made to declare Russian as a State language alongside Ukrainian. For instance, in February 1994 local authorities held a consultative referendum. People were asked to answer whether Russian should be recognised along with Ukrainian as a State

Language, and whether it should be used alongside Ukrainian at work, in business, administration, science and education. In spite of the fact that the majority of those who voted showed their approval for such a proposal, the central officials apparently overlooked it. It seems as if Donetsk region is only temporarily being allowed to use Russian, which constitutionally has become the language of an ethnic minority.

Obviously, those who would attempt to Ukrainianise Donbass 'aggressively' reveal their flat misunderstanding of the significance of the Russian language for the vital inter-ethnic transmission in the area. The Donbass preference for the Russian language is a result of historical and geo-political factors, rather than just a local anomaly. The industrial specialisation of the region, along with the territorial proximity to Russia, favoured close economic co-operation, and led to a high level of industrial migration to Donbass both of 'native' and 'extrinsic' Russian-speakers. Consequently, even now, when the Ukrainian language is constitutionally established as the State one, the number of people who can speak it fluently is quite low. According to the results of the sociological survey conducted by the Sociological Service of the Donetsk Center for Political Studies in 1997, only 42· 5 per cent of respondents 'speak Ukrainian fluently', 49· 5 per cent 'have good reading and comprehension skills', and 7· 4 per cent 'don't understand Ukrainian at all'. There are some peculiarities when looking at different ethnic groups. For instance, the number of those who speak fluently is considerably lower among Russians and Byelorussians (less than 30 per cent). No respondent of Tatar nationality speaks fluent Ukrainian. Moreover, about 15 per cent of the Russian, Byelorussian and Jewish respondents note that they don't understand any Ukrainian at all. It is interesting to point out that only some 17· 5 per cent of respondents consider 'knowledge of Ukrainian to be obligatory for all the citizens of Ukraine', 46· 6 per cent think that 'it is desirable but not necessary', and 34· 5 per cent think that 'there is no necessity at all'. The majority of those who hold the first of these opinions do already speak the language fluently. Furthermore, among Russians, we find not only the lowest number of those who know Ukrainian pretty well (27 per cent), but also the biggest number of those who do not consider this knowledge to be obligatory (40 per cent). This sluggishness of Russians as to learning the Ukrainian language illustrates the phenomenon of the low cultural adaptability of this once-dominant ethnic group – rather than a case of linguistic prejudice and intolerance.

According to the results of the sociological survey cited, no more than 10· 6 per cent of respondents agree that only Ukrainian should have status of State language all over the Ukraine. The overwhelming majority of the respondents (85· 3 per cent) adhere to the opinion that both Russian and Ukrainian should have this status and about 2 per cent argue that it should be only Russian. It is noticeable that no representative of the non-dominant ethnic groups suggests that Russian alone should have status of State language, although, according to the results of the previous survey, we see that it is considered as a native tongue by 75 per cent of Greek and 91 per cent of Jewish respondents. This could be thought of as a good example of how non-dominant ethnic groups easily identify the official State language with the State of residence, while once dominant groups are often reluctant to choose something other than their native language, because this choice might in itself lower the status of their own native tongue (for the official data on the language composition of the Donetsk region see Table 5.1). For the present, this difference is not so serious. However, one can anticipate it deepening as fast as the process of Ukrainianisation is accelerated. Russian obstruction of the expansion of the official language in Donbass is commonly considered as one of the most dangerous and potentially conflictual issues in Ukraine. So far, the 1997 academic year was marked with a remarkable precedent when an attempt to Ukrainianise one of the Donetsk central secondary schools failed: a demonstration by passionate parents meant that 'rejections' looks possible.

Table 5.1 Ethnic and Language Composition of the Donetsk Region

Nationalities	Number of representatives (% of the whole population of the region)	% of people speaking an ethnic language as a mother tongue[a]	% of people speaking Russian as a mother tongue[b]	% of people speaking Ukrainian as a mother tongue[c]
Ukrainian	2693432 (50· 7)	43	56	-
Russian	2316091 (43· 6)	98	-	1
Greek	33691 (1· 58)	11	86	1
Byelorussian	30935 (1· 45)	28	70	2
Jewish	28135 (0· 53)	4	94	0· 5
Tatar	25495 (0· 43)	50	49	0· 4
Moldovian	13332 (0· 35)	43	53	2
Armenian	10147 (0· 19)	45	53	0· 2
Bulgarian	7217 (0· 14)	24	74	1

Polish	6897 (0· 13)	11	73	12
German	6323 (0· 12)	14	84	1
Gipsy	4806 (0· 09)	59	24	14
Azerbaijani	4316 (0· 08)	70	29	0· 3
Georgian	3779 (0· 07)	57	43	0· 4
Uzbek	3133 (0· 06)	67	30	0· 5
Mordovian	3004 (0· 06)	27	72	-
Chuvash	2636 (0· 05)	38	61	-
Lithuanian	2217 (0· 04)	43	55	0· 6
Udmurtian	1268 (0· 02)	25	75	0· 3
Kazakh	1189 (0· 02)	74	22	1
Bashkhir	1118 (0· 02)	41	50	0· 3
Marijnian	1097 (0· 02)	50	50	-
Lazgin	1078 (0· 02)	65	32	0· 2
Korean	1072 (0· 02)	32	67	0· 3
Ossetian	1002 (0· 02)	42	54	0· 3
Latvian	988 (0· 02)	43	55	0· 6
Others	11368 (0· 21)	-	-	-
Total	**5187631(100)**	**73**	**28**	**2**

a) This number includes all the people who speak their own ethnic languages, including Russians and Ukrainians.
b) This number includes people who are not ethnically Russian but who speak Russian as their native language.
c) This number includes people who are not ethnically Ukrainian but who speak Ukrainian as their native language.

Source: Отчет за 1996/1996 гг. отдела по делам национальностей, Донецкая областная государственная администрация; *Материалы Всесоюзной переписи населения по Донецкой области* (1989) Донецкое областное управление статистики.

Guarantee of National Cultural Autonomy (*National Minorities Law, Article 6*): 'The State guarantees all the national minorities the right to national-cultural autonomy, to the use of and instruction in their native language in state educational institutions or through national cultural societies, the development of national cultural traditions, the use of national symbols, the celebration of national holidays, the practice of their religion, the satisfaction of their needs in literature, art and mass media, the creation of national cultural and educational institutions and any other activity that does not contravene existing legislation'. (*National Minorities Law, Article 7*): 'The State shall provide training of cultural and teaching staff through the network of educational institutions, and shall promote international agreements concerning national staff training abroad'. (*National*

> *Minorities Law, Article 8*): 'State institutions, social associations, enterprises, etc., located in places where the majority of the population belongs to a certain ethnic minority, shall use its native tongue alongside Ukrainian as a language of instruction'.

Obviously, this is one of the most substantial pieces of Ukrainian minority legislation. However, on the question of national autonomy as applied to Donbass region, one can stress the obvious double standard in public opinion, which is conditioned by the ambiguity of the local issue itself. In a territory where different ethnic groups co-exist in close proximity, the right for autonomy, even if it does not exceed the limits of cultural and educational provisions, can hardly be observed without infringing somebody's interests. Obviously, the question of political autonomy could not be raised, for the reasons that, firstly, at the moment there is no apparent reason for such a claim to be made; secondly, mechanisms for practical decision-making and other state procedures are not yet established; and thirdly, even if there were a legal precedent for it, no sufficient experience of self-government by national units is available. Even the implementation of purely cultural programs sometimes suffers not only from financial difficulties but also from the puzzles of organisation. The normal establishments of the national societies are often far from being well-structured, and many of the associations tend to disintegrate due to irreconcilable contradictions between their leaders.[13] According to the data of the Nationalities' Committee of the Regional State Administration, by 1st July, 1997, there were 53 national-cultural organisations: 2 of those are of all-Ukrainian status; among the rest 10 are of regional, 28 of city, 9 of district and 4 of rural levels. When looking at their national profiles one can observe that the levels of self-organisation vary among the groups[14] – see Table 5.2.

---

[13] Author's interview with Tatyana Bolbat, Chief Expert in the Political Parties Department of Donetsk City Council of People's Deputies, May 1997.

[14] Громадські організації національних меншин Донецької області за станом на 1.07.1997, *Донецкая областная государственная администрация.*

Table 5.2 National-cultural Societies in the Donetsk Region

Nationalities (% of the whole population of the region according to the Census of 1989)	All-Ukrainian organisations	Regional organisations	City level organisations	District level organisations	Rural organisations
Greek (1· 53 %)	2	2	16	7	4
Jewish (0· 53 %)	-	3	6	-	-
German (0· 13 %)	-	1	3	1	-
Armenian (0· 19 %)	-	1	1	1	-
Russian (43· 6 %)	-	1	1	-	-
Daghestani (no data)	-	1	-	-	-
Spanish (no data)	-	1	-	-	-
Assyrian (no data)	-	-	1	-	-
Total	**2**	**10**	**28**	**9**	**4**

Source: *Громадські організації національних меншин Донецької області за станом на 1.07.1997*, Донецкая областная государственная администрация, Отдел по делам национальностей.

> **Financial Assistance** (*National Minorities Law, Article 16*): 'Special allocations for national minorities development are provided in the State Budget.' (*National Minorities Law, Article 17*): 'Ukraine facilitates the development of international co-operation for provision and support of national minorities' interests, specifically, concluding bi-lateral and multi-lateral agreements in this area.'

The data just given illustrate not so much the degree of ethnic self-consciousness but rather the financial possibilities of the various groups – which differ considerably. For instance, when answering the question if state financial assistance for ethnic groups is needed, only about 12 per cent of the respondents of Greek nationality gave an affirmative reply, while for the over-all sample there were 30· 4 per cent of such replies. Greeks have been relatively more successful in their applications for assistance from their historical motherland than other ethnic groups. Speaking of state support to minority groups and their national-cultural organisations, one should mention that at present, financial difficulties create serious obstacles to the implementation of this task. However, many leaders of Donetsk national-cultural societies have mentioned great consultative assistance from local authorities, and particularly from the Nationalities Committee of the Regional State Administration. Thus, though facing many problems, the cultural national development of different ethnic groups in the region seems to be accelerating. What will be the results of these developments? Are non-dominant groups preparing themselves for exodus, striving to participate in the new system in order to demand more autonomy, or integrating themselves into the state system? As yet, no definite answer is feasible, but any path forward will demand competence and tolerance from both from the State and from the representatives of the different ethnic groups.

> **Political Access**. (*National Minorities Law, Article 9*): 'Citizens of Ukraine belonging to national minorities may be elected to State institutions of all levels, and have the right to take up any post in all governmental bodies, enterprises, establishments and organisations'. (*National Minorities Law, Article 14*): 'National civil associations have the right to nominate their candidates for elections to governmental bodies according to the Constitution of Ukraine, the Statute of the Peoples' Deputies and Local Soviet Deputies Elections.'

(For the distribution of representatives in the local Soviets see Table 5.3)

Table 5.3 Ethnic Composition of People's Deputies (Regional level)

Nationalities	Regional Soviet of People's deputies	% of the whole no.	District Soviets	% of the whole no.	City Soviets	% of the whole no.	Rural Soviets	% of the whole no.
Ukrainian	47	62· 7	253	64· 2	445	54· 5	2415	75
Russian	24	32	98	24· 9	328	40· 2	560	17
Jewish	1	1· 3	-	-	17	2· 1	1	0· 03
Ossetian	1	1· 3	-	-	2	0· 2	-	-
Bulgarian	1	1· 3	1	0· 2	1	0· 1	6	0· 1
Greek	1	1· 3	41	10· 4	12	1· 5	180	5· 6
Lithuanian	-	-	1	0· 2	1	0· 1	-	-
Byelorussian	-	-	-	-	3	0· 4	22	0· 6
Azerbaijani	-	-	-	-	1	0· 1	3	0· 09
Armenian	-	-	-	-	1	0· 1	1	0· 03
Georgain	-	-	-	-	2	0· 1	-	-
Latvian	-	-	-	-	1	0· 1	-	-

Tatar	-	-	-	-	1	0·1	2	0·06
Assyrian	-	-	-	-	1	0·1	-	-
Tajik	-	-	-	-	-	-	4	0·1
Polish	-	-	-	-	-	-	3	0·09
German	-	-	-	-	-	-	2	0·06
Marinian	-	-	-	-	-	-	1	0·03
Lezgin	-	-	-	-	-	-	1	0·03
Total	**75**	**100**	**394**	**100**	**816**	**100**	**3201**	**100**

Source: Отчет за 1996/1997 гг. Отдела по делам национальностей, Донецкая областная государственная администрация.

So far, no serious problems concerning political access for ethnic minorities have occurred. However, this situation scarcely illustrates the flourishing of political pluralism in Ukraine. It rather demonstrates that political access itself should not be seen as the most important measure of the operative, (Kuzio, 2000, p. 145) commonly held, set of public values. In 1998 in the Donetsk region there were more than 30 political parties and movements representing diverse concepts of development. Many of those have tended to use some questionable ethnic issues in their political agitation. (Jung, 1994, pp. 51-56) However, no sign of any active intercourse between political parties and national movements is observed. The only exception has been the All-Ukrainian Party of Muslims, founded in Donetsk in September 1997. To what extent will it pursue ethnic goals? Taking into account that party leaders are quite influential persons on the local level, some challengeable results may be expected. The next pre-election period in Donbass will probably present some new tendencies in public political attitudes, which will contribute to the agenda and future prospects of both State and Regional politics.

To sum up, State regulation of the most crucial issues of inter-ethnic relations in Ukraine are couched largely in the universal language of the Declaration of Human Rights, providing a wide spectrum of opportunities for the social, cultural and educational development of different ethnic groups. However, some quite debatable issues have arisen in particular cases. So far, all the inconsistencies between State priorities and regional (ethnic) interests, as well as their ever-increasing internal contradictions, have impeded the improvement of existing mechanisms of decision-making in the field of inter-ethnic coexistence when applied to the particular territories.

Conclusion

As Ernest Gellner said concerning the phenomenon of nationalism, 'the theoretical understanding is an open and contentious field in which there is little that is firmly established. The current situation has stimulated the debate: we need both ideas and information'. (Gellner, 1995, p. 7)

This is obviously true when we look at the whole field of inter-ethnic relations. When contemplating the maturing of the multi-ethnic nation state, we can speculate on the point of contact between the integration process and the development of particular ethnic groups and regions as one of the dilemmas of coexistence. Having been involuntarily drawn into this discourse, one can only look at the available choices and try to verify if any of them is acceptable.

Having briefly analysed the particular case of Donetsk region, one can make the following statements:

The specific geo-political environment and distinct economic characteristics of the area have been essential factors in forming its unique ethnic composition. As a result of the linked processes of intensive urbanisation and rapid industrial development, the population of the region has been deeply integrated into modern economic infrastructure. Merging into an integrated community like this has resulted in a fairly high level of cultural assimilation in this territory. However, during the early Soviet period, ethnic peculiarities were maintained due to the 'compromise tactics' described above, and a number of national-cultural autonomous units emerged. Since the late 1930s, though, and up to the Independence era, any ethnic or regional autonomy in the country was of a symbolic nature. Donetsk region has been shaped as a highly industrialised area with a large proportion of multi-ethnic but predominantly Russified working class. The call for national independence brought about a new growth of social, regional and ethnic consciousness in the region and this, consequently, added to the already 'pro-Russian' reputation of the area the new epithets of 'wilful' and 'hard to control'.

In spite of the fact that the State's treatment of nationalities problems is based on quite a liberal approach, some debatable issues have been observed as applied to the regional case. The most challenging of those are the definition of the minority group, language status and the realisation of the National-Cultural Autonomy principle. All the difficulties that have sprung from the mentioned issues and problems, which cause alarm now or may perhaps cause alarm later, could possibly be overcome under the condition that the regional peculiarities are taken into account when formulating general principles of inter-ethnic coexistence in the State. This equally refers to all the decisions adopted on the regional level, which should take into account the interests of the non-dominant groups.

In spite of the lingering economic and political crisis in Ukraine, and notwithstanding the somewhat ephemeral and artificial character of the ideology of Nationhood that is being constructed, the country is managing, so far, to maintain a semblance of relative stability in inter-ethnic relations. So far, this might be explained rather as a lucky chance than as an authorised regularity. For if it is not to resemble a house built of cards, Ukraine as a young unitary democratic State should take concrete steps for maintaining its inherent ethnic diversities within the National Unity its government is keen to promote. This demands a high level of mutual tolerance and, consequently, high levels of competence and political culture both from the State authorities and from national and regional activists. So far as it is a matter of live-and-learn; but quick decisions are indispensable. And so, 'we need both ideas and information'...

References

Arel, D. (1995), 'The Temptation of the Nationalizing State', in V. Tismaneanu (ed.), in *Political Culture and Civil Society in Russia and the New States of Eurasia*, Armonk, N.Y. and London, pp. 157-188.

Birkh, S. and Zinko, I. (1996), 'The Dilemma of Regionalism', in *Transition*, 1 November 1996, pp.22-29.

Bremmer, J. (1994), 'The Politics of Ethnicity: Russians in the new Ukraine', in *Europe-Asia Studies*, vol. 46, n. 2, pp. 261-283.

Gellner, E. (1995), 'Introduction', in S. Periwal (ed), *Notions of Nationalism*, CEU Press.

Holdar, S. (1995), 'Torn Between East and West: The Regional Factor in Ukrainian Politics', in *Post-Soviet Geography*, no.2, pp.112-132.

Janmaat, J. (1999), 'Language Politics in Education and the Response of the Russians in Ukraine', in *Nationalities papers*, N.Y., vol. 27, no. 3, pp. 471-479.

Jung, M. (1994), 'The Donbass Factor in the Ukrainian Elections', in *RFE/RL Research Report*, vol. 3, no. 12.

Juska, A. (1999), 'Ethno-political Transformation in the States of the former USSR', in *Ethnic and Racial Studies*, vol. 22, no. 3.

Kuzio, T. and Wilson, A. (1994), *Ukraine: Perestroika to Independence*, London, Macmillan.

Kuzio, T. (2000), 'The national Factor in Ukraine's Quadruple Transition', in *Contemporary Politics*, vol. 6, no. 2, pp. 43-164.

Prizel, J. (1998), *National Identity and Foreign Policy. Nationalism and Leadership in Poland, Russia and Ukraine*, Cambridge University Press.

Rex, J. (1997), 'The problematic of multinational and multicultural societies', in *Ethnic and Racial Studies*, vol. 20, no. 3.

Solchanyk, R. (1991), 'The Politics of State Building: Centre-Periphery Relations in Post-Soviet Ukraine', in *Europe Asia Studies*, vol. 46, no. 1, pp.47-68.

Stewart, S. (1993), 'Ukraine's policy towards Its Ethnic Minorities', in *RFE/RL Research Report*, vol. 2, no. 36, pp. 55-60.

Wilson, A. (1995), 'The Donbass Between Ukraine and Russia: The Use of History in Political Disputes', in *Journal of Contemporary History*, vol. 30, no. 2, pp. 265-89.

Wilson, A. (1995), 'The Growing Challenge to Kiev from Donbass', in *RFE/RL Research Report*, 20 August 1993, pp. 8-13.

Wilson, A. (1997), *Ukrainian nationalism in the 1990s*, Cambridge University Press.

Костюк Г. (1995), *Сталінізм в Україні: генеза та наслідки* [Stalinism and Ukraine: its Genesis and Aftermath], Смолоскип, Kiev.

Вінниченко В. (1920), *Відродження нації: Революція і національне питання* [Renaissance of the Nation: Revolution and the Nationalities Issue], vol.1, Kiev- Vienna.

Громадські організації національних меншин Донецької області за станом на 1.07.1997 [NGOs of the National Minorities in the Donetsk region up to 1/07/1997], Донецкая областная государственная администрация.

Донбасс: через века (1996) [Donbass: through the ages], Кардинал, Donetsk.

'Закон про громадянство України' [Law on Citizenship in Ukraine], in *Правда України*, November 14, 1991.

'Закон про мови' [Law on Languages], in *Радянська Україна*, November 3,1989.

Зиза Н. (1990), 'Люди более ста национальностей: как им живется в Донбассе?' [Peoples of over one hundred nationalities: how do they live in Donbass?], in *Возвращаясь к истокам*, Donetsk, pp.131-165.

Лаврів П. (1992), 'Цей «русский» Донбасс, або Спроби неупередженого погляду на історію населення донецьких степів' [Russian Donbass, or An Attempt at an Unbiased View of the History of the Donetsk Steppe Population], in *Дніпро*, No. 1, pp. 26-29.

Ленин В. (1956), *О национальном и национально-колониальном вопросе* [On the National and National-Colonial Questions], Moscow.

Мала енциклопедія етнодержавознавства [Small Encyclopedia of Ethnic and State Studies](під ред. Римаренко Ю., Андрющенко В. та інш.) (1996), Генеза, Kiev.

Материалы Всесоюзной переписи населения по Донецкой обласги [Census for the Donetsk region] (1989), Донецкое областное управление статистики.

Материалы конференции по последствиям депортации народов СССР [Papers of a conference on the consequences of the deportation of peoples in the USSR] (1993), Харьковский государственный университет, Kharkov.

Національний склад населення Донецької області за 1996/1997 [National composition of the population of the Donetsk region in 1996/1997], Донецкая областная государственная администрация, Отдел по делам национальностей.

Національні меншини в Україні у 1920- 1930 роки: історико-географічний атлас [National minorities in Ukraine in the 1920s: a historical-geographical atlas](1996), Головна спеціалізована редакція літератури мовами національних меншин, Kiev.

Неизвестное об известном: краеведческие очерки [The Unknown on the Well-Known: local lore essays] (1978), Donetsk, pp. 6-24.

Пірко, В. (1991), 'К вопросу об основных этапах заселения Донбасса в эпоху феодализма' [On the issue of the main stages of the colonisation of Donbass in the epoch of feudalism], in *Сборник докладов, представленных на VII-ой Всесоюзной конференции по исторической географии*, Донецкий государственный университет, May 14-16 1991, Donetsk, pp. 37-44.

'Про національні меншини в Україні' [National Minorities Law of Ukraine], in *Правда України*, May 21, 1992.

Резник И. (1990), 'Национальные районы в Донбассе в 20-е гг.' [National Regions in Donbass in the 20th century], in *Тези доповідей і повідомлень Республіканської наукової конференції*, Donetsk.

Рижков В. (1995), 'Третина населення України не хоче вважати себе меншиною' [One third of the population of Ukraine does not want to consider itself a minority], in *Демос*, No. 5, pp. 6-8.

Римаренко Ю., Курас І. (1993), *Єтнонаціональний розвиток України* [Ethno-national development of Ukraine], Юрінком, Kiev.

Саєнко Ю. (1995), 'Доєдності розмаїтостей: соціокультурні орієнтації етносів' [The unity of diversities: the socio-cultural orientations of ethnic groups], in *Політика і час*, No. 2, pp. 73-79.

Сорока Т. (1973), 'Некоторые формы праздников металлургов Донбасса', [Some forms of holidays of Donbass metal-workers], in *Народна творчість і етнографія*, No. 4.

Хмелько Ю. (1995), 'Діва береги- два способи життя: лінгво-етнічні структури та соціальні орієнтації правобережної та лівобережної України' [Two banks - two modes of life: linguistic-ethnic structures and social orientations of right-bank and left-bank Ukraine], in *Демос*, No. 1, pp. 17-20.

Чірко Б. (1990), 'Національні меншості на Україні у 20-30 рр.' [National minorities in Ukraine in the 1920s and 1930s], in *Український історичний журнал*, No. 1.

6   Quo Vadis?
The Case of Russia
OLGA STRIETSKA-ILINA

The society of the Russian Federation (RF) is undergoing a period of complex cultural, social and political uncertainties, against the background of a deep economic crisis. An identity vacuum and a general re-orientation in the system of values have negative implications for interethnic relations. Ethnic and social phobias, with a lack of civic and political culture, do not lead to the level of social solidarity necessary for democracy. This essay is an attempt at answering the question of how to harmonise the various parallel cultures in a polycultural society such as the RF. Examples of political measures are considered, and ethnic attitudes are studied, as an indicator of the chances for sustaining a cosmopolitan society in Russia. The essay also looks at urban centres as examples of the urban culture of dispersed settlements of diverse ethnicities.

Quot homines, tot sententiae.
Quot nationes, tot mores.

Introduction

There are hundreds of definitions of culture, none of which, however, adequately or completely reflects the notion in all its complexity. But one feature is a kind of common ground for all definitions, being at the same time an explanation of their complexity. This is the abstract, transcendent character of the notion, and its relationship with some other existential characteristics, including other cultures themselves. A logical continuation of this approach leads us to the thought that cultures are never independent entities: they are all 'parallel', because they co-exist with other cultures. In the industrial societies, especially in the post-modern world, with its globalisation of the 'world' cultures, technological innovation, and information exchange, the single supranational culture exists hand in hand with the more static ethnic (or religious, or language-based) cultures, based in a more stable way on self-identity and the existential division between 'we' and 'they'. At the same time, the subjectively static nature of ethnic identity is itself defined in relative terms, being the result of a continuous interaction with other supposedly 'static' ethnic or other cultural group identities. Therefore, in the contemporary world anyway, cultures are rarely pure or free-standing.

This applies to those areas of the world which are not necessarily post-modern in terms of the system of values of the society generally, but whose societies are nevertheless highly complex due to historical factors in their formation. We can see this pattern in societies like India, with its complex ethnic and social structures that do not have a direct territorial implication, or Russia, with its historically very mixed population, and constantly increasing inter-regional migration in the post-Soviet times across the whole territory of the former 'empire'. In such countries some kind of pluralism is a must, as it is a structural feature of the whole society.

Simplifying the definitions of cultural or, in particular, ethnic 'sameness', it is possible to distinguish two basic types: first, communities, meaning groups, nationalities, or ethnic, linguistic or cultural communities, living in a compact area, and second, dispersed populations of ethnic, linguistic or other cultural minorities, living in an alien environment with different cultural values. The theory of nationalism and its 'ultimate goal' – the nation state (Winderl, 1999) – refers to the first type. Nationalism of the second type is an issue largely neglected by social scientists. At the same time, a dispersed population, distinct from the national majority, is almost always present. In our analysis we try to address both types.

The question of what forms a nation is a long-standing dispute between the proponents of ethnocultural and modernity schools. This debate, however, lies beyond our scientific interest. What is crucial for our line of reasoning is that '[the] nation is not a historical reality, it is a deeply political entity, constantly shifting and mutating' (Winderl, 1999, p. 19).

There are very few homogeneous nations in the contemporary world and none of them is of an absolute purity. There are, however, examples of a homogeneity which is sufficient for bringing together different ethnicities into one nation without questioning the very idea of such belongingness. This implies, however, a considerable degree of loyalty to the national majority from the side of representatives of other ethnic groups (and we are not yet speaking here about ethnic minorities, because, for instance, some of the 'titular' nations of the republics of the Russian Federation are methodologically majorities and minorities at the same time). This loyalty provides the grounds for integration of the ethnic group in the society and the culture of the majority, and in many cases leads to assimilation. What makes an Italian-origin émigré identify himself as American or an ethnic Arabian citizen of France claim himself to be French? These issues are closely connected to the question of the model of citizenship in a given country. Brubaker considers two crucially different approaches and their implications for the notion of identity as well as institutional and political arrangements of the state:

> ...while the French understanding of nationhood – state-centred and robustly assimilationist – engendered an interest in the civic incorporation of second-generation immigrants, the German understanding of nationhood engendered an interest in their civic exclusion.
>
> (Brubaker, 1992, p. 15)

In the somewhat technical analysis by Brubaker the French and the German models are considered as assimilationist versus ethnocultural respectively as a logical consequence of their historical roots and from the point of view of current institutional and policy practices. However, Brubaker admits that identity is a corner-stone of citizenship in a nation-state, and that the modern politics of citizenship is primary a politics of nationhood, and therefore a politics of identity. The whole meaning is therefore highly *ideological*, and the political decisions and self-interest of the state are not the only factors of importance. State policy itself is often driven by *self-understanding of the nation* (Brubaker, 1992), and while becoming a citizen in France means to become French not only *de jure* but also *de facto*, becoming German as an idea is bizarre for Germans, as one can only be born German (no matter whether in or outside Germany). The *ethnocultural* approach to the German origin makes the idea of cultural assimilation, which occurs alongside the civic inclusion of immigrants, humiliating in the perceptions of the Germans. Therefore the proponents of inclusion have adopted a postnational approach that can allow immigrants to become citizens while avoiding becoming German, i.e. enjoying the whole spectrum of political and civil rights avoiding 'symbolic or cultural violence against immigrants' (Brubaker, p. 184). The ideological nature of the notion of citizenship, however, makes the border between the two models somewhat blurred in a number of perspectives. Indeed, does a converted (read 'assimilated' according to Brubaker's language) Algerian fully identify himself with the French? Or, putting it in a different way, what is his self-identity: purely French, Arabian-origin French, Algerian-origin French, Algerian, Algerian-French, and so on and so forth. Social integration is not equal to cultural assimilation, and its reflection in the process of identity evolution is not unambiguous. What if the Czech Roma declare themselves Czechs or Slovaks, and in many instances not for reasons of mere convenience? What if they indeed think of themselves as Czechs in the first place and Roma only in the second? Brubaker's logic, however, is important for understanding the preparedness of the majority society to accept such a line of self-identity by representatives of other ethnic groups. Indeed, the above example of the Roma population in the Czech Republic is tightly linked to the history of the Czech lands, which have been incorporated into the enclave of the German cultural influence for centuries and where perhaps the ethnocultural perception of the Czech nation prevails. It is therefore difficult for the Czechs to accept the idea of Gypsies being Czech to the same extent as the rest of the population. The situation in this concrete example is further worsened by a sharp cultural difference of the Romany minority from the majority population, including the system of values and the way of life, and a lack of emancipation (political but especially cultural) of the group. But the same kind of approach may be observed in other countries, including successor states of the Soviet Union, where majority/minority cultural differences are not that distinct and where possibly the recent political history creates special circumstances. In such a country as Latvia, the Russian national minority, numerous and in some localities outnumbering the majority population, has a long way to go to be perceived in the country as (Russian ethnic-origin) Latvians. Even granting full-fledged citizenship does not lead to such perception. The self-understanding of the nation is still highly ethnocultural in this case.

In fact this evidence is not surprising, as the Soviet Union was a multinational state, based on the principle of the nationhood of its structural parts, a principle which was highly institutionalised (Brubaker, 1992). The ethnic heterogeneity was deliberately established in national codifications, where ethnicity at a sub-state level was given a chance to experience nationhood, and where nationality enjoyed state-sponsored codification exclusively on a sub-state rather than a state-wide level (Brubaker, 1996). In spite of meticulously elaborated scientific theory and active propaganda, both propounding the existence of a unified and indivisible Soviet people, a multinational, multicultural perception of the society prevailed. This was all against the background of suppression of some cultures and artificial support for others, a policy that created a hierarchy of cultures according to their supposed maturity and thus political status. Although the Russian people always remained the dominant nationality, an emperor for the empire, the Soviet Union was never a Russian nation-state (see also

Brubaker, 1996). It merely provided the political and cultural conditions for Russian dominance.

There is another set of issues, connected to our analytical focus. When there is not the necessary degree of loyalty from a sub-nation, or, on the contrary, where there is a high degree of national identity and rising nationalism, it often leads to interethnic conflicts, secession, or a special status within the state. This can tend to foster the creation of another nation state, if and only if there are appropriate territorial conditions for this (we know many examples, such as the new states on the territory of the former Yugoslavia and the former Soviet Union, and the Czech Republic and Slovakia, successor states to Czechoslovakia). This tendency is advanced by another important criterion: a regional economy which can facilitate a local ethnic, semi-ethnic or purely regional identity, making the vision of regional independence and its consequences more positive. Western Europe has faced this tendency in recent decades (as in Belgium, Spain, and Italy). This tendency leads to the fragmentation of states which can never fully satisfy national aspirations. The simple fact that there are about 3000 ethnic groups in the world and only 180 states militates against the 'one nation – one state' approach. The contemporary world is not the one of nations (Smith, 1991). At the same time, the alternative idea of the nation state with 'one nation – two or more ethnic groups with the same national identity', implies a loyalty and willingness for integration which is not always present. The provision of a special 'semi-national' status within the state (e.g. in a federal republic) often simply relegates the same range of problems to the sub-national level. As Brubaker (1996) puts it, we live in 'a world in which nationhood is pervasively institutionalised in the practice of states and the working of the state system'. (p. 21)

In the Russian Federation there are 89 federal subjects (out of these only 21 republics, and 11 autonomous *oblast* and *okrug*), and 176 ethnic groups,[1] and it is clear that not all of these could be provided with a special status within the state. Moreover, there are millions of people living as part of a dispersed population of different ethnic origin, living outside its original territorial limits, whose cultural aspirations clearly cannot be satisfied on an ethnic territorial basis (unless ethnic expulsion and mass migration occurs).

The type of social structure of mixed ethnic components is typical to urban settlements which attract population of different ethnic origin, with different beliefs, faith and languages. This is the functional mission of a

---

[1] Data released by the Minister of Nationalities and Federal Relations, V. Mikchaylov, in 1996.

city, and is related to its role in technological development, information flow and mass media. It implies a special cosmopolitan culture or polyculture of city-dwellers. The concept of cultural boundaries in urban society do not refer only to compact cultural communities in cities, but also to individuals, each of whom is a cultural micro-cosmos, with an individual system of values, and sometimes differences of language, religion, etc. The mega-cultural space of a city is, however, subject to other values also: to the overall degree of tolerance of its society, its political culture, and policy itself. The provision of an urban anthropology of parallel cultures is therefore practically useful if and only if this model has the potential to provide such a polysocium with a full range of cultural and language institutions, adequate to its polycultural aspirations, and if the society does not already suffer from a too high level of ethnic/cultural intolerance. Urban culture presupposes a higher social organisation and a more civilised manner of social living, but its sophisticated character is somewhat ambiguous. Perhaps it is not a mere linguistic accident that *urbanus* in Latin means, depending on the context, not only urban, but also cultural, fine, part of the inner polity, and... insolent. By its functional role, a city, and especially a capital, and even more, a world level capital may become a mediator of tolerance and polyculturism, or of a xenophobic clash and the monoculturism of exclusion.

Going back to the problem of institutionalisation of the state nationhood and the two models which we would call state-centred (and not necessarily assimilationist) versus ethnocultural, we put a question whether there is a hypothetical capacity to establish a state-centred, civic, but polycultural state, providing that all peoples of the state form one nation but enjoy cultural heterogeneity supported at the state level. Does Russian federalism have a chance in a longer term to provide for prosperity of the whole nation rather than momentous satisfaction of political aspirations of sub-nations and other nationalities on its territory?

Noah's Ark

National formation is a process during which the dominant nation includes some ethnic groups and excludes others. This is certainly an oversimplification, since it is, in fact, never a one-way process, but it is circumscribed by the nationalisms of smaller groups and their resistance to the dominant nation, and also by the opposed tendencies of inclusion of the dominant nation. There are nations that historically have an inclusive tendency. In the process of national formation such nations suck in not only culturally close ethnic groups, but also alien cultures that are difficult to absorb and which, in fact, are often rather resistant to this treatment. Such dominant ethnic groups are sometimes defined as 'empire-forming', or as having special prerequisites or inclinations towards domination (Яковенко, 1996). Russians could be seen as belonging to this type of ethnic formation. It is, however, a very arguable concept, as we know many examples where such dominating and inclusive tendencies have turned out to be only temporary (Byzantine, Ottoman, Habsburg). Empires are not just abstract; once established, they are political creations, based on a kind of a common Idea. These Ideas (especially in empires of modern period) offer pure examples of the much-discussed invention of tradition (see works by Eric Hobsbawm, 1983, 1992, Benedict Anderson, 1983 and others). The Byzantine Empire was based on an idea of Christianity and the Hellenic culture. The Russian Empire was based on the idea of *sobornost'* – the principle of assembling people on the basis of religious faith in a harmonious diversity. The weak point of the concept was its explicit reliance on the Orthodox Church, and basically the idea of *sobornost'* was the Russian Idea, whereas the composition of the Russian Empire was highly heterogeneous in ethnic and religious terms. In the USSR, the Idea was a Soviet culture of the socialist state, involving the creation of a new society of *Soviet people*, but preserving the diversity of sub-national cultures.[2] This is how empires operate, and ethnic communities within empires either share the Idea and accept a corresponding common Belief, or they become 'dissident' cultures in the empires. The rationale of an economic justification for colonialism is combined with the irrational Idea (or invented tradition) in order to stick the separate parts together. If the economic rationale creates prosperity in all parts of the empire, it will usually be easier to consolidate the whole nation under the Idea, but with economic failure (or with the failure of the economic model) the effort of keeping the whole together becomes more costly than is justified by the effects, and the economic part of the package of reasons is no longer attractive either. The empire then falls apart, completely or partially, but it can then take decades for the former dominant nation and the *new* nations

---

[2] The preservation of heterogeneity was not typical for all empires. For instance, the Austrian and the Hungarian parts of the empire undertook different paths in approaching the ethnic and cultural aspirations of the peoples inside the empire after 1867, where the Austrian part largely followed the ethnocultural principle of nationhood, while the Hungarian part considered groups which were different in cultural and linguistic terms as still being an integral part of the Hungarian nation, with the corresponding Hungarian identity: and this would eventually lead to assimilation.

to accept a new model (or even to create one). The new nations undergo the rise of national identities and cultures, while the formerly dominant nation suffers a crisis of identity, with nostalgic feelings of the former greatness of the old times and the Idea, or searches for a new kind of identity to compensate for its losses. In the Russian case, the former Idea is, in fact, of a dual character: on the one hand it was *sobornost'*, as the basis of the former greatness of the Russian Empire, and on the other, the Soviet ideology, as the basis of the Soviet empire. Both these ideas have important implications in the present cleavage structure of the society.

Looking at the process of the ethnic genesis of the social space in the territory of Russia, it is difficult not to agree that Eurasia is not a purely geographical term. The philosophers of Eurasianism, which was an ideological concept of Russian émigrés of the 1920s and 1930s (Piotr Savitsky, Nikolay Trubetskoy), tried to explain the tragedy of the *Bolshevik* revolution by the adverse results of the promotion of European values in Russia. They argued that the Revolution was a logical consequence of the Europeanisation of Russian society since Peter I under the Roman-German standard. This concept stressed the role of the geopolitical zone, with its natural and economic landscape and the cultural core, formed in the so-called Mongolosphere, which corresponded closely to the territory of the Russian Empire. They underlined the importance of the nomadic culture in this zone and the special ethnopsychological configuration of eastern Slavs and the Turkic element. The theory, like all theories, was certainly a kind of oversimplification but, in fact, did reflect the real basis of the ethnic formation. The theory argued that the Russian state system was borrowed from the Tatar state system, but with a special cultural role for the Orthodox confession, which introduced a high culture and which appears to have been a uniting element and a creative inspiration throughout Russian history.

This theory has received some new attention nowadays, being, however, famous rather for its weakest postulates than for the real creative and positive idea of Eurasianism. Instead of relying on the special place of the Orthodox religion and therefore stressing the Russian Idea, it is necessary to look at the supranational character of the theory. Eurasianists actually never stipulated the idea of Russian superiority or the national domination of the largest ethnic group. The Russian ethnicity was seen as the first among equals, as the ethnicity that integrated but did not assimilate other ethnic groups, and which created a supranational state (Карлов, 1997). The Eurasian ideology points to the common history of the ethnic groups living in the territory of the Russian state, to their interaction and to the necessity of reflecting their interests in the national policy. Eurasia is a geographical, economic and historical unity (Трубецкой, 1993, p. 97). The internationalism of the theory is impossible to deny. The basis of Eurasianism is actually the idea of the existence of parallel cultures within the territorially integrated political unit. The objective of supranationalism in the Russian state positively evaluated some aspects of the Soviet experience. Nikolay Alekseyev stated in his publications in the 1920s that the principle of the federation should not be a nationality but a real geographic and economic unity in the framework of regions. This idea has received some partial reflection in the contemporary concepts of the national system of territorial administration and ethnic cultural development (Валентей (ed.), 1997).

Contemporary efforts in the conceptualisation of interethnic relations are undertaken in the logical framework of federal relations, *i.e.* the division of power between the centre and periphery, and the suggestion of a concept of a common ground of identity. Article 3 of the Constitution of the Russian Federation states:

> The multinational people of the Russian Federation shall be the vehicle of sovereignty and the only source of power in the Russian Federation.

The absurd terminology of the definition (*the multinational people*) gives an idea of the central paradox: on the one hand there is an attempt at creating a nation state with a common citizenship, the Russian Federation, but the concept of the federal composition of the Russian state based on the nationality principle, on the other hand, calls the whole idea of this into question: the paradox is that between the nation state and federal nations. The heart of this problem lies in the administrative divisions of the former USSR.

Unlike the Soviet Union, the country's predecessor, the Russian Empire, was organised on the basis of a simple administrative territorial division (*губерния, область, уезд*), with the possibility of free movement of people (with an exception for the Jews, who had special limits of settlement). This excluded the possibility of any establishment of mononationality in the parts of the territory of the Russian Empire. The provision for participation of other than ethnic Russian representatives in administrative and political structures was a part of the policy. This of course, does not mean that the ethnic question was resolved. The ideology of the Russian Empire was based on three pillars: *самодержавие* (autocracy), *православие* (Orthodox religion), and *народность* (in the sense of national roots or *nationness*), which were all actually a basis for the domination of the Russian ethnicity and the suppression of other ethnic cultures, which brought about considerable antagonism between the dominant and local ethnic cultures. This was effectively manipulated by the communists for the purpose of dissolving the empire and then for the establishment of initially pro-ethnic Soviet power in regions.

The ethnic question, however, was not resolved in the Soviet times. The totalitarian regime suppressed some cultures, but artificially supported other ethnic groups (which would otherwise have been naturally assimilated – like, for instance, some of the small peoples of the Russian north); created high cultures and standard languages in cases of some ethnic groups, and closed all schools working in other local languages, or simply deported whole ethnic groups. The national policy of the totalitarian regime was based on the arbitrary rule of the communist elite (which was multiethnic, but not importantly representative, and the ruling elites were anyway dominated by ethnic Russians). For example, a census for the Russian Republic of the USSR recorded one hundred and ninety four ethnic groups in 1926, ninety seven groups in 1939, one hundred and twenty six in 1959, one hundred and twenty two in 1970, one hundred and twenty three in 1979, and one hundred and twenty eight in 1989 (Вайнонен, 1996). These figures do not really demonstrate the physical disappearance or revival of nationalities, but merely decisions regarding their existence or their merging with other nationalities, taken on their behalf by the central authorities. The ruling political elites had a multiethnic *façade* but the real power was concentrated in the hands of ethnic Russians, who, unlike other nationalities, had an exclusive right of being in their home country no matter which corner of the former Soviet Union they were in. The end of such practice had a severe impact over identity and nationalism in Russia at a later stage (see further). It is, however, important to see another side of the coin, where multinationality of the state introduced a certain degree of multinationality in political representation within the territory of the former Russian Soviet Federal Socialist Republic, and where internal political and territorial arrangements provided for representation of nationalities and ethnic groups. In addition, a natural mixture of the population made the existence of a pure Russian bigger town or city virtually impossible, and the same went for the institutions of political representation and employment. This later engendered a myth of under-representation of Russians in Russia and supported an element of nationalism in the country after the collapse of the Soviet Union. The myth is strongly encouraged by the situation in which the Russian majority has to re-think their new place among the 'nations' of the newly emerged state, as well as their links to *former compatriots* in terms of the citizenry but, so to speak, *still compatriots* in terms of ethnic and cultural belonginess–the Russian minority in the newly independent states.

The policy for defining the boundaries in the territorial-administrative division of the USSR was based on the national-regional principle. Republics of the Soviet Union were conceptualised as regions based on the notion of the homogeneity of the endogenous nationality which gave its name to the republic. In fact, there were no really homogeneous republics (except for Armenia) and most of the regions defined like this actually represented polyethnic entities. During the unitary polity of Soviet times (it was a federation in a formal way, but not in practice: a so-called *façade* federation), the composition of the population in the whole territory of the Union became even more polyethnic, heterogeneous in an ethnic sense, and finally, sometimes simply mixed in demographic terms as the result of movement of people during the industrialisation of the country and as a result of national cadre policy (e.g. in the 1930s, and especially after the Second World War, many nationalities' representatives were put forward for jobs in industrial and administrative centres of the Soviet Union, where they moved), quota policy in enrolments to higher education with a preferential approach to republics' nationalities, forced migration (deportation) and mixed marriages.

So, although the territory was officially organized on the one nation (nationality) – one region principle, with a real multinational factor in almost all the regions, different ethnic groups in fact had different degrees of sovereignty. The hierarchy of national-territorial organisation (national republic, autonomous republic, autonomous *oblast (область)*, autonomous *okrug (округ)*, etc.), implied a multi-step subordination of smaller ethnic groups situated within republics associated with other titular nations. The whole approach was based on Stalin's theory of nations, which assigned a particular form of territorial organization to a particular level of national development. For instance, according to Stalin's theory, an autonomous *oblast* was assigned for ethnic groups which had not achieved the level of nations in their development, and although most *oblasts* were later transformed into autonomous republics, the principle remained the same. In spite of the proclamation of the USSR as a federal state, even the union republics which were theoretically on the top of the ethnic pyramid never enjoyed the sovereignty theoretically guaranteed them by the Constitutions of 1936 and 1977, and the state was in reality a unitary state (similar features of *façade* federalism were also seen in Yugoslavia). The Soviet Union, however,

> established nationhood and nationality as fundamental social categories sharply distinct from the overarching categories of statehood and citizenship. In doing so, it prepared the way for its own demise.
>
> (Brubaker, 1996, p. 23)

The Soviet federalism, therefore, neither satisfied the aspirations for sovereignty within the federation, nor provided for a stability of the union.

The situation in the field of language policy, where on the official level the equality and flourishing of all languages was proclaimed, had a similar logic. However, in reality there were several patterns of language policy in the Soviet Union. First, the predominance of the Russian language as the fundamental communication tool led to a characteristic 'socialisation' of the language, where it started to fulfil also a functional role of cultural transmission, broadened social opportunities, and finally prestige. This resulted in many cases of *preference*[3] for Russian in the education of children, and to an absolute prevalence of Russian in the urban centres of many republics (Uzbekistan, Kyrgyzstan, etc.). On the whole this tendency was an outcome of industrialisation and an increased role for information in the society. The choice of Russian as the language of instruction for children was often defined by parents as giving the best chances for social and professional adaptation, especially in urban areas. The tendency was towards a growing preference for Russian in education, and consequently towards a growing number of Russian-language schools, with the closing down of schools using other languages of instruction, leaving the local national language only as a medium for communication in everyday life (the *de-socialisation* of national languages), which led to a virtual inability to address professional issues in the national languages, and, in the end, to assimilation in many cases (Алпатов, 1995). Although this pattern was rather widespread, being to some extent natural in a unitary state, it was not absolutely general. For instance, according to the 1989 census, about 30 per cent of Bashkirs and Tatars, 35·6 per cent of Latvians, 39·5 per cent of Kazakhs and 52·9 per cent of Armenians did not identify themselves as Russian-speakers (Алпатов, 1995, p. 88). In rural areas, people generally preserved their national languages.

---

[3] The *preference* in many cases was a forced choice of a lesser evil for the sake of the future of the children.

The second pattern was support for national languages, sometimes even in an artificial way. This policy was mainly adopted in the 1920s and 1930s, when more than seventy new alphabets were created, the number of new national schools was steadily increased, and when there were even attempts to operate bureaucracy in the national languages of small ethnic groups, and to provide translations of works of world literature into these languages. In general this policy failed, largely due to objective reasons of state unity and the need for a common language (Алпатов, 1995, p. 89). After the war this pattern was adopted mostly for languages of titular nationalities of republics, with support for their literature, press and theatre.

The third pattern was an oppressive one, adopted mostly in the second half of the 1930s, being in line with the general style of the Stalinist authoritarian rule of that period. After the resolution *On the compulsory education of the Russian language in schools of national republics and oblasts* of 1938, and a later resolution for Union Republics, hundreds of schools with national languages of instruction were closed. Already in 1938 in Bashkirya, a resolution on the abolition of German, Estonian, Russian-German, and Latvian schools, and their reorganization into Soviet standard schools with the Russian language of instruction, and with the nomination of Russian teachers was issued (Алпатов, 1995). The results of such policies were astonishing. For example, in 1930 95 per cent of Komi-Zyryan children were studying in their national schools, but after the war they all studied in Russian schools (Алпатов, 1995, p. 89). The impact of adopting such a policy should not be underestimated, since the echo of this cultural suppression is heard in today's revival of ethnic identities and growing *ethnocracy* (see further in this chapter). In the worst position in terms of cultural development appeared the ethnic minorities in a number of republics which implemented their own assimilation policies (e.g. the Svans and Megrels in Georgia, or the Abkhaz language, which was persistently suppressed in favour of Georgian and for some time even converted to the Georgian codification). In such cases several ethnic groups happened to be under a double pressure of assimilation and some part of this population lost their identity entirely (like some deported Germans, Poles or Crimean Tatars).

As we have seen, the national and language policy of the Soviet Union was based on a totalitarian approach, where the state took the determining role in decisions to promote some cultures and languages, and to assimilate or expel others. The cultural and language policy was directly linked to the system of territorial administration, with its hierarchical and in most cases accidental arrangement. An attempt to build up a unitary state, covered by the *façade* of federalism, and based on the principle of nationality, was combined with the promotion of a common identity for the whole nation – the Soviet people – with common values, culture, and language (to a different extent) and history (recent or longer-term), where the role of a common high culture could in reality be filled only by the Russian culture. This was accepted by many nationalities (e.g. half of the Karel population, and more than one third of the Bashkir, Komi, Mordva, etc. perceived Russian as their native language (Алпатов, 1995, p. 91)) but not by all. The creation of the doctrine of the Soviet People (*советский народ*) was also supported by a scholarly theoretical elaboration, which not only analysed the attributes of 'the new historical community', but also precisely defined a hierarchy between internal ethnic communities with the help of allegedly scientific arguments (see works by e.g. Бромлей (Bromlej), 1980, 1983, 1987). Both the theory and the practice, however, conceived the entity of the Soviet People as supra-national rather than national (Brubaker, 1996).

Most groups have always had a distinct identity and a certain degree of political and cultural nationalism: something which exploded immediately with the weakening of the Soviet bonds at the beginning of *perestroika*, and which eventually led to declarations of independence (in the Baltics, Ukraine, etc.). Other groups had a similar but latent nationalism, which still affects the design of policy on the territory of the Russian Federation at present. The interesting fact is that oppressive actions under totalitarian regime, especially during Stalin's period, such as depressions of ethnic intelligentsia, deportations of the whole nationalities, genocide, or better to say ethnocide, served as a reinforcement of collective identities, and provided a substitute for the 'lacking collective memories' (Winderl, 1999, p. 81). This eventually had the reverse of the intended effect, and strengthened otherwise latent nationalism. Mass deportations of the Chechens, Ingush, Karachay, and Balkars in 1944

> left the strongest marks in the collective memory of North Caucasian people... The watershed event of persecution changed the status of Chechen nation building by weakening the Pan-Caucasian identity in favour of an ethnically based self-perception.
>
> (Winderl, 1999, p. 119)

Winderl names this type of nationalism

> a bottled-up nationalism, a repressed nationalism that had existed for some time and re-emerged when the pressure from outside declined...
>
> (Winderl, 1999, p. 127)

At the same time, in the case of the present composition of the Russian Federation we mostly deal with *small nations* (not necessarily in terms of numbers but in terms of location of their culture and institutionalisation of their nationhood, mainly given by the institutional hierarchy of nationalities under the Soviet regime). The *small nations*, dominated by the Russian or pro-Russian ruling elites, 'were in subjection to a ruling nation for such a long period that the relation of subjection took on a structural character for both parties.' (Hroch, 1985, p. 9)

The lack or inadequacy of institutionalisation of their nationhood under Soviet federalism, supported by their revived collective memories, leads to a contemporary political appeal, where their nationalism is in at least a majority of cases of a cultural nature. If the latter is not properly addressed in the contemporary national policy of the RF, it can easily be transformed into a political nationalism, with a demand for more political autonomy, self-defining foreign policy and finally, even secession, as has already happened in Chechnya. Other republics in the RF have a tendency towards independence and may come up next in the row. When such a cycle is already in place, it turns into an incurable disease, and the best treatment is granting independence. The introduction of independence, however, is a very sensitive question from the point of view of both domestic and international politics. The fear of atomisation of the statehoods and eventual instability and unpredictability on the territory of the former Soviet Union threatens the West and prevents it from recognition of independence of seceding states. Economic interests in the given territory and presence of a numerous Russian speaking population, as is the case in Chechnya, are a driving force for military resistance to secession in Russia. At the same time economic interest may turn to be insignificant at a closer look, and long-lasting warfare in fact appears to be the main destroying factor for both economic reasons and the presence of the Russian population in the country. Timely negotiations of the self-interests of the formerly ruling nation in the seceding territory may in such cases turn out to be more effective.

According to the new Constitution of the Russian Federation, ratified on December 12th, 1993, there are in total 89 federal subjects: 2 federal cities (Moscow and St. Petersburg), 21 republics, 6 territories (*край*), 49 areas (*область*), 1 autonomous region and 10 autonomous areas (see a full list in the Annex). Republics, autonomous regions and autonomous areas are organised on an ethnic principle (although it does not mean that they are monoethnic). The design of the federation was highly determined by the institutional frame nationalities were granted during the

Soviet period, where the former Union republics received entire independence. This led to a somewhat absurd situation, where one million Estonians received independence, while six million Tatars were denied sovereignty (Winderl, 1999, p. 193). Such an arrangement, however, perfectly corresponded to the Soviet theory of ethnicity, which recognised the former republics as nations, and therefore sponsored institutionalisation of their nationhood in the frame of the Soviet Union, and in fact involuntarily supported their nationalism and aspirations for an independent statehood. This was not the case of the former autonomous republics, which therefore form most of the present republics of the Russian Federation. Territories and areas are mostly concentrated in geographical regions or around big cities. The RF may be defined as a constitutional-contractual type of federation. Its unique character is the result of an attempt to divide the power of regions (republics, areas, etc.) according the federal principle, rather than joining together formerly independent states. The basis of the federation is the Federal Treaty of March 1992 (two republics did not sign the Agreement – Tatarstan and Chechnya), which is incorporated into the text of the Constitution, and individual agreement between the centre and the federal subjects, concluded in the framework of the existing Constitution.

The Federal Treaty defines the status of regions-signatories as of constituent units of the Russian Federation, where ethnic republics are given the clause of sovereign states (Polishchuk, 1996, p. 14). The disparity of statuses of regions in the RF in the Federal Treaty is demonstrated in Article 5 of the Constitution, which states:

> The Russian Federation shall consist of republics, territories, regions, federal cities, an autonomous region and autonomous areas, which shall be equal subjects of the Russian Federation. The republic (state) shall have its own constitution and legislation. A territory, region, federal city, autonomous region and autonomous area shall have its own charter and legislation…

Furthermore, Article 66 states:

> The status of a republic shall be defined by the Constitution of the Russian Federation and the constitution of the republic in question. The status of a territory, region, federal city, and autonomous region and autonomous area shall be determined by the Constitution of the Russian Federation and the Charter of the territory…

The contradiction is contained in claiming that all federal subjects are equal, and immediately stating a possibility for republics to have their own constitutions, and therefore to be prototypes of states, unlike other federal subjects. There has been an active discussion among Russian scholars and politicians regarding this asymmetry of status of federal subjects. Some argue that the Constitution gives considerable and unnecessary extra sovereignty to republics as compared to other subjects, while others argue that this asymmetry is necessary for the functioning and viability of a federation (Зорин, 1996, p. 24). Both arguments seem to be justifiable; however, the real asymmetry is not in the formulations in the Constitution regarding the status of federal subjects, but in the territorial organization itself. Certainly, it is fully justified to give a higher status to the republic, organised on the basis of a nationality with its own identity, cultural aspirations, and very often a will of a considerable degree of political sovereignty, than to a region, even if it has a kind of regional identity. But several questions immediately arise: How far should the degree of sovereignty be defined? How to keep a balance between federation and confederation? How to preserve state unity and avoid secessions? What will be the position of minorities in the (semi-) sovereign republics?

Two basic approaches could be suggested: one is ethno-territorial federalism with 'a state-sponsored codification of nationhood' (Winderl, 1999, p. 145), which may however justify a marginalisation of the regions based on purely territorial principle. Another approach is to organise federal relations on the pure state-centred, regional, principle, minimising political institutionalisation of the nationhood of sub-nations, but preserving its cultural institutionalisation.

The first approach would most probably end up with a hierarchical composition for the federation, as was so typical of Soviet rule, would lead to a rise of political nationalism in the republics, and very often to secessionism and discrimination against minorities in the republics. It is possible to say that this approach has been applied in the policy of territorial division so far. If before 1991 the federation was based on a national-territorial principle, now this principle has merely been augmented by a regional-territorial principle. The disparity in status between republics and regions fuels the escalation of demands of regional elites, who have been increasingly influential in the local economies, public finance, and have been intervening into such exclusively federal areas of authority as foreign trade, immigration and international relations, along with active campaigns of local governments to elevate the status of their territories to republics, a process known as the 'sovereignty parade'. (Polishchuk, 1996,

p. 14) Tatarstan, with its pronounced nationalistic and regional appeal, has received a real special status in the federation under an agreement with the centre. It has proclaimed the priority of its legislature over the common federal legislature. It now has the right, and in some cases it has already implemented the right, to have its own diplomatic representative institutions (embassies) in other countries. Tatarstan has become actually a state inside the state, on the grounds of its separatist tendencies since the early 1990s, with a clear-cut ethnic dimension to the ideology of the new 'state'. At the same time one should bear in mind that in Tatarstan the Tatar nationality represents only about half of the population. Furthermore, 68 per cent of Tatars live outside the territory of their republic (as well as 71 per cent of Mordva, 88 per cent of Evenks (Валентей (ed.), 1997), more than 50 per cent of Mari and Chuvash, 40 per cent of Buryats, one third of Bashkirs and Udmurts) (Зорин, 1996, p. 26). The 'more sovereignty' tendencies are also evidenced in Tuva, Bashkorkostan, and North Ossetia-Alania. Giving more sovereignty will actually lead to more risk of destroying any degree of unity. The larger the share of the titular nations in the republic, the stronger are sovereignty demands. But even a republic which is relatively homogeneous in its ethnic composition, Tuva, has only about 60 per cent of the titular nationality (Зорин, 1996, p. 25).

Structural distortions inherited from the central planning, and the immaturity of Russian markets create sharp regional economic disparities, spatial disproportions of population and labour, and eventually inequality of opportunity of populations in different regions of the Federation (Polishchuk, 1996).

> This unfairness not only threatens social peace and prompts attempts of extra-market redistribution of wealth, but also undermines national unity. The integrity of the state, unless kept by force, rests upon the feeling of being a member of a community where everybody has certain rights, guaranteed and protected by this community. Otherwise those who feel themselves discriminated against would be trying to find an identity with a smaller group which guarantees some fairness to its members. In Russia, where the place of living is one of the main factors of social and economic discrimination, regions become natural candidates for the role of a community which maintains reasonable standards of fairness, unavailable nationwide. The federal structure of the Russian state provides a conductive framework for political ramification of these sentiments, which are originally brought to existence by economic forces.
>
> (Polishchuk, 1996, p. 6)

Instead of market re-allocation of investments, jobs and labour force, broad-scale extra-market measures of redistribution of the national product take place (Polishchuk, 1996, p. 12). This adds regional dissatisfaction, especially among those regions, which are resource-rich, populated, and relatively well performing economically. The ethnicity factor is often skilfully manipulated by regional administration politicians, who use economic hardship and the rise of national identities for the manipulation of the electorate, by means of a typical populist appeal. The simple struggle for power leads to the emergence of an ethnocracy: a group of people with power in a region, which serves the interests of their own ethnic group rather than the economic and social development of the region as a whole, just in the same way as regional bureaucracy often serves the needs of the region but does not contribute to the interests of overall prosperity of the country. In most cases, the individuals involved get into power due specifically to their initial administrative position, or where applicable due to a particular ethnic origin, manipulating ethnic feelings and generously promising a better life to their own, 'discriminated' nationality in a typical populist way. Ethnocracy is an evil, as in most cases it overlooks the real needs of regional development in economic terms, and mixes these up with the need for cultural consolidation of a particular nationality, prioritising this activity as the key to regional development.

> Soviet and post-Soviet 'national struggles' were and are not the struggles of nations, but the struggles of institutionally constituted national elites – that is elites institutionally defined *as national* – and aspiring counter-elites.
>
> (Brubaker, 1996, p. 25)

The question of the enhancement of cultural life of ethnic, linguistic or confessional communities is no doubt extremely important, especially in such a multicultural society as the RF. Nevertheless, it cannot be directly bound to the question of regional organization, since the territories are multiethnic anyway. Thus, the argument is that territorial organization and matters of cultural recognition of ethnicity should not be decided as one issue. Moreover, the promotion of community cultures is a broader issue anyway, as it concerns not only ethnic or linguistic communities but also, for instance, confessional groups. The parallel cultures are not bound to interstate or intrastate boundaries; they overlap, crossbreed and penetrate.

Opinions about the development of federal relations according to a model of the United States or Germany, with the highest possible degree of power decentralisation, and asymmetry in delegating power to different regions, are frequently heard, but cannot be completely applicable to the situation in the RF. Neither the US nor Germany organise their federal relations and power sharing between the federal subjects with ethnicity as a principle of federal territorial organisation. Therefore these models can be seriously considered only if the Russian Federation applies a different than ethnic principle of sub-state formation. It must be noted in this respect that a majority of contemporary federations have been unsuccessful, and in most of those successful ones (Germany, USA, Austria, Australia) ethnicity is not a basis of organisation. Neither can the example of Switzerland be directly adjusted to the RF: the number of ethnic communities in Switzerland and in the RF is not comparable. In Switzerland, for example, the state language policy is based on equal status of all languages, which in practice means the ability of a state functionary to answer all letters in German, Italian or French. In the RF, with its more than 100 languages, such an approach would clearly be inappropriate. Conversely French centralism is also inapplicable, as Russia's immense geographic diversity and economic impoverishment of the centre preclude full control by Moscow (Ordeshook, Shvetsova, 1995).

Admitting the necessity of applying the best practices in federal relations from the countries of mature democracy, it is perhaps necessary to acknowledge that a country with such a degree of divergence and mixture of the population all over its territory – in ethnic, confessional and linguistic terms – paradoxically but precisely due to the divergence, should not build its administrative structure on the nationality principle in the first place. Different ethnic and cultural groups have been dispersed throughout the whole territory in its previous and recent history, and therefore its cultural geography does not coincide with the boundaries of the present federal subjects. On the other hand, a higher degree of power to the regions could be granted if the territory were to be reorganised on a purely regional basis. The present branch structure of industry in the RF has a specificity, where on the territory of each republic the principal enterprises are not subjects of regional administration but of ministries of the RF, which means that these enterprises do not participate in the creation of local industrial complexes (Хакамада, 1996). The principle of subsidiarity should be granted to the regions, and in case of economic success an alternative, regional identity may come into view (e.g. Nizhny Novgorod). Greater decentralisation can also serve as a regional buffer against economic disturbances and political uncertainties in Moscow for the local population. Political representation, responsive party system and sensitive politics of accountability for the regional electorate must, however, precede or go along with the implementation of the principle of subsidiarity. This may help to preclude bureaucratisation of regional administration with limited control of power and maximum access to regional resources. The current state of the art still derives from the command system of the Soviet regime, where the absence of political culture, the systemic arrangements and the lack of civil society allow regional governors to abuse their power. Only under certain conditions the regional power may have a potential to act in favour of development of its territory and its people, and only then can the equalisation of status of all parts of the Russian Federation up to the level of the present republics prove useful. Furthermore, the reorganisation of the territorial administration of the whole country on a purely regional principle, with a possible reduction of the number of regions, undermining the principle of ethnicity, may assist the preservation of the state integrity. The loyalty from the side of its citizens can be achieved through cultivation of a civic culture on the one hand, and through diminishing the grounds for political nationalism by satisfaction of the *cultural* nationalistic appeal, on the other hand.

The suggested approach to territorial organisation would certainly require very careful application, with gradual, flexible and variable implementation. In the contemporary situation, nationalities are simply not prepared for this kind of reform. The attempted introduction of new internal passports, with common citizenship of the RF for all its inhabitants, immediately provoked an active discussion, followed by opposition from the side of republics. The new RF passports were designed to show only the citizenship (of the Russian Federation) and not the nationality of the holder. The president of the Republic of Adygey (North Caucasus) expressed opposition to the fact that data in the new passports will be only in Russian, while Adygeya (like many other territories) has two state languages.[4] In the Altai Republic, the chairman of the government followed the Tatar parliament in claiming that the decision to omit the holder's nationality in the new passports was premature and contrary to the wishes of many Russian republics and regions. So, the long-awaited scrapping of the *fifth column*[5] in favour of what is supposed only to be a normal and civilised

---

[4] The titular nation in the Adygey Republic forms now only 22 per cent of the population; 70 per cent were evicted during the Tsarist and Soviet times (Nationality Policy, 1992).

[5] The so-called *fifth column* was the definition of nationality recorded in passports, based not on residence, but purely on ethnic descent. The claimant, however, had a choice of nationality between the descent of two parents. The practice therefore often became the choice of 'a lesser evil', *i.e.* a nationality that provided for a trouble-free life. This explains a decreasing demographic record for some nationalities, the Jews being the most typical case.

concept of citizenship has provoked fears of the liquidation of the republics and eventually of the corresponding nationalities. This simple example actually indicates how far the contemporary society is from perceiving itself as a common entity without political subdivisions on the basis of nationality. It would also be extremely difficult for ethnic representatives to start identifying themselves as *rossiyane* (*россияне*) – a term which could be directly translated into English as citizens or inhabitants of the Russian Federation, but which is mostly translated as simply Russians (which is *russkiye* – *русские*). The term *rossiyane* itself, even in Russian, has a semantic bias towards the route word *rus/ros* (*рус/рос*), implying a high degree of association with Russians. And such semantic notions clearly have an impact on feelings of identity: indeed, would a Scot be happy to be called English?

The political explosions of the last decade in respect to national feelings and ethnic conflicts have created a basis for a common assumption that there is a real crisis in ethnic relations, and a great probability of further ethno-political conflicts in the Russian state. This assumption has become the starting point for the formulation of the state's nationalities policy, and is in fact reflected in a number of governmental documents. At the same time, the national policy remains very inflexible, and is based on a formal understanding of the principle of equality. Instead of suggesting an adaptable mechanism that can provide equality of opportunity for ethnicity, the state is trying to draw up its nationalities policy based on the egalitarian principle. The preamble to the Constitution uses the formulation 'proceeding from the commonly recognised principles of equality and self-determination'. Equality of federal subjects is no doubt an important issue, but as long as the subjects are formed according to very different criteria – national in one case, regional in another, or a conglomerate around an urban centre in a third case – real equality cannot be achieved. The state policy should rather be concentrated on achieving equality of opportunity for an adequate development of all cultures, ethnicity, languages, etc. The right of self-determination, guaranteed to all peoples of the RF under the Constitution, has actually been questioned for a long time now by international scholars. The reality shows that invoking the right to self-determination is a way of expressing sovereignty aspirations which frequently leads to a point of no return: to a demand for secession. The right of peoples (i.e. ethnic groups) to self-determination, as formulated in the Constitution, actually implies a struggle to attain mono-ethnic statehood. But what 'people' would count: at the level of a republic? autonomous area? tiny ethnic groups? titular but minority nationality in the given compact area? Or how would such an approach assist to meet the cultural aspirations of dispersed or highly mixed populations?

The society and the government of the RF alike seem to have been unprepared for the degree to which various nationalities would push for full territorial separation. Therefore, the policy measures in the first years of the existence of the RF displayed a desire to preserve the unity of the RF at any cost, whether this meant giving in some cases a special status with significant devolution of sovereignty (as, for instance, for Tatarstan, after a referendum on sovereignty there which showed 68 per cent of the population to be in favour of secession (Nationality Policy, 1992)), or in others suppressing separatist movements by force, a pattern which led to the continuing war with Chechnya. The case of Chechnya is not itself a general pattern, though, since the warfare has changed the situation dramatically, turning a political problem into a chronic and apparently incurable disease. It is too late now to suggest any alternative solution but a full separation of the republic, and all ideas about political and cultural measures, which should have been developed by Moscow instead of starting the armed conflict, are now nothing more than idle speculation. It is necessary to create a situation which can prevent the illness from developing in the first place, rather than trying to cure it once it is already in place. It seemed that the first war of 1994-1996 turned the Chechens into heroes in the eyes of millions of people inside and outside Russia and, peculiarly enough, the war has had only one positive implication: people learned what an ethnic war was like, and became somewhat more tolerant in consequence. The later events of 1999, however, demonstrated how fragile this attitude was and how easy it was to manipulate the feelings of people by a national-patriotic appeal and skilful sketching of inter-nationality aversion for the sake of momentous political achievement.

The separatist movements are connected with the explosion of ethnic identities, resulting from the hunger for justice among various ethnic groups on the territory of the RF after 70 years of cultural subjugation and frequent forced assimilation. There is no doubt however that the hunger for justice is mostly the hunger for cultural justice, which simply evolves into a hunger for political sovereignty if the cultural demands cannot be accommodated within the state. The principle of a political and territorial organisation of the Russian state based on the ethnic principle is a dead end. The history of the Russian Empire, as well as the history of the Soviet period, determined the polycultural nature of society in the entire territory of the RF, which makes it impossible to conceive political sovereignty for the republics on an ethnic or cultural basis. Cultural contiguity and interplay have been essential for the Russian milieu. As a result of forced and free migration, today, some 60 million people live outside the confines of their 'home' republics (Starovoitova, Nationality Policy, 1992). In many republics, a significant number of other ethnic groups are represented, both in-comers and endogenous people. For example, in the Khakaz and Buryat Republics there are over 100 such groups. A large Russian population in the non-Russian republics is another feature: in Buryatia 24 per cent of the population is Buryat and 48 per cent Russian, while Bashkirs make up only 23 per cent of the population of Bashkorkostan. In Khakazia the titular nationality makes up only 11·5 per cent of the total (Nationality Policy, 1992). Taking all these factors into account, who will be served by political nationalism and secessionism? The ethnocracy, and patrons of 'ethnic' politics, are the only ones who can rise to the peak of the power on the waves of ethnic aspirations.

The real crisis, perhaps, is not in the interethnic relations in the RF, but in the nationalities policy supported by the system of territorial and administrative division. If this is so, an alternative way for cultural accommodation among all peoples in the territory of the RF should be a priority, rather than the definition of modalities for meeting the demands of political sovereignty. The next section will look at the dynamics of inter-ethnic relations at the beginning of the post-Soviet period.

Inter-Ethnic Crisis or Identity Crisis?

Interethnic relations are a point of intersection for all sides of political and economic life in the RF. They have implications for employment issues, the behaviour of the electorate, social policy, institutional development, etc. Ethnic phobias and attitudes can therefore be considered as indicators of the real existence of a crisis in ethnic relations, with implications for the moral health of society, and for its potential for development in a democratic direction. The existence of such a crisis would certainly call into question the very possibility of national solidarity, at least in the short run. Simply assuming that there is a real crisis of inter-ethnic relations in the country may therefore lead the national strategy badly astray in respect to ethnic policy.

Ethnic phobias are not best understood as isolated attitudes towards a particular ethnic group. The analysis of statistics shows that groups with a high level of negativism towards one particular ethnic group usually manifest relatively stronger negative attitudes to other ethnic groups as well, and moreover, demonstrate less tolerance to different cultural or political formations and to any expressions of their aspirations. For example, respondents with a clear anti-Caucasian feelings recorded a higher negativism toward Roma, Estonians, Jews or Americans; while those who expressed negativism toward Estonians, had twice as high indicators of negativism toward Chechens (Гудков, 1996, p. 25). Xenophobic feelings usually work hand in hand with general intolerance. Thus, indicators of ethnic tolerance could become indicators of the overall level of societal solidarity, its chances for democratic consolidation and the advancement of civil society.

Expressions of ethnic attitudes are not always unambiguous. They correspond to the double standard of self-image: one standard for the person him/herself and another standard for everyone else. Therefore, the data on ethnic attitudes must be considered very carefully and mostly treated as mere indicators of trends rather than robust statistics. The double nature of attributions of ethnicity should be also taken into account: 'we' and 'they', which in fact indicates not only a self-identity but also a way of being identified by outsiders (a Roma can claim himself as Czech or Slovak but he will still remain a Gypsy for Czechs). Thus, ethnic stereotypes may at the same time express peculiarities of the vision of the ethnic group or the community about the common 'self'. Another side of this is their vision of their own ethnic group in comparison with other ethnic groups (Гудков, 1995, pp. 23-24).

In this context, the dynamics of self-description of Russians in 1989-1994 was expressed in the fact that not only did the signs of 'modernity'[6] become considerably stronger in the self-image, but also the indicators of remoteness, and of the alienation of the Russians from any other ethnic groups. The rise of Russians' estimates of self-worth coincides with the strengthening of ethnic isolationism groups (Гудков, 1995, pp. 24-25). The most typical feature of this period is the identity crisis, expressed among Russians in two main dimensions: self-pejorative characteristics on the one hand, and feelings of self-esteem and alienation towards other ethnicities and cultures on the other hand. 73 per cent of respondents in 1994 answered that Russia has always been a country of a great culture, but at the same time 41 per cent considered that Russia lagged behind most developed countries, while 31 per cent considered that Russia is developing according to its own, distinct way. At the same time, in their ranking of features of character which they saw as typical for this or that ethnic group,

---

[6] The word 'modernity' is used in a positive sense, reflecting a democratic orientation, economic liberalism and, to a certain extent, a pro-Western alignment.

the Russians demonstrated a significant increase in positive self-estimation, whereas from 1994, the negative features start being mostly seen as typical for other ethnic groups. The closer the distance to other ethnic groups, the more negative the vision of the group in 1994 (e.g. of Lithuanians or Jews compared with Americans) (Гудков, 1995, pp. 24-25). Another peculiarity is that in 1994 the association of Russians with the national community diminished, compared to the data of 1989. The growing tendency toward an individualist vision and individual-orientated values is noticeable.

**Table 7.1 Do you Feel Responsible for the People of your Nationality?
(in % of the number of respondents)***

	Certainly yes	Certainly no
1989	21	27
1994	10	40

* Comparative results of the all-Russia survey of 1989 (representative sample N=1250 people) and 1994 (N=2957)

Source: *Экономические и социальные перемены: мониторинг общественного мнения* [Economic and social changes: monitoring of the public opinion], ВЦИОМ, 2/1995.

It is interesting that the national self-consciousness had significantly decreased its linkage with the state by 1994, instead seeing ethnicity in terms of such traditional characteristics as common language, territory, history, culture, etc. There was also a shift in the system of personified values in the society in this period: from Soviet toward Russian, and from Marxist toward Russian-patriotic (the popularity of e.g. Lenin and Gagarin diminished, but that of Catherine II and Kutuzov increased) (Левинсон, 1995, p. 28). In general, the anti-Semitic tendencies in ethnic stereotypes marginally increased in 1989-1993, linking the Jews with moral defects as the features of character slightly more often in 1994 than in 1989 (Левинсон, 1995). The highest rate of increase in the fears of Russians in the period of 1989-1994 was connected with three basic issues: unemployment and poverty, criminality, and violence on ethnic grounds (the latter fear increased by eight percentage points between 1989 and 1994) (Голов, 1995, p. 31).

Comparison of surveys of October 1993 and March 1995 showed that a significant increase of mutual ethnic aversion between different ethnic groups in the period of the break-up of Soviet political and administrative structures, connected with the ideological and ethnic

consolidation among practically all nationalities, stagnated in 1992 –
beginning of 1993. There were no notable changes in 1994 and 1995
(Гудков, 1995a, p. 14). Attitudes toward such ethnic groups as Tatars,
Armenians, Azerbaijanis and Uzbeks slightly improved, towards Jews they
remained almost unchanged, and they marginally worsened toward
Estonians and Chechens. The Chechen war of 1994-1996 did not provoke
anti-Chechen phobias (the rate of increase in anti-Estonian sentiments was
higher than that of anti-Chechen ones), but due to propaganda in the mass
media, the fears of terrorism organised by Chechens did increase in some
places even already in 1995, largely affecting big urban centres, including
Moscow. However, anti-Chechen phobias *per se* were the strongest in
southern Russia (33 per cent), as compared to northern Russia (24 per cent)
(Гудков, 1995a, p. 14).

There were two basic groups of objects of ethnic negativism in
Russian society: first, *traditional* ethnic negativism (toward Jews, Tatars,
Uzbeks, and to some extent Ukrainians), and second, more recent ethnic
negativism (toward Armenians, Chechens, Roma, or Caucasians in
general). The strongest ethnic negativism was directed towards Caucasians
and Roma, but in general, for the period of 1993-1995 the anti-Caucasian
and anti-Roma phobias were either stagnating or diminishing (Гудков,
1995a, p. 16), except for anti-Chechen feeling, as mentioned above. In the
latter case, as well as in the case of negativism toward the Balts, we see
clearly that this reaction is the result of the national domestic and foreign
policy and of the *state* propaganda: blaming the Chechens for terrorism and
naming them as responsible for the war, and exacerbating the issue of the
Russian minorities in the Baltic States.

**Table 7.2 Attitudes of Russians Toward People of Other Nationalities
(in % of the number of respondents)**

	1993		1995		1996	
	Positive	Negative	Positive	Negative	Positive	Negative
Chechens	35	48	30	51	53	47
Roma	39	48	36	48	59	41
Azerbaijani	43	43	42	39	72	28
Armenians	41	45	46	35	n.a.*	n.a.
Uzbeks	61	20	59	18	n.a.	n.a.
Estonians	64	16	58	19	88	12
Jews	68	17	64	17	90	10
Tatars	71	13	74	12	n.a.	n.a.
Ukrainians	81	7	83	7	n.a.	n.a.
Russians	91	2	92	2	n.a.	n.a.

* 'n.a.' means not available in the publications

Source: Гудков Л. (1995a), all-Russian surveys of October 1993 and March 1995. The results of the survey of July 1996 were published in Гудков Л. (1996). The comparison of the three surveys is constructed on the basis of data available in these publications.

According to the results of 1996 all indexes of ethnic negativism fell, reaching the level of 1993 or even the earlier period of 1989-1990. This was not a result of increasing sympathy toward other ethnic groups, of anti-xenophobia or of tolerance exactly, but rather reflected a higher number of respondents who expressed ethnic and nationalistic indifference (the most frequent answer was 'I don't have a particular attitude toward...') (Гудков, 1996, p. 22). As a matter of fact an important factor for society is not the low percentage of anti-Semites, but rather a higher percentage of open and conscious anti-anti-Semites, i.e. people who do not stay indifferent. The resistance of society toward xenophobia and ethnic/cultural negativism, and the moral, cultural and political resistance of individuals, groups and institutions against all forms of chauvinistic and racial expressions, are essential factors.[7] This is an indicator of the level of social solidarity and the potential for the establishment of a cultural and political 'welfare state'. Thus, ethnic indifference is not really an indicator of the level of tolerance of the society. However, it certainly does show the relief of tension in inter-ethnic relations and the improvement of the situation after a peak of nationalistic tensions in 1993-1995. Therefore, if the assumption of the existence of a crisis of inter-ethnic relations was ever correct at the beginning of the transformation period, we can still say that by 1996 it could have been a matter of the past.

The latter supposition cannot, however, be fully confirmed by the data on some cities in the RF. A specific feature of urban settlements lies in their highly ethnically mixed populations, and a complex aggregation of issues connected with this, such as migration problems, cultural and social accommodation, etc. The level of ethnic tension in multi-ethnic cities was still high in 1995, but a certain stagnation of the process was evidenced, where the presence of inter-ethnic tensions in Moscow was recorded at

---

[7] The importance of this factor is seen in the analysis *Attitudes toward Jews in the Soviet Union: Public Opinion in Ten Republics. Working Papers on Contemporary Anti-Semitism* by Singer, D. (ed.), NY, 1993 (quoted from Гудков, 1996, p.23).

around 68 per cent of respondents between 1993[8] and 1995. The same data in Ufa and Orenburg decreased, while Stavropol demonstrated an increase in interethnic tension (63 per cent of respondents in 1993, 84 per cent in 1995). In general, the urban respondents ranked interethnic conflicts in the fourth, or mostly fifth place as a possible source of insecurity for Russia, following economic collapse, the struggle between political forces, corruption, and criminality (Иванов et al., 1996, pp. 89-90). In 1995, taking part in a conflict in the interest of one's own ethnic group was considered as possible only by 8 per cent of respondents in Moscow, 7 per cent in Ufa, and 12-15 per cent in other examined cities. Nevertheless, at the same time a notably higher number of people claimed non-participation in violent conflicts against other political forces or power groupings (78 per cent in Moscow), and non-participation in strikes (62 per cent in Moscow), unlike rejection of participation in ethnic conflicts (only 25 per cent in Moscow) (Иванов et al., 1996, p. 91). This tendency was indicated among the Russian respondents as well as among representatives of other ethnic groups (Ibid., p. 92). This issue should not be underestimated, because it demonstrates a pronounced ethnic cleavage of the society compared with other political issues, and can only confirm that cultural dissatisfaction and ethnic tensions may eventually lead to political nationalism and open conflicts. The survey indicated general ignorance about the interests of different ethnic groups in the work of state institutions of different levels, mass media, etc. Respondents claimed the under-presentation of the history, culture and traditions of endogenous ethnic groups (Ibid., p. 95), inequality of opportunity of different ethnic groups in educational attainment and financial conditions of living, and the lack of conditions for developing the national cultures and languages of different ethnic groups (Ibid., p. 96). At the same time there was an opinion expressed by respondents that granting different kinds of rights of sovereignty only 'separates the peoples of Russia'. Negative ethnic stereotypes and prejudices were demonstrated by 41 per cent of Muscovites (increased from 21 per cent), 57 per cent of respondents from Stavropol, mentioning Caucasians as the main subjects of dislike (Azerbaijani, Chechens, Armenians) (Ibid., p. 97). Comparing the results of the survey in the five

---

[8] The results of a survey by the Centre of Sociology of Interethnic Relations of the Russian Academy of Sciences are used. The questionnaire survey was conducted in Moscow, Stavropol, Orenburg, Samara and Ufa, based on a quota sampling, addressing representation of ethnic groups, social-professional status, gender, age, etc. (Sample: Moscow N=837, Stavropol=908, Ufa=593, Samara=800, Orenburg=320) (Иванов et al., 1996).

cities, the tensest inter-ethnic situation was in Stavropol, and to some extent in Moscow. Both centres accepted significant flows of immigration from the Caucasus from the second half of the 1980s, when the ethnic situation became unpredictable, ending up indeed in numerous violent ethnic conflicts. The present imperfect situation in Moscow and Stavropol is a reflection of inability to serve the interests of all incoming ethnic groups (expressed mostly in cultural demands and in a lack of social provisions) as well as an inability to address an increased concern from the side of the native population (mostly on security issues, employment, etc.). It is also important to relieve the immigration burden from centres like Moscow, by creating incentives for migration to regions with low population density and a natural potential for growth (e.g. natural resources, labour, and the development of new branches of activity, including the use of sophisticated technologies, in order to accommodate immigrating intelligentsia).

Statistical analysis of the results of public opinion polls shows that xenophobic and negative reactions are more frequent among politically active respondents, while, vice versa, respondents who are politically indifferent, passive, and disappointed in politics are generally indifferent when it comes to ethnic attitudes too, and they can be said to demonstrate a higher degree of tolerance (Гудков, 1995a, p. 16). This is particularly important to take into account when examining the results of the elections, where populist programmes, meaning either the pronouncedly nationalistic appeal of Zhirinovsky in 1993 or the national-patriotic charismatic campaign of Lebed' in 1996, or the populist pro-stability, pro-security appeal for the display of power and against the imaginary terrorists of Putin received a high percentage of votes. If the most tolerant electorate is at the same time the most passive, then it is quite possible that this electorate does not go to election polls, while the votes of the nationalistically-minded and more 'aggressive' part of the electorate would be most likely to be cast. The peculiar fact is that the electorate of Zhirinovsky's Liberal Democratic Party of Russia and the electorate of Alexander Lebed' showed almost the same high level of xenophobic feelings as the electorate of the Communist Party of the Russian Federation (Гудков, 1996, p. 26), in spite of the quite different political programmes of the parties and leaders. The common feature of these programmes, though, was a clear populist appeal, orientated toward the national-patriotic feelings of an electorate suffering a crisis of national identity, and subject to nostalgia about the 'quiet' and 'reliable' past. The vast majority of the electorate of the mentioned populist plea, however, did not seek turning back to communism. They were rather searching for an alternative which would at the same time provide for a better economic situation and fill the identity gap – giving them back the lost sense of 'greatness' of the times of the Russian Empire and the Soviet Union. This electorate expected a charismatic, strongly personified politics, and presents a vulnerable, easily directed, elastic mass, which could be attracted by both left- and right-wing parties, or eventually 'no-name' party or politician depending on the skilfulness of political leaders and their surrounding, and on the concrete political-economic situation. This *ductile society* is certainly a danger for future democratic consolidation and the advancement of tolerance in the society, as it could be manipulated by a nationalistic, chauvinistic or separatist, appeal.

Analysis shows that the expressions of inferiority complexes among Russians, which have been directly related to the crisis of national identity, correlate with xenophobic beliefs also. These expressions had been escalating since 1989, as stated in the form of fears about the plundering of national resources, a conspiracy against Russia, military threats, etc., but finally began to weaken after 1996 (Гудков, 1996, p. 23). The basis for Russian great-patriotic or *homeland* sentiments (following Brubaker's language, 1996) has diminished since then.

The identity crisis throughout the post-Soviet space is a common feature, connected with global changes in world politics. This is not a notion specifically inherent to Russians. The same identity crisis is also seen in the United States, where it is mostly evidenced in the political attempts by high officials to project its weight on the international and particularly European scene. Russian foreign policy features similar attempts at creating an image of greatness, although the results are far less magnificent. As for Russian domestic politics, the crisis of identity is utilised by politicians in their populist appeals and manipulation of ethnic feelings. This sharpens the existing phobias, and eventually helps to provoke ethnic conflicts.

The identity crisis in the post-Soviet space is directly related to two notions: first, the reduction in the weight of the Russian state on the international level, and second, the loss of the common identity of *the multinational Soviet people* as a consequence of the break up of the Soviet Union. The international character of the Soviet identity, although artificial and not always reflecting the reality, was carefully cultivated in people's minds for seventy years. This long-standing self-delusion was only interrupted by the collapse of the USSR. The ideological and identity gap which resulted from the break up of the Union was filled by the revival of ethnic identities, something which is mostly manifested in ethnocultural nationalism and sometimes in striving for political independence on the side of non-Russian ethnic groups, and the *homeland* nationalism of the Russians. The latter has been typically supported by often unresolved or inadequately tackled problem of the ethnic Russian population on the territories of the newly independent states, whose destiny is still perceived by the majority of Russians as a destiny of the Russian people (regardless of the existence of any citizenship arrangements). The *homeland* nationalism in Russia was expressed in typical fears, such as the fear of plundering of national resources (reaching its peak in 1993, when it was mentioned by about 75 per cent of respondents, this figure decreasing to 60 per cent in 1996), or the fear of losing power in the homeland (54 per cent of respondents considered in 1993 that non-Russian nationalities enjoy too much influence in the RF, while in 1996 the figure dropped to 40 per cent) (Гудков, 1996, p. 27). It is important to mention that a too big influence of non-Russians was much more feared in big cities than in the rest of the territory, confirming the suggested hypothesis about big urban centres as an important cultural and political mediator, which may have a positive as well as negative semantic weight. The result of such fears is, for instance, the creation of the Parliamentary Commission for the Analysis of the Cadre Policy of the Highest Echelon of the State Power in the Light of the Interests of the Russian Statehood (something pushed by Zhirinovsky's party). The argument behind the sophisticated title of the newly created commission was simple: too many non-Russians (i.e. Jews) in power. In other words, the Russians, accustomed to being the masters of their huge empire-state, are now afraid that they could stop being masters even of their homeland. As Brubaker puts it,

> Like Weimar Germany, post-Soviet Russia has suffered a 'humiliating' loss not only of territory but of its status as a Great Power, creating an opening for political entrepreneurs with a variety of remedial, compensatory, or restorationist political agendas.
>
> (Brubaker, 1992, p. 15)

Apart from political debates, the ideological stance after the collapse of communism has been suffering a moral gap, which is being filled to some extent by a revival in the moral values offered by religions. The dynamics of the growth of various confessions on the territory of the RF is as follows:

**Table 7.3 Number of Believers by Faith in the Russian Federation in
1990 – 1996 (thousands)**

	1990	1993	1996
Russian Orthodox church	3450	4556	7195
Islam	870	2537	2494
Buddhism	12	52	124
Other confessions	111	168	534

Source: Adapted from Зорин В. (1996), p. 30.

However, against this background of a general religious revival, the
transformation of the Orthodox Church into almost a state religion is of
special importance. In September 1997 a law on the freedom of conscience
and religious association was adopted, after some marginal presidential
corrections of the parliamentary version of the document. Although the
document names the 'respected' religions of Christianity, Islam, Buddhism
and Judaism, which constitute 'an integral part of the historical heritage of
people of Russia', it also underlines 'the distinguished role of the Orthodox
religion', which affronted representatives of other confessions. The
Orthodox Church retains some dogmatic positions which, if more closely
connected to the state, may create feelings of cultural/religious
discrimination among other confessions. The stronger the trust given to the
Orthodox Church among the respondents, the higher the level of ethnic
negativism and xenophobic attitudes (31 per cent of respondents who fully
trust the Orthodox Church indicated ethnic negativism) (Гудков, 1996, p.
25).

The growing ideologization of the Orthodox religion on the one
hand, and the identity crisis in society on the other, sometimes has an
impact on the attempts among the population to search for an alternative
identity. For example, there is a pronounced revival of small
ethnoconfessional communities. The St. Peter and Paul Lutheran
community, which has a German tradition, was founded in Moscow in the
17th century. In 1904 the congregation numbered 14 000 Germans, 2 000
Latvians, 600 Estonians and 150 Finns and Swedes.[9] The church was

---

[9] The information on this religious community is taken from the published results of a case
study of the St. Peter and Paul community in Moscow (Курило, 1995) and from in-depth
interviewing by the author.

practically closed in 1936, and a lot of community members, being in the majority Germans, were deported *en masse* or arrested. The community was re-established in 1991, and by mid 1990s it already counted 300 people. Most of them are ethnic Germans or their descendants, who would like to re-establish the Lutheran cultural traditions. The interesting feature of the composition of the community is the increasing number of young members, which seems typical for the current period with its ideological uncertainty. There is a renunciation of the ideology of materialism on the one hand, and a denial of traditional religious ideology (Orthodox religion) on the other hand. More than half of the community's members do not speak any German, and their native language is Russian, though many of them do now study German. The striking fact is that the community includes representatives of many different nationalities: besides Germans, who represent about half of the community, there are many Russians (or assimilated, Russified Germans), and also Finns, Latvians, Jews, Hungarians, Tatars, and Ukrainians. The descendants of Russified Germans who join the community are striving for a revival of cultural traditions and national-confessional identity. On the other hand, representatives of other ethnic groups are attracted by the relative radicalism of Protestantism, its openness and orientation toward Western values, and they are specifically trying to find an alternative to the 'ideologised' Russian Orthodox Church. In their case their aim could be defined as a search for an alternative cultural identity through spiritual pursuits, and the invention of tradition. Regular participation in services by representatives of other confessions, and a growing number of polyconfessional families have become a typical feature of the recent times (Курило, 1995). The sister Lutheran community of Sts. Ann and Peter of St. Petersburg counts about 600 people, also mostly people of German origin, coming back to St. Petersburg from the deportation settlements. Various ethnic groups are represented in the community, especially among the young people. These are only examples of the revival of cultural communities and the search for an alternative identity which have become typical: hundreds of ethnic or confessional community newspapers and new language schools have been established. So far, this has been a result of bottom-up initiatives, but the provision of a system of legal norms for the support of cultural autonomy should intersect with this public initiative.

As far as the crisis of national identities is concerned, the elite crisis should not be discounted. It is one component of the destruction of the socio-cultural orientation of society. Speaking of this elite crisis, it is necessary to bear in mind that the elite could be considered in three clusters: as a political elite, a social elite and a public elite. The social elite continues to be a base for economic reform (in 1994, for example, 40 per cent of the social elite considered continuation of the economic reform necessary, compared with only 28 per cent among all respondents) (Левада, 1994, p. 10). The social elite has been augmented by a new stratum, the so-called new Russians, a group which is economically successful in the market economy, but which mostly remains indifferent to other aspects of the development of society. The moral gap within the national identity could hardly be filled by this social group.

The crisis in society has had an important effect on the public elite that had experienced a short period of flourishing in the first years of *perestroika* (Левада, 1994, p. 95). The Russian public elite, the *intelligentsia*, which has been historically so important and functionally meaningful for society, has been suffering a pronounced level of moral crisis in recent years, when the society has clearly re-orientated itself towards the world-wide mass culture, thus distancing itself from historical traditions and roots. It has lost its formerly important influence on the orientation of society, and this gap has been partly filled by a new type of political elite – the new type of politicians, with their populist, demagogic appeal. Because of the fact that a lot of present political elite, especially in the regions, came from members of the former *autocracy*, the general de-politicising of society is quite natural. The new democratic values have not yet become an integral part of the society's system of beliefs, whereas the former pseudo-democratic tradition actually serves to discredit these values themselves. In this setting, populist political success is very conceivable.

The merging of xenophobia and the ideology of ethnic nationalism became a general feature in the 1990s, which also saw the crisis of the public elite, and the loss of its role in formulating and directing the moral values of the society. The striking and worrying fact is that the only group of respondents which still suffers from the complexes of national degradation, the fear of plundering of national resources, the loss of the great national and state power are those respondents with complete higher education: during the period 1989-1996 the share of such fears among this group almost doubled (from 39 per cent to 69 per cent) (Гудков, 1996, p. 26).

Concluding this look at the basic features of the recent history of the development of ethnic phobias, it is possible to say that anti-Semitism, so traditional for Russian society, though still in place in the 1990s, gave way to anti-Caucasian xenophobic feelings. The history of the dissolution of the Soviet Union has also introduced a 'new external enemy' – the Balts and other people of former Union republics, who now belong to independent states. Already in 1995 we saw a stagnation in the development of ethnic intolerance, and there was a decline in xenophobia in 1996, in spite of attempts in the media to create a negative image of Chechens. The latter, however, proved more effective during the media campaign of 1999, when the image of Chechen terrorists violating the population in different parts of the territory of the Russian Federation was successfully manipulated. Where the truth ends and a lie starts is unknown but the result was certainly achieved: the population almost unanimously said yes to the war. What caused such a sudden change after a tendency of stabilisation of inter-ethnic relations and general relief in ethnic tensions? The skilful manipulation of aspirations for a stronger and more stable power in the framework of the electoral campaign was undertaken against the background of other objective factors, such as aggression on the side of Chechen nationalists, vivid fundamentalist Muslim appeals on their side, coincidence with the social upheaval among the Russian-speaking pensioners and the widely broadcast reports of harsh suppression of their claims in Latvia, as well as efficiently escalated media campaign concerning terrorist actions of Chechens (the liability of the latter was never proved, but proof was never needed in a society with an embryonic political culture and an immature legal state). This was precisely an expression of Brubaker's (1996) concern about mutual influences between the *nationalising nationalism* of successor and pro-independence states and the *homeland nationalism* of Russia, which present a great danger for future stability, especially, we may add, when they become a plaything of elite interests and a tool in their struggle for power.

Instead of Conclusions

As we have seen the nationalism of the society (among both the non-Russian and Russian populations) is closely connected with the crisis of identity. Therefore the crisis in fact takes place at the level of ideology rather than reality, which confirms that the cultural/national aspirations should be addressed in the first instance. This demand cannot be fully satisfied in the framework of the current system of territorial organisation. Although the territorial-administrative organisation of the country is based on the principle of ethnicity in case of republics and grants a high level of sovereignty to them, it still cannot address the whole spectrum of ethnic divergence on their territories. The distorted structure of the present federation gives grounds for greater sovereignty aspirations to territories organised on a purely regional basis, but does at the same time provide some basis for *national* solidarity and civic culture.

The present organisation of republics and areas is based on the principle of nationality, where in fact a Western approach to ideas of federations and nation states has been applied. As analysis shows, the composition of the population of the Russian Federation is so heterogeneous in ethnic terms that a one nation – one territorial unit approach cannot be implemented. At the same time it is clear that at present a revival of nationalism among the titular nationalities of the republics has raised the issue of cultural aspirations to a political level. Therefore the purely regional principle of territorial division cannot immediately be applied either. This dilemma has found scholarly reflection in some recent scientific attempts. For example, Valery Tishkov on the one hand criticises the provision of ethnicity as 'the basis for "socialist federalism", which was promoted as radically different from "bourgeois" (read: territorial) federalism' (Tishkov, 1997, p. 237), and on the other hand, proposes 'a strategy of gradual de-ethnicisation of the state and of de-etatisation of ethnicity', but (!) 'without questioning the system of ethno-territorial autonomies' (Tishkov, 1997, p. 260). He places civic nation-building and individual rights in opposition to the collective rights of communities and argues that the provision of both is the key to success. Without really aiming to question the need to address both civic rights of individuals and the rights of communities, let me express a reservation concerning the practical chances for implementing 'a major project of civic nation-building' (Tishkov, 1997, p. 260) while maintaining the existing ethnicity-based territories. This would lead to addressing the needs of ethnoterritorial autonomies, mainly in a political sense, and would eventually also support their nationhood and nation-building in institutional terms. But cultural communities are not equal to ethnically defined territories, and their needs should be addressed in some other way. The dilemma will never be resolved unless the state applies a very flexible and very gradual approach in reforming the system of territorial administration. This means in practice that the decentralisation of power, and re-assigning political power to ethnicity-based territories, should be provisional; and the stress should be gradually put on *regional* representation and power sharing where the ethnicity factor should be slowly undermined. Where necessary, major ethnic groups should be represented in political arrangements, but this issue must not be stressed, otherwise it will be realised in the form of ethnocracy.

Asymmetric federalism is not an evil by definition, but *ethnic* asymmetric federalism might turn out to be. This has been proved throughout the socialist period. The degree of sovereignty should be balanced throughout the territory where regions can accommodate the same degree of power as the republics. The federal organisation needs to undergo steady de-ethnicisation at the same time. Nevertheless, because the process may be long-lasting, the immediate stress should be put on addressing the cultural aspirations of all ethnic groups without exception, with a system of provision of legal norms granting equality of opportunity to all cultural demands. In such a big and economically weak country, the local needs and the cultural diversity of the society can best be addressed at a lower level. This could be partly realised by the Federal Law on National-Cultural Autonomy, adopted in June 1996.

The history of the concept of national-cultural autonomy originated at the beginning of the 20th century in the ideas of Austrian social democracy. The concept was elaborated to provide an approach to the nationality question in Austria-Hungary, basing this on the principle of the territorial federal arrangement (as opposed to a national federal approach). The concept was criticised by the Marxists and especially by Lenin, who argued that the idea of national cultural autonomy undermines the territorial settlement of ethnic groups. This misleading argument had a negative impact on the nationalities policy in Soviet times, when the principle of national territorial autonomy was applied.

The idea of national cultural autonomy was elaborated especially for areas with a high mixture of ethnic groups to stimulate various forms of development of ethnic traditions, language and culture. As it is formulated in the Federal Law on National Cultural Autonomy (1996), one of the principles of national cultural autonomy is self-identity, with a certain ethnic commonality. In spite of every positive potential which the concept can bring in, it is still necessary to say that the theory underestimates the complexity of cultural issues. The cross-cultural analysis employed in the Parallel Cultures project has fostered an advantageous multi-disciplinary approach, which shows that in many cases the border between ethnic and religious, or ethnic and language identity is minimal, that one factor actually facilitates another, and finally that a confessional or language community today may claim itself an ethnic group in several years. If the Jews in Russia have transformed their identity from a confessional commonality to an ethnic one, it may be logically questioned why this should not occur in other cases too. Cultural issues should certainly be approached from a broader, multidisciplinary perspective.

The concept of national cultural autonomy implies public support for the initiatives of ethnic cultural communities, associations, etc. in their intentions to organize language education, to preserve historic cultural traditions, to participate in mass media and in decision making, and to maintain cultural values, crafts, etc. The concept, however, cannot be fully implemented without provision for the functioning of civil society and advancement of the civic culture in general. The virtual absence of the libertarian and cosmopolitan tradition (except for a short period during Stolypin's reforms) created the preconditions for the existence of continuous ethnic cleavage expressed in a nationalism based on an exclusive definition of citizenship.[10]

At present the Russian nation (if a one can speak of such an organism at all) suffers from the lack of 'a common sense of solidarity' (Winderl, 1999, p. 36). The nation-building should not be concentrated around a single ethnic group, which in the case of the Russian Federation can be only Russians, but should rather be directed at state-centred, civic, nation-building with respect for the multicultural environment. The Russian Federation has to face a challenge of nation *formation* with perhaps very basic problems of strategy, in which the very balance between an ethnic and cultural divergence of national minorities and their belonging to one common nation needs to be found. It is, however, important to recognise that the process can in no way be built on the dominance of the Russian nation, nor on the embracing of the ethnic minorities by the dominant nation. The Russian Federation should not take the path of forming a Russian nation-state, nor of *nationalising*[11] the Russian state. The latter is certainly especially difficult to achieve against the background of the manifest identity crisis among the Russian population, where (re-)creation of a myth, a tradition, a *Russian* Idea, is in a way necessary for the national emancipation, but radically contradicts the objective of creating the ideology and identity of a civic state. Furthermore, the government and its federal parts should be ethnically neutral. Perhaps even a more ethnically

---

[10] Here the definition of citizenship by Kitschelt (1992) is employed. He associated inclusive views of citizenship with libertarian procedural preferences and exclusive views with authoritarian ones. However, this perception of views on citizenship is only partly applicable to Russian nationalism, since in terms of border possessions and the historical incorporation of other independent states under relations of dependence, those views are not entirely satisfactory in this case.

[11] According to Brubaker (1996) *a nationalising state* is understood as a state *of* and *for* a particular ethnocultural 'core nation' whose language, culture, demographic position, economic welfare, and political hegemony are protected and supported by the state (p. 103).

neutral name of the country and therefore of the nation may be suitable. In many respects such a line of ideas may appear to be wishful thinking and certainly somewhat utopian at present. Nationhood needs to be up-graded from the sub-state to the state-wide level, whereas ethnicity should be addressed not at a sub-state, but rather at a local or community level. A positive feature and a critical potential of the civil society in the Russian Federation is its poor support to homeland nationalism and populist demagogy alike. On the other hand, it has a potential for supportive actions in the provision of minority cultural rights. Only a full range of civil society institutions, and the participation of the public in the life of the state, will uphold the full support of development of ethnic divergence, with the various cultural aspirations of minorities addressed through non-governmental organisations, communities, publicly supported institutions, private firms, etc. These institutions, rather than political bodies, should become a platform for ethnic and cultural representation. The creation of grounds for civil society will advance the national solidarity, where cultural tolerance should become a norm. Without implementation of the principles of civil society, it is impossible to preserve the national unity; without awareness from citizens of personal responsibility for the destiny of the state, an ideal of tolerance among citizens of the state cannot be achieved; without tolerance there is no loyalty to the state. It is necessary to put the individual at the focal point of a conception of the legislature where an individual is not a kind of *homo novus*, but a transmitter of culture (ethnicity, religion, language, etc.). In the Soviet Union the principle of nationality was established and expressed in an obsolete manner: the so-called *fifth column* (the nationality definition in passport) had become the same kind of natural routine as the ascription of gender. Identity had become one of the addictions of modernity, and to take a distance from this approach in the 'post-colonial' times will demand not only elaborate civic education but also the introduction of an alternative, civic, model of identity, distanced from the ethnic one.

Nationality is not an abstract model for citizens of the RF, it is a given prerequisite for personal identity, even if it no longer has the stability of modernity and the natural need of an individual to be affiliated, a part of a whole. Identity develops, changes over time, and often poses unresolvable puzzles: for instance, in the case of 'border cultures' (Bhabha' 1996) and double/triple identities. The crisis of identities in the post-Soviet space is multiplied by the conflict of identities in the post-modern world. And the question of addressing cultures is no longer easy to answer: what actually are we trying to address? The concept of parallel cultures implies a corresponding *existential* approach to identities, where one or more 'selves' may be superimposed and where self-identity and outside definition may not always coincide (Hall, Bauman, 1996). The parallel cultures approach considers an individual as a part of a whole, and the whole as comprised of individuals. It does not, though, disregard the role of the 'common', posing in fact the cultural 'common' as an object of study, where the object is understood as changeable, diffuse, and influential as well as influenced. Parallel cultures formulations should not be in fact recall the over-simplifications of theories of 'partial' or 'minority' cultures (Bhabha, 1996), but should eventually provide an analysis of the global multicultural environment.

The parallel cultures approach does not have as an object of research a community as a 'monolithic fixed category' (Bhabha, 1994), nor a binary opposition of identity – we/they, self/other – but attempts to see the individual versus the global, the ethnic versus civic culture, where an individual is considered a central issue, a focal component but also a cultural transmitter in a harmonious rather than conflicting self-identity and societal perception.

Annex

Federal Subjects According to the Constitution of 1993

Republic of Adygeya, Republic of Altai, Republic of Bashkorkostan, Republic of Buryatia, Republic of Dagestan, Ingush Republic, Kabardin-Balkar Republic, Republic of Kalmykia – Khalmg Tangch, Karachayevo-Cherkess Republic, Republic of Karelia, Republic of Komi, Republic of Mari El, Republic of Mordovia, Republic of Sakha (Yakutia), Republic of North Ossetia, Republic of Tatarstan (Tatarstan), Republic of Tuva, Udmurt Republic, Republic of Khakasia, Chechen Republic, Chuvash Republic;

Altai Territory, Krasnodar Territory, Krasnoyarsk Territory, Maritime Territory, Stavropol Territory, Khabarovsk Territory;

Amur Region, Arkhangelsk Region, Astrakhan Region, Belgorod Region, Bryansk Region, Vladimir Region, Vologograd region, Vologda Region, Voronezh Region, Ivanovo Region, Irkutsk Region, Kaliningrad Region, Kaluga Region, Kamchatka Region, Kemerovo Region, Kirov Region, Kostroma Region, Kurgan Region, Kursk Region, Leningrad Region, Lipetsk Region, Magadan Region, Moscow Region, Murmansk Region, Nizhny Novgorod Region, Novgorod Region, Novosibirsk Region, Omsk Region, Orenburg Region, Oryol Region, Penza Region, Perm Region, Pskov Region, Rostov Region, Ryazan Region, Samara Region, Saratov Region, Sakhalin Region, Sverdlovsk Region, Smolensk Region, Tambov Region, Tver Region, Tomsk Region, Tula Region, Tyumen Region, Ulyanovsk Region, Chelyabinsk Region, Chita Region, Yaroslavl Region;

Moscow, St. Petersburg – federal cities;

Jewish Autonomous Region;

Aginsky Buryat Autonomous Area, Komi-Permyak Autonomous Area, Koryak Autonomous Area, Nenets Autonomous Area, Taimyr (Dolgan-Nenets) Autonomous Area, Ust-Ordynsky Buryat Autonomous Area, Khanty-Mansi Autonomous Area, Chukchi Autonomous Area, Evenk Autonomous Area, Yamal-Nenets Autonomous Area.

References

Anderson B. (1983), *Imagined Communities: Reflections on the Origin and Spread of Nationalism*, Verso, London.

Baumann, Z. (1996), 'From Pilgrim to Tourist – or a Short History of Identity', in Hall, S., du Gay, P. (eds), *Questions of Cultural Identity*, SAGE Publications, London, Thousand Oaks, New Delhi, pp.19-36.

Bhabha, H.K. (1994), *The Location of Cultures*, London-NY, Routledge.

Bhabha, H.K. (1996), 'Culture's In-Between', in Hall, S., du Gay, P. (eds), *Questions of Cultural Identity*, SAGE Publications, London, Thousand Oaks, New Delhi, pp. 53-60.

Bromlej, J.V. (1980), *Etnos a etnografia* [Ethnicity and ethnography], Bratislava.

Brubaker, R. (1992), *Citizenship and Nationhood in France and Germany*, Harvard University Press, Cambridge-Mass., London.

Brubaker, R. (1996), *Nationalism Reframed. Nationhood and the National Question in the New Europe*, Cambridge University Press, Cambridge.

Gouré, L. (1994), 'The Russian Federation: Possible Disintegration Scenarios', in *Comparative Strategy*, 13:4, pp. 401-417.

Hall, S. (1996), 'Introduction: Who Needs Identity?', in Hall, S., du Gay, P. (eds), *Questions of Cultural Identity*, SAGE Publications, London, Thousand Oaks, New Delhi, pp.1-17.

Hobsbawm E. and Ranger T. (1983), *The Invention of Tradition*, Cambridge University Press, Cambridge.

Hobsbawm E. (1992), *Nations and Nationalism Since 1780*, Cambridge University Press, Cambridge.

Hroch, M. (1985), *Social Preconditions of National Revival in Europe. A Comparative Analysis of the Social Composition of Patriotic Groups among Smaller European Nations*, Cambridge.

Kitschelt, H. (1992), 'The Formation of the Party System in East Central Europe', in *Politics and Society*, v. 20, 1992/1, pp.7-50.

Nationality Policy in the Russian Federation, materials of the Moscow conference of September 1992.

Ordeshook, P., Shvetsova, O. (1995), *If Hamilton and Madison Were Merely Lucky, What Hope is There for Russian Federalism?*, Social Science Working Paper 888, California Institute of Technology, Pasadena, California.

Poleshchuk, L. (1996), *Russian Federalism: Economic Reform and Political Behavior*, Social Science Working Paper 972, California Institute of Technology, Pasadena, California.

Smith, A. (1991), *National Identity*, London, Penguin.

Tishkov, V. (1997), *Ethnicity, Nationalism and Conflict in and after the Soviet Union*, SAGE Publications, London.

Urban, M. (1994), 'The Politics of Identity in Russia's Postcommunist Transition: The Nation Against Itself', in *Slavic Review*, 53:3, pp. 733-763.

Winderl, T. (1999), *Nationalism, Nation and State*, WUV, Vienna.

Алпатов, В. (1995), 'Языки в советском и постсоветском пространстве' [Languages in the Post-Soviet Space], in *Свободная мысль*, 4, pp. 87-98.

Бромлей, Ю. (1983), *Очерки теории этноса* [Essays on theory of ethnicity], Moscow.

Бромлей, Ю. (1987), *Этносоциальные процессы: теория, история, современность* [Ethnosocial processes: theory, history, contemporaneity], Moscow.

Вайнонен, Н. (1996), 'Лучшая гарантия от новых "Ичкерий" в реализации идеи национально-культурной автономии' [The best guarantee from the new '*Ichkeryas*' in realization of the idea of national-cultural autonomy], in *Российские вести*, 28.09.1996.

Голов, А. (1995), 'Постоянные страхи россиян' [Permanent fears of Russians], in *Экономические и социальные перемены: мониторинг общественного мнения* [Economic and social changes: monitoring of public opinion], ВЦИОМ, 2, pp. 30-32.

Губогло, М. (1996), 'Три линии национальной политики в посткоммунистической России' [Three trends in the nationalities policy of post-communist Russia], in *Этнографическое обозрение*, 5, pp. 110-122, 6, pp. 137-144.

Гудков, Л. (1995), 'Динамика этнических стереотипов' [Dynamics of ethnic stereotypes], in *Экономические и социальные перемены: мониторинг общественного мнения* [Economic and social changes: monitoring of the public opinion], ВЦИОМ, 2, pp. 22-26.

Гудков, Л. (1995а), 'Этнические стереотипы населения: сравнения двух замеров' [Ethnic stereotypes of the population: comparison of two measurements], in *Экономические и социальные перемены: мониторинг общественного мнения* [Economic and social changes: monitoring of public opinion], ВЦИОМ, 3, pp. 14-16.

Гудков, Л. (1996), 'Этнические фобии в структуре национальной идентификации' [Ethnic phobia in the structure of national identification], in *Экономические и социальные перемены: мониторинг общественного мнения* [Economic and social changes: monitoring of the public opinion], ВЦИОМ, 5, pp. 22-27.

Зорин, В. (1996), 'Национальные аспекты Российского федерализма' [National aspects of Russian federalism], in *Свободная мысль*, 10, pp. 19-30.

Иванов, В. et al. (1996), 'Что думают россияне о межнациональных отношениях' [What do citizens of Russia think about inter-ethnic relations], in *Этнополитический вестник*, 2, pp. 87-100.

Карлов, В. (1997), 'Евразийская идея и русский национализм' [The Eurasianist Idea and Russian Nationalism], in *Этнографическое обозрение*, 1/1997, pp. 3-12.

Козлов, В. (1995), 'Проблема этничности' [The problem of ethnicity], in *Этнографическое обозрение*, 4, pp. 39-54.

Конституция Российской Федерации [Constitution of the Russian Federation] (1993).

Курило, О. (1995), 'Прошлое и настоящее евангелическо-лютеранской общины немецкой традиции в Москве (этносоциологическая характеристика)' [Past and present of the German tradition Evangelical-Lutheran community in Moscow (ethno-sociological profile)], in *Этнографическое обозрение*, 6, pp. 137-130.

Левада, Ю. (1994), 'Элита и масса в общественном мнении: проблема социальной элиты' [The elite and the 'mass' in Public Opinion: the problem of the social elite], in *Экономические и социальные перемены: мониторинг общественного мнения* [Economic and social changes: monitoring of public opinion], ВЦИОМ, 6, pp. 7-10.

Левинсон, А. (1995), 'Значимые имена' [Names as symbols], in *Экономические и социальные перемены: мониторинг общественного мнения* [Economic and social changes: monitoring of public opinion], ВЦИОМ, 2, pp. 26-29.

'Политические лидеры о национальном вопросе' [Political leaders – about the nationalities question], in *Этнографическое обозрение*, 1/1996, pp. 95-103, 2/1996, pp. 125-132.

Валентей С. (ed.) (1997), *Федерализм. Энциклопедический словарь* [Federalism. Encyclopedia], ИЭ РАН, Центр социально-экономических проблем федерализма, ИНФРА-М, Moscow.

Трубецкой, Н. (1993), 'Общеевразийский национализм' [All-Eurasian Nationalism], in *Россия между Европой и Азией: Евразийский соблазн* [Russia Between Europe and Asia], Moscow.

'Федеральный закон Российской Федерации о национально-культурной автономии' [Federal Law of the Russian Federation on National Cultural Autonomy], (1996), in *Российская газета*, 26.06.1996.

Хакамада, И (1996), interview, 'Политические лидеры о национальном вопросе' [Political leaders on the nationalities question], in *Etnograficheskoye obozreniye*, 1.

Яковенко, И. (1996), 'От империи к национальному государству (Попытка концептуализации процесса)' [From Empire to Nation State (An attempt to conceptualise the process)], in *ПОЛИС*, 6, pp. 117-128.

Index

References from Notes indicated by 'n' after page reference